THE ROAD TO GLORY

Confederate General Richard S. Ewell

by Samuel J. Martin

Guild Press of Indiana, Inc.
6000 Sunset Lane   Indianapolis Indiana 46208

Library of Congress
Catalog Card Number
91-058045

Book Design
Jeane M. Gaiennie Real Quack Designs

Hardcover Edition   ISBN 1-878208-07-1
Paperback Edition   ISBN 1-878208-08-X

Lieutenant General Richard S. Ewell

Acknowledgments

At one of the three crossroads in the village of Spring Hill, Tennessee, a sign points west, saying, "Ewell Farm. One Mile.This was the last home of Lt. Gen. Richard S. Ewell, CSA." I wanted a photograph of the house for this book, so I retrieved my camera from the trunk of my car and started driving slowly down the country lane.

After traveling about a mile, I spotted a large, white, rambling home perched atop a distant knoll. It was the only logical dwelling within view to have been Ewell's house, but there was no identifying sign nearby. As I debated whether to climb the muddy slope to get close enough to snap a picture, (risking an attack from the herd of cows eyeing me with curiosity from their field on the hill), a sheriff's car approached from the east.

"Can you tell me, "I called as I flagged the cruiser to a stop, "Is that General Ewell's house up on the hill?"

"Oh," the deputy replied through the open window of his car, "I don't know any folks who live around here."

I would like to thank that officer for so uniquely confirming the need for a biography of the "famous" Confederate general, Richard Stoddert Ewell. It has been over fifty years since the only book on Ewell was published, *Old Bald Head,* by Percy Hamlin, and since that time, new evidence has come to light that allows a more complete examination of his life. This would include the probable psychological affects on Ewell due to the amputation of his leg, refutation of the smears on his performance by Jubal Early and John B. Gordon, and new light on his "treason" during the last days of the war.

I wish to acknowledge many friendly and competent individuals who have helped in my research. These include Sue Rainey, Hilton Head Island Library, Hilton Head Island, South Carolina; C.M. Keener, U.S. National Archives, Washington D.C.; Kathleen Francis, University of Richmond Library, Richmond, Virginia; Marylin Bell Hughes, Tennessee State Library and

Archives, Nashville, Tennessee; Margaret Cook, Earl Gregg
Swem Library, College of William and Mary, Williamsburg,
Virginia; Richard Shrader, Louis Round Wilson Library, The
University of North Carolina, Chapel Hill, North Carolina; and
the people working at the Indiana University Library,
Bloomington, Indiana, Carmel Public Library, Carmel, Indiana
and Indianapolis Public Library, Indianapolis, Indiana.

I must also thank the many used book stores across the
United States. Through the mail and innumerable visits, I was
able to obtain copies of books, which while secondary sources,
are so rare as to make finding and reading them as valuable as
utilizing first person accounts.

I am grateful to Larry Turner of Minneapolis, Minnesota,
for suggesting the book; to Wallace and Katherine Fennell of
Rock Hill, South Carolina, for their continuing interest and
encouragement; to J.E. Gessler of North Hollywood, California,
Editor-in-Chief of *The Kepi,* who published my first article on
Ewell; to Adam Banks of Boston, Massachusetts, for his special
efforts on Fort Warren; and to Dr. Stephen Wise of Parris Island,
South Carolina, who so graciously read the manuscript and
offered constructive criticism.

I would like to thank Richard Day, archivist for the Lewis
Library of Vincennes University (Indiana) for drawing the maps
for the book; Susan Hormuth of Washington, D.C. for her assistance in obtaining most of the photographs, and Susan Sneller of
Austin, Texas, who aided in the final editing process.

I must also acknowledge the many friends who so often
asked, "How's the book coming?" Such questions made me feel
guilty enough to keep working on the manuscript.

I especially want to thank Nancy Niblack Baxter of Guild
Press of Indiana Inc., without whose editorial guidance this book
would not have been possible. Her concise criticism, always
given with encouragement, is wholly responsible for whatever
literary credit may accrue to this manuscript.

And I truly appreciate the patience and silent support of
my wife, Katherine, an "author's widow," who spent so many
evenings alone while I read and typed in my basement cubicle.

Prologue

The "flower of Virginia aristocracy" had assembled that warm, humid evening in late May, 1863. The Taylors, the Lees, the Turners, the Fitzhughs, the Beverleys, the Randolphs, the Carters—all had come to William Yerby's elegant, brick house perched atop a small hill five miles south of Fredericksburg, Virginia. "Ladies rode up in coaches with [their] outriders of . . . still faithful negroes," remembered one of the guests. "The beaux arrived from every direction. Men not in the army were unpopular, and the gentlemen were all in uniform."[1]

"[And] what a supper! Home-cured hams and home-raised turkeys. Little roasted pigs and saddles of mutton. Oysters in every style sent up from Norfolk, chicken fried and roasted . . . stuffed mangoes, spiced pears, beaten biscuits, hot rolls, fruit cakes, angel cake, wine, mint juleps, punch, and coffee."[2] The reason for the gathering of Southern aristocrats, an almost fairyland escape from the lengthening, dreary realities of life during the Civil War, was to celebrate the recent wedding of Lieutenant General Richard S. Ewell and Leczinska McKay Campbell Brown, the sweetheart he had waited over twenty years to marry. Just eight days earlier, Ewell had been promoted to replace Lieutenant General Thomas "Stonewall" Jackson (mortally wounded in the Battle of Chancellorsville) as head of the Second Corps in Robert E. Lee's Army of Northern Virginia. Ewell had demonstrated his capability for high command since the start of the conflict, but he had been out of service for the past nine months, recuperating from the amputation of his right leg, the result of his being shot during the Battle of Groveton toward the end of the Second Manassas Campaign.

As the newlyweds circulated among the guests, Ewell exhibited a mildly bizarre trait which no doubt had some of the ladies whispering behind their fans that the General was, as people said, a little odd. He insisted on presenting his new bride as, "My wife, the Widow Brown."[3]

III

Ewell had loved "Lizinka" (the Americanized version of her unusual name, given because she was born in Russia while her father was serving as the United States ambassador) all his life. But he had lost her in his youth to James Percy Brown, and now at age forty-six he had at long last realized his dream of marrying her. He could not bring himself to call her "Mrs. Ewell." It was as if he could not believe his good fortune.

About midnight the older folks either left the party for their own homes or sought beds within the spacious Yerby house. The young, unmarried couples slipped outside to sit on chairs strewn along the wide veranda. "Candles were our only light," Hattie Brown Turner, Lizinka's daughter, fondly recalled, "and the wind blew them out as fast as they were lighted."[4] The party was over all too soon. Six days later, Ewell drove Lizinka to the railroad station at Hamilton's Crossing. She rode the train back to Richmond; he started preparations to take his 20,000 men north, to lead the way for Lee's march into Pennsylvania. Their few, precious days of marriage were only an interlude in the bloody contest fast approaching its climax. For Dick Ewell, his grand wedding was a personal triumph, the highest point in a tempestuous life, a giant step on "The Road to Glory",[5] (his sarcastic term for the South's struggle to make good its break from the Federal Union). Much of import had preceded the event; much yet remained for one of the most noteworthy, yet controversial careers of the Civil War.

THE ROAD TO GLORY

Antebellum

Richard Stoddert Ewell was born on February 7, 1817, in Georgetown, D.C., the sixth of ten children of Dr. Thomas and Elizabeth Stoddert Ewell. Two boys and three girls preceded Richard; two sisters and two brothers followed. The family's roots were in Wales, amidst the fighting Llewellen clan, whose surname was abridged when Thomas, the first of the Ewells to emigrate to America, came to Maryland about 1640.[1]

That first ancestor's son John moved south to Virginia in 1680 and began to develop family holdings that at one time totaled about 18,000 acres of prime farmland. Charles, John's only heir, had three sons, one of whom (also named Charles) married Sarah Ball, a first cousin of George Washington's mother.[2] His sons, James, Charles, and Jesse (Ewell's grandfather, a colonel in the Revolutionary War), proved to be prolific sires, so much so that when their children (including Thomas, Ewell's father) became of age, the dividing and sub-dividing of the properties among the many siblings had shrunk the Ewell inheritance to almost nothing. Ewell's mother Elizabeth Stoddert was descended from James Stoddert, a Scotsman who had settled in Maryland in 1665.[3] The Stodderts moved later to Virginia, but unlike the Ewells, they continued to prosper. Benjamin Stoddert, Elizabeth's father, was a rich merchant, owner of fifty sailing ships, and a member of George Washington's first cabinet (Secretary of Navy).[4]

While Elizabeth brought a goodly dowry to her marriage, Thomas Ewell was not at first dependent upon her wealth to support his growing family. He had graduated with high honors in medicine from Pennsylvania University and had made a good start at building his practice, centered on the Navy Department in Washington, D.C. By the time Dick was born, though, the family had fallen on hard times, mostly due to difficulties evoked by Thomas' acrid personality. Even in his youth, he had been intractable. His grandfather had scornfully written him, "[Your] pride . . . derogates respect," and he reproved the lad for having "extreme irritability, too often roused by unfounded suspicions."[5] These traits Thomas never seemed to lose. He made so many enemies that his medical practice eroded, reaching a point so low that Thomas Ewell was forced to sell his home in Georgetown and move to a rundown farm located close to Centreville, Virginia. Here his children grew up.

The days at Bellevue (more often called Stoney Lonesome because of its remote location and barren soil) were carefree for young Dick. He spent his time outdoors doing all that a boy would do in those days, hunting, fishing, but most often galloping horses about the hills and valleys of northern Virginia. He became a superb rider, a skill he used to advantage the rest of his life. But while Dick prospered in the pastoral simplicity of Stoney Lonesome, the rest of the family suffered. Not only was money (and the necessities it provided) scarce, but also Thomas Ewell grew increasingly bitter because of his failures. He blamed others, not himself, and tormented discontent probably contributed to his early death in 1826. His widow was faced with the problem of rasing nine young children with most of her inheritance gone. To support her large family, Elizabeth Ewell began teaching school.

Son Dick was her prize student (especially expert in math and science). He was not a particularly docile pupil, however. Having absorbed some of his father's obnoxious traits, Dick was, as reports had it, unduly morose and rudely outspoken. For example, when a family friend gave him a book, he refused to say anything about the gift.

"Aren't you going to thank Mr. Lloyd?" his mother said trying to urge a response.

"I never asked him for it," Dick glumly retorted.[6]

Later, his sister, Rebecca, described him as being "as caustic and cynical as anyone need be with all of his perfections."[7] His mother feared this attitude would prevent Dick from receiving an appointment to West Point, the poor boy's sole opportunity for education and advancement. Her worries proved groundless. Dick obtained entry to the military academy when he was nineteen years old.

Ewell's record at West Point from 1836 to 1840 was good. Unlike many Southern boys who were ill-prepared for the extensive curriculum, causing them to struggle to keep up with their better-educated Northern counterparts, Dick found the majority of his courses undemanding. He finished thirteenth in a class of forty-three.[8] Future Union generals William T. Sherman and George Thomas scored higher than Ewell, but he graduated ahead of later Confederate compatriots Bushrod Johnson and Thomas Jordan. Given a choice between the infantry, the artillery, or the dragoons, Ewell chose the dragoons because this branch would take him to the Far West where the opportunities for a "more independent way of getting a living"[9] might be found. Ewell planned to resign soon from the army anyway to make his fortune as a civilian.

Ewell had a special reason for wanting wealth. He had expected to marry his first cousin, "Lizinka" McKay Campbell (the daughter of his mother's sister, his chief playmate and his best friend when he was growing up), after finishing college. While Dick had always assumed they would wed, she was ignorant of his scheme. In a letter to his mother, he repeated a boast he had no doubt made to Lizinka, that he would "never marry . . . my heart [is] very susceptible, yet . . . too tender to retain an impression long enough . . . to lead to any dangerous consequences."[10]

Lizinka either believed him or never really considered Dick as a suitor, for in 1839, during his third term at West Point, she married James Percy Brown, owner of a large plantation outside of Spring Hill, Tennessee. Like his father, Ewell ascribed his losing Lizinka to circumstances beyond his control. He considered himself poor and undistinguished as compared to his wealthy and more socially advantaged rival. He became determined not to remain impoverished throughout the rest of his life, even though it was obviously too late for him to gain Lizinka's hand, seemingly lost to him forever.

Life in the army proved unexciting. After training for dragoon duty at Carlisle Barracks, Pennsylvania, Ewell began a career of chasing Indians. He served at Fort Wayne in the Cherokee Territory (now Oklahoma) from 1840 to 1842, spent a few years at Fort Scott, Kansas (interrupted only by a jaunt to Santa Fe, New Mexico in 1843, escorting traders and their wagons to the far away post), then returned east in 1845 for a short term of recruiting.[11] Reassigned to Fort Scott that same year, Ewell remained in Kansas until 1846 when war with Mexico loomed. While most of his fellow officers rushed south to prepare for the coming conflict, Ewell went east to serve with the Coastal Survey on Chesapeake Bay. He was suffering from malaria, and his superiors assumed that exposure to the salt air would provide a cure.

Stopping for a few days at Jefferson Barracks just outside of St. Louis, Ewell found himself delayed en route east, and was put in temporary charge of the garrison until a new commandant arrived. As Dick began attending to details, a stubby second lieutenant burst into his office with an impassioned plea. He had orders to hurry south to Mexico, but needed a few days before reporting to go and propose to his sweetheart. Would Ewell give him a pass? Little did Dick know that granting the furlough would pay off in years to come. Having Ulysses "Sam" Grant in his debt proved most beneficial during very difficult times twenty years later.[12]

Ewell probably gave Grant his pass because he was feeling romantically sentimental himself. For the first time in six years, Dick was exposed to society and suitable women he might wed if he so desired. But the ghost of Lizinka overcame all competition. "This is the worst country for single ladies," Ewell groused about St. Louis. "I have not seen a pretty girl or an interesting one since I have been here."[13]

After spending only a month on the East Coast, Dick was reassigned to Louisville, Kentucky, on recruiting duty. He no doubt thought he had lost his chance for glory in Mexico. Soon, however, he received orders bringing him into the conflict. Captain Philip Kearney requested that Ewell be named as his second in command of "F" Company, First Dragoon Regiment, which would escort the army commander-in-chief, General Winfield Scott. Ewell rushed south, expecting that being near the seat of power would open the path to heroic exploits and brevet promotions. He quickly learned this was not to be. The ground was too rocky for cavalry and Scott was not about to venture close to the front.

Ewell, watching the war from a safe distance, took part in just two skirmishes. One, a foolhardy pursuit of the Mexican retreat at Churubusco, saw Dick lose two horses and Phil Kearney his arm.[14] Ewell did, however, earn brevet promotion to captain because of "gallant and meritorious conduct" during the foray. "I wish I had known . . . there was to be such an over-whelming quantity of brevets made out," Ewell would later moan. "I should certainly have tried hard for another . . . ."[15]

When the war ended, Ewell was assigned recruiting duty, first in Boston, then in Baltimore, where he remained until 1850. He was promoted to captain that August, put in charge of "G" Company, First United States Dragoons, who were posted at Rayado, New Mexico. This tour out west lasted ten years.

Ewell's personal life had been necessarily kept in the background during these years of intense career involvement. He had, however, stayed in touch with Lizinka, and knew that she had been widowed in 1844. He was finally drawn to visit her in 1855 when Lizinka asked that he resign from the army to manage "Tarpley," one of her plantations situated about a mile west of Spring Hill, Tennessee.[16] Her offer implied that they renew their long ago romance. He arrived that November, met her two teenaged children, and saw that she was immensely wealthy, having inherited the properties of both her husband and her father. And Lizinka had changed. Where once she had been a coy Southern belle, now she was a strong-minded woman, used to having her own way. Independence, born of widowhood and nurtured by affluence, had had its effect on her.

Ewell, of course, was no longer the idealistic boy that she remembered. Years of army service had turned him into a hard-bitten, taciturn man, devoid of social graces. Each of them, however, found the other more appealing because of these evolutions, and he was sorely tempted to accept her proposal that he remain in Tennessee to become overseer of her planta-tion. But he refused her plea. His pride would not let him match his fortunes as a poor soldier to those of an opulent dowager.

Ewell returned to New Mexico with Lizinka uppermost in his mind. Determined to finally make himself wealthy enough to seek his former sweetheart's hand, he sought riches by invest-ing his meager savings in a silver mine called "The Patagonia."[17] His military duties (riding tens of miles a day in frequent but futile forays against renegade Indians) occupied most of his time, but every spare moment was spent prospecting the lode. His frenzied effort to build a fortune took its toll. Ewell's health collapsed. Emaciated by dyspepsia (probably a stomach ulcer), he sold his share in the silver mine, and on January 31, 1861, set out on sick leave for Virginia. Ewell came home to the Civil War.

Profile of a Soldier

The man who donned Confederate gray on April 24, 1861, scarcely resembled the boy who had graduated from West Point twenty-one years before. Now bald and bearded, Ewell was still taller at five feet, ten inches, than most of his contemporaries. Hard times serving out west, however, had shrunk his weight to only one hundred and thirty pounds. His "bright, prominent eyes, a bomb-shaped bald head, and a nose like that of Francis of Valois," reminded General Richard Taylor, one of Ewell's fellow officers, of a woodcock.[1] His not so handsome features were accented by a disinterest in dress. "His clothes . . . ," according to John Wise, the son of a former Virginia governor, "looked as if made for a larger man."[2] Wise also wrote that Ewell seldom combed his beard; "his grizzled mustache [stuck] out like . . . the muzzle of a terrier."

General John B. Gordon, another subordinate of Ewell's, described him as "a compound of anomalies, the oddest, most eccentric genius in the Confederate Army."[3] Ewell was bright, "far above [others] in common, healthy sense," according to Thomas Gantt, a lawyer cousin.[4] And even as a child, Ewell had been "peculiar," a trait that had intensified as he grew older. Was it an act? The answer is, probably at times. He enjoyed shocking people and had no desire to do what society found "acceptable." But on the other hand, Ewell had a tendency to forget his surroundings, to concentrate only on his thoughts. Campbell Brown, Lizinka's son and Ewell's principal aide throughout the war, tells a story that supports this premise. "I heard one day of a place where honey could be had . . . [so] General Ewell and I rode there . . . . We found they had just churned so we asked for some buttermilk, and while the woman stepped into the house to get it . . . Ewell picked up her large scissors and began cutting his own hair. He [was] half-finished when she came out . . . He laid down the scissors, drank his milk, then took off [with] the hair on one side of his bald head short, on the other untouched."[5] Several days passed before

Campbell could harass Ewell into finishing his self-barbering.

Ewell's eccentricities extended to his dietary habits. To ease the pain of the ulcer, he usually ate a strange concoction he called "frumenty." The ingredients, raisins, egg yolks, wheat grain, and sugar, were mixed and boiled in milk.[6] His men joked that Ewell's suffering was no doubt the result of this weird diet.

Another of Ewell's oddities was an inability to say what he was thinking when unusually excited. "His thoughts would leap across great gaps which his words never touched . . . which he expected his listener to fill up by intuition," Gordon remembered. "And woe to the dull subordinate who failed to understand him!"[7]

Ewell's voice was high and squeaky, often punctuated by a pronounced lisp. Perhaps to compensate for these feminine-like traits, Ewell was a proficient swearer. "His profanity did not consist of a single oath or even double oaths," Gary Eggleston, a private under Ewell, wrote in his memoirs, "but was ingeniously wrought into whole sentences."[8]

Such irreverence attracted (or repelled) the chaplains. One especially interested in saving Ewell's soul followed him to the hills above Winchester just before a battle began. As the two watched the combat unfolding below, an alert Northern artillery battery sent a shell whizzing close by their heads. "As I can be of no service where I am," the chaplain hastily intoned, "I will seek a less exposed place."[9]

"Why chaplain," Ewell answered, "You're the most inconsistent man I ever saw . . . you're anxious to get to heaven, [but] now that you've got the best chance to go, you run away from it as if you'd rather not make the trip after all."

Ewell had a droll sense of humor. At best an agnostic, he took special delight in teasing the staunch believers, interested in introducing religion to the heathens. "Ask a red man, 'Indian, is that a white child?' " he would admonish them with a sly smile, "You get the answer,' part missionary, part Indian.' "[10]

While Ewell would regale comrades seated around a campfire with his humor, he was a different man during a battle. "Fighting was beyond question the ruling passion of his life," Taylor reported. "He always feared lest someone would get under fire before him."[11] Ewell not only sent his troops into battle but also would often grab a musket and join the skirmishers on the front line. "Refreshment," was the rationale he offered for his actions. And despite his fragile appearance, Ewell had the stamina of a mule. "He was regarded as . . . the most enduring man in the [Southern] army," remembered Wise, "and as a horseman, he had no peer."[12] Ewell was noted for invariably leaving the road, preferring to gallop through timber and water.

Ewell was not only hard on himself but also demanded as much from his troops. "His men were more afraid of him than of Yankees," one of his scouts recalled. "[Those] detailed for duty at the General's headquarters went with fear and trembling."[13] They expected to be berated for their mistakes, big or small.

The first to suffer the shock of Ewell's demanding ways were the members of his initial command. When he reported for duty in April, 1861, assigned to train a cavalry regiment made up of sons of the Southern aristocracy, located near Ashland, Virginia, he declared that the young troopers, not their negro servants, would stand guard at night.[14] These scions of Virginia's First Families were infuriated by this change in procedure, and had they complained to their politically-connected fathers, they might have created trouble for Ewell. He was soon through with training cavalry, however. The bluecoats were threatening Fairfax Court House, Virginia; Ewell was needed there.

He took command of the Fairfax Court House outpost late in the afternoon of May 31, 1861. After arraying his men (two cavalry companies plus an infantry regiment) into a perimeter defense, Ewell retired to a room in the lodging house located on the village square. At 3:00 a.m., he was awakened by the thunder of hundreds of hoofbeats approaching the area from the east, out of Washington, D.C. Ewell leaped up out of his bed, and without pausing to dress, rushed outside.

He found his inexperienced soldiers milling around in terrified confusion, trying to assume form as enemy cavalry in columns of fours galloped toward them. Ewell was standing in the middle of the street when the Northern horsemen bore down on him. Clad only in a white nightshirt, the barefooted, bald-headed Ewell swore and shook his fists at the bluecoat cavalry as they raced past him. They ignored what appeared to them to be an old, irate, local citizen. Shooting their pistols into the air, the enemy raiders frolicked off into the darkness west of the town.

After the Yankees had disappeared, Ewell hurried back to his hotel room where he dressed, stuffing his nightshirt into his trousers. He then returned to the town square, gathered up his men, and herded them west of the village. Putting them in ambush, hidden behind rows of fence rails on both sides of the road, Ewell awaited the probable return of the Federals.

When the enemy horsemen, headed back to Washington, rode up at 3:30 a.m., their confident canter was disrupted by Ewell's bushwhackers. The first blast of Rebel muskets caused the Union to fall back. They re-grouped to try a second dash through the gauntlet, but once again were repulsed by Ewell's troops. Deciding not to risk any more casualties, the Yankees collected their wounded and wound their way back home through the fields instead of the pike.

During the melee, Ewell was nicked in the shoulder by a stray Minie ball. An observer, seeing blood staining Ewell's nightshirt, offered sympathy.

"I'm sorry to see you wounded, Sir."

"I should like to know," Ewell snarled, "if it's any of your goddamn business."[15]

Such stories of Ewell's being bellicose, disheveled in appearance, physically inexhaustible, eccentric, as touchy as an old dog with a new bone, were typical during the early days of the war. Ewell offered many sides for people to see. All of the facets to his enigmatic personality, however, were not yet visible, and many would change before the war ended.

First Manassas

Ewell's encounter with the enemy at Fairfax Court House was, of course, only one of a number of bitter incidents between adversaries in the weeks following the shelling of Fort Sumter. At dawn on April 12, 1861, the South had opened the bombardment with a solitary mortar shell that arched high before dropping into the harbor bastion that faced Charleston, South Carolina. When it exploded, flinging iron fragments throughout the Federal bulwark, the sounds of hot metal ricocheting off brick walls echoed all across the United States. In the North, men bellowed with indignation at the new Confederacy's impertinent "firing on the old flag," and they swarmed into the hastily set up recruiting stations to enlist as soldiers, dedicated to putting a quick end to the insurrection. "One Rebel can whip ten Yankees," the Southerners angrily replied, and they rushed to enroll in their companies, regiments, and brigades of war. One had to choose sides.

Richard Ewell had elected to join the South and his state, Virginia. Resigning his captain's commission in the U.S. Army, he volunteered for Confederate service, and was commissioned a lieutenant colonel.[1] Ewell left no written word as to why he sided with the South, but his actions spoke louder than a fiery declaration. Duty and honor called Ewell: duty to protect his people, his home, from the expected onslaught by the armies of the North, and honor according to the Nineteenth century code for being a gentleman. His reasons were the same as for the hundreds of thousands of others, both North and South, who answered the clarion call for troops.

In another regard, however, Ewell had a unique incentive, grounds which influenced his behavior as a military leader and which remained compelling throughout the war. No other officer (North or South) had a similar cause, was so dominated by personal intents as was Ewell. The war offered him what he wanted most from life, what he had found impossible in the peacetime army, the status of a high-ranking officer, an elevated

Lizinka Brown

Campbell Brown

Tarpley Plantation

Photograph of Tarpley Plantation by the author.
Photograph of Campell Brown courtesy of *Civil War Times, Ill.*

station from which he could rightly court his rich, widowed, childhood sweetheart, Lizinka Brown.

Lizinka had always held an influential sway over Ewell, and in these troubled times, she asked for his help. Her only son, Campbell Brown, had enlisted as a private in a Tennessee infantry company a few days after Fort Sumter. But after a month in the field, he concluded that "rheumatic knees" would preclude his serving as a soldier on the front lines.[2] Through a letter from his mother, Campbell asked Ewell for a staff assignment, a "safe" place where he could serve out the war.

Ewell, promoted to brigadier general on June 17, 1861—a reward for conspicuous performance in defending his Fairfax Court House post—received Lizinka's note at Manassas Junction, Virginia, where he now commanded the Second Infantry Brigade in General Pierre Gustave Toutant-Beauregard's army. He recalled the lad. In 1855, when he had last seen Lizinka, Campbell was a typical teenager—opinionated, overindulged, an insufferable brat. With that image still in mind, Ewell could not visualize himself nursemaiding such a boy throughout the war. Still, he did not want to refuse Lizinka. Unsure how he should confront this dilemma, Ewell turned to his aides for advice.[3]

If he had hoped to find a good excuse to keep Campbell off his staff, Ewell was disappointed. His aides pointed out that the boy was no longer a teenager, he was twenty-one years old, had been well educated, and was certain to be an asset to their group. When that logic failed to move Ewell, a more persuasive issue was introduced. What better way to a mother's heart than through her only son? Seeing Campbell as a means for advancing his romantic aims, Ewell capitulated, and sent Lizinka a letter inviting the boy to join him in Virginia.

Campbell reported for duty on July 20, 1861. Ewell was away from camp at the moment, and when he returned, he was told the boy was waiting to see him. Ewell had no trouble recognizing Campbell, who was sitting under the shade of a large tree. He had changed little over the past six years, and was ordinary in every way except for his hair. With golden curls smothering his head (a painful but innocent taunt to one as bald as Ewell), Campbell was the spitting image of his father, Ewell's one-time rival, James Percy Brown. As he advanced to greet his new aide, all of Ewell's initial apprehensions returned.

"Well, Campbell," he sniffed with cruelty in his voice, "I'm sorry you've come."[4]

"I'm sorry, too," the young man replied, "if I've embarrassed you in any way, Sir."

Ewell blinked with surprise. This was not the same whelp —lazy, flippant, and arrogant—that he remembered. Regretting that he had been unfriendly, Ewell tried to make amends.

"We'll probably have a fight tomorrow," he said, forcing a laugh. "I had hoped you'd stay away long enough to miss it."

Having made a sort of an apology, Ewell dismissed Campbell from his mind and avoided further contact with the aide. But when he was finally compelled to use Campbell's talents, Ewell was pleasantly surprised. Campbell proved a congenial, capable aide. The two rapidly grew close, and their relationship became like that of father and son.

Ewell had told Campbell when they first met that a battle was brewing. While this may have sounded like an excuse (over three months had gone by since Fort Sumter, and the adversaries had yet to come even close to seriously clashing), the opening fray of the war was indeed at hand, although neither North nor South was ready for combat. Both armies of volunteers had had little training, and huge risks faced the general who dared to fight with "green" troops. Brigadier General Irvin McDowell, commanding the Union soldiers stationed about Washington, D.C., noted this in a letter to his civilian superiors. "Our regiments are exceedingly raw," he reported, "and the best of them, with few exceptions, not over steady in line."[5] But President Abraham Lincoln, stung by newspaper headlines screaming "On to Richmond," insisted that McDowell must attack the Rebel forces under Beauregard, posted at Manassas Junction. So against his better judgment, McDowell started to advance his 35,000 men on July 16, 1861. "It was a glorious spectacle," Captain Fry, an aide of McDowell's, recalled. "The various regiments were [all] brilliantly uniformed . . . and the silken banners . . . flung to the breeze were unsoiled and untorn."[6]

The Confederates had taken up a position along Bull Run, a tidal stream that rambled southeast toward the Potomac River. Only six usable fords were available for crossing the water, and Beauregard had posted a brigade on the west bank of each. His other five brigades lay behind in reserve.

McDowell, marching his men in column, first contacted the Confederates on July 18th. McDowell quickly withdrew to form his battle line, and by Sunday morning, July 21st, he was poised for attack.

Ewell's brigade was located at Union Mills Ford, one of the Bull Run crossings, the southernmost point on Beauregard's line. The spot was five miles away from Ewell's boyhood home near Centreville. "A small, wooden house of two rooms served to accommodate (Ewell) and part of his staff, "Campbell Brown remembered, "while the rest slept in a tent close by." [7] Above the tiny cabin, a road (actually a dusty footpath) wound down toward the stream, passing unbridged through the water to the opposite shore. Four hundred yards to the north, the Orange and Alexandria Railroad tracks (running west to east) came to an abrupt halt at the stream, where the blackened remains of a wooden trestle loomed. The bridge had been torched several days before, a fiery spectacle with flames devouring not only the dry timbers but also the overhanging leaves of trees, to deny access by the enemy to Ewell's position.

Across the run, the land climbed in a steady incline to the center and to the left, its peak hovering above the elevation enjoyed by Ewell. The summit was covered by a dense forest— the only significant woods in sight.

The ford by Ewell's cabin plus another shallow spot near the former railroad bridge were the only places in the immediate area where the waters could be crossed. All other points along the stream were impassable, both because of steep banks and impenetrable brush on each side of the water.

Ewell's position looked like a very insignificant spot, yet it was the most strategic part of Beauregard's line. If the Union decided to turn the Confederate's flank, they were likely to come straight for Ewell.

While the Yankees were massing to engage the South that Sunday morning, Beauregard was also intending to assault. He was not willing to wait and accept McDowell's blow. His brigade leaders were well aware that an attack on their part was imminent, but Beauregard had not yet passed on the details of

17

his plan.

Ewell was up before dawn. He sat alone in front of his cabin, anxiously awaiting orders from Beauregard. His reverie was interrupted when Major John B. Gordon, executive officer for one of the regiments, approached him. "Come eat a cracker with me," Ewell chirped loudly, "We'll breakfast together here and dine together in hell."[8]   Ewell's loud, irreverent greeting shocked Gordon, an ex-lawyer from Georgia with no military experience. He sat down timorously next to Ewell, and as they talked in the dim light, Gordon recognized that his brigade commander was filled with a "flutter of exultation."[9] Ewell obviously looked forward to the coming battle.

Day was breaking when Beauregard's courier finally rode up with Ewell's instructions. The order read:

> *General,*
> *You will hold yourself in readiness to take the offense on Centreville at a moment's notice—to make a diversion against the enemy's intended attack on Mitchell's Ford, and probably Stone Bridge. You will protect your right flank against any attack from eastward. General Holmes' Brigade will support your movement. If the enemy be prepared to attack in front of your left, leave it (said brigade) in a proper position, with orders to take the offense when it hears your engagement on the other side of the run. I intend to take the offense throughout my front as soon as possible.*
>
> > *Beauregard[10]*

Beauregard's orders to Ewell were a bit baffling. While he expected McDowell to attack his front to Ewell's immediate left, he was also planning on mounting his own assault at the same time. Ewell, however, saw his role clearly: his troops would move against the Federals' southern flank, but would hold in place until an order to attack was received. He started to rally his force.

Ewell's brigade of 2,500 men included three infantry regiments. The Sixth Alabama, headed by Colonel John J. Seibels, a former newspaper editor (the *Montgomery Confedera-*

18

tion),[11] was camped behind Ewell's headquarters cabin. All but two hundred of the men were asleep; those missing were on picket duty along the run, some in rifle pits dug into the downward slope toward the stream, the rest behind the huge boulders that were strewn throughout the area.

The Fifth Alabama was bivouacked above Seibels, close by the charred railroad bridge. Their leader was a young man who would eventually prove to be one of the most competent leaders in the Confederate army. A graduate of the Virginia Military Institute, Colonel Robert E. Rodes had served as professor of engineering for his alma mater prior to the war.[12]

Further upstream, beyond the torched overpass, the Sixth Louisiana was bedded down. Their colonel, Isaac Seymour, a New Orleans publisher before joining the Confederacy, had previous military experience, having seen action in both the Indian and Mexican Wars.[13]

Ewell's infantry was supported by both artillery and cavalry. Four twelve-pound, smooth bore Napoleon cannons were managed by a young lieutenant, Thomas Rosser. A strapping man (6'2" tall and weighing over 200 pounds), he had resigned his appointment to West Point from Texas before graduation to join the Confederacy.[14] His guns, emplaced above the torched railroad bridge, were unlimbered, ready to fire.

The cavalry (four companies) was led by Lieutenant Colonel Walter Jenifer. Campbell Brown remembered him as "worthless as an officer—a great dandy but small man."[15] Jenifer would soon leave Ewell's command.

Immediately after the receipt of Beauregard's dispatch, Ewell began forming his men. The raw troops fell into position amidst much noise and confusion, their eagerness making up for a lack of training. Before all the men had found their places, the roar of cannons exploded to the northwest. It was 6:00 a.m. The battle had started, but instead of opening on Ewell's left as Beauregard had anticipated, the fray raged at a distance, to Ewell's rear.

For an hour and a half, while the crescendo of combat rose behind him, Ewell waited for his orders to advance over the run. But no messenger came from Beauregard. Unable to bear the suspense any longer, Ewell decided to send Gordon with a company of Seibels' infantry across the water to "feel" the ground opposite their station.

Gordon forded the stream, then led his small force north toward the tree-covered heights. As he approached the railroad tracks, his advance was contested by Yankee soldiers, emerging from the woods to his front. The enemy troops came slowly forward. Falling back to the rail embankment, Gordon ordered his men to open fire. While this served to halt the oncoming bluecoats, Gordon was clearly outnumbered. When the Federals realized that they held an advantage, they were sure to envelop the Georgian's company and cut it to pieces.

Ewell, watching from his hillside, had three choices: he could leave Gordon on his own, hoping that somehow the Georgian could avoid disaster; he could rush reinforcements across the stream to Gordon's aid; or he could call back the skirmishers. Having no authority for bringing on an engagement on his front, Ewell, always a believer in adhering strictly to orders, reluctantly decided to abandon the foray. He sent a man to retrieve the company.[16]

After Gordon was safely back over the run, he attempted to report to Ewell. This was not an easy task as Ewell was in perpetual motion—first mounting his horse, then climbing off, and all the while muttering to himself, "No orders!" When he finally noticed Gordon trying to approach him, Ewell halted in his tracks. "Send me a mounted man," he shouted to Gordon, "with enough sense to go and find out what's the matter."[17]

Gordon hurried to his regiment where he picked a member of the Horse Guard for Ewell's mission. The soldier selected, a former university student clad in the foppish style of a cavalier, galloped up the hill to report to Ewell. But before he could even salute, Ewell was sputtering directions, slashing the air with a finger, emphasizing words that lagged far behind his anguished thoughts. Ewell's orders were incomprehensible. He had omitted most of what the private needed for fathoming his wishes.

"Do you understand, Sir?" Ewell demanded as he finished his discourse.[18]

"Not entirely, Sir," was the quizzical answer. "Do you mean that . . . . "

"Go away from here!" Ewell interrupted. Turning to his watching (and no doubt astonished) staff, he cried, "Send me a man who has some sense!"

Captain Fitz Lee, Robert E. Lee's nephew, serving as an aide to Ewell, volunteered to ride north to see if Brigadier General D.R. Jones, stationed at the next ford, had received any orders. Another officer was sent to the rear, to ask if Brigadier General T.H. Holmes had gotten instructions.

While waiting for his couriers to return, Ewell spotted enemy artillery being rolled out of the forest, northeast of his station. It was obvious that the Yankees meant to begin shooting at him. Ewell leaped onto his mount and spurred the horse toward Rosser and the Confederate guns.

When he arrived at the cannons, emplaced just above the former railroad bridge, Ewell started spouting orders again, his instructions liberally spiced with profanity. His tirade came to an abrupt stop when a young girl unexpectedly rode up and dismounted before Ewell. Oceola Mason, who lived in the forest harboring the Yankees,[19] had ridden her horse across the stream and up to the Rebels to warn them about the enemy's actions. Hundreds of Union soldiers were axing trees to obstruct the road to Centreville. As Oceola paused a moment to catch her breath, Ewell seized the chance to react to the incongruous scene.

"Look there, miss," he growled, pointing to the hill on the far side of the stream. "Don't you see those men in blue clothing?" Speaking with exaggerated courtesy, omitting his usual oaths, Ewell went on, "Look at those men loading those big guns. They're going to fire, and fire quick, and fire right here. You'll be killed." His voice rising with each word, Ewell delivered his final point with a shout. "You'll be a dead damsel in less than a minute. [Go] away!"[20]

The seventeen-year-old Oceola glanced at the rise where the enemy was arming their weapons. Sniffing at the threat, she returned her gaze to Ewell to repeat her story of Yankee activities.

Ewell was astonished. Shaking his bald head in despair, he muttered an aside to his audience. "Women—I tell you, Sir, women would make a grand brigade—if it weren't for snakes

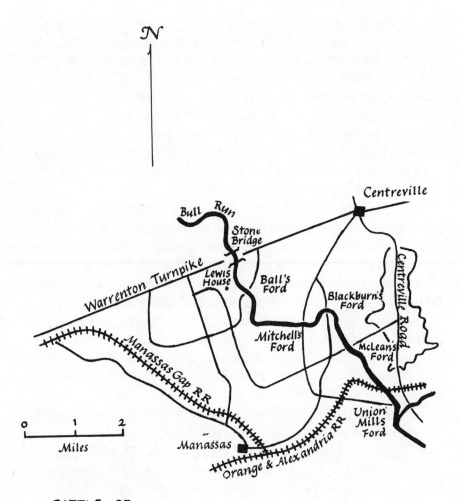

BATTLE OF
FIRST MANASSAS

July 21, 1861

and spiders . . . women are not afraid of bullets; but one, big black snake would put a whole army [of females] to flight."[21]

The Union opened their cannons on Ewell about 8:00 a.m. His artillery returned fire, but neither side was close enough to the other to do much damage. To add to Ewell's frustration, the battle continued to rage to his rear, but the anticipated orders from Beauregard for him to join the fray still had not come. The only word received came from the man sent to Holmes, who had returned to report Holmes had not heard from army headquarters either. If Ewell began to wonder if he had been forgotten, these fears were soon dispelled when Fitz Lee rode up after visiting the adjacent brigade. He informed Ewell that about 7:00 a.m., over two hours ago, Jones had received the following dispatch:

> *General Ewell has been ordered to take the offense upon Centreville. You will follow the movement at once by attacking him in your front.*
>
> *Beauregard*[22]

Beauregard's long-awaited order to take the offense had been issued hours ago. Ewell had been assigned a key role in the assault, but the messenger carrying his instructions had somehow gone astray. As a result, his troops had not advanced on schedule. Clearly, the rest of Beauregard's army was waiting on him. Ewell felt he had to move at once, to make up for lost time, so he ordered his command across Bull Run.

Had Ewell paused for a moment, he might have noted that Beauregard's orders must have been issued before the fighting had opened in his rear, and therefore they no longer applied. There was no reason for his hurrying forward. The battle was roaring behind him, not to his front. But Ewell did not stop to consider these facts; his past military experience had taught him to obey without question. He wrote a quick note to Beauregard, explaining why he was late, sent two messengers (each carrying a copy of his letter) to army headquarters, then rode to the run. He found utter chaos!

While two fords were available for Ewell's twenty-five

hundred to cross Bull Run, the bulk of his troops had jammed the road below his cabin. The Sixth Louisiana were the only ones passing through the waters by the railroad bridge. And since the path past the headquarters house was "[so] narrow, winding, and precipitous . . . [we] could only march by twos," a cavalry officer recalled, "it required . . . hours for the whole brigade to get over."[23]

The brigade finally started out in column, headed north for Centreville with Rodes leading, Rosser and the guns next in line, then Seibels and Seymour. The march had barely begun when it was interrupted by a rider, galloping toward the van. When Captain Rhodes (one of the couriers sent to Beauregard) reached Ewell, he dismounted and handed over instructions that read more like a cipher than a commanding general's orders:

> *On account of the difficulties in our front, it is thought preferable to countermand the advance of the right wing. Resume your forward position.*
>
> *Beauregard*[24]

Despite intense questioning by Ewell, Rhodes was unable to identify the "difficulties" Beauregard had mentioned. He had not seen any fighting; he had not learned anything about the battle. He could only say that fierce combat was raging to the northwest, a fact painfully obvious from the continuing roar of cannons.

Ewell had every man turn about in place, which put the the tail of the column in front. Seymour's Louisianians led the discouraged regiments back across the ford. The troops retired to their bivouacs; Ewell and his staff resumed their posts around the headquarters cabin. As the day progressed, growing hotter with each passing minute as the sun shone down overhead, they sat and listened to the battle. "With nerves at such high tension . . . " Campbell Brown wrote in his memoirs, "every moment we seemed to hear the guns nearer and nearer."[25]

About noon, a messenger brought Ewell new instructions from Beauregard. He was to take his brigade over Bull Run, follow the creek north to McLean's Ford, and attack a Union artillery battery posted there. While Ewell hit the enemy flank, both Longstreet and Jones would charge the Federals' front.

Ewell quickly, and this time efficiently, sent his men over the water and headed north. Skirting west of the woods enveloping the Centreville Road, his progress was soon intercepted by bluecoat pickets, protecting the cannons that had shot at him earlier. Ewell began shifting from column into battle line. Rodes took the center and started firing, which allowed Seibels to slip into position on the right. Seymour hurried up from the rear to assume the left, but before his troops were positioned to join in an attack northward toward the Union battery, yet another envoy from Beauregard arrived with verbal orders.

"Move by the most direct route at once, and as rapidly as possible for the Lewis House!" the messenger said.[26] The site was northwest of Ewell's bivouac, where the fighting had been raging since early morning. After adding that Ewell was to report directly to Brigadier General Joseph Johnston, who was assisting Beauregard by deploying reinforcements into the fray, the messenger also admitted that he was late getting to Ewell. He had been delayed by the lame horse of a friend who accompanied him part of the way. "Who is winning the battle?" Ewell demanded. The courier had no idea.

Ewell sent Fitz Lee and a scout forward to inform Johnston he was starting for the front. Once again reversing the direction of his regiments, turning the men around in place, putting Seymour in the lead, Ewell broke off skirmishing to start for the front. He left the enemy wondering why he was retreating. It was 3:00 p.m.

As the men trudged westward, Ewell grew uneasy. He did not know why, but something was wrong, different, changed in the air. Then it came to him. He no longer heard the sounds of battle! Ewell assumed the worst. The Rebels had lost the fight, and he was on his way to cover a retreat. Because of the confusion of orders, Ewell had thought for some time now that he would be called into the fray "only in case of defeat or as a forlorn hope to prevent it."[27] Further, he was late, maybe fatally so, because the courier had been slow in finding him. Hiding his concern, Ewell asked the men to pick up their pace. Seymour's hard-striding Irishmen leaped forward as if freed from a tight leash. Despite the burning sun and billowing dust raised by their hard-striding feet, the troops from New Orleans quickly outdistanced the trailing regiments. Ewell had to stop Seymour's Irish twice to allow Seibels and Rodes to catch up.

As Ewell closed on the Stone Bridge about 5:00 p.m., he was intercepted by Colonel Preston, assigned to Cockes' brigade. "The Yankees are entrenching by the crossing," the excited officer cried. "You must take your command [there] at once."[28]

Ewell, desperate for action, was very tempted to divert his columns, but he refused the plea. His orders were to report to Johnston. Ewell promised Preston, however, he would ask his superiors for permission to return.

As Ewell and his men neared the Lewis House, they found Fitz Lee waiting with word of what had happened at the front that day. McDowell had attempted to turn the Rebel left, the furthest point from Ewell's post. When Shanks Evans, covering the northern flank, spotted the bluecoats approaching, he alertly wheeled his brigade west to block their path. Evans held his ground for awhile, but as the enemy pushed more and more men against his line, he was forced to retreat to Henry Hill where the Confederates made their stand. First Bee and Barton rushed into the battle, then Jackson, Elzey and Early from Johnston's army, who had been brought to the field from the Shenandoah Valley by train, entered the fray.

The enemy advance stalled, held its place, then started to give ground grudgingly. Their withdrawal was orderly at first, but panic seized a few, which caused the rest to start running. Suddenly, the Union army became a mob of terrified individuals, stumbling across fields, clambering up and down the rolling hills, splashing through Bull Run in a desperate flight to save their lives.

Fitz also informed Ewell that it was not necessary for him to report to Johnston, who had already issued orders for the brigade to assume the reserve. Ewell's troops were not needed for mopping up the ground. Infuriated because he was still denied any role in the battle, Ewell refused to accept the mundane assignment. He put his men at rest, then rushed alone to

the Lewis House to confront Johnston. He poured out the story
of the Yankee bushwhackers by the Stone Bridge, and begged
Johnston to let him drive them away.

Johnston, a small, wiry man with gray and thinning hair
that contrasted with a white goatee, gazed through his field
glasses toward the assumed point of danger. "Our troops are in
pursuit [of the enemy] beyond . . . Stone Bridge," he quietly
observed.[29]

Ewell, too, had raised his binoculars. He saw hosts of
Yankee soldiers running from the battlefield. In their wake along
the Warrenton Turnpike, military debris such as haversacks,
muskets, and blankets lay abandoned. The gear strewn along
the ground was more than enough to accouter Ewell's entire
brigade. And although he had to concede that a Federal ambush
was highly unlikely, Ewell did note that the enemy retreat was
mostly unimpeded.

"Let me go in pursuit of the enemy," Ewell pleaded.[30]

"No," Johnston replied curtly as if to tell Ewell that he
should cease making such requests.

As Ewell agonized over his being denied combat, an aide
to Beauregard arrived and reported that enemy troops had been
spotted approaching Union Mills Ford, Ewell's post along Bull
Run. They were reputed to be enroute to Manassas. This was
most improbable: the badly battered Yankees were not capable
of resuming further assaults. Ewell, however, was willing to
accept any tale that provided him the chance to fight his men.

"Let me take my brigade back . . . he insisted.[31]

Johnston finally acceded to his request.

Ewell rushed down the hill to where his brigade waited.
Thinking he was short of time, that he had to move as many of
his men back to the ford as soon as possible, Ewell concocted
an inventive strategy. He mounted an infantryman behind each
of his troopers.[32] Riding two men per horse, the cavalry with
their passengers galloped on ahead to Union Mills Ford. Those
still on foot followed with the same rapid pace they had taken to
the front.

It was dark by the time Ewell (riding with the cavalry)
arrived at Bull Run. He found his camp empty. There were no
bluecoats approaching his position. When the troops on foot

marched into camp, Ewell had no choice but to send them on to their bivouacs for the night. And if he had hoped that dawn would provide a last chance to engage the Federals, Ewell was doomed to disappointment. Heavy rain began at 3:00 a.m. The storm continued past daybreak, whose gray light revealed that the water between Ewell and his adversary had risen, blocking any further confrontation. The Battle of First Manassas had ended.

* * * *

Newspapers, trying to interpret from afar the confusing aspects of a major battle, found fault with the Confederates' success. A Columbus, Georgia, publication singled out Ewell for a scapegoat, citing him for disobeying Beauregard's order to initiate the planned Southern assault. Moving quickly to defend his reputation, Ewell gathered all his correspondence with Beaureard. "Take this with you [to Richmond]," he instructed George Harrison, an aide on his staff. "You . . . have it in your power to vindicate me."[33]

The potential slur was put to rest, and Ewell's performance at First Manassas was remembered as creditable, a microcosm of his Civil War career. He displayed his eagerness for combat, a propensity for odd behavior, blind obedience to orders, and a cunning resourcefulness under pressure. Throughout the day, under difficult battlefield circumstances, Ewell held the trust of his men. He had made an auspicious start.

Lizinka Brown

Losing the Battle of First Manassas taught the Federals a lesson. They would not fight again until they had trained and organized their troops into a real army, a task given to Major General George McClellan. The new Union commander set up camps around Washington, D.C. where he began the daily drilling of over 100,000 soldiers.

His well-managed efforts were closely monitored by the Confederates, who advanced their defensive line up to the outskirts of the Northern capital. Johnston (now in command of the Southern force) was so close that his men picketing the front could watch civilian workers constructing the dome on the Capitol Building.[1]

Ewell's brigade was located on the far right, where the mouth of Pope's Head Run met the Occuquan River. Johnston's front stretched from that point northwest, following the Potomac River for fifty miles to Leesburg, Virginia. Infantry provided the pickets, serving twenty-four hour shifts on the line; the Rebel cavalry was permanently stationed along the perimeter.

Through the rest of the summer, Ewell's days were spent in dull but important routine training of his men. When the brigade was not covering the line, they practiced regimental drill (marching and mastering the formations used in battle) in the morning, rested throughout the afternoon, then held a formal parade every evening. The work of turning the volunteers, mostly farmers and small town boys, into soldiers went slowly. Everyone was trying hard, but the ranks were seldom full. Coming from rural settings, the men had never been exposed to mumps, chicken pox, or measles, so when one soldier contracted any of these childhood diseases, an epidemic soon followed.

Worried that the enemy would soon assault and overwhelm their weakening line, the Confederates moved back to a safer spot on August 11th. Ewell's brigade retreated twelve miles to Sangster's Crossroads, situated on the Orange and Alexander Railroad. He made his headquarters in a partially-built house, already occupied by fierce yellow jackets who resented his intrusion and had absolutely no respect for rank.[2]

When he was not swatting bees or training his troops, Ewell was entertaining guests such as the Carys, two pretty sisters and their equally beautiful cousin. Late in September, Fitz Lee and Major Benjamin Greene of Ewell's staff had gone to Fairfax Station on an errand. While there, they met Constance, Hettie, and Jennie, and invited the young ladies to visit Ewell's headquarters. They agreed to come the following evening.

It rained heavily throughout the next day. That night, when the ladies arrived, they found the path to Ewell's door sloppy with mud. Fitz Lee, holding a brand new blanket, met their carriage, and with a flourish, unfurled the as yet unsoiled mantle at their feet. Lieutenant John Taliaferro, an aide of Ewell's whom Campbell Brown described as having "the heart of a lion and the brain of a sheep,"[3] groaned out loud at Lee's attempt to make a grand impression. Fitz Lee was using Taliaferro's blanket.

Inside the house, the conversation centered on the hardships of the field, especially the illnesses that had shrunk the ranks of so many men. Fitz Lee slyly alluded to a "home remedy" used for curing coughs. Without much urging, he mixed up a batch. Each of the girls tasted only a spoonful of the whiskey, sugar, and water, hardly enough to make them drunk, but an act so titillating that the officers hosting the fete, including Ewell, were pleasantly shocked.[4]

During the dinner, the men kept stealing glances at the three young ladies. Hettie, tiny, brown-haired, with an exquisite figure,[5] was very beautiful, and her sister, Jennie, was just as bonny. But neither was a match for their cousin Connie, a masterful flirt who demanded and received the most attention. She dominated the after meal festivities, shooting a hand gun and serenading an army regiment as they moved past the house.[6]

While Ewell had been content to just watch the animated banter of his aides and the female guests, he must have seen the

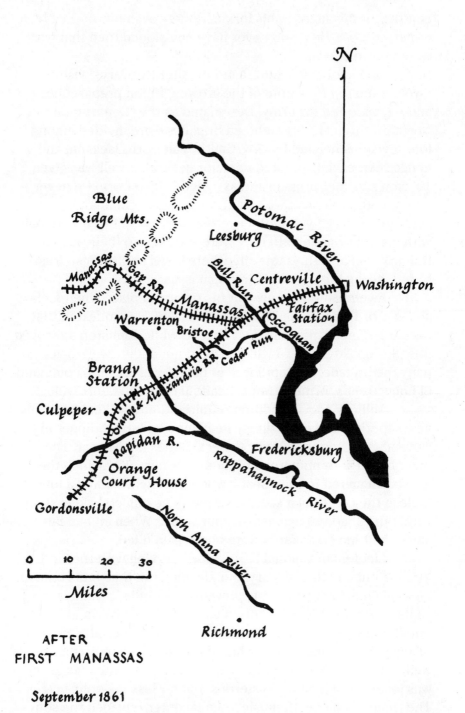

N

Blue
Ridge Mts.

Leesburg

Potomac River

Manassas Gap RR

Bull Run

Centreville

Washington

Manassas

Fairfax
Station

Warrenton

Bristoe

Occoquan

Cedar Run

Brandy
Station

Orange & Alexandria R.R.

Culpeper

Rapidan R.

Fredericksburg

Rappahannock River

Orange
Court House

Gordonsville

North Anna River

0   10   20   30
Miles

Richmond

AFTER
FIRST MANASSAS

September 1861

contrast of this night to his former, lonely evenings in the old army out West. He could never have envisioned then that war would be so social.

On October 22, 1861, a month after the Carys' visit to Ewell, Johnston took note of the growing Union preparedness and restructured his army. Designated as the "Department of Northern Virginia," his eighteen brigades were divided among four divisions headed by G.W. Smith, Van Dorn, Jackson, and Longstreet, each promoted to major general.[7] Ewell was given Jackson's former brigade and assigned to Van Dorn. He never assumed the role. As Ewell was about to take command, Johnston ordered yet another retreat and asked Ewell to remain with his old brigade until they were settled into their post at Union Mills Ford, the same site where Ewell had been so frustrated during the Battle of First Manassas.

Ewell had no sooner put his troops in place when Jackson was ordered to the Shenandoah Valley. He requested that his old regiments accompany him, and while Johnston approved this plea on November 11th, he would not allow Ewell to accompany the brigade. He kept Ewell at hand by giving him command of Longstreet's former troops, headquartered in Centreville.

Military social tradition required that Ewell entertain his new superior, and accordingly he planned a formal dinner in late November in honor of Major General James Longstreet. The night began with numerous rounds of drinks, after which the guests staggered to their seats, wooden benches lining a long table in the center of a spacious room. The officers' aides stood within the shadows against the four walls.[8] When all had finished their meal, tankards were once again filled.

Lieutenant Colonel F.E. Skinner, serving with the First Virginia but a native of Maryland, decided the time had come for musical entertainment. He bellowed for Woodie Latham, a captain with the Eleventh Virginia, to sing "My Maryland," a popular new song. Latham came forward and offered a breathtaking performance. "I never heard it rendered a tenth part as well," Campbell Brown wrote.[9] As Latham began the chorus, he was joined by a host of boisterous, but far less melodic, voices. The room swelled with music, then laughter replaced the song. Longstreet, a heavy-set man lacking all sense of rhythm, had climbed onto the table to dance a teetering jig, tiptoeing as he tried to avoid stomping on the plates Ewell had borrowed.[10]

All at once, conflicting notes were heard. Beauregard, in the spirit of the moment, mounted the wooden bench to sing the only song he knew, the "Marseillaise."[11] Ewell could have marveled again at the disparity between his prior peacetime service and the sociability of this Confederate army of volunteers.

Several days after the party, Campbell Brown left Ewell to go to Richmond. He was sick, suffering from jaundice, and had gone to the capital to recover. When Lizinka learned her son was ill, she hurried east to nurse him. Campbell quickly recovered and returned to Ewell; Lizinka stayed on to visit with her friends and relatives over the holidays. She spent Christmas at Stoney Lonesome, Ewell's boyhood home, fifteen miles from his current headquarters.[12]

Looking to take advantage of her being close by, Ewell invited Lizinka to attend a review of his brigade, where she would see him in command of thousands of men marching in formation and saluting his leadership. He could have hoped that the parade would impress Lizinka with his credentials as an eligible suitor, creating the perfect aura for allowing him to ask for her hand in marriage.

The regiments were in line at the appropriate hour that cold, January day, but Major Greene was late. He was bringing Lizinka and her daughter, Hattie, to the parade grounds. When he finally appeared, Greene was driving their wagon at top speed. As he tore past the first ranks of men, standing at attention, the front seat broke loose, tumbling backward, sending Lizinka and Hattie flying high through the air. The men nearest to the accident were treated to the rare view of stockinged legs and multiple petticoats in the brief seconds before the ladies and Greene landed softly in the hay-filled back floor of the wagon. "The [troops]," Campbell gleefully recalled, "cheered them."[13]

Both Lizinka and Hattie escaped injury. In fact, after scrambling out of the back of the wagon and shaking the straw from her clothes, Lizinka began to laugh about the incident. Her good humor probably saved Greene a profane tongue lashing from Ewell, who must have been infuriated at seeing the accident infringe on his carefully planned scheme to impress his lady.

That night, after they had eaten dinner, Ewell gazed at Lizinka and saw a beautiful woman. Still slim at age forty-one, her dark hair combed in the fashion of the day (parted in the center with long curls nestling on white shoulders), she returned Ewell's amorous stares with deep-set, sparkling eyes. Her nose, straight, perhaps a bit long, added to her loveliness. Only her lips, pursed tightly together, hinted at her stubborn character, a steely determination unusual in ladies of the South.[14] They talked, and at last, when the time seemed right, Ewell asked Lizinka to marry him.

"I think perhaps it was meant that we be united, if not in this world, then surely the next," was her answer.[15] This was not a firm commitment (she even insisted that Ewell keep their possible engagement from her children), but he thought himself betrothed, close to attaining his impossible dream.

Lizinka left for Nashville the next day, leaving behind a changed man. Ewell, still a non-believer who continued to swear, began attending church. He evidently considered attendance at Sunday services a requirement for an agnostic married to a religious-minded lady.

Perhaps he did say a prayer or two; others throughout the South were certainly appealing to the heavens because although the eastern front was still calm, trouble was brewing out west. Kentucky, neutral from the onset of the war, had been occupied by both adversaries. Albert Sidney Johnston was in charge of a Confederate force whose long line stretched from the Appalachian Mountains to the Mississippi River; Ulysses S. Grant was poised with a Federal army, ready to attack the Rebel center just below the Ohio River, where the Cumberland and Tennessee Rivers terminated. Ewell was especially fretful because he had known Grant since West Point, and had always been impressed by his quiet, determined nature. "He is the one man I fear," Ewell had written Richmond, "and I hope the enemy does not discover him."[16]

The enemy did. Grant captured Fort Henry early in February, 1862, opening the way to Fort Donelson, the Tennessee river, Nashville, and eventually Lizinka. Ewell was incensed

over the military ineptness that had brought the war and its
perils to the doorstep of his beloved. "It is perfectly inexpress-
ible that you should have been left in Tennessee with two rivers
perfectly open leading to the heart of the country," he complained in a note to Lizinka. "Large sums were appropriated . . .
for the defense of the Tennessee and Cumberland . . . Johnston
has been badly out-generaled."[17]

Apprehensive for Lizinka's safety, Ewell decided to
resolve the issue himself. He put Campbell on leave to go to
Nashville to convince his mother to shut down her plantation
and return to Richmond. From a distance Ewell added a voice of
warning, writing Lizinka, "If the Yankees conquer Tennessee,
your Negroes go . . . you would be left without a protector. They
[the enemy] don't respect private property . . . after they get a
foothold . . . ."[18]

In the midst of his campaign to manage Lizinka's escape
from Tennessee, Ewell was interrupted by the demands of a new
position. He was made a division commander, replacing Kirby
Smith, reassigned to East Tennessee, and promoted to major
general on February 21, 1862.[19] Although Ewell had wanted a
high rank, this role may have been more than he thought necessary for impressing Lizinka. He groused about his added responsibility, openly complaining, "Why do you suppose President
Davis made me a major general?"[20] Two short years ago, he had
led fifty dragoons; now Ewell was in charge of 8,000 men, split
into three brigades.

The post was, of course, a real plum, and Ewell knew it.
The officers he would command were experienced, among the
most competent in the Confederate armies. Brigadier General
Isaac Trimble headed the Seventh Brigade. A graduate of West
point, Trimble served ten years in the army, then resigned in
1832 to begin a career as a civil engineer, working for the railroad.[21] Trimble was capable, a "dandy" in his dress (he looked
like a general), but not a man for details. His brigade was loosely
trained.

By contrast, the Fourth Brigade, led by Brigadier General
Arnold Elzey was an excellent outfit. They had fought at First
Manassas and had made the last charge that day, the one that
broke the Yankee's line. But while his troops were well disci-

plined, Elzey himself was somewhat suspect. He was open to drinking a dram or two of whiskey if the occasion demanded it— and it usually did.[22]

Such allegations could never be leveled against Brigadier General Richard Taylor, commander of the Eighth Brigade. He was straight-laced to a fault. Only thirty-two years old, the son of Zachary Taylor, the Mexican War general who was later elected President, and the brother-in-law of Jefferson Davis, Taylor was reputed to be aloof, self-assured, a most competent commander of men.[23] His leadership capabilities at this moment were being severely tested by an attached battalion known as the "Louisiana Tigers." Headed by Major Rob Wheat, a mercenary with unsavory experience from all over the world,[24] they were a rowdy collection of thieves, cutthroats, and hoodlums from the wharves of New Orleans. The day after the battle of First Manassas, Tigers in their gay Zouave uniforms of white gaiters, red-stripped pantaloons, short blue jackets, and red fez hats, had plundered the bodies (both North and South) lying on the sunlit field. Taylor gained the Tigers' respect in a gruesome fashion, executing two members of the battalion via a firing squad taken from their own ranks. The culprits had stormed the stockade in an unsuccessful attempt to free other Tiger comrades in jail for looting the quartermaster's stores.[25]

While Ewell was not envisioning executions, he probably did consider taking some sort of drastic action against the volunteers he commanded when he took charge of his division. The enlistments for many had expired; they were of a mind to go home. Anticipating the problem, the Confederate Congress had enacted the Furlough and Bounty Act which granted both a sixty day leave and a fifty dollar bonus to those who signed a commitment to serve for the duration of the war. The noncoms could also change companies or elect new officers.[26]

The latter incentive, of course, caused negative results. The natural inclination of the soldiers was to throw out the "disciplinarians" in favor of leaders who offered to be more lax. Although many outfits were decimated by this approach, Ewell's division survived the changeover without disruption, mostly through the clever efforts of his brigade commanders.

"Taylor wanted [a battery] to reelect their old captain,

but instead they chose their first lieutenant . . . whom he declared worthless," Campbell Brown wrote. "[Taylor] relieved the whole concern from duty and sent them off to Richmond."[27]

Faced with a similar situation, Trimble kept a battery in formation until they agreed to elect the chief he wanted, Lieutenant Joseph Latimer, a slim, silent teenager who would soon prove himself a fearless hero.[28]

At the peak of this complex Confederate reorganization fiasco, McClellan suddenly showed signs of finally beginning his offense. The bluecoats were sure to march south, but the Southern leaders were uncertain of the route they would select. McClellan had three options: he could come through Manassas on the west; he might chose a center path along the Potomac River; or he could sail down the Chesapeake Bay to the peninsula, east of Richmond, between the James and York Rivers. Johnston's position at Centreville was too far north to protect all these avenues, so he decided to withdraw southwest, behind the Rappahannock River, where he could better contest any of McClellan's alternatives.

Three weeks passed before Johnston was able to complete his withdrawal, leaving behind a large stockpile of supplies that he considered too unwieldy to carry. Because Ewell was the last to head south, abandoning his encampment on March 9th, he was given the task of burning the provisions. He lit his fires, then led his troops on a miserable march through cold and rain to their new position. It was below the Rappahannock, close by the mighty Orange and Alexandria Railroad bridge crossing the stream. He posted Elzey's brigade to the right, a half mile downriver from the wooden trestle, Trimble's troops at the span, and Taylor's regiments to the left rear in reserve. Brigadier General Jeb Stuart's cavalry, picketing the ground across the water, lay between Ewell and the enemy.[29]

On March 17, 1862, McClellan made his move, sending his troops by boat down Chesapeake Bay toward the Peninsula east of Richmond. Thinking this might be a feint, that McClellan might still come overland, Johnston decided against hurrying to the capital. Instead, he drew back to the Rapidan River, leaving Ewell on the Rappahannock to blunt any Yankee thrust from above. Ewell was also given the task of gathering provisions to be sent south to the rest of the Rebel army.

Ewell took his assignment seriously, and soon thousands of chickens, beef, hogs, and bushels of grain were headed to the rear. His effort was so vigorous that surrounding farms and fields were quickly stripped, leaving little for his men to eat. Considering the area inexhaustible, Ewell could not believe Richard Taylor when he came to division headquarters (Dr. Cunningham's ornate mansion) to report the problem. To prove that Taylor was wrong, Ewell set out on his own to forage. He returned hours later towing an undernourished bull.

"That's a most respectable animal," Taylor remarked sarcastically, "but he'll hardly afford much subsistence to [our] eight thousand men."[30]

"Ah!" Ewell moaned with recognition, "I was thinking of my fifty dragoons."

A few days later, Campbell returned from his mission to Nashville to evacuate Lizinka. The city had fallen as Ewell had feared, but she had escaped, fleeing south before either Campbell or the enemy arrived. She found refuge in Alabama, in the home of her brother-in-law, Major Hubbard.

Ewell was greatly relieved. With Lizinka safe, he now could concentrate on the war, and he had a devious scheme in mind. He planned to torch the railroad span across the Rappahannock, and he wanted the enemy for an audience. Federal Brigadier General Oliver O. Howard's men lay posted nearby.[31] He would lure Howard to the burning bridge by tearing up the tracks north of the river.

Trimble's Fifteenth Alabama was given the mission with Stuart and his cavalry accompanying them as a guard. The infantry regiment was split into two teams: one would rip up the tracks from their bed, separating the rails from the tar-soaked ties, the second would stack the wooden ties into square piles, balance the long, iron rails on top, then set the heap on fire. Flames, licking the center of the rails, would soon turn that section of the bars red-hot, twisting and bending the metal because of the cold weight hanging at each end. The track would literally self-destruct.[32]

Ewell watched from a small hill south of the river as Trimble's men, working with a professional cadence, headed

Isaac Trimble

Arnold Elzey

Richard Taylor

George Steuart

Photographs from the Library of Congress Collection

toward the horizon. They moved rapidly out of sight, with only the now barren road bed, dotted with piles of smoldering ties, remaining in their wake. All was quiet.

Soon, however, the bark of muskets rose to the north, and the Rebel infantry, shielded by Stuart's horsemen, reappeared, running for the river. Federal soldiers were in hot pursuit. As the Fifteenth Alabama approached the span, they converged to cross, looking like water poured into a funnel. The cavalry followed, Jeb Stuart bringing up the rear. When he reached the south shore, Stuart leaped off his horse and scooted down the bank to where huge struts held up the span. He put a match to the dry hay that had been stuffed between the wooden girders, and the fire ignited immediately.[33]

As the flames soared high into the cold, afternoon air, the Yankees unlimbered their cannon to begin shelling Ewell, still observing from his knoll on the opposite shore. "They fired solid shot at us," Campbell Brown recalled, "which came pretty close."[34] Ewell remained under the barrage for a few minutes, then ordered his men to fall back out of range. He "rode off at a walk," Campbell proudly noted.

All the while, the bridge was burning. As its massive, supporting timbers blackened, sagged, then began giving way, the floor—piece by piece—fell into the stream below. Each fragment spit and splashed when it hit the water. Less than an hour later, all that remained was a stark, smoldering set of beams protruding from each shore.

Ewell returned to the river to check out his handiwork. As he looked at the vacant space over the water, Taylor came to his side to frown at the waste of what had once been a magnificent bridge. He seemed shocked by the destruction.

"You don't like it?" Ewell asked.[35]

"At the close of the Napoleonic wars," Taylor began, "Bugeaud, a young colonel, commanded a French regiment on the Swiss frontier. A stream separated him from an Austrian force four times his strength. He . . . determined to [burn] the bridge, but reflected that if left [standing], it might tempt the enemy . . . to neglect the fords. Accordingly, he masked his regiment as near the end of the bridge as the . . . ground permitted, and waited. The Austrians moved to the bridge, and Bugeaud fell upon them in the act of crossing, and destroyed [their] entire force. Moral: 'Tis easier to defend one bridge than many miles of fordable water."

"Why did you keep that story," Ewell grumbled, "until the bridge was burned?"

With the Yankees in force just across the Rappahannock, Ewell decided to seek a safer position. On March 30, 1862, he left pickets to cover the river as he moved the rest of his division a mile back from the stream. While establishing his headquarters in the Barbour House, close by Brandy Station, Virginia, Ewell learned that McClellan's advance by sea was not a feint. He had landed on the Peninsula and was advancing toward Richmond. Johnston had interposed his army between the enemy and the Rebel capital, but was retreating under the pressure of the Federal assault.

Ewell was exempted from this action. Reinforced by two cavalry regiments under Colonels Flourney and Munford, his orders gave him the choice of joining Brigadier General C.W. Field at Fredericksburg, Virginia or Stonewall Jackson in the Shenandoah Valley. Ewell turned to Field first, writing him to suggest that they combine forces and march on Washington. Ewell repeated this proposal a number of times before finally receiving Field's reply. He informed Ewell that he had just burned the bridges over the Rappahannock River at Fredericksburg. There was no way of crossing the stream to get at the Federals.[36] Left with no other alternative, Ewell looked to Jackson.

* * * *

His engagement to Lizinka, the developing father/son relationship with Campbell Brown, and the comradeship of fellow officers each contributed to an awakening sociability in Ewell the spring of 1862. Eccentricity was the spice with which he enhanced his new-found reputation. Those he came in contact with regarded Ewell as being a bit odd, yet they recognized his intellectual abilities, a provocative combination to both the men who followed him and those he served under. If Ewell thought he had devised a unique way of showing individuality, however, he soon found his match. That was in Stonewall Jackson, the rising star of the Confederacy.

Stonewall Jackson

When Ewell and Jackson began discussions about joining forces in the Shenandoah Valley in April, 1862, the outlook for the Confederacy was bleak across all fronts. The Rebels had seen their line in Kentucky broken at Mill Creek in January, followed by defeats at both Fort Henry and Fort Donelson in February, forcing a withdrawal into lower Tennessee.

The Union successfully established a beachhead in North Carolina that same month. In March, a Confederate advance in Arkansas ended in failure at Pea Ridge. Back east a temporary Southern advantage in ironclad ships was neutralized when the Virginia (Merrimack) failed to oust the Monitor from the waters of Hampton Roads. Control of the Mississippi River began slipping away that April, starting with the fall of Island Number Ten above Memphis, followed by a Yankee down-stream campaign against New Orleans. Fort Pulaski (just outside of Savannah) surrendered to the bluecoats on April 14th, tightening the Yankee blockade along the Georgia coast. And in a bloody April battle in Tennessee, a Federal force under Ulysses S. Grant crushed the Rebels at Shiloh Church.

The combined casualties of the North and South in that April 6th/7th battle exceeded 23,000.[1] General Albert Sidney Johnston was among the Rebel dead, bleeding to death after a stray bullet severed an artery in his leg. "In his fall . . . " President Davis proclaimed sadly that, "the best hope of the South lay buried."[2]

Worst of all, Richmond was surrounded, its people panic-stricken, expecting Federal attack from any of several directions. McClellan with 100,000 troops was inching up the Peninsula from the east; McDowell and 30,000 men were poised north at Fredericksburg; Major General Ambrose Burnside with 11,000 troops was in North Carolina, threatening the city from below; and to the northwest, Major General Nathaniel P. Banks and his 22,000 men were in control of the Shenandoah Valley.

Southern military leaders disagreed on the best means

for coping with the enemy forces encircling Richmond. Should they concentrate for one, main battle (as proposed by Johnston) or divide the Confederacy's meager numbers to attack the Federals in detail, as urged by Robert E. Lee, serving as an advisor to President Davis?[3] Lee's view prevailed, and plans were laid for Jackson to move against Banks in the Valley.

There was merit to the idea. If Stonewall could rout his adversary, he would not only eliminate Banks' threat from the northwest but also sever the supply lines to McDowell, pinning his force to Fredericksburg, allowing Johnston to concentrate on his main threat, McClellan. Ewell was the key pawn in the game. His troops, when added to Jackson's numbers, would provide the strength needed to initiate the campaign.

When Ewell was advised of his role, he contacted Jackson at once. Plans for the consolidation of their forces were begun (couriers riding furiously to and fro), but before commitments were made, Ewell was mortified by a local incident.

"Some [Federal] stragglers were picked up by the cavalry and brought in." Campbell Brown remembered. "Among them, one squad of seven . . . had gone into a yard, stacked [their] muskets against a tree, and left one to watch while the six plundered [the house]. One of our cavalry suddenly rode up to the fellow by the tree, who surrendered at once, and the whole seven were captured and brought off . . . . He got in just as they were breaking open doors, cursing its ladies, and smashing crockery, etc. All were low Germans—what are called 'Black Dutch.' "[4]

Ewell forgot about Stonewall and the Valley for a moment. "Their troops are . . . ill treating the people," he reported indignantly to Richmond, "robbing and stealing . . . committing more wanton injury than they did [during] the Mexican War."[5] Ewell asked for permission to attack the bluecoats to his front, to punish them for their barbaric acts. Robert E. Lee replied if "you feel reasonably assured you can strike a successful blow . . . do so."[6] Johnston was more wary, counseling Ewell to evaluate "relative forces, the enemy's position, and . . . facilities for crossing the river . . . . If you [still] feel confident after considering these things, attack!"[7] But just as Ewell started to develop his strategy, Jackson intervened with a series of conflicting communications.

This was the first incident in what would soon grow into a pattern of confusion in Ewell's relationship with Stonewall. Both had served under Johnston during the onset of the war, so Ewell knew Jackson and was familiar with the background of his new superior. A graduate of West Point, breveted to major for bravery during the Mexican War, Jackson had left the army soon after that conflict ended to become a professor at the Virginia Military Institute. He joined the South when the Civil War began, earning laurels (and his nickname, "Stonewall") for intrepidity during the Battle of First Manassas.

What Ewell did not know (but would soon realize) was that Jackson was more reticent than usual for one born and raised in the isolated, mountainous areas of western Virginia. His growing, intense commitment to Presbyterian beliefs had turned his personality inward, so that he often failed to communicate with others. Stonewall knew just what he meant to do, but he seldom shared his plans. Jackson seemingly had no confidants.

Ewell discovered Stonewall's reluctance to fully communicate immediately. While preparing to assault the Federals to his front, he received a message from Jackson. "The bearer of this letter," Stonewall wrote, "is . . . to guide you to Swift Run Gap in the Blue Ridge [as] I am falling back to that position."[8] Ewell's attack, approved by Lee and Johnston was off; he must go to Jackson. And he must hurry because his orders, noted as sent "In haste," were late. The courier, Lieutenant R.K. Meade, "a one-armed, hapless, well-meaning fellow,"[9] had taken almost twelve hours to deliver the message. Ewell instructed his men to be ready to march by first light on April l9th, but at 3:00 a.m., just as the division was assembling, Lieutenant J.K. Boswell rode up out of the darkness to hand Ewell a different plan. He was to head for Fisher's Gap instead, stopping for a day en route so the troops could observe the Sabbath.[10]

What about the orders that Meade had brought him? What about "In haste"? Boswell knew nothing about the disparity in Stonewall's instructions. Ewell was no doubt exasperated, not only because of Jackson's inconsistency, but also because time would be wasted (his agnostic opinion) on religious services. One can almost hear Ewell's profanity that same day when yet a third courier from Stonewall arrived. Lieutenant Kyd Douglas trotted into camp at 1:00 p.m., fresh and jaunty[11] despite his doleful tale of how arduous his ride through the mountains had been.[12] He brought orders from Jackson telling Ewell to move through Swift Run Gap after all. Kidder Meade would be his guide.[13]

Three hours later, despite the cold, pouring rain, and before Jackson could change his mind again, Ewell was marching. Elzey's men moved out of Brandy Station at 4:00 p.m. on April 19th, 1862. The other two brigades, camped below Elzey, closer to the journey's end, waited until the following morning to leave camp. Ewell left last. Staying past noon to be sure that the division's supplies and baggage were all loaded on trains for Gordonsville, where he would turn west to climb the Blue Ridge, Ewell and his aides mounted once every piece was safely stowed, and rode south to Culpeper to board a rail car that would pass by his marching men to put him at the van ahead of his columns.[14]

Ewell's plan worked perfectly. He reached Gordonsville ahead of his division. But shortly after beginning his march west, he received word from Jackson to hold at Liberty Mills, forty miles short of Swift Run Gap. He waited there for two days, then received orders to advance as far as Stanardsville. "It was a long and hard day's march," Campbell Brown admitted, "and we were glad enough . . . to rest there."[15] The following day, April 28th, Jackson called for only Ewell to come ahead.

The ride to Jackson's headquarters was an arduous, twenty-five miles across the towering Blue Ridge. To Ewell, however, used to the rough trails and rocky ground of the deserts out west, the trek was little more than an outing. On a crystal clear, chilly Sunday afternoon, Ewell rode his blowing mount through Swift Run Gap and down the steep slopes that hovered over the village of Conrad's Store.

Ewell met Jackson outside his headquarters, a clapboard cottage, owned by Mr. Argenbright. As unassuming as the tiny house he occupied, Stonewall was medium in height, dressed in a faded, dark blue uniform. "Cavalry boots covering feet of gigantic size, [and] a mangy cap with visor drawn low," were

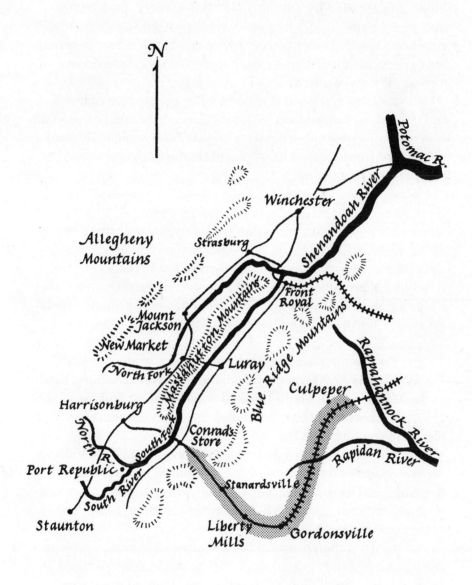

N

Potomac R.

Winchester

Shenandoah River

Allegheny
Mountains

Strasburg

Massanutton Mountains

Front
Royal

Mount
Jackson

New Market

North Fork

Luray

Blue Ridge Mountains

Culpeper

Rappahannock River

Harrisonburg

North
R.

South Fork

Conrad's
Store

Port Republic

South River

Rapidan River

Stanardsville

Staunton

Liberty
Mills

Gordonsville

EWELL'S ROUTE
TO
CONRAD'S STORE

April 19-30, 1862

SHENANDOAH VALLEY

0   5   10   15   20

Miles

highlights recalled by Taylor. "[He had] a heavy, dark beard, and weary eyes . . . . "[16] Jackson's scrubby appearance no doubt reminded Ewell of tales he had heard. Stonewall was renowned for his eccentricity. "I never eat pepper," he was quoted as saying, "it causes a weakness in my left leg."[17]

Jackson had good reason to be apprehensive of Ewell, too. Stonewall's obsession with religious purity must have made him wary of a new subordinate who was both an agnositc and a celebrated master of oaths. A placid relationship between the two seemed highly unlikely.

Whatever they thought of each other, Stonewall and Ewell were soon seated inside Argenbright's house, talking about strategy. Their discussion probably started with a review of the Valley's topography. Three parallel mountain ranges defined the area: the soaring Alleghenies lay to the west, the mesa-like Massanutton rose in the center, and the craggy Blue Ridge sat poised to the east. Two branches of the Shenandoah River, the North Fork and the South Fork, rippled between alternate peaks as they flowed north toward the Potomac River.

Two Federal armies were massed in the Shenandoah. Banks with his 22,000 men was posted near Harrisonburg, south of the Massanutton; Major General John Fremont and his 20,000 troops were west of the Alleghenies, headed southeast for Staunton to unite with Banks.

The Confederates also held two positions in the Valley. Jackson had 6,000 troops with him at Conrad's Store; a small force of 2,500 led by Brigadier General Edward Johnson waited west of Staunton. Ewell's 8,500 men increased the total Confederate numbers to 17,000.

Jackson then presented his strategy. He had to prevent the juncture of the Federal armies. If he could keep Fremont from entering the Valley, then with Ewell's added numbers, he had a chance to defeat Banks alone in battle. Stonewall proposed to slip southwest, join with Johnson in pushing Fremont deep into the Alleghenies, then return to unite with Ewell to deal with Banks. While he was thus involved, Ewell would occupy this place, Conrad's Store. Stonewall's cavalry, led by Colonel Turner Ashby, would picket between Ewell and Banks.

Ewell asked what he should do at Conrad's Store. "Watch

Stonewall Jackson

Photograph from the Library of Congress Collection

Banks!" Jackson tersely replied.[18] Although Ewell probed for a
more definitive answer to his query, Stonewall disdained to say
more, only repeating, "Watch Banks!"

On April 30th, two days after returning from his meeting
with Jackson, Ewell led his troops up the Blue Ridge, through
Swift Run Gap, and down the steep slopes into Conrad's Store.
When the brigades had started out that morning, they shivered
under cold, leaden skies, but as they approached the crest of
the mountain, the clouds began to part. The sun suddenly
appeared, turning the afternoon into a balmy day. Winding
downhill through myriads of orange and blue wildflowers, the
men found their spirits lifted by the inspiring beauty surrounding them, and they sang and laughed as they moved along the
rock-strewn trail toward Conrad's Store.

Jackson and his force had already vacated the town, but
that evening, braving a driving rain storm, Stonewall returned to
make sure Ewell was safely ensconced.[19] Ewell seized the opportunity to badger his superior for more freedom, to be allowed to
do more than just "Watch Banks!" Jackson bent a bit. While he
did not think Banks would leave his position outside of
Harrisonburg, if the enemy shifted south toward Staunton or
east as if to leave the Shenandoah Valley, Ewell should follow
and stop him. Ewell wanted more. Could he attack the Yankees if
Banks carelessly exposed any portion of his army? Jackson
reluctantly agreed, but added that the risks must not be great;
Ewell had to confer with him before opening any action.[20] On
that less-than-positive note, Stonewall galloped off into the rainy
night.

Eager to find a reason to take the offensive, Ewell spent
the next two days spying on the bluecoats. He put his scouts,
"White's Commanches," on top of the flat, barren Massanutton
to watch the Yankee camps. Although they kept Ewell informed
about every minute detail of the daily life of the Union men, the
Comanches were unable to report Banks' intentions, which was
the unreasonable reason Ewell had sent them up on the mountain. He became increasingly irate, berating the scouts for their
incomplete (in his opinion) observations. "One of [Ewell's]
abominations was to receive 'don't know' for an answer," remembered one of the harried cavalrymen, "[but] there were a

great many things which [we] really did not know, and when asked about them . . . could not say anything else."[21]

Ewell decided to contact Jackson, to find out how he had gathered intelligence about the enemy's plans. In his letter to Stonewall, Ewell also outlined an elaborate scheme that he had drawn for disrupting Banks' communications, and asked for permission to proceed. Several days passed before the scout carrying Ewell's message found Jackson (deep in the Alleghenies) and returned with his answer. "I have been relying on spies for my information," Stonewall replied tersely. "The attempt [you propose] is too hazardous."[22]

Enraged by Jackson's brief response, which arrived just as Ewell received word that Banks seemed intent on attacking his position at Conrad's Store, Ewell released his wrath on Colonel James Walker, the leader of the Thirteenth Virginia. "Did it ever occur to you," Ewell raved, "that General Jackson is crazy?"[23]

"I don't know," Walker replied. He could easily relate to Ewell's frustration because as a schoolboy studying under Stonewall at the Virginia Military Institute, he himself had become so infuriated at his teacher, he had challenged Jackson to a duel. As a result of this episode, Walker had been expelled. "We used to call him 'Tom Fool Jackson' . . . but I do not suppose he's really crazy."

"He is as crazy as a March hare!" Ewell insisted. "He has gone away, I don't know where, and left me here with instructions to stay until he returns. But Banks' whole army is advancing on me, and I have not the most remote idea where to communicate with [him]. I tell you, Sir, he is crazy and I will just march my division away from here. I do not mean to have it cut to pieces at the behest of a crazy man."

The report that the Yankees were moving on Ewell proved just a rumor, one of many that came to him over the next few days. And Jackson was not incommunicado, as Ewell had related to Walker. He was not only supplying most of the rumors, but also advising Ewell how he should handle them. "Do what you can . . . to prevent Banks [from] giving assistance to the forces in front [of me and] Johnson . . . "[24] he urged in a letter sent May 4th. Ewell had no idea what Stonewall had in mind. When Jackson repeated his fears the next day, that Banks was going west to reinforce Brigadier General Robert Milroy at the head of Fremont's columns, "Do anything to call him back," Jackson begged.[25] Ewell saw his chance to escape the chains binding him to Conrad's Store. He sprang to action, eagerly planning an assault on Banks' rear. Ewell had barely begun his preparations when Stonewall sent yet another dispatch. Ignoring the perils he had supposed yesterday, Jackson surmised that Banks might be moving north to Strasburg; if so, Ewell must follow him.[26] As Ewell considered this scenario, Stonewall sent his fourth letter in three days, this time warning that Banks was planning to march east, to cross the Blue Ridge at Luray, to join forces with McDowell at Fredericksburg.[27]

That same day Robert E. Lee wrote Ewell, repeating that Banks was said to be leaving the Valley. He instructed Ewell that if Banks moved east, Ewell must cross over the mountain, get between the enemy and Richmond, and strike a blow.[28]

By sifting through this stack of conflicting communications, Ewell found a common thread, the basics of his bizarre situation. He was tied to Banks. As long as the Yankees remained by Harrisonburg, Ewell could not leave Conrad's Store. But if Banks moved, no matter where, Ewell must follow.

Stonewall had been gone for ten days, longer than Ewell had expected. Thinking that perhaps Ashby knew when Jackson would return to unite with him against Banks, Ewell wrote the cavalryman to come and visit him. "I should like to see you very much," he begged, "as I am tired of waiting here . . . . If I hear nothing definite from [Jackson] . . . I expect to be obliged to go back [to Richmond]."[29]

Ashby showed up on May 11th. "I've been in hell for three days," Ewell said as he welcomed the cavalier. "Been in hell . . . . What's the news from Jackson?"[30]

" . . . The Lord has blessed our arms with another glorious victory," Ashby answered.[31] He went on to report that on May 8th, Stonewall had intercepted Fremont's van under Milroy and fought a battle at McDowell, a tiny village twenty-five miles west of Staunton. The combat had raged from 4:30 p.m. until late that night; the Confederates had suffered twice as many casualties as the Federals (Edward Johnson had been wounded, taking a ball in the foot); but in the end, Jackson held the field.

Ewell was ecstatic upon hearing Ashby's news. Fremont's defeat meant that Jackson would soon return to Conrad's Store to begin the campaign against Banks. Ewell's improved disposition was gratefully noticed by his men. "The boys began to think there might be a warm place somewhere away down in his . . . iceberg of a heart," one of the scouts recalled, "and they decided that he wasn't such a savage old bear after all."[32]

But Jackson did not reverse his course. He did not return. Instead, he chased after Fremont, driving him deep into the mountains, making sure his adversary would not cross the Alleghenies to unite with Banks' force in the Valley. Worse yet, the latter was rumored to be preparing to leave New Market (a town fifteen miles north of Harrisonburg where he had recently consolidated his force). His men were said to be cooking three days' rations.

Ewell's distress returned, and he poured out his bitter frustration in a letter to his niece, Lizzie. "I have spent two weeks of the most unhappy I [can] ever remember," he began. " . . . I have been keeping one eye on Banks, one on Jackson, all the time jogged up from Richmond . . . I ought to be en route to Gordonsville, at this place, [or] going to Jackson, all at the same time . . . . I have a bad headache, what with the bother and folly of things . . . . As an Irishman would say, 'I'm kilt entirely.' "[33]

On May 12th Banks suddenly added to Ewell's vexation. He split his army, one group staying with him at New Market, the other, troops under Major General James Shields, heading east, planning to leave the Valley and reinforce McDowell at Fredericksburg.[34]

By dividing his force, Banks placed Ewell in a terrible quandary. According to Jackson's precise orders, as long as Banks remained at New Market, Ewell could not leave Conrad's Store. But Lee had written if the Federals left the Valley, Ewell was bound to follow over the Blue Ridge to block their advance toward Richmond. Banks had both stayed in place and moved to vacate the Valley. Whose orders should Ewell obey? On the surface, the predicament was easily resolved; Lee was the superior officer, his word should prevail.

But Ewell did not want to take his troops from the Valley.

He had come to assault Banks, and now that the bluecoats had reduced their army, the campaign was all the more promising. Obviously, without Ewell's division, Jackson lacked the numbers for making the attack they'd all been waiting for. Ewell had to stay in the Valley. He saw that his only chance of doing so was somehow to find a means (within the restraints of Jackson's instructions) of keeping Shields' half of the Northern force there, too.

Ewell immediately sent a note to Jackson, informing him of the problem. He hoped Jackson would come to his locale. He then turned to deal with Shields. Although his orders forbade his leaving Conrad's Store unless Banks with his whole army also left New Market, Ewell reasoned he could at least direct a small portion of this command after Shields. Colonel Thomas Munford's four cavalry companies, two cannons from Brokenbough's artillery, and two cavalry companies from Lieutenant Colonel Thomas Flourney's regiment were given the mission. Munford was in charge, but before going, he was to call on Ewell for last minute instructions.

Munford knocked on Ewell's bedroom door about midnight. "Before I knew what he was after," Munford related, "[Ewell] sprang out of bed, with only a nightshirt on . . . and spreading the map open . . . down on his knees he went; his bones fairly rattled, his bald head and long beard [made Ewell] look more like a witch than a Major General."[35] After pointing out the positions of Jackson, Shields, and McDowell, Ewell spoke his mind.

"This great wagon hunter is after a Dutchman, [the] old fool," he raved, referring to Jackson. "General Lee at Richmond will have little use for wagons if . . . these people close in around him; we are left out . . . in the cold. Why, I could crush Shields before night if I could move from here . . . Jackson is certainly a crazy fool, an idiot."[36]

Seeing that his tantrum made no sense to Munford, Ewell produced a letter just received from Jackson, who wrote that with the help of God, he had captured Milroy's wagon trains.

In that same note, Jackson admonished Ewell to stay by Swift Run Gap. "What has Providence to do with Milroy's wagons . . . " Ewell fumed. "Mark my words, if this old fool keeps this

54

up, and Shields joins McDowell, we will go [to] Richmond . . . . "[37]
Having vented his wrath at Stonewall, Ewell returned to the
dilemma with Shields. He implored Munford to do all he could to
prevent the Federals from leaving the Valley, and he insisted
that he be kept informed.

After the Colonel departed, Ewell went back to bed. He
was soon interrupted again when an aide of Munford's stomped
up the stairs, opened Ewell's door, and asked loudly for
his superior.

"Look under the bed," Ewell shouted as he leaped to his
feet. "Do you see him there?"[38] Before the surprised officer could
reply, Ewell bellowed, "Do you know how many steps you
came up?"

"No, Sir."

"Well, I do, by every lick you gave 'em with that thing
[sword] you have hanging about your feet . . . . " Continuing to
berate his visitor, Ewell barked, "Do you know how many
ears you have?"

"Sir?"

"You'll go out of here less one, and maybe both, if you
ever wake me up this time a night [again]!"

While that evening of May 12th was trying, the next day
was the longest so far of Ewell's life. Hour after hour, he waited
in vain for word from Munford. He had no clue as to whether the
cavalry had been able to catch up with Shields, much less
impede his path out of the Valley. And despite the desperate
letter sent to "the enthusiastic fanatic" (as Ewell had come to
call Stonewall),[39] he had received no acknowledgment from
Jackson that he understood that their scheme to attack Banks
was at risk. Finally, late that day, the communications dam
broke, and four letters came to Ewell.

Johnston's was the first to arrive. He advised, "Should
(Shields) cross the Blue Ridge . . . Jackson and yourself should
move eastward . . . . "[40] Next, a dispatch from Stonewall was
received. Giving no recognition of Ewell's warning that Banks
had divided his force, Jackson repeated his oft-given advice, "If
Banks goes down the Valley, follow him."[41] Ewell rejoiced over
this note. His scouts had just informed him that Banks had
begun withdrawing to the north. Here was his opportunity to

escape the confinement of Conrad's Store. He would evacuate the dreary town before Stonewall changed his mind again, and take his division to Luray, halfway down the Valley, east of the Massanutton. This path gave Ewell three options: he could turn west from that point to intercept Banks moving to Strasburg; he could go north to Front Royal to keep Shields from leaving the Valley; or he could march east using Thornton's Gap to cross the Blue Ridge if called to Richmond.

As the troops began to assemble, Ewell sent Campbell to Gordonsville with orders for Brigadier General L.O.B. Branch, heading a brigade just assigned to Ewell, to hurry forward, meeting the division at Luray. Ruefully mindful of Jackson's seeming preoccupation with wagons, Ewell added a poetic postscript: "The road to glory cannot be followed with much baggage."[42]

All this effort was in vain. Before the day ended, Ewell received his third message. Stonewall had realized at last that Shields was about to leave the Valley, but instead of allowing Ewell to use his whole force to thwart the enemy movement, he authorized only employing cavalry, a step Ewell had already taken. By inference, and despite Banks' movement north, the rest of the division was to continue to remain at Conrad's Store.[43]

Robert E. Lee sent the fourth letter, received by Ewell the morning of May 14th. In his terse dispatch, Lee ordered Ewell to stay in place, to await Stonewall's return from his western foray against Fremont.[44] Ewell was encouraged by the note. While Lee knew that Shields meant to leave the Valley, he had not sent Ewell (as had Johnston) after the bluecoats. The original strategy to assault Banks had not yet been cancelled. There was still hope of a good fight. Still, Ewell was nervous, worried that generals and politicians far from his post amidst the rugged mountains of the Shenandoah Valley would neither understand the potential within his grasp nor appreciate the need for a quick, positive decision.

Three days later, still glued to Swift Run Gap, Ewell's flagging spirits were sent soaring by Jackson. Writing from Mount Solon, twelve miles from Harrisonburg, he offered, "I design moving, via Harrisonburg, down the Valley, and it may be that a kind Providence will enable us to unite and strike a suc-cessful blow."[45] Jackson was almost at hand, and he was finally aiming to fight! In just a day, no more than two, the long-delayed offensive would finally start. But as dusk came on, bringing with it a cold, steady rain, a courier from Munford destroyed Ewell's ardor. Shields, after eluding the cavalry, had moved out of the Valley.

Ewell knew he must go after Shields. Johnston (Ewell's and Jackson's immediate superior) had specifically noted that if the enemy left the Shenandoah, Ewell must follow, and his directives allowed no discretion. But after ordering his men to start preparing to leave Conrad's Store, Ewell hesitated. Banks, weakened by the reduction of his army, was quite temptingly vulnerable, and even if Shields did reach McDowell, routing Banks within the week would cut the enemy's supply line to Fredericksburg. McDowell, despite Shields' reinforcements, could not advance on Richmond without bread and bullets. So the initial reason for Ewell's entering the Shenandoah Valley in the first place was still sound. Ewell made the only decision he could under the circumstances; he called for his horse to ride to Stonewall to discuss how they might salvage the original pur-pose and execution of the campaign: to attack and defeat Banks.

After an all night gallop, Ewell reached Mount Solon on Sunday morning, May 18th. His view of Stonewall's camp must have evoked his ire. Instead of preparing to hurry to Conrad's Store, to unite with Ewell in attacking the enemy, Jackson's troops were resting—taking naps, washing clothes, cooking food, waiting for church services to be conducted later that afternoon. With only a few, precious days available for engaging Banks, Jackson was willfully wasting one on observing the Sabbath.

Stonewall, dressed in a crisp new uniform of Confederate gray, greeted Ewell in front of his headquarters, but he quickly decided that the two should talk elsewhere (not only for secrecy but also to move Ewell's blasphemous tongue away from the ears of his pious men). They rode to an old mill. Once settled in the dank, cobwebbed building by a country stream, Ewell poured out his plight, that Johnston's orders required him to leave the Valley to intercept Shields' passage toward McDowell.

"Providence denies me the privilege of striking a decisive blow for my country," Jackson concluded sadly. "I must be satisfied with the humble task of hiding my little army about these mountains, to watch a superior force."[46]

Ewell would not accept Jackson's maudlin rationalizing. He blurted out the idea that had filled his troubled mind all through the long night's gallop to Mount Solon. All was not lost. He would simply disobey his orders to leave the Valley, to pursue Shields—the orders from Johnston. He, they, would go for Banks. As Stonewall no doubt stared with disbelief, Ewell went on to explain his plan. He was assigned to the Valley where Jackson was his superior. If Stonewall would issue an order for him to remain, Ewell was willing to risk rank and career by assuming responsibility for following that directive over Johnston's. Stonewall gladly accepted Ewell's proposal. It would put them both in a position to defeat Banks and salvage the flagging campaign. He wrote out instructions directing Ewell to "move your command so as to encamp between New Market and Mount Jackson on next Wednesday night." He then added a critical proviso, "unless you receive orders from a superior officer and of a date subsequent to the 16th."[47]

Having settled that issue, the two then started to plot their attack on Banks. Stonewall proposed a fast march down the Valley, west of the Massanutton. Ewell disagreed. Noting that the bluecoats had built strong fortifications below Strasburg, he favored marching east of the mountain to Front Royal, which was guarded by only a tiny Union force.[48] After capturing the garrison, they could hurry west for Winchester and take Banks from the rear.

Jackson agreed with Ewell's plan, but added a modification. To deceive the enemy into believing that he and Ewell intended to join and attack from the south, Ewell would send a brigade (Taylor's) to Stonewall, who would start advancing on Banks' rear west of the Massanutton. When he came to New Market, Jackson, screened from the Federals view by Ashby's cavalry, would suddenly veer right, over the Massanutton, to unite with Ewell, marching north along the eastern slopes of the mountain, to swoop down on Front Royal.

A much relieved Ewell paid a high price for his role in

saving the campaign. Stonewall insisted he delay his return to
Conrad's Store to attend Sunday services. As he settled in the
grass with the men of the Twelfth Georgia, Ewell may have
listened with suspicion to the words of Reverend Robert
Dabney, seemingly speaking directly to him. "Come ye that are
weary and heavily laden . . . . " the minister/soldier began his
sermon.[49]

Upon arriving back at Conrad's Store, Ewell gave Taylor
his orders to join Jackson, then started the rest of his division
north. They halted for the night at Columbia Bridge, just below
Luray, on May 20th. That same evening the carefully preserved
campaign began to unravel. Ewell received a note from Branch,
(supposedly on the way to join him) which said that he would
not be coming after all; he had been recalled to Richmond. And
the next morning, a messenger rode up with new directives from
Johnston. "If Banks is fortifying near Strasburg, attack would be
too hazardous. We must leave him in his works," Johnston
wrote. "[Let] Jackson . . . observe him . . . you come eastward."[50]
The orders were dated May 17, 1861, subsequent to the instructions Stonewall had given to Ewell. A senior officer had intervened. Ewell could no longer stay in the Valley.

Johnston had added at the bottom of his message that it
should be sent on to Jackson. Ewell called Lieutenant Frank
Myers to his headquarters, gave him a parcel including
Johnston's note, and ordered, "Mount the best horse you can
find and carry [this] to General Jackson."[51] Myers had no inkling
as to where Stonewall was located, but from past experience, he
knew better than to say, "I don't know." He took the pack of
letters and without uttering a word, rushed outside to ask
others if they knew Jackson's whereabouts. Ewell, realizing that
Myers required directions, followed. "Go to New Market and
take the turnpike [south] to Harrisonburg," he bellowed. "I want
to see you again today."[52]

Myers ran to his horse and rode off. Ewell should have
started assembling his troops for the march back to Conrad's
Store, but he held back. What would Stonewall's reaction be to
Johnston's letter? Was there any chance of salvaging the campaign, after all this frustration and planning? Thorton's Gap was
nearby. Several hours could be saved using that pass, time to

linger, hoping for a miracle. Ewell decided to wait until Myers returned with Jackson's reply. As the minutes of the morning slowly ticked by, Ewell, his stomach churning and burning from its aroused ulcer, kept glaring up the Massanutton, looking for Myers to appear. By early afternoon, when he could no longer stand the suspense, Ewell asked for his horse. He had decided to go up the mountain and intercept his scout. Winding his way along the zig-zag trail, Ewell spotted Myers approaching from above. They met. The scout handed Ewell an envelope. It was the letter from Johnston that he had forwarded to Stonewall. Along the bottom of the page, Jackson had scrawled, "Suspend the execution of the order for returning to the east until I receive an answer to my telegram."[53]

Jackson had joined Ewell in insurrection! To question a superior's orders was tantamount to disobeying them. With the problem now in Stonewall's hands, Ewell could only worry and wait. His vigil lasted well into the night. Before the sun rose, a courier stole into camp. He sought out Ewell to give him a message. Lee had interceded. Impressed with the inspired plan Ewell had convinced Jackson to support, he had authorized continuing the campaign. Come morning, Stonewall would cross the Massanutton to join with Ewell in their move against Front Royal and the long-sought goal of engagement with the forces of Nathaniel Banks.

* * * *

The weeks of waiting on Jackson brought out an unseemly side of Ewell. Frustrated by Stonewall's secrecy, the often conflicting orders from Richmond, and his lost opportunities to attack an unenterprising enemy, Ewell acted as his father often had, irrationally blaming others. In this case, he mostly blamed Jackson for being unable to handle his own problems. Worse yet, he vented his fury on his troops. They obeyed him more out of fear than respect.

But while his men trembled under his anger, Ewell's reputation soared with the Confederate command. Stonewall was pleased with a subordinate who followed all his orders without a question. Lee respected Ewell's every suggestion.

None of this was particularly important. What mattered was that Ewell had not yet been tested under fire. And when he did finally go into battle, Ewell would have to prove himself— perhaps more to his troops than either Jackson or Lee.

The Valley Battles

While Jackson and his men were crossing the Massanutton to unite with Ewell to attack Banks' outpost at Front Royal, the Northern menace to Richmond approached the crisis stage. McClellan had maneuvered Johnston up the Peninsula to within a few miles of the Southern capital, putting the Federals in position to open what many thought would be the final battle of the war. A Yankee victory could be assured if the 40,000 men under McDowell (including Shields' Division, en-route from the Valley) came down from Fredericksburg, adding their numbers to McClellan's assault. President Davis was so concerned that he had evacuated his wife to Raleigh, North Carolina, where she would be safe.[1] If the Valley Campaign was to have any meaning and eliminate both Banks and McDowell as factors in the enemy's strategy for taking Richmond, then Jackson and Ewell had to move now!

Jackson reached Ewell at Luray the evening of May 21st. He spent the night reorganizing his army, assigning the men formerly under Brigadier General Edward Johnson (wounded during the battle with Fremont's van at McDowell) to Ewell. A new brigade was formed, led by Colonel W.C. Scott; Elzey's command was strengthened by the addition of three regiments; and the "Maryland Line" was created (a battalion composed of troops, natives of that state) for Brigadier General George Steuart.[2]

Rising early the next morning, the army—17,000 strong —finally began its march to Front Royal. The road leading northward, tucked between the jagged Blue Ridge on the right and the flat Massanutton to the left, was so rutted that the troops found it difficult to keep in step. And when the sun rose over the mountain, its sultry rays began to take a toll. Even Jackson's formula for marching (fifty minutes of striding, then ten minutes of rest) could not keep men from falling by the wayside. The ranks thinned as the exhausted and thirsty left the columns to seek shade and water. Stonewall harried those left in line, "Close up!" By nightfall, the survivors of the difficult trek were about ten miles from Front Royal. Twenty lung-searing miles lay in their wake.

The dawn of May 23rd presented an azure, cloudless sky. As the anxious eyes of the weary troops scanned the horizon, they saw that it would be another sunny, sizzling day. As the troops fell into line, Stonewall changed his order of march. Ewell's division, which had trailed yesterday, took the lead with Taylor first, then Elzey, Trimble, the Maryland Line, and Scott. The army moved forward. Several miles up the road, Stonewall and Ewell, riding with the van, received word that Front Royal was being garrisoned by the First Maryland, a bluecoat regiment. Jackson was so intrigued by this news, that he stopped the column to order Colonel Bradley Johnson to "Move [the Maryland Line] to the front with all dispatch."[3] He would let his Marylanders test their manhood against their treacherous cousins.

When he reached Spangler's Crossroads, Jackson sent his cavalry under Ashby and Flourney splashing through a ford in the South Fork, heading west. While the troopers would have been useful in the upcoming fray, Stonewall had in mind for them the more important role of cutting the telegraph wires from Front Royal to Strasburg. He did not want Banks to discover that he was in peril.

Four miles from Front Royal, Stonewall stopped. Noting that the main pike into town was likely to be fortified, he wheeled the Maryland Line and Taylors' brigade right onto the Gooney Manor Road. They would follow this lesser route into the village to attack the Yankees' flank from the east. The rest of the army would hold in place, advancing only after the way ahead had been cleared. Jackson and Ewell would accompany the strike force.

The Gooney Manor Road was a formidable challenge in itself. A broken, muddy trail winding up a rise into a forest of pine, it proved a difficult path to climb. When the panting, sweating men finally reached a plateau, they swung left to follow a trail through giant evergreens. The troops were protected from the blazing sun by the trees, but beneath the needled canopy, the air was saturated with moisture. Lungs already test-ed by a nine-mile hike now labored to breathe in the humid atmosphere. Except for the soldiers' gasps, there was no sound. The woods were as still as an empty church.

When Johnson's Marylanders finally came out from under the tall, closely spaced trees and into a meadow, a soli-tary enemy sentinel, relaxing in the thick grass by a rail fence, saw them coming. The astonished soldier leaped to his feet, fired a warning shot into the air, then ran down the heights to alert his comrades in the village below.

Urging their mounts onward to the knoll's edge, Jackson and Ewell looked down on the charming village of Front Royal, whose houses were clustered like children's blocks, arranged in rows, the symmetry broken only by several church steeples reaching for the sky. The Gooney Manor Road descended into the town from the south. The Valley Pike ran west, parallel to this route, until it came abreast of the hamlet, where it turned east into Front Royal, then exited above, swinging to the north-west. To the east, beyond the village, the Manassas Gap Rail-road crawled out of the foothills of the Blue Ridge. A spur ran south into the town while the main line continued west, crossing the South Fork just below the point where the stream joined the North Fork to become the Shenandoah River. Three bridges were in sight: an old, rickety wagon span led the Valley Pike across the South Fork below the railroad; a wooden viaduct carried the tracks over the same stream; and above the railroad, a third bridge took the Valley Pike over the North Fork.

Front Royal, a mile beyond and beneath the viewpoint of Jackson and Ewell, was swarming like a wasps' nest as men in blue, roused by their surprised picket, scurried through the streets, leaving their defensive positions along the pike to form a new line across the Gooney Manor Road. As he watched the drama unfold, Ewell was distracted by the sudden appearance of a young woman running toward him. Dressed in a white frock, waving her bonnet to catch his attention, Belle Boyd (already infamous as a Confederate spy) came up to report breathlessly that the Federals had just one regiment at hand, supported by two cavalry companies, and a few cannons. "Charge right down," she urged, "and [you will] catch them all."[4]

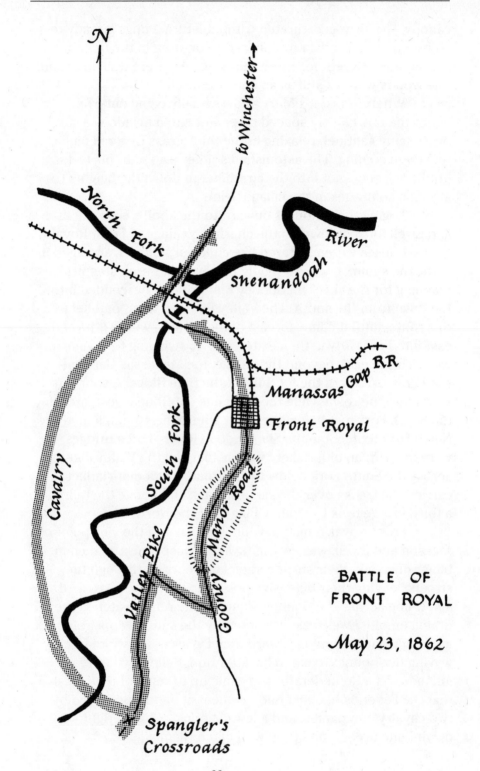

N

to Winchester →

North Fork

River

Shenandoah

Manassas Gap RR

Front Royal

Cavalry

South Fork

Valley Pike

Gooney Manor Road

BATTLE OF
FRONT ROYAL

May 23, 1862

Spangler's
Crossroads

As if on cue, Richard Taylor rode up, ready to lead his brigade against the enemy. The Louisiana Tigers, dressed in their preposterous Zouave uniforms, were up front; the rest of the regiments followed behind. Jackson laid out his plan for attack: the Sixth Louisiana under Colonel Isaac Seymour would charge on the left; the Tigers with the Maryland Line would swing right, to assault the enemy from the flank. The other troops would hold in reserve.

At first the men made their descent toward Front Royal at deliberate speed. But their frustrated yearning to fight could not be stemmed for long, and with a shout from Taylor, the whole force surged forward, screaming as they raced down the hill to engage the bluecoats. "I shall never forget the style in which the [Tigers] passed us," Campbell said in his memoirs. "[Wheat] was riding at full gallop, yelling at the top of his voice . . . [his men] strung out according to . . . speed or 'stomach for the fight' . . . . All running, all yelling, all looking like fight."[5] The Yankee line melted into the town, then beyond to the plain above where the Confederates caught up to them. The combat was individual, hand to hand, man to man.

Suddenly, a shrill whistle split the air. The fighting faltered as all eyes turned east to see a locomotive roaring out of the mountains toward them. Rocketing down the hill at top speed, the engineer saw that he was about to drive right into the center of the battle. He hit the brakes, but could not stop because of the steep grade of the track and the load of his cars, pushing from behind. With its wheels locked and screeching, the engine slithered into the middle of the fray.

An ominous thought swept through the Rebel ranks. Had reinforcements arrived in the nick of time to save the enemy? The Louisiana Tigers answered their question. With practiced ease, they swarmed the train, opening the doors of box cars, stripping tarpaulins off flat beds, exposing an immense load of equipment and supplies. A few of the men, more interested in fun than looting, climbed into the cab, booted the engineer from his seat, and began tooting the whistle to celebrate their conquest.[6]

All the while, only yards to the northwest, Seymour and Johnson continued the fight, driving the enemy toward a ridge fronting the rivers where the Yankee cannons were unlimbered, waiting to fire. As the enemy soldiers raced past the guns, their artillery opened with deadly canister against the pursuing Rebels. The Confederates stumbled to a stop under the hail of lead pellets, then fell back as the withering blasts took their toll.

Wheat's Tigers were retrieved from the train and became part of a new line that charged the bluecoat position again. This advance was also repelled by the enemy cannons, leaving a scattering of gray-clad bodies sprawled on the ground to mark the high point of the impetuous attack.

Watching from the knoll south of Front Royal, Stonewall found the repulse more than he could bear. He ordered Ewell to hold while he hurried forward to take charge of the front. If Jackson needed reinforcements, he would send word back to Ewell to bring up the reserves, posted on the pike four miles away.

As Ewell watched Jackson gallop down the hill, a Yankee artillery round whizzed overhead. The Federal batteries had switched to Ewell as their target. Puzzled as to why the enemy gunners would waste ammunition on a lone officer and his tiny staff, Ewell whirled in the saddle to see twenty riders and their mounts assembled close behind him. Their presence had drawn the Union's fire. Ewell galloped up to the gathering.

"What do you mean . . . by making a target of me . . . with these men?" he demanded of Lieutenant Myers and his band of scouts known as "The Commanches."[7]

"Why, General," Myers protested in innocence, "you told me to stay near you, and I'm trying to do it."

"Clear out, Sir, clear out!" Ewell shouted. "I did not tell you to get all your men killed, and me, too."

As the Commanches scattered, Ewell galloped back to the brow of the knoll where he saw that the Federal artillery had stopped firing at him. The Yankees had limbered their guns to join their infantry in running pell-mell for the bridges crossing the two forks of the Shenandoah. Rebel cavalry was approaching from the west, and if the bluecoats did not get over the streams now, before the Southern horsemen arrived, they would be cut off without a means of escape. The Yankee soldiers won the race, racing first across the narrow wagon structure, then turning north to cross the pike bridge.

The last of the Union men to reach the far shore of the North Fork stopped for a moment to set the span on fire. Hot flames burst skyward as the Tigers, close on the heels of the withdrawing enemy, poured onto the bridge. Wheat and his men, however, stopped on the opposite bank, giving up their chase to fight the fire. Then Seymour's troops, the Maryland Line, and Flourney's cavalry arrived on the scene. They, too, joined in battling the blaze, forming bucket brigades, using hats to throw water onto the smoldering embers. By the time the fire had been extinguished, the enemy was out of sight.

Stonewall refused to let the Federals escape. Despite their head start, he was determined to catch them all, and he ordered Flourney and his troopers to chase after the Yankees. Jackson himself would lead the pursuit. As the sun vanished below the western horizon, the Rebel cavalry returned, herding 650 disconsolate prisoners plus two of the Yankee's guns into Front Royal. Ewell was especially pleased with the capture of "a fine Parott piece . . . brought off within sight of the enemy pickets by Privates Fontaine and Moore." Describing the feat in his battle report, he wrote, "Using two plow horses from a neighboring field, [the men] brought it back to Front Royal—a piece of cool daring, hard to match."[8]

The Confederates had no time to celebrate their victory; they had to move quickly if they were to take advantage of their hard-won position on Banks' flank. Jackson issued his orders: Campbell Brown was placed in charge of the captives, arranging for their movement south to Richmond and prison; the Twelfth Georgia under Colonel Z.T. Conner would garrison Front Royal; and as soon as the other brigades (still waiting on the Valley Pike, four miles away) came up, Stonewall would head west for Winchester.

Ewell led the army out of Front Royal, moving as far as Cedarville before halting for the night. Just before dawn on May 24th, a cold rain started to fall. Ewell woke his troops and began marching again, but Jackson soon ordered them to a stop. Banks surely knew by now that the Rebels were on his flank. He had three options: remain at Strasburg; go north to Winchester; or slip by Stonewall to exit the Valley through the pass west of

Front Royal. Jackson had to know which path the enemy would take before he moved any further.

Ewell's cavalry, just assigned to Steuart, was sent west, to scout Banks and discern the enemy's plan. At about noon, one of the troopers returned to report that Banks was withdrawing toward Winchester, his wagons filled with supplies strung out up and down the Valley Pike. Hoping to catch the bluecoats in column, Stonewall led four brigades toward Middletown (halfway between Strasburg and Winchester). Ewell, his three brigades, and the Maryland Line stayed behind to guard against the Yankees' using their trains as bait, sacrificing wagons so troops could make the dash east for Front Royal.

About 2:00 p.m., the thunder of cannons told Ewell that a battle had started. While the fighting raged throughout the afternoon, Ewell suffered the agony of ignorance: he had no idea who was winning the fray; he received no orders to come ahead from his remote post. Finally, at 4:30 p.m., Stonewall sent word that he had pierced the enemy's columns. But Banks had started only his wagons for Winchester; his infantry had stayed behind at Strasburg. Jackson wrote that he intended to capture the trains, then attack Banks. Ewell was to send two of his brigades (Elzey's and Taylor's) to join in the charge; his remaining regiments (Trimble's) and the Maryland Line were to remain at Cedarville with him.

A half an hour later, Steuart and the cavalry rode back into camp to report that Banks had just arrived in Winchester. He was not at Strasburg; his infantry had marched at the van of his columns, not at the tail as Stonewall had said. Ewell was incensed. Jackson was again obsessed with wagons instead of the enemy's troops.

While his orders were to hold in place, Ewell recognized that he should be confronting Banks. He decided he must rush to Winchester. Trimble's brigade, the cavalry, and the Maryland Line started out at once. Ewell knew that he was taking a great risk by willfully disobeying instructions, but he manfully faced the issue by sending word of his movement to Jackson. As it turned out, Ewell escaped censure. At almost the same time that Ewell started for Winchester, Stonewall learned that Banks' infantry had eluded him, and he issued orders for the step Ewell had just taken on his own.[9]

As the sun slowly sank in the west, Ewell's troops moved rapidly forward, but their pace soon slowed. Dusk, then night and its blackness arrived. The men could barely see the path ahead. All at once, bursts of flame flared from both sides of the road. Enemy ambush! Ewell quickly formed a skirmish line, put himself in command, and charged after the unseen Federals. They proved to be only Union pickets, who disappeared into the darkness when challenged. In a succession of such stops and starts, Ewell's force crept ahead. When they were within two miles of Winchester, Ewell came to a halt for the rest of the night.

Before sunrise on Sunday, May 25th, Ewell rose and rode with his aides toward Winchester to reconnoiter the village. Less than a mile from the town, they wheeled left to scramble up a high knoll that overlooked the coming battle arena. The village below was larger than Front Royal, its houses (enough for 5,000 people) arrayed in an oblique rectangle. Above the town and to the west, a series of strong forts perched each on its own ridge, covering the approaches into the town from the south. Banks obviously anticipated Jackson's attack from that direction as he had put most of his men in these emplacements. East of Winchester, no Yankee troops could be seen. The road from Front Royal appeared undefended.

Ewell decided to attack at once. Calling his artillery forward, he positioned a battery of four guns on each side of the Front Royal road, then formed his battle line. His force included the Twenty-First North Carolina led by Colonel W.W. Kirkland, the Maryland Line under Colonel Bradley Johnson, and the Twenty-First Georgia commanded by Colonel John T. Mercer. Ewell's cannons opened at 5:40 a.m.; Kirkland led the charge.

Surging forward, smugly confident that no one would contest their attack, Kirkland's impetuous troops were staggered when Yankee soldiers, crouched behind a stone wall, leaped up and fired a blistering volley into their flank. Kirkland, at the head of the charge, fell first, and within a few seconds, seventy-five of his men lay dead or dying on the ground, too.[10] The Maryland Line, following Kirkland, veered eastward, away from the town, but Mercer and his Georgians, also trailing,

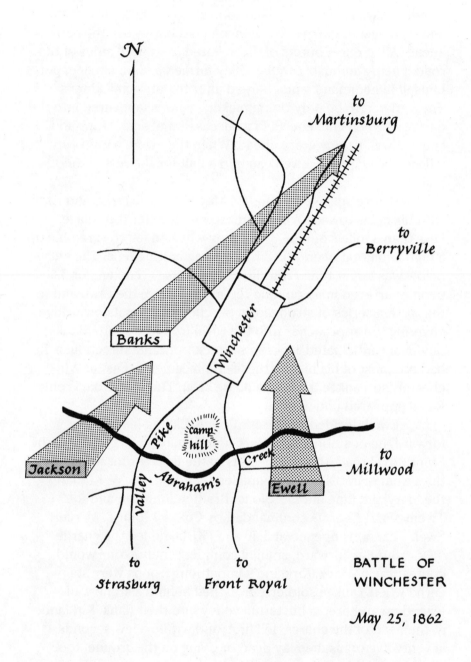

N

to
Martinsburg

to
Berryville

Banks

Winchester

camp
hill

Valley Pike

Abraham's

Creek

Jackson

Ewell

to
Millwood

to
Strasburg

to
Front Royal

BATTLE OF
WINCHESTER

May 25, 1862

turned west and got behind the enemy position. The Federals, seeing the threat to their rear, abandoned their rocky barricade and fled into Winchester. The Rebels did not pursue them. Noting that they were within range of the Union guns, posted high in the forts to the west, Johnson and Mercer elected instead to dig in. The Maryland Line entrenched below the village; the Georgians assumed a position behind the slopes east of town. The fight disintegrated into a languid exchange of artillery.

As the opposing cannons threw shell after shell at each other, the valley below Ewell filled with white, acrid smoke. Unable to see each other, both artilleries stopped firing at the exact moment, as if someone had suddenly thrown a switch to deaden the thunder.[11] But the eerie stillness was only an illusion, because once the clamor of cannons was eliminated, the rattle of muskets on the left filled the air. Stonewall and his men had come up the Valley Pike to join the fray.

Ewell was jubilant, but his joy was short-lived. Jackson's arrival coincided with an impenetrable fog that slowly dropped from the sky to settle like a blanket on Winchester. The town vanished from view.[12] As Ewell glared at the interfering cloud (as if his scowls could wish it away), Trimble rushed up and warned that Banks would use the mist to conceal his withdrawal to the northeast.[13] He begged Ewell to allow him take his reserve regiments forward to block the road to Berryville, the most likely way for an enemy retreat. Ewell agreed.

Trimble took Cantey's and Posey's regiments forward in column. After fording Abraham's Creek, a shallow stream below Winchester, the men groped toward their objective. The fog was so thick that they could see only about three feet ahead. As the troops filed one by one into the mist, they appeared to be entering a netherland. All the while, the battle continued to rage to Ewell's left. Stonewall was evidently not beset by clouds.

For half an hour, Ewell agonized over his being denied the chance to fight. Then, just as suddenly as the mist had come, it lifted. Ewell saw from his vista that while Banks' infantry was still in position, he had started his retreat. His wagons filled the road running north toward Martinsburg, bypassing the trap set by Trimble.

Directly to Ewell's front, his men (freed from the fog) had reentered the fray. Their efforts were sluggish as eyes and interest focused northwest of Winchester, where Taylor charged his brigade up the hill left of the Federal forts. "Steadily and with fine order, mounting the hill, and there fronting the enemy, where he stood in greatest strength," Stonewall described in his report, "[Taylor's] . . . whole line magnificently swept down the declivity and across the field, driving back the Federal troops and bearing down on all opposition before it."[14]

The fall of the bastion and the sight of victorious men in gray surging toward them from every direction aroused the citizens of Winchester. As the Union soldiers swarmed in retreat through the village streets, the local populace joined in the fight. "Males and females vied with each other . . . (in) firing from . . . houses, throwing hand grenades, hot water, and missiles of every description," one of the Northern officers bitterly wrote. "This record of infamy is preserved for the females of Winchester."[15]

Seeing the enemy running away using a different route than expected, Ewell raced down his hill, then east to where Trimble's men waited to intercept the bluecoat soldiers who were not destined to come their way. He led the regiments north after the frightened Federals, but although the Rebel troops marched in double time, they could not close on their quarry. Ewell forced the pursuit for about six miles before halting to wait for the cavalry, his only chance of nabbing the fast-running Federals.

No horsemen came. Instead, Captain Sandie Pendleton, an aide to Stonewall, rode up to report a problem. He had delivered orders to Steuart to "move as rapidly as possible to join [Stonewall] on the Martinsburg Turnpike to carry on the pursuit of the enemy . . . ."[16] Steuart had refused to obey because the instructions had not been confirmed through Ewell, his immediate superior. Infuriated with Steuart's insistence on petty protocol during a crisis, Ewell turned the air blue with oaths as he endorsed Jackson's directive. The troopers under Steuart finally went after Banks, but their effort was too late. By the time the horsemen finally caught up, Banks with most of his force had safely crossed the Potomac River. The contest was over. Only the harvesting of the stores remained to be done.

Banks left behind a vast quantity of much needed goods, including food, clothing, medical supplies (dressings, drugs, and surgical instruments), and 9,300 new rifles. But before Stonewall attended to these spoils, he issued orders for the troops to thank Providence for their victory. The army would spend the next day in prayer.[17] On May 27th, the wagons were loaded and started south while the infantry marched north for the shores of the Potomac to confront the enemy. Ewell's men were put in reserve, located at Charlestown, five miles south of Harper's Ferry and the river.

Ewell spent the next four days training his battle-weary troops. Hour after hour, the men marched in formation. They would start out in column, then shift with a yell into battle line to mount a bayonet charge. When not out drilling on the field, they stayed in camp and cleaned their weapons.

On May 30th Ewell received orders to bring his division south immediately. Concerned because he had been so urgently recalled, Ewell had his troops moving before evening, then he rode on ahead in the rain alone. The drizzle that had started about noon suddenly changed to a downpour with winds so strong Ewell was almost blown off his horse. By the time he arrived in Winchester, the General was soaking wet. His soggy wool uniform smelled, and if he had had hair, it would have been plastered against his forehead. Jackson, headquartered in a local hotel, met Ewell in the lobby, greeting him by displaying a dispatch from Colonel Conner, leader of the Twelfth Georgia, posted at Front Royal.

> *Enemy in close pursuit, Shields has been crossing at*
> *Berry's Ferry with a large army all day, at least 12,000 men.*
> *Unless you can throw re-enforcements here by morning, all*
> *will be gone.*[18]

Stonewall explained that Shields' division had returned to the Valley with McDowell's troops supposedly close behind. When Conner saw the bluecoats streaming through the pass east of Front Royal, he had fled. Shields was, Stonewall thought, heading for Strasburg to join with Fremont, hurrying east out of the Appalachians. Although McDowell's rumored approach was good news (it meant that he was not going to Richmond to reinforce McClellan), the potential uniting of Shields and Fremont was bad for Jackson. If the two Federal armies came together below his current position, they would trap him between their troops and Banks, said to be re-grouping to come down from the north. The only chance for escape was to rush south and pass through Strasburg before the Fremont/Shields pincer closed on them. If he could slip past this peril, Stonewall planned to stop, select a ground suitable for defense, and offer battle. Major Harmon, the army's quartermaster, and his wagons had already started to trek south. He would be followed by the captives taken at Winchester, two of Stonewall's three brigades, and then Ewell's troops. Windner would bring up the rear.

Ewell objected.[19] The plan was viable, but he grumbled over being stuck in the middle of the columns. He wanted to be up front, where fighting was more likely to occur. While Stonewall no doubt appreciated Ewell's ardor for combat, Jackson had to refuse the request. His march order was based on the location of his brigades; there was no time to shuffle troops.

Ewell, being a good soldier, agreed to the lesser role and returned at once to Stevenson's Depot where his men had bivouacked for the night. He roused his division and had them heading south before sunrise. Upon reaching Winchester at mid-morning, they fell into line behind Jackson's parade. The sky had cleared, and the sun blazed down on the men plodding along the macadamized pike. Moving at a fast pace, many started to falter. Their shoulders sagged from the weight of heavy packs, and their feet blistered from walking the hard, stone-surfaced road. Jackson's limping army looked more like a column of cripples than the potent host of just a few days ago.

At first, only the clever slackers dropped out of line, slipping obtrusively off the road into the cool woods nearby to catch their breath. But soon even the dependables began falling to the side, groups of twenty, thirty, then hundreds openly deserted, unable or unwilling to continue the punishing gait. Ewell screamed and swore as the stragglers melted away from the columns, but his anger could not stem the tide. By the time it was dark, when Jackson finally halted for the night, several thousand were missing from his ranks.[20] Those remaining were so tired that they collapsed in place, too exhausted for even one more stride. But the wearisome, thirty-mile retreat proved worth its physical price, because scouts sent ahead to check out Strasburg, only two miles away, came back to report that the route was still open. The Federals' pincer had not closed.

Jackson was not safe yet, however. Fremont's army was camped just west of Strasburg, positioned to pounce on Stonewall's columns as they passed by. Ewell was given the chore of falling out of line to hold the enemy off until the tail of the Confederate procession (Winder's brigade) had cleared Strasburg. After holding Fremont at bay, avoiding combat if possible, Ewell was to rejoin the Rebel column, bringing up the rear.

On June 1st Ewell roused his men at 3:00 a.m. and guided them through Strasburg, then west on the Capon Springs Road. His skirmishers soon made contact with the enemy, whose pickets fell back to seek refuge in a dense woods of laurel and oak. Fremont was in force in this forest, a fact he quickly announced by opening his artillery against the oncoming Confederates. Ewell halted, put his troops in battle line, and waited for the Union attack. Two hours passed without any change in the stalemate.

"I can't [perceive] what these people are about," Ewell groused to Richard Taylor, whose troops fronted the Yankees. "They won't advance but stay out there in the wood, making a great fuss with their guns."[21]

Taylor smiled sheepishly. Fremont's reticence was fine with him, because at that moment he was "no more good than a frightened deer." He told Ewell that he had "ducked like a mandarin" when the enemy had started their bombardment.

Ewell roared with laughter. Taylor had often ridiculed him because he would not drink the spicy, Creole coffee that Tom Strothers (Taylor's negro) brewed. Here was a chance to get even. "It's Tom's strong coffee!" Ewell cried. "Better give it up." Turning serious, he then ordered, "Remain here while I go out to check on the skirmishers."

Taylor suspected what Ewell had in mind. On the way to Winchester, his superior had shouldered a musket to join the infantry on the front line. The men, of course, knew Ewell's secret, that he thought of skirmishing as "refreshment." He had bragged to his fellow officers that his only concern was that "Old Jackson would catch [me] at it."[22]

The bark of muskets revealed that Ewell had reached the front and was personally pressing the enemy, trying to evoke a response. But the promising chatter soon ebbed, then died away. "I am completely puzzled," Ewell complained after returning to his command post. When Taylor suggested flanking the enemy position, Ewell snapped, "Do so! I'm sick of this fiddling around."[23]

Taylor quickly moved his brigade into position, and advanced on the bluecoats. His foe melted backwards, "It was so easy," Taylor related, "I began to think of traps. Sheep would have made as much resistance as we met."[24] Because the Federals faded so fast, Taylor's troops had burst across the front, drawing fire from their fellow Rebels on the skirmish line. The action had to be stopped.

For four frustrating hours the bluecoats continued to cower in the woods, seemingly afraid to mount a charge. And while Ewell waited on Fremont to his front, Winder slipped by his rear, through Strasburg and into line behind Stonewall's column. The army had escaped the Federal pincer. Ewell had no reason to remain in place.

Disappointed at not being able to bring Fremont into an engagement, Ewell reluctantly withdrew his men. He returned to Strasburg, then marched south on the Valley Pike to catch up with the rest of the army. He moved only a short distance. Thinking that the Federals might be following him, Ewell saw a chance to lure them into combat. He placed his men on both sides of the road, hiding in ambush, where they lay throughout the afternoon. Fremont, however, failed to show, and as darkness fell, Ewell assembled his troops and resumed his retreat up the Valley.

About 9:00 p.m., as Ewell hurried to catch up to Stonewall and the rest of the army, a cruel storm suddenly opened on the weary Rebels. Thunder rumbled overhead and lightning flashed across the sky. Suddenly, a rattle of musketry rose to the rear. Fremont was trailing the Rebels, and the Union cavalry

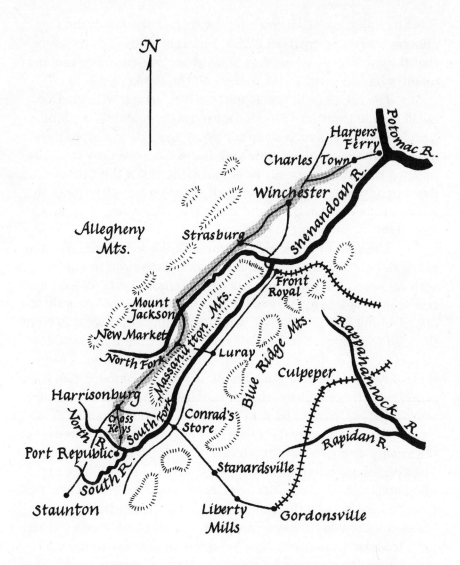

N

Potomac R.

Harpers
Ferry

Charles Town

Shenandoah R.

Winchester

Allegheny
Mts.

Strasburg

Front
Royal

Rappahannock R.

Mount
Jackson

New Market

Massanutton Mts.

North Fork

Luray

Blue Ridge Mts.

Culpeper

Harrisonburg

Cross
Keys

North R.

South Fork

Conrad's
Store

Rapidan R.

Port Republic

South R.

Stanardsville

Staunton

Liberty
Mills

Gordonsville

EWELL'S ROUTE
TO
PORT REPUBLIC
May 30 – June 9, 1862

SHENANDOAH VALLEY

0   5   10 15 20

Miles

was attacking! Ewell's horsemen, protecting the tail of the column, were so surprised by the Federals' unexpected charge that they scattered when they saw the enemy. Seymour and his infantry had to whirl about to fend off the Yankees.[25]

The retrograde was restarted. Proceeding with caution, Ewell trudged south to Mount Jackson where, about 3:00 a.m., he halted to let his men sleep for five hours. They started moving again the morning of June 2nd, but were slowed by both the pouring rain and the pesky hit-and-run tactics of the Union. Ewell finally caught up to Stonewall's troops that afternoon. He followed the column throughout the rest of the day, stopping that night in place on the road.

The retreat resumed on June 3rd. While his men trudged at the tail of the long column, Ewell rode to the van to confer with Jackson. Stonewall was worried. Fremont was close on his heels; Shields was also traveling south, east of the Massanutton, approaching Luray where he would probably whirl west to come through the gap to New Market and assault their flank. And the Rebels were exhausted. They had, after all, been running for three days with no rest. As a result, over 5,000, one-third of their army, had straggled from the ranks.[26] If Jackson was to hold his army together, he had to stop and let the troops sleep.

"How can we rest?" Ewell certainly must have asked, with the enemy so close and threatening. Stonewall had a solution. The continuing rain had raised every stream in the Valley to a flood stage, precluding anyone from crossing except by bridge. If the Rebels burned the two spans across the South Fork by Luray, Jackson could keep Shields from coming through the gap to New Market, and force him to march all the way to the end of the Massanutton before he could get at the Confederates. And once Jackson's men were over the North Fork below New Market, if they torched the only bridge spanning that river, they could offer a barrier to Fremont's harrying. Tomorrow would be a day of rest.

After crossing the raging North Fork, Ewell pitched his tent close by the stream. He needed sleep as much as anyone, but Ewell anticipated that the Yankees would try to ford the river that evening. He and his staff would stand guard. The water rose rapidly during the night, and before "headquarters knew what was going on, [they] were on an island," one of the aides recalled. "Ewell mounted his old gray horse . . . plunged into the water without coat or hat, and swam over to the camp of his cavalry, leaving the staff . . . to get out as they could."[27] By deserting his associates during the crisis, Ewell no doubt added to the resentment some held for him.

The rain continued on June 4th. Rebel spirits, already dampened by the leaden skies and soggy ground, were further tested by news brought by messenger from Richmond. Johnston, battling McClellen at Seven Pines (close by the Southern capital), had not only failed to dislodge the Yankees from their forward position but also had been hit in the chest by a shell fragment toward the end of the contest. He would recover from his wound, but a new commanding general to lead the army would be needed. The camp buzzed with speculation as to whether Jackson might succeed Johnston. "I don't know who'll be [chosen]," Ewell declared, "but I shan't be scared . . . if the choice falls on Lee."[28]

Jackson started moving again on June 5th. When the van neared Harrisonburg, Stonewall wheeled southeast on a country lane that led toward Port Republic. His advance soon came to a halt. Unlike the stone-surfaced pike, this road oozed with thick, sticky muck that seemed to swallow both man and beast. Ewell's columns, bringing up the rear, were held up short of Harrisonburg throughout the day, unable to proceed because of the delays ahead.

June 6th was greeted with a warm sun that first steamed, then dried the road, allowing the ranks to creep ahead. Late that afternoon, musketry exploded to the rear. Ewell hurried back to learn that Fremont had caught up. Ashby and his men had been fighting with enemy cavalry. The bluecoat parry had been thwarted, but Ashby expected a renewed attack, and he had a plan. A thick grove of trees stood north of the road; if the Rebels concealed some troops inside the forest, they could bushwack the Yankees when they returned.[29]

Ewell liked the idea. He had the Fifty-Eighth Virginia fall out of line, and Ashby led them toward the copse. But just as the Rebels approached the woods to assume their post, they were blasted by a sheet of flame. The would-be ambushers had walked into the snare they had envisioned for the enemy.

Ashby lost his horse during the initial barrage, but he refused to retreat. Waving his sword over his head, he called loudly to the scattered regiment to re-form and follow him on foot in a charge. His bravery recalled a few, and they advanced, only to be ravaged by a second swarm of bullets. Ashby went down. Ewell saw it all, but not as a spectator. The Yankees' opening flash of musketry was still burning bright when Ewell seized command, directing troops to the right to drive in the flank of the hidden enemy. His men plunged into the forest, using their rifles as clubs to bludgeon the bluecoats out of their grove and into the arms of oncoming Rebel cavalry. The fury lasted only minutes, but when Ewell galloped up to where Ashby lay face down at the edge of the woods, he saw that his first apprehensions were confirmed. Ashby was dead.

That evening, although the Confederate campfires burned bright, conversations were muted. The men, still stunned by Ashby's death, found it painful to discuss their fallen comrade. So they talked about Ewell, about a previously unseen side of his surly character. After the skirmish was over, Ewell had personally loaded the wounded into ambulances and ac-companied them to a nearby farmhouse where he tenderly put them to bed. He then dug into his meager purse and gave all his money to the farmer. The dollars were for the men's individual needs.

"I hadn't cared [much] for Ewell before," noted Captain Goldsborough with the Maryland Line, "but after this evening, my regiment will go anywhere . . . for him. I love him!"[30]

The next morning, June 7th, Jackson and Ewell discussed their situation. Fremont was closing on their rear, and with the end of the Massanutton in view, Shields was sure to show at their front any moment. They were about to be trapped in the pincer they had avoided earlier at Strasburg. To escape the enemy's trap, they decided to split their forces. Ewell would remain in place to meet Fremont's advance, slowing his pursuit by bringing him to battle; Jackson would move ahead to seek out Shields.

In looking for the best available position to intercept Fremont, Ewell sought out his subordinates' opinion. Asking for advice was typical of Ewell. "He was never content with his own plan," Taylor related, "until he had secured the approval of another's judgment."[31] Elzey recommended they form behind a low ridge that crossed the road near Cross Keys, and Ewell quickly accepted his proposal. Trimble posted his men in a thick woods on the right flank; Elzey's troops defended the center; Steuart (assuming command of Scott's undermanned brigade) hid his force in a grove of pines on the left. The artillery was unlimbered on the road in front of Elzey, below the crest of the hill. Taylor's regiments stayed in the rear as the reserve.[32]

Ewell waited all day for Fremont to approach and accept battle, but the enemy remained by Harrisonburg, not about to risk a confrontation. If he wanted a fight, Ewell would have to bait his hook. He did so by sending the Fifteenth Alabama ahead early the next morning, Sunday, June 8th, with instructions to find the Yankees and start an engagement. When the enemy pressed them, the regiment was to fall back, pretending to be driven from the field.

Ewell's scheme worked to perfection. About 10:00 a.m., the sounds of skirmishing arose up front, and an hour later, the Rebel pickets came in view, retreating, firing listlessly toward their pursuers. As the Alabama troops slipped out of sight into the woods where Trimble lurked, Fremont halted to align his men for the assault. In the interim, his guns rumbled up, unlimbered, and started a steady barrage that roamed left to right across Ewell's front. The Southern cannons replied, revealing their position along the road, inducing Fremont to believe he could flank the Confederates from the east. When he finally advanced, with Brigadier General Julius Stahel leading the charge, Fremont headed straight for Trimble, hidden underneath the trees.

"I ordered [my] three regiments to rest quietly . . . until the enemy . . . [came] within 50 steps of our line," Trimble recalled. "A deadly fire was [then] delivered along our whole front, beginning on the right, dropping . . . deluded victims of Northern fanaticism and misrule by scores."[33]

The volley tore gaping holes in the bluecoat alignment. Shocked by the unexpected onslaught, the Federals stopped in place, their numbed, shattered formation offering a stationary

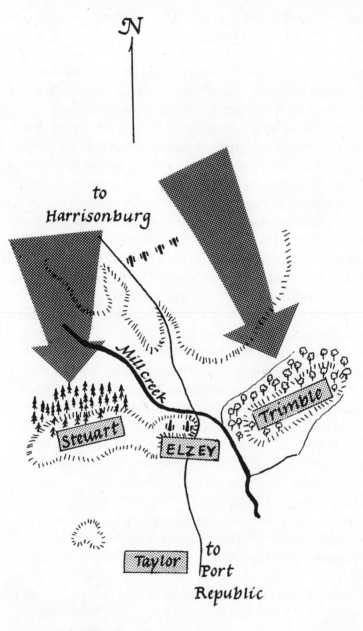

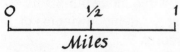

N

to
Harrisonburg

Mill Creek

Stewart

ELZEY

Trimble

Taylor

to
Port
Republic

0   ½   1

Miles

BATTLE OF
CROSS KEYS

June 8, 1862

target to Trimble's second file. They fired a withering blast that decimated the Union's ranks, causing the Yankees to retire from the field, running as a disorganized mob.

Desperate to restore his shattered left, Fremont called for artillery fire into the forest where Trimble was posted. The shelling was fierce, but instead of retreating to escape the bombardment, Trimble attacked. He sent his brigade forward after the fleeing bluecoats and their impertinent guns.

When the Federal reserves saw the Rebels coming, they joined the retreat. The entire eastern wing of Fremont's army collasped, with Trimble's troops following in hot pursuit.

While Ewell was pleased with Trimble's success, he knew the battle was far from over. Union cannons were now firing all across his front, and scouts reported bluecoats gathered on the left, preparing to attack. Ewell decided to head for Steuart's line to personally take charge of his defense.

An hour passed with no sign of the enemy. All at once, a riderless mare trotted out of the east and into the clearing where Ewell had installed his field headquarters. A few minutes later, Campbell Brown emerged on foot from under the trees, caught and mounted the loose horse, and then galloped up to report to Ewell. Embarrassed by the inept behavior of his aide, Ewell offered a sarcastic remark.

"Where's your hat?" he sneered "And how did your horse get away from you?"[34]

"I lost them both when the shell hit me."

Ewell turned pale as personal concerns immediately took precedence over irritation. He had not noticed that Campbell's shirt was bloody and torn. What would his beloved Lizinka think? Would she blame him because her son had been wounded? Ewell helped Campbell down off his mount, and gingerly probed the young man's bloody, bruised shoulder. He found a minor puncture. There was no threat to life.

"Go to the rear!" Ewell ordered. Once he knew that his aide had not been seriously injured, Ewell's only concern was keeping Campbell away from further danger.

"Let me stay."

"No!"

Recognizing that his demand was personal, not military,

Ewell made a lame attempt to rationalize his order. "If you meet General Jackson," he added, "let him know where Taylor's Brigade [is] located."

As Campbell reluctantly remounted, one of the watching officers held up a flask, offering whiskey to quell the shock of Campbell's wound. Ewell would not allow even a sip. Any moment now, the Yankees might attack, and he could not stand seeing Campbell exposed to combat for a second longer. Ewell shooed his aide toward the rear. And from that moment on, he made sure that Campbell never came under hostile fire again. Allowing Lizinka's only son to face peril was to gamble with his own romantic fortunes, a risk that Ewell dared not take.

If Fremont had attacked while Ewell was so engrossed with Campbell's wound, he probably would have won the battle. The Northern commander held a two-to-one advantage in troops over the Confederates, and he was in an excellent position to charge. The brigades led by Schenck and Milroy had safely penetrated the woods to the west. Their pickets were engaged. They were set to make an assault. With Ewell upset and distracted, an advance was bound to succeed. But at the opportune moment, Fremont lost his nerve. Still shaken by Stahel's repulse to the east, he ordered a general retreat.

Ewell waited until 4:00 p.m. for the bluecoats' charge, then cautiously crept forward himself. Finding that Fremont had retired out of view, he hurried back to Port Republic to report to Stonewall on the events of the day. Jackson first congratulated Ewell, then shared an audacious plan with him. Come morning, he would battle both of his adversaries. Outlining his strategy, Stonewall noted that three streams were bounding the area: the South Fork of the Shenandoah, formed by the intersection of two lesser waters, the North and South Rivers. He intended to cross the latter at dawn, rush north, and engage Shields. Once that contest was won, he would retrace his steps back over the water to meet and beat Fremont. If Shields proved too formidable a foe, holding the Confederates at bay, allowing Fremont's force to close on their rear, Stonewall would torch the bridge over the North Fork to keep Fremont from entering his fight with Shields. He would then retire into Brown's Gap, an impenetrable location high in the Blue Ridge.[35]

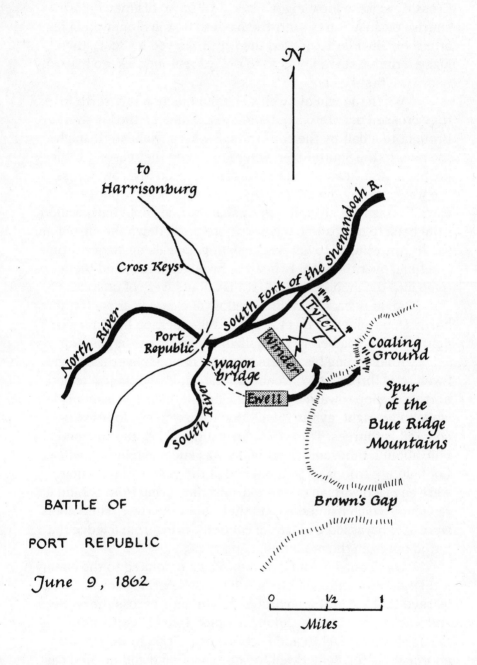

N

to
Harrisonburg

Cross Keys

South Fork of the Shenandoah R.

Tyler

North River

Port
Republic

Bridge

Coaling
Ground

wagon
bridge

Ewell

Spur
of the
Blue Ridge
Mountains

South River

Brown's Gap

BATTLE OF

PORT REPUBLIC

June 9, 1862

0   1/2   1

Miles

After agreeing to the daring scheme, Ewell returned to Cross Keys for a short night's sleep. He woke his men before sunrise on June 9th to start them south to join Stonewall in his attack on Shields. Taylor led the way, followed by Scott, then Elzey. Trimble stayed behind to delay Fremont, to keep his army out of the first battle.

When the van of Ewell's column reached the North River, they crossed over into a mass of milling men on the far shore. Brought to a halt by the confusion, Ewell rode ahead through the mob to the South River, where he found the reason for the problem. A makeshift span of wagons, parked in a row across the water, was connected by just single planks laid between each. Though the stream was so shallow one could have waded from bank to opposite bank anywhere up or down the shoreline, the troops refused to get wet, insisting on walking gingerly, one at a time, over the wobbly boards. Ewell tried to speed them up, to go into the muddy water, but his shouts were of no avail.

All at once, the muffled bellow of cannons arose to the north. Determined to meet his schedule, Jackson had started to fight with Shields before the bulk of his army was in position.

Abandoning his efforts to hurry the men over the river, Ewell rode through the stream, up the bank, and then wheeled north to gallop toward the battle. The South Fork was on his left, while to his right lay the Blue Ridge whose steep slopes were covered with trees. The field between the water and the mountain, about a thousand yards wide, was knee-high in ripe wheat. Confederate troops were crouched in the yellow grain. They were engaged with an enemy skirmish line firing from behind a rail fence which fronted a road that ran to the river. The Rebels were also harassed by Federal cannons, firing from a ledge that jutted out from the mountain.

Ewell quickly found Stonewall, who pointed to the enemy artillery. Those guns had to be silenced! Returning south, Ewell learned that Taylor had marched his brigade across the water, and was headed for the Union cannons. Two of Scott's regiments (the Fifty-Eighth and Forty-Fourth Virginia) were just approaching the field. Ewell took them in hand and hurried east, up the tree-clad hillside after Taylor. Picking his way right then left, jumping over and riding through the dark green, thickly clustered laurel, Ewell led his men north toward the continuing rumble of cannons. The growth was so dense Ewell could see nothing but the tall trees and short shrubs that blocked his path.

As he rode into a shaded glen, Ewell heard elated cries from the open ground to his left. He leaned low on his mount squinting through the leaves to see who was cheering. Bluecoats were celebrating! Supported by their cannons (Ewell's objective), they had shattered Stonewall's line in the wheat field, and were driving the Rebels' ranks backward. With no thought that his small force was too insignificant to make a difference, Ewell threw his troops into the fight. "The two regiments, bravely led by Colonel Scott, rushed with a shout upon the enemy, taking him in flank," Ewell reported, "[and] for the first time that day, the enemy was driven back . . . for some hundreds of yards."[36] Stung by Ewell's impetuous charge, the Union soldiers forgot about Jackson and whirled to assail their new aggressor. Their counterattack sent Scott and his men scampering for the protection of the nearby woods, where they stopped to form and face the oncoming Yankees. But the enemy pursuit had evaporated.

Having done what he could for Jackson, Ewell turned his attention to the Northern guns. He rode on ahead of his men, down a steep ravine, up the sheer opposite slope, and into a level clearing—a coaling ground, a place where charcoal was made. Five silent cannons, surrounded by the dead and dying of three previous encounters, were held by Taylor's brigade. They were threatened by an overwhelming line of enemy troops, determined to recapture their cannons. Taylor recalled the moment.

> *[The Federals] marched straight upon us. There seemed nothing left but to set our backs to the mountain and die . . . . At that instant, crashing through the underwood, came Ewell, outriding staff and escort. He produced the effect of a reenforcement.*[37]

Ewell galloped ahead to join in the fight. Suddenly, a shell swooped down from above, dove under Ewell's horse, and exploded, killing the animal instantly. Ewell was not hurt, nor

was he slowed. Stepping deftly from mount to ground, he continued his charge on foot. The Federal attack stopped in its tracks.
While Ewell's personal bravery was a reason for the bluecoats to
hesitate, the menacing spectacle of Scott's regiments pouring
into the clearing after Ewell was the more likely cause for their
holding back.

Ewell rushed up to one of the cannons, put his shoulder
to a wheel, and spun the piece around, aiming the gun toward
the watching Yankees. Willing hands armed the weapon. Ewell
yanked the lanyard. The cannon fired, sending a ball screaming
into the enemy's ranks. They turned and ran.

Ewell was not finished. Grabbing the reins of a nearby
artillery horse, he mounted bareback and led a pursuit after the
fleeing Yankees. Jackson's troops (able to re-group because of
Ewell's earlier flank attack) came up from below to join in driving the bluecoats north.

Close on the heels of the enemy, Ewell spotted a Yankee
officer on a white horse directing the retreat, drawing fire on
himself to protect his troops. "[Don't] shoot that man," Ewell
cried.[38] His attempt to save his adversary's life, to reward such
bravery, was in vain. As Ewell was shouting his warning, Rebel
rifles dropped both the dauntless officer and his superb animal.

The enemy retired in reasonable order. Ewell, his cumbersome mount too slow to keep pace with the pursuit, turned
back to meet Stonewall approaching from the south. "He who
does not see the hand of God in this," Jackson insisted, his pale
blue eyes blazing with excitement, "is blind!"[39]

Ewell was not interested in the Almighty's involvement in
their affairs. He wanted orders to recross the North and South
rivers to open the engagement with Fremont. But when Ewell
asked for these instructions, Jackson calmed down and revealed
that he had abandoned his plan to assault Fremont. The struggle
with Shields had lasted much longer than he had anticipated, so
he had recalled Trimble and burned the span over the South
River. With Fremont isolated on the opposite shore, the fighting
was over for the day. Ewell should tend his wounded, bury the
dead, and when the men chasing Shields returned with their
prisoners, join the rest of the army in marching east, up the
mountain, into Brown's Gap where they would spend the night.

By late afternoon, the pursuit of Shields was over. He had escaped, losing only 450 men to Jackson's trailing Rebels. Fremont, however, was still nearby, massed along the western banks of the South Fork. When he discovered he could not get over the water to close with the Confederates, Fremont vented his frustration by shelling a provisional hospital tent that Jackson had set up along the river to house the wounded enemy soldiers. The canvas had been unmistakably identified with a yellow flag. Ignoring the ignoble intrusion, Stonewall left the scene and marched for the Blue Ridge.

A cold rain fell that night. Huddled inside his rubber cloak, seeking the warmth of the campfire sputtering just outside his tent, Ewell talked with Colonel Munford. "Look here, Munford," he piped in his high, squeaky voice, "remember the conversation we had one day at Conrad's Store?"[40]

"To what do you allude?"

"Why, to . . . General Jackson . . . . "

"Very well," Munford recalled with a smile.

"I take it all back . . . Old Jackson's no fool," Ewell alleged."He [keeps] his own counsel, and does curious things; but he has method in his madness." Grinning to show that he was about to make a wry comment, Ewell added, "He's disappointed me entirely."

Ewell's good humor was in part due to his happy reunion with Campbell Brown. The boy was fine, not only recuperated from his shoulder wound but also eager to discuss his treatment by a young lady at a nearby farmhouse.

"I found [it] a real luxury to get shot," Campbell told Ewell after they met. "I never had such a fuss made over me in my life." Thinking that perhaps Ewell did not appreciate being tended by a pretty girl who was receptive to his flirting, he boasted, "Not that I . . . failed to use my advantages."[41]

While Ewell probably chuckled, picturing the naive lad, attended by an adoring, ministrant female, he may have filed the conversation in his mind. The odds were likely that any of them could be wounded and need the attention of a beautiful woman.

The next morning, Stonewall summoned Ewell to his headquarters to deliver a reprimand for his attempt to spare the life of the Federal officer on his white horse. "[Never] do such a thing again," Jackson insisted. "This is no ordinary war, and the brave and gallant . . . are the very kind that must be killed. Shoot the brave officers and the cowards will run . . . [taking] their men with them."[42]

While Stonewall's advice was certainly sound, Ewell may have questioned it. He believed in a code of honor between gentlemen; he certainly had a tender spot for heroes in his heart, demonstrated more than once during the just completed Valley Campaign, and he must have known that had the enemy followed Jackson's tenet, he himself could well be dead now.

* * * *

The Valley Campaign was a test of Ewell's abilities as a commander, and his scores were high. By leading his men into combat, joining them on the front line, sharing their danger, he had earned their respect. His troops came to love him because Ewell seemed so concerned when they were wounded. And because he won battles, Ewell gained their unquestioning support. As Goldsborough had said, "We will go anywhere [with] him."[43]

Jackson recognized Ewell's emerging military ingenuity. While he remained reticent, refusing comment on Ewell's performance, his actions expressed an unprecedented reliance on a subordinate. Allowing Ewell to conduct the battle against Fremont at Cross Keys was the highest of compliments from an egotistical commander like Stonewall.

Certainly Banks, Fremont, and Shields were impressed by Ewell. Although they could not know it at the time, each of them would became infamous as victims of the whirlwind Valley Campaign. Ewell's performance was the principal reason history would remember them as confused, indecisive, or even stupid.

Ewell was actually embarrassed by his success. In his battle reports of the period, he credited others rather than himself. For example, his men captured Front Royal, but he wrote that the Rebels were victorious because of "Jackson's personal superintendence."[44] Ewell anticipated Banks' withdrawal from Winchester, moved on his own to obstruct the way out of town, yet acknowledged, "I adopted . . . [Trimble's] suggestion."[45] And while thrashing Fremont at Cross Keys was a personal triumph for him, Ewell lauded Elzey for "selecting the position."[46] Ewell's words were not offered as flattery. "He never bestowed [praise] unmerited," Myers recalled, "and he meant everything he said."[47]

In refusing to accept personal laurels, Ewell may have been expressing an objection to war, to the sudden death and maiming he saw in battle. He was deeply touched by the loss of Ashby, and cried out aloud when his men shot at the Union officer on the white horse. Perhaps his growing aversion to the war's brutality was behind his sharing the danger of the front line with his men. By putting himself at risk, Ewell felt less pain when others fell.

One can, of course, fault Ewell for avoiding the truth that his own life was more important to the Confederacy than that of an enlisted man. He was one officer that the Rebels simply had to keep alive. He had proven that he was both an excellent tactician and superior leader of men. Would Ewell perform as well in the future? With his known eagerness for being under fire and disregard for his own safety, his aides must have wondered if he would even survive. Whatever the answer, this part of the war was over, and Ewell's fame was forever enshrined in the Valley as a tough, persistent fighter.

The Seven Days Battles

Waiting for either Shields or Fremont to make the next move, Jackson's army watched from their aerie in Brown's Gap above Port Republic for three days. But both of their foes had had enough. Fremont retired to the north to Mount Jackson; Shields fell back to Luray. Given the respite, Stonewall emerged from the mountains on June 12th and set up his camp along the South Fork of the Shenandoah River. The army was looking forward to rest and recuperation, but Jackson had other ideas in mind for them. He worked them hard, insisting on daily drills to keep the men battle-ready. He did loosen his usually rigid discipline somewhat, allowing his soldiers to slip into town at night for a drink in the local taverns, to explore nearby Weyer's Cave, or to court the young ladies living in the neighborhood.[1] Jackson himself spent his time in secretive communication with Robert E. Lee.

As Ewell had envisioned, Lee had been chosen to replace the wounded Joe Johnston, to defend Richmond from McClellan's army. But rather than await the Federals' attack, less fearsome now that Jackson's Valley success had pinned McDowell's 30,000 Yankee troops in Fredericksburg instead of on the way to reinforcing McClellan, Lee was planning his own assault to drive the enemy from the doorsteps of the capital. Stonewall's men would play an important role in the game.

Including Stonewall in Lee's assault would not be easy. If he openly set out for Richmond, the Federals would quickly follow to offset his numbers. Jackson's move had to be surreptitious, a rapid sprint for the capital under the noses of the unsuspecting bluecoats. He would mislead the enemy into believing that he meant to renew his offensive in the Valley. To aid in this vital deception, Lee sent Whiting's troops by train to Staunton as if to reinforce Stonewall's army.[2] Only Jackson knew that after Whiting reached the Valley, he would turn back, joining the rest of his force in a run to Richmond to attack McClellan. The night of June 17th, before he left to meet Whiting, Jackson called on

Ewell and gave his subordinate instructions to take his brigades south. Upon reaching Waynesboro, Ewell would march eastward and cross the Blue Ridge through Milan's Gap. He would continue on to Charlottesville, where he was to wait under the shadow of the mountains for Stonewall.[3]

"Why?" Ewell asked. Was Jackson meaning to hurry north along the eastern edge of the range to attack Washington, or was he going to Richmond to unite with Lee against McClellan? Ewell felt that his performance and loyalty during the Valley Campaign had earned his superior's trust, that Jackson would surely share his plans with him. But Stonewall refused Ewell even a hint at their destination.

Others were equally uninformed about Jackson's proposed itinerary. The next morning, a troupe from Stonewall's staff came to Ewell, saying that their superior had vanished without assigning them duty. Perhaps they could do something for him. Ewell glared balefully at the clique of smiling, confident officers, suspecting that they were only laughing at his ignorance of Jackson's plans. He knew they had no desire to serve under him.

"I'm only commanding a division, marching under orders, I don't know where," he sniffed, cloaking his chagrin by being brusque. "[And] I've more staff than I've any use for."[4]

Shortly after heading out the next morning, Ewell found Jackson unexpectedly at his side. He had come to order Ewell not to stop in Charlottesville but to go on to Gordonsville. He then disappeared again, without a further word about their objective. Ewell's humiliation was increased by the snub because he had just heard that John Harmon, Jackson's quartermaster, was boasting that Stonewall had told him that the men were marching to Richmond. Growing more dispirited with each minute of the day, Ewell's distress boiled over that evening.

"[Jackson] has gone off . . . without entrusting to me, his senior major general, any order or . . . hint of [where] we are going," he complained bitterly to R.L. Dabney, both chaplain and chief of staff for Stonewall. "But Harmon, his quartermaster, enjoys his full confidence, I suppose, for I hear . . . he is telling the troops that we are going to Richmond . . . ."[5]

"You may be certain . . . you stand higher in General

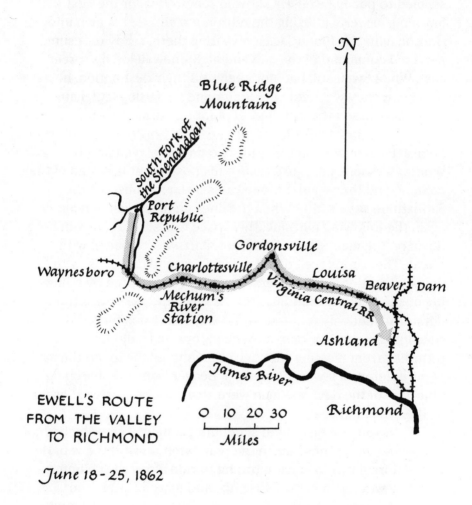

N

Blue Ridge
Mountains

South Fork of
the Shenandoah

Port
Republic

Gordonsville

Waynesboro

Charlottesville

Louisa

Beaver Dam

Virginia Central RR

Mechum's
River
Station

Ashland

James River

EWELL'S ROUTE
FROM THE VALLEY
TO RICHMOND

Richmond

0   10 20 30

Miles

June 18 - 25, 1862

Jackson's confidence than anyone else, as your rank and service entitle you," Dabney insisted. "As for Major Harmon, he has not heard a word more than others. If he thinks we are going to Richmond, it is only his surmise . . . ." Dabney's assurances seemed to pacify Ewell. He showed renewed vigor the next morning, cleverly utilizing the railroad to shuttle his men into Gordonsville. He found Jackson waiting there, ready to resume personal command of the movement. Stonewall led his force east. While Ewell still had not been told their destination, he now knew they were going to Richmond to battle McClellan. They had passed the last, logical point for turning north.

Ewell bivouacked that night east of Gordonsville, short of Louisa. He remained in place for two days, delayed first by Whiting's troops passing to usurp his position at the head of the column, and then (under Stonewall's order) to observe the Sabbath on June 22nd.[6] When the lines finally began moving again the following morning, their pace was slow. A hot sun bore down on the men, whose butternut shirts were stained with sweat. The troops reeled under the glare, and canteens were quickly emptied. The soldiers' thirst was aggravated by billowing dust, raised by plodding feet. As dusk approached, a thunderstorm suddenly erupted, and heavy raindrops turned the road into a quagmire of mud. When Stonewall galloped up, returning from meeting with Lee in Richmond, he found the van of his columns a few miles short of Beaver Dam, the marching objective of the day. The men were strung out to the west as far as the eye could see.

Despite being behind schedule, Stonewall knew he had to halt awhile to let those far to the rear catch up with the van. He rose before dawn the next morning to ride along the column, pleading with his men to "close up" and march faster. The troops tried to step out, but yesterday's steady rain had muddied the road, and shallow runs, once easily forded, were now raging streams to be bridged. When the army finally came to a halt that night, their goal of Ashland lay five miles ahead.

Ewell met with Jackson that evening. Their discussions were brief, because Stonewall was exhausted, suffering from a lack of sleep during the past few days. While seeing Lee in Richmond, he had had no chance to lie down, and the night before, he had rested only a few hours, having risen at sunrise to direct the day's march.

Jackson began his briefing by noting that McClellan had made a serious tactical mistake by dividing his force outside of Richmond, placing one element of his command north of the Chickahominy River, the other south of the swampy, meandering stream that flowed southeast across the Peninsula. His base of supply was located at White House, a village on the Pamunkey River, a tributary of the York. By attacking the Union emplacement above the Chickahominy, driving the Yankees below the river, Lee could sever McClellan's line to his provisions and force the bluecoats to abandon their campaign to capture the Confederate capital. When he retreated, McClellan would be exposed to possible annihilation by a vengeful Rebel army.[7]

Continuing his presentation, Stonewall revealed that he would trigger Lee's assault. He would advance from the north, opening the battle by charging the Union flank. As the enemy turned to ward off the blow, A. P. Hill would attack from the west, followed in echelon by D.H. Hill and then Longstreet.

After completing this summary, Stonewall gave Ewell his orders for the morning march to battle. His division would lead the army, taking the country lane south out of Ashland. Since they had not yet reached their planned starting point, an early assembly would be necessary. Ewell's men had to be up and ready to go by 2:30 a.m.

Shortly after Ewell had returned to his headquarters to begin preparing for the pre-dawn march, Major General William Whiting stormed into his tent. An outspoken critic of Stonewall (having recently stated that "Jackson has no more sense than my horse!"),[8] Whiting objected vociferously to the plan for the army to move in a single column. In his view, splitting their force into parallel groups would get the troops to the front much faster. Ewell agreed, and the two went to see Stonewall to offer this suggestion. It was past midnight, and in a few minutes the men would be roused, but Jackson would not make an immediate decision. "I'll think over your proposal," he promised, "and . . . communicate [my answer] . . . later."[9]

Whiting was incensed at being so summarily dismissed by Jackson, and as he and Ewell walked back toward camp, he

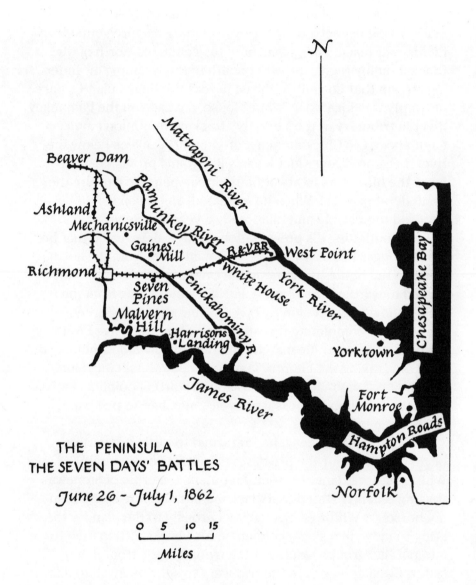

THE PENINSULA
THE SEVEN DAYS' BATTLES

June 26 – July 1, 1862

100

complained about Stonewall's vacillation. Ewell laughed. "Don't you know why 'Old Jack' would not decide at once?" he asked. "He's going to pray over it first," he chortled.

A few more paces down the path, Ewell suddenly recalled that he had left his sword in Stonewall's tent. Returning to retrieve the saber, Ewell halted just outside his superior's quarters. If Jackson was sleeping, he did not want to awaken him. Ewell peeked inside, and as he had predicated to Whiting, Stonewall was on his knees, his eyes uplifted to heaven.

Ewell roused his men at the appointed hour, but the move south was delayed. Provisions expected from Richmond had not yet arrived, and while waiting for breakfast, the troops had broken ranks to fill their canteens. They spread across the countryside looking for scarce wells.[10] Five hours passed by before everyone had returned, ready to move out. Whiting's troops advanced at 8:00 a.m., followed by Ewell, who trailed the column until reaching the Virginia Central Railroad tracks, where he turned right to parallel Jackson and the rest of the army. "Providence" had prodded Stonewall into accepting the two path suggestion that Ewell and Whiting had posed earlier.

The trek was pure drudgery. The land was flat, swampy, and heavily wooded. The hot, humid air, smelling of decaying leaves, was hard to breath. And adding to the men's discomfort, clouds of mosquitoes swarmed the ranks, buzzing and biting at will.[11] Even worse, the enemy was obviously aware that Stonewall's army was approaching: Northern pioneers had felled trees into the path of the oncoming Rebels. From time to time, enemy pickets nipped at Ewell's flanks. His troops persisted, however, showing high spirits and making good progress. Ewell was so pleased with their effort that he halted at noon for a full hour to let the division eat lunch.

Resuming the march at 1:00 p.m., Ewell continued moving south. Two-and-one-half hours later, when he arrived at the intersection marked by the Shady Grove Church, Ewell turned east to rendezvous with Stonewall. The men plodded steadily ahead, concentrating on their objective. Suddenly, the relative quiet was shattered by the sounds of battle opening below their position. Lee's plans called for Jackson to begin the clash by attacking McClellan's flank. Had Stonewall already passed by up front and started to fight? Should Ewell wheel to join in the fray? Although tempted to hurry toward the melee, Ewell resisted the lure, continuing to move east. About 5:00 p.m., approaching Hundley's Corner, Ewell knew he had made the right decision. Stonewall with the rest of the army was just coming in from the north.

Anxious to learn if they were going to join the battle still raging to the south, Ewell galloped up to Jackson. The two leaders had barely begun to talk when, without warning, a rattle of musketry, aimed at the Rebels, burst out of the brush to the south.

"Make them keep quiet," Stonewall growled.[12]

Ewell dispatched two regiments, the Thirteenth Virginia and the First Maryland, into the glen where the Federals lay hidden. The troops filed into the dense foliage; there was a quick flurry of gunfire; then it was still. The quiet was soon broken. Colonel Bradley Johnson came out from under the trees to rush up to Ewell and report that his men had routed a band of Northern pickets. The bluecoats had retreated up a hill, then over a creek that flowed below the slope. As the Yankee skirmishers scampered up the opposite shore, they were met by thousands of their comrades coming forward. The enemy lay in strength nearby.[13]

Jackson ordered two guns unlimbered. While the cannons disposed of the Yankee troops, the rest of the army would retire for the night. Not too many days ago, Ewell would have been outraged by Stonewall's indifference to the Union threat, and demanded that he be allowed to smash through the enemy's screen to join in the fray still heard to the south. But the Valley Campaign had made Ewell a believer. While others, especially Trimble, openly grumbled at Jackson's reluctance to mix with the enemy,[14] Ewell accepted his superior's decision without complaint.

As the sky darkened and night came on, the troops built fires and prepared their suppers. They sat in the shadows of the flickering flames, their conversations hushed as all eyes and ears were drawn to the carnage, still crackling so close to their bivouacs. They could smell the gun powder. Billows of thick, black smoke hovered overhead. The contest finally ebbed about

9:00 p.m.

Rising at dawn on June 27th, expecting orders to gather up his men and set out at once for battle, Ewell found he was held in place while Stonewall's columns—strung out for miles to the north—closed on the van of the army. The long delay seemed to fill the men with lethargy. With everyone finally in place about 8:00 a.m., the Rebel lines began moving south in the direction of yesterday's fray. Ewell's men headed the parade. Jackson advanced cautiously, halting often to remove the felled logs and heavy brush that the Federals had heaped on the road to block his path. Two hours after the march began, the languor evident in the morning vanished, as fighting exploded directly up front. Shelling and musketry grew in intensity as Ewell, anxious to get under fire, urged his troops toward the clash. But about 11:00 a.m., the sounds of combat faded away. Minutes later, as the columns approached the crossroads marked by the Walnut Grove Church, Ewell saw his way blocked by gray-clad troops. He had to halt his men to wait for the path to clear.

Stonewall rode forward alone to sort out the situation. He met first with A.P. Hill (in charge of the Rebels who were blocking Ewell's lane) and then Robert E. Lee, who arrived as Hill was leaving to rejoin his force. When his hurried conversation with Lee was finished, Jackson returned with explanations and new plans.

Lee had expected Jackson to reach the Yankee's flank at 9:00 a.m. yesterday and launch the Confederate assault. But Stonewall, delayed on the road, failed to show. After six hours of waiting, A.P. Hill (commanding the advance division) lost patience. Acting without orders, Hill opened the conflict by charging the enemy's defenses at Beaver Dam. His engagement brought both D.H. Hill and Longstreet into the battle, which, while fiercely fought, failed to dislodge the Federals. When A.P. Hill resumed his combat that morning, (the noisy shelling heard earlier by Ewell and his men), he found only token resistance from Yankee pickets, covering their comrades' retreat. Hill was pursuing the Union. Lee had asked Stonewall to move east in parallel and north of Hill to again threaten the bluecoat flank.

With Ewell's Division (Taylor, Trimble, and then Elzey) in the lead, Stonewall began marching. When his van came to the

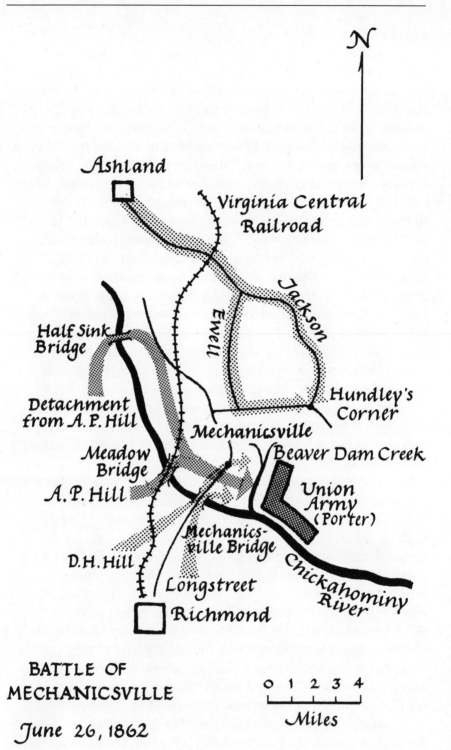

BATTLE OF
MECHANICSVILLE

June 26, 1862

next intersection, he wheeled south "at right angles . . . to [his direction] of the evening before, and as it turned out, two or three miles wrong," Campbell Brown recalled.[15] A mill pond blocked the path ahead; their guide had sent them down a dead end road. Jackson would have to retrace his steps to the junction passed about an hour ago.

Even though he had lost critical time, Jackson insisted on keeping the same order of march. He ordered Ewell to turn around (putting Elzey's troops up front), then held his other divisions stationary while Ewell passed by on his way back to the north. When Ewell reached the intersection where Jackson had made his wrong turn, he ran into yet another delay. D.H. Hill's division was trudging by, and he had to wait until the route had cleared. The halt was all the more frustrating to Ewell because to the south, the low rumble of cannons shaking the ground announced that battle had begun again. A.P. Hill had brought the enemy to bay.

Finally on the right road, Ewell hurried eastward, then south. A mile west of Old Cold Harbor, Jackson called a halt, and cocking an ear toward the riotous clash seemingly concentrated in a thick grove of trees just ahead, declared, "Those woods are full of the enemy."[16] Ewell needed no direct order. He quickly formed his lead regiment into a skirmish line and sent the men into the ominous forest.

"Everyone seemed holding their breath—waiting for the crash—but all was silent," Campbell Brown recalled.[17] The troops sprinted through the trees, then out into the clearing beyond, still without opposition.

Assuming Ewell would soon be engaged, Jackson had moved to the rear to advance his other two divisions (Whiting's and Winder's troops). Ewell, with no one to fight and no orders, sent an aide after Stonewall for further instructions. As he impatiently marked time, Ewell spotted a small, dapper horseman charging toward him. Major Walter Taylor, Lee's Chief of Staff, galloped up to Ewell to say that A.P. Hill was engaged and in serious danger up ahead. Ewell was to advance at once to divert the bluecoats' attention by attacking their flank.

Ewell immediately pushed his troops forward. He looped through several series of forests and fields, pushing his men toward the ever closer sounds of battle, before finally finding the front one mile past New Cold Harbor. There, under a cover of thickset elms, he peered out toward the arena he had committed to enter. He faced a ravine. A corn field, knee-high in green stalks, grew on the gentle downward slope; the bottomland was marshy, covered with brambles, vines, and small trees. A dusty road led to the swamp, vanished inside the wallows, and then reappeared to climb the opposite bare hill. Yankee artillery crowned the far crest.[18]

There was no time to organize the division into a solid set of battle lines. Turning to Elzey, who had hurried up to take his own look at the ground, Ewell ordered him to charge the Federals, entrenched behind tiered breastworks on the far slope. Elzey rushed his brigade left of the road, then down into the swamp. Seconds later, the sudden crackle of muskets announced that the Marylander had met the enemy.

Ewell missed the clash. Planning to order his force into the battle by echelon, he had wheeled about, anticipating Trimble's brigade coming into view. The timberland to his rear was deserted. Trimble, who had "a talent for mistakes,"[19] had lagged behind Elzey's column, missing the last turn in Ewell's meandering course to the front. At that moment, he was actually marching his troops away from the fray. To make matters worse, Taylor's brigade (under Colonel Isaac Seymour, filling in for the Louisianan who was sick) had followed Trimble astray.

With irritated impatience, Ewell and his staff galloped back into the forest and through to the meadow beyond, where he encountered an agitated Robert E. Lee. "Hurry [your] division as rapidly as possible," Lee begged, "and send someone back to bring up [Stonewall and his other divisions]."[20] Realizing that Lee's request was his chance to keep Campbell out of danger, Ewell dispatched his aide to the rear after Jackson, then rode off to round up his missing brigades.

When he finally found Trimble, Ewell was distraught to learn that only two of the former railroader's four regiments were nearby. Both the Sixteenth Mississippi and the Twenty-First North Carolina had wandered off during the disoriented march.[21] Fortunately, Seymour had kept his men in line; all of his regiments were at hand.

Ewell ordered Trimble to assemble his available troops
and hurry with him back to the front. When Ewell arrived, he
learned that Elzey's lonely attack had been thrown back. The
Marylanders had charged, thinking that the bluecoats had only
two breastworks—one halfway up the slope, the second located
along the crest. They could not see the third Northern line
hidden at the bottom of the knoll. Not expecting opposition, the
men were shocked when a blast of muskets shattered their
formation. Elzey, leading the attack, had been dropped by a ball
to the head.[22]

Ewell had no time to tend to his seriously injured subordinate; Lee wanted an immediate assault. Taking personal
charge of his force, Ewell led them into combat, putting the
Louisianans under Seymour right of the road. Trimble's regiments (the Fifteenth Alabama and Twenty-First Georgia) began
to charge left of the path. Seymour never reached the morass at
the bottom of the ravine. As he galloped through the corn in
front of his men, he was hit in the chest by a ball fired by a
Yankee sharpshooter on the crest of the far slope. Seymour
toppled off his horse and died amidst the green stalks. His men
ran by, reaching the swamp without their leader.[23]

When the Rebels entered the marsh, they faced a mesh
of close-growing trees and brush fronting a broad creek imped-
ing their advance. Ewell pushed them through the thickets, into
the murky waters, and on to more heavy undergrowth. Still in
the semblance of a battle line, they crept forward. As their ranks
emerged into the open, they were greeted with a hail of bullets.
The burst was ignored. Ewell's troops charged, expecting the
enemy to run from their answering fire. But this was not the
Valley. Whereas both Banks' and Fremont's men had scattered
when confronted, these more seasoned bluecoats held their
ground. Their withering salvos forced the Confederates back
into the cover of the marsh.

Stalemated in the swamp, Ewell soon learned that he was
in a precarious position. Disaster had unfolded on the right.
After the attack had been checked, Rob Wheat, leading the
infamous Louisiana Tigers, had decided to personally check out
his front. He had foolishly ridden out from under the trees into
the open, presenting a singular target to the bluecoats. A fusil-

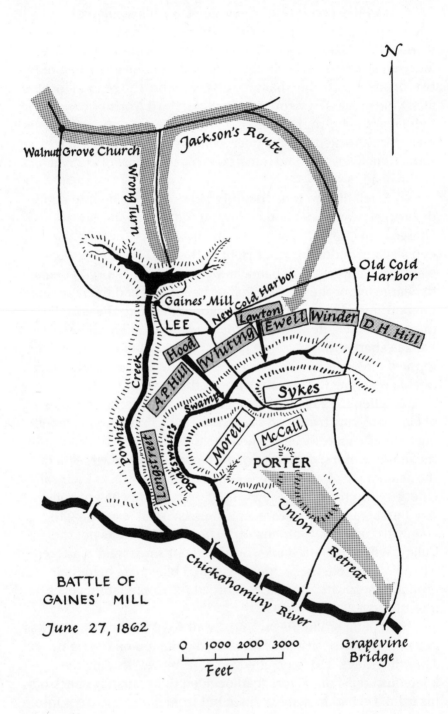

BATTLE OF
GAINES' MILL

June 27, 1862

0   1000 2000 3000
Feet

lade followed that toppled Wheat from his horse.[24] As their major fell, the unpredictable men from New Orleans panicked and broke for the rear. The other Louisiana regiments, rattled by Seymour's death, were primed for flight, and they followed the Tigers back through the marsh and up the hill to safety. Ewell was left with just two of Trimble's regiments to face what seemed like the whole Union army.

"[We were] opposed to constantly renewed forces . . . advantageously posted," Ewell remembered.[25] But if he withdrew to safer ground, a gaping hole would open in Lee's line. The enemy might well pour through and roll up the Rebels from behind. If the Confederates were to win the battle, Ewell had to stay and fight.

Improvising an audacious strategy, Ewell sent Trimble to go look for his missing troops while he bought time by spreading the few men left at hand, about 1,000 in total, in a line along the edge of the swamp. They were told to open a steady fire that would deceive the bluecoats into believing they were a larger force, capable of stemming any assault. To encourage his uneasy soldiers to hold their post, Ewell brazenly walked his horse back and forth along their front, drawing the enemy's fire to himself rather than his troops.[26]

On the left, Lieutenant Colonel John F. Trentlen, acting commander of the Fifteenth Alabama, followed Ewell's example by pacing his mount in and out of the trees crowding the skirt of the marsh. Even a lowly private joined the act. Seeing Ewell and Trentlen defying the enemy, Frank Champion seized a horse and gleefully impersonated an officer by prancing in full view of the astounded Yankees in a similar manner.[27] Bullets flew past the trio of riders, but miraculously, none hit their target as a hail of answering fire by Ewell's men hurried the aim of the Federal sharpshooters. For over two hours, the daring strategy held the Union at bay. "I cannot speak too highly of [my] troops," Ewell wrote in his official report. "Their ammunition was exhausted, and their pieces [grew] too hot to load . . . [yet they] held their ground."[28]

Reinforcements finally came at 4:30 p.m. Hood's Fifth Texas and Hampton's South Carolina Legion scurried down from the hill to Ewell's rear and slipped into place in the tenuous line.

About 5:00 p.m., the corn field behind the Southern position filled with Confederate gray. Dressed in brand new uniforms, Lawton's Georgia Brigade—3,500 strong—roared into the marsh and through, joining both Hood and Hampton in charging the Yankee emplacements. As they bounded by Ewell, he raised his sword and waved them on, cheering, "Hurrah for Georgia!"[29] The Federal resolve was as stubborn as ever, but the Confederates' front was too broad for the entrenched enemy. Lawton's ranks overlapped the Union breastworks on the right, flanking them, forcing a retreat. The hole opened by Lawton was quickly matched both to Ewell's left and right as other brigades of Lee's force advanced en masse, driving the bluecoats from the field.

Ewell attempted to take part in the rally. But just as he started to gallop up the battle-strewn hill to his front, his horse staggered and fell, hit by an errant shell, killed in its tracks. Ewell was thrown clear, but when he tried to continue on foot, he felt a sharp twinge in his leg and what seemed to be a large pebble under his toe. He plopped down, pulled off his boot, and turned it upside down. A flattened ball dropped out. The bullet had evidently ricocheted off a tree, hitting Ewell in the leg before falling into the boot. His calf was badly bruised, but there was no blood.[30]

Just then, Campbell Brown rode up, and the two walked to the top of the hill. No Yankees were in view. McClellan had been routed.

While some might have relaxed at this point, Ewell disdained his chance for rest. "Find . . . General Jackson and get leave to withdraw our troops to . . . [this] . . . spot," he ordered Campbell. "Collect stragglers, try and find my spare horse, and . . . send my saddle to this point."[31] Ewell remained on the field on foot (his second mount could not be found until past midnight), helping sort out Lee's scattered force by guiding regiment after regiment into position for action the following day.

On the morning of June 28th, the bulk of Lee's army was positioned north of the Chickahominy, ideally located to cut McClellan off from his supply base at White House. The Yankees had no choice but to retreat. But McClellan seemed not to realize his problem; he was calmly entrenching his troops below the river.

Confused by this maneuver, Lee held back for a moment while he evaluated the alternatives available to the Yankees. McClellan could attack Richmond. The route was clear, as only two Rebel divisions, Huger's and Magruder's, guarded the lines below the Chickahominy. Lee quickly rejected this probability. The enemy had approached the capital so tentatively (planning to lay siege instead of attack), he was certain McClellan was too timid to seize this opportunity. Yet, although they were not likely to advance, the bluecoats could not remain in place. McClellan needed to replenish his food and ammunition. With Lee crowding his flank, threatening the supply depot at White House, the Union general had to either fall back and protect his provisions or head south to establish a new station along the James River.

Whatever McClellan decided was vital to Lee's strategy. If the Union marched south toward the James, Lee had to cross the Chickahominy quickly before the bluecoats slipped safely away. Catching them with their columns strung out, Lee could attack in detail, possibly destroying the entire enemy force. But if the Rebels forded the river, only to find McClellan on his way eastward, retreating for White House, then Lee would have needlessly abandoned his hard-won advantage of position. He would have to recross the water to get at McClellan, but with the Chickahominy (a formidable barrier) protecting their rear, the Yankees could probably make good their escape.

Lee decided to hold until McClellan made a move. He did take one precaution, however, by sending a unit east to block the path to White House. This force could delay the enemy if McClellan chose this way out of his predicament. Since Ewell was the only division commander who had his men assembled and ready to march that rainy Saturday morning, June 28th, he got the choice assignment to move to Dispatch Station.[32]

Ewell started to advance about dawn. At 10:00 a.m., as his men trudged along the northern banks of the Chickahominy, clouds of dust and smoke were spotted soaring above the tall pines, blocking the view south of the stream. Was McClellan heading for the James River? Ewell ordered Trimble to check out the Yankees' intentions.

"[I] sent an officer up a tree," Trimble related. "[He]

111

could . . . plainly see the Yankee forces moving southward . . . the Federal Army was certainly retreating."[33] Ewell immediately sent this news on to Lee.

A little after noon, the division approached its objective, Dispatch Station. The site was in flames. Large piles of wooden boxes were burning briskly, their contents obvious from the appetizing smell of bacon permeating the air. Ewell was infuriated that the enemy destroyed food that his troops could have eaten. His oaths were even louder when he learned that Jeb Stuart with his cavalry had arrived before him, and they were the ones who had started the fires.

Stuart shrugged off Ewell's shrill invectives by noting that there were plenty of provisions available for the taking at White House. He was going there now. Would Ewell and his hungry men care to join him? Refusing Stuart's offer, Ewell stated that his orders from Lee did not include discretionary ventures.[34]

Jeb's instructions were as explicit as Ewell's, but he was sure that Lee would not object if he pushed "down the White House Road . . .   to find out what force was in that direction and, if possible, rout it."[35]

After Stuart's departure, Ewell put Trimble's troops to work tearing up the railroad tracks that ran above the river. "Trimble," Campbell Brown reported, "[had gone] astray as usual,"[35] during the march to Dispatch Station, and dispensing extra duty was Ewell's way of punishing his wayward subordinate. As Trimble's men labored all that afternoon, the others relaxed, bothered only by an occasional sniper's bullet from across the stream where a few bluecoat stragglers amused themselves by harassing the Rebels. That night, the division bivouacked in the immediate area.

Ewell continued to rest his men on Sunday morning, June 29th. He had no orders except to remain in position. To the south, below the stream, clouds of billowing smoke hung over the trees as McClellan continued to destroy his stores. Now and then a clarion blast would signal ammunition blowing up. About noon, "the most fearful explosion took place . . . like the simultaneous discharge of many guns, and the woods between us and the river were felled with falling shells."[36] Suspecting an enemy attempt to ford the river, Ewell and his troops ran for the water where they watched two railroad locomotives pulling a line of cars storm into view. The train was coming at top speed, headed straight for the Confederates' camp. Its cars were aflame, and its load of artillery shells, ignited by the fire, spiraled upward in every direction.

Without noting that the bridge connecting the tracks to their position was gone, destroyed by the enemy just prior to their retreat, the men by the river panicked, scattering in their haste to elude the oncoming train. Ewell stayed to see the locomotives soar into the air, high over the bridgeless Chickahominy. Hovering for just a second, presenting a still picture like a photograph, the lead engine dropped nose down into the water, landing with a gigantic splash, pulling the second locomotive and the rest of the cars after it. "It was one of the grandest sights I ever [saw]," Campbell Brown recalled.[37]

Excited discussion about the train was soon interrupted by new orders. Ewell was to take his troops one mile further east to Bottom's Bridge, to contest any bluecoat attempts to cross. The march was made quickly, the division falling into a defensive position upon arrival. About 3:00 p.m., another series of explosions erupted to the west, from the area Ewell had just abandoned. But the issue this time was not supplies being destroyed, nor were trains being set on fire. A fearsome battle had started. The sounds of combat seemed to grow with every minute, causing Ewell great anguish as he debated with himself whether he should rush to join in. The temptation (and perhaps Stuart's advice on discretion with orders) proved too much, and at 4:00 p.m., Ewell called his troops to arms.[38]

But before the excited men could assemble, a courier arrived with new instructions. Ewell was to join Jackson at Grapevine Bridge (to the west, above the Chickahominy, halfway back to the site of their first day's battle).

The division started the trek at 6:00 p.m., arriving at Grapevine Bridge after dark. Jackson had already crossed in pursuit of the bluecoats; Ewell was to follow. But with the moon hidden behind gray, swirling clouds, Ewell could barely see the way ahead. He decided now was not the time to grope blindly into Yankee territory. He pushed his troops over the water, but halted on the opposite shore for the night.

Sleep was almost impossible. The warm, motionless air was laden with humidity, the spongy ground was damp with dew, and swarms of flies, gnats, and mosquitoes eagerly vied with each other to bite the men. If that were not enough to keep one awake, a thunderstorm broke before dawn. Few complained when Ewell called them into formation for an early start to find Jackson.

The rain soon ended that June 30th. Marching under the broiling sun, the division reached Savage Station about 10:00 a.m. where the Federals had once maintained a field hospital, amply supplied with food and medicine. The men looked hungrily at mounds of still smoldering provisions, set afire by the enemy before fleeing the area. Even more painful to see were the Union maimed and dead, left behind after yesterday's fierce battle (the fray they had almost joined). Magruder's Division had attacked the flank of McClellan's retiring columns, fighting a bloody but indecisive affair.

Ewell finally caught up with Stonewall's force at noon. They were camped just above White Oak Swamp, getting ready to deliver an artillery barrage to blast away irksome resistance to their pursuit. Twenty-three cannons were unlimbered, and at Jackson's signal, they roared in unison, sending a deadly spray of canister into the thick brush across the murky run that meandered through the marsh.[39] The bluecoats hiding in the thickets seemed to scatter, but a fast reconnaissance by the cavalry revealed that the Federal skirmishers had not run but only changed position. Expecting orders from Jackson to find a way to flank the Union out from their posts, Ewell was shocked when he was told to accept the stalemate. Stonewall had returned to his field headquarters where he plopped down against a tree and began to nap. Throughout that afternoon, although valid plans for dealing with the Federals were proposed by a number of officers, Jackson refused to do anything. Even the renewal of combat, starting at 3:00 p.m. and continuing for over two hours up ahead, would not move him. He was done fighting for the day, and that was that.

Dawn found the Federals gone. Stonewall roused his men and marched them south through the now empty swamp.

Emersing from the marsh above Frayser's Farm, the troops passed by the site of yesterday's fight. Even though less than twenty-four hours had elapsed, "[The area] smelt horribly," Campbell Brown said in his memoirs. "The weather was oppressive and the unburied dead putrefied at once."[40]

Campbell Brown recalled decaying bodies; Robert E. Lee thought back to lost chances. He had aligned his whole force parallel to McClellan's moving columns, and ordered a charge that should have decimated the bluecoats' ranks. But Jackson had not attacked. Neither had Holmes to the south, nor Huger on the north. Only the center divisions of Lee's army (Longstreet and A.P. Hill) had answered his call, and their troops were too few. McClellan had fought them off and escaped that night to a point below the Southern position. Now, with his flank free of future threats, the Yankee commander would probably make good his change of base.

Lee would not give up the chase. On July 1st, he began moving down the Willis Church Road after the Federals. Stonewall took the lead with Ewell at the rear of his columns. As he plodded south through the dust raised by the marching columns to his front, Ewell saw an unkempt horseman blocking the division's way ahead. The rider painfully dismounted, waving his hand to halt the van. Jubal Early was reporting for duty, replacing the wounded Elzey.[41] Ewell barely knew his new subordinate. Their paths had crossed only twice in the past: at West Point where Early had graduated ahead of Ewell, and then at First Manassas where Early had come late that day by train from the Valley to make a charge. Noting Early's slouch, his straggly beard, and his tobacco-stained teeth, Ewell may have wondered if this disheveled officer really merited a general's stars. But when he heard Early speak, Ewell's uncertainty probably disappeared. Early swore as often and almost as skillfully as Ewell did.

Proceeding down the Willis Church Road, Ewell's division suddenly came under fire. Huge projectiles looking like lamp posts, so massive they could be spotted even when a great distance away,[42] dropped out of the sky. Wondering how he could have attracted the enemy's attention, in this case, Union gunboats on the James River, Ewell looked back to see clouds of dust rising above his soldiers' heads. The billowing shroud,

115

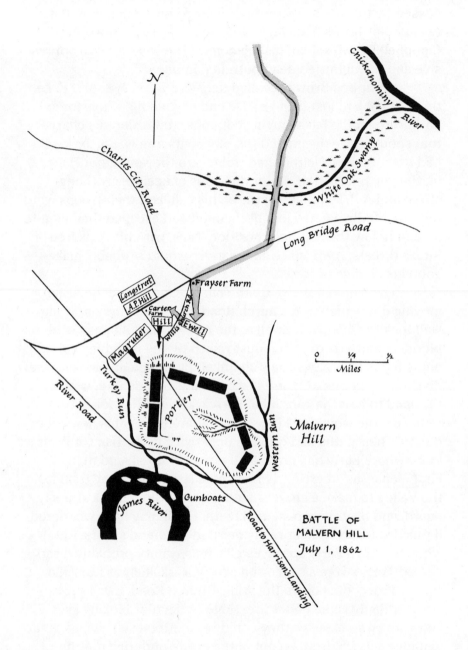

Chickahominy River

Charles City Road

White Oak Swamp

Long Bridge Road

Frayser Farm

Longstreet
A.P. Hill

Carter Farm

Hill

Magruder

Willis Church Rd.

Ewell

N

0   ¼   ½
Miles

Turkey Run

River Road

Porter

Western Run

Malvern Hill

James River

Gunboats

Road to Harrison's Landing

BATTLE OF
MALVERN HILL
July 1, 1862

lifted by thousands of marching feet was pinpointing his position for the Federal navy. Ewell immediately split his men into two columns, directing them off the road to move through the pine thickets on either side of the path. The dust ebbed, but the heavy shelling persisted. Having found a viable target, the shipborne artillery continued to pound away.

As the division crept forward, rumors of heavy fighting ahead passed from mouth to mouth. The Federals were making a stand atop Malvern Hill, the last formidable barrier between the Confederates and the James River. And while Ewell's men were not yet engaged, they began to fight the battle in their minds. "[The] shells crashing through the pines, their noise and terror greatly exaggerated by . . . falling limbs, the sound of the large guns on the boats . . . additionally deep and solemn [because of] the closeness of the threat,"[43] made everyone wary. Then the division started to encounter refugees returning from the front. "Litter bearers with wounded, the frightened stragglers, and broken . . . ambulances . . . met them in their advance," Campbell Brown wrote. "The morale effect was [one of] defeat."[44]

Unlike his men, Ewell eagerly anticipated charging into the fray, and he rode ahead to the van to look for Stonewall. He found him at the intersection where the Willis Church Road met a narrow lane to Carter's Farm. Jackson, pointing to the slope that started its rise about a hundred yards ahead (Malvern Hill), related that the Yankees were entrenched atop its peak. Lee planned to attack the heights. Magruder would advance from the west; Jackson would charge from the east with Whiting left of the road, D.H. Hill on the right. Ewell and Winder would hold in reserve. But before he committed to the assault, Jackson would make a personal reconnaissance.

Stonewall and Ewell rode east, picked up Whiting, then headed south into a small forest. The three horsemen trotted through the glen before emerging into a broad field, planted in wheat. Riding through the yellow stalks, Jackson and his two companions stood out against the grain, presenting an inviting target to the Northern gunners posted on the far side of the clearing. The enemy artillery opened fire. Coming to a halt, Stonewall ignored the noisy cannons as he studied the knoll that rose to the south. Both Ewell and Whiting stayed quietly beside their commander. No one flinched when shells burst and flared nearby. But when a solid ball came bounding directly toward Ewell, he jerked his mount's reins to escape the path of the rolling shell.

Pleased with himself for having won the joust of nerves with Ewell, Whiting pressed his advantage. He requested that one of Ewell's brigades be assigned to him as reinforcements. Ewell objected, leading to an interchange of caustic comments and insults between the two officers.

"Come, gentlemen," Stonewall interrupted. "Don't let us have any quarreling."[45]

Jackson turned his horse and led Ewell and Whiting away from the enemy's still-firing cannons. When they reached the Rebel camp, Stonewall told Ewell to have Trimble and his brigade report to Whiting. The order was belittling (given the recent exchange), but Ewell complied without comment. Before another hour had passed, Whiting asked for still more troops, and Ewell was forced to further dilute his division. He sent Stafford (leading Taylor's Louisiana regiments) to the front, leaving himself just Early's brigade at hand.

Ewell had expected the battle to begin momentarily, but the hot afternoon dragged on and on with no sign of a Confederate attack. The only action came from the continued shelling by the Union. Finally, about 3:00 p.m., when Ewell could no longer stand the waiting, he rode ahead to ask why the delay. He was told that Magruder had made a wrong turn coming to the front, and that he was only now getting into position. The attack had been rescheduled for 5:00 p.m.

When he arrived back at his post, Ewell spotted Colonel Stapleton Crutchfield, Jackson's Chief of Artillery, casually conversing with other officers. He approached Crutchfield to find out why the Rebel guns were not contesting the annoying and continuing Northern barrage. Crutchfield replied with an insolent question.

"Have you seen my ammunition trains?"[46]

"Don't you know where they are?"

"No," the colonel sighed with an unconcerned shrug. "I told Jackson this and I reckon he's sent [someone] . . . to look for them."

Ewell was both incredulous and furious at Crutchfield's indifference in the face of battle. But before he could give vent to his anger, the relative quiet was shattered by the eruption of weaponry to the southwest. The battle had finally begun.

Ewell raced to Early to determine the readiness of his brigade. As they talked, an aide of D.H. Hill's galloped up. Hill had led an assault against the enemy's left on Malvern Hill, had been thrown back, and now was in desperate need of immediate assistance. Hill had sent the aide to Jackson, who had authorized committing Ewell's available reserve.

While Early assembled his regiments, Ewell had Campbell Brown ride ahead to find the quickest path to the front. The young man soon returned to report that due to the enemy's shelling, the only viable route was a circuitous way. The brigade was formed by now, and they moved out.

Traveling west through a series of woods and clearings, the columns gradually turned south to follow a narrow, dusty lane that ended abruptly at Turkey Run—a marshy creek lying at the bottom of a steep ravine. The ominous clamor of muskets and cannons rose nearby, but the battlefield action was not visible because of the brush surrounding the stream.

A fast inspection of the marsh revealed a problem. Although the men could wade through the bog, the ground was too soggy for horses. Ewell made a prompt decision. As Early reported later, "[My] brigade was started across the bottom . . . [while the] officers [took] a detour to the right over an old dam."[47] Doubling back to where he expected his troops would exit the brush proved more difficult than Ewell had thought. The way was blocked by fugitives fleeing from the front, the sun had set (it was too dark to see which men were his), and the land beyond the marsh was forested, further hampering his search. Ewell and Early agreed on a solution to the dilemma. Early would locate the missing regiments; Ewell would gather up stragglers and send them back to fight. They parted, each off on his own separate mission.

Riding in circles in the dark and confusing glen, Ewell exhorted the deserters to form and follow him back to battle. His loud oaths finally convinced a small band from Kershaw's brigade to turn around, and they started entreating others to join them. Soon, a sizeable force was on hand and Ewell took them forward. Winding his way through the thick woods, Ewell came out from under the trees and into a clover field at the foot of Malvern Hill. From the heights, Federal cannons fired through the gloom on the Confederate position. The flash from the Yankee artillery acted as a strobe light, revealing in a series of still pictures hundreds of dead and wounded men lying on the steep slope.

As Ewell gazed, dismayed by the carnage, D.H. Hill came up beside him to suggest quietly that there was no reason for continuing the assault, that Ewell use his force to fill the gaps in what remained of the Confederate line. Ewell agreed, and when Early finally arrived with his brigade, his men were added to the thin rows of Rebel ranks. Seeing that the numbers were too few to fend off a Federal counterattack, Ewell left the front to find Jackson and ask that reinforcements be forwarded at once. When he reached the rear at 9:00 p.m., Ewell, joined by Campbell Brown, started searching for Stonewall. It was a hopeless task. Although the woods and trails teemed with Southern soldiers, the wandering mobs were disorganized. Lee's army had disintegrated into hordes of individuals whose only intent was to escape the ever-firing Federal guns.

To compound Ewell's troubles, it began to rain, a fearful gale whose lightning and thunder seemed to echo the Union artillery. Ewell abandoned his search at 3:00 a.m. Seeking refuge from the downpour, he lay under a tree to catch a few hours of sleep.

By morning, the rain had slackened to a cold, miserable drizzle. Ewell found Hill, who had come back from the front about dawn, and the two generals started to search for Jackson. They finally found him far to the rear, protected from the weather in a covered wagon, eating breakfast. Ewell and Hill offered their fears of Yankee counterattack, and begged Stonewall to reinforce their line. "If McClellan knows what he's about," Ewell warned, "he'll take the aggressive and . . . we are in no condition to meet it."[48]

"Oh, no," Stonewall replied with confidence, "McClellan will clear out [this] morning."

Neither Hill nor Ewell agreed with Jackson's intuition, but

they were unable to persuade him to change his mind and take action. Leaving without the help they had sought, Hill returned to his lines while Ewell looked for Campbell Brown. "Have [the] thirty ammunition wagons [captured] at White Oak Swamp moved back to the Richmond side of it," he ordered after locating his aide. "[They'll] be safe [there] in event of our retreat."[49] Jackson could be apathetic to their danger, but Ewell was not about to be caught unprepared.

Returning to the front, Ewell went to Early to get him to withdraw his brigade to safer ground. He was amazed to find Early in no peril. Stonewall had been right in his assumptions. The enemy had indeed retreated to the southeast along the James River during the hours before dawn.

Leaving Early's men in place, Ewell rode north to check on Trimble, who had moved behind Hill late the night before, taking a reserve post. His troops had never been called to action, and except for those wounded by artillery fire, had taken no casualties.

Ewell's last stop was to the left where Stafford's men were camped. He had attacked yesterday, but his assault had been dispersed so quickly that his losses were minimal.

At this point it began to rain again, a heavy downpour that forced Ewell to seek shelter in a small farmhouse. He sat alone on the dirt floor, thinking about the battles contested during the past week. While his division had escaped almost unscathed, the rest of Lee's army had been devastated. Over 20,000 men had fallen, 5,000 when D.H. Hill and Magruder made their disjointed and unsupported charge on Malvern Hill. Ewell could not forget his vision of the many dead and dying on just that one slope the night before. Moxley Sorrel vividly described Ewell's despair over the Rebel losses. "I found him doubled up on the floor of a little shanty, his head covered up, the ground was covered with our slain," Sorrel wrote in his memoirs. "[Ewell] . . . recognized me, and lisped . . . 'Mather Sorrel, can you tell me why we had five hundred men killed . . . on this field yesterday?' That was all; the soul of the brave general was fit to burst for the awful and useless sacrifice."[50]

All day on July 2nd, Lee reassembled his force. Companies returned to their regiments, regiments found their brigades, and brigades became divisions again. By nightfall, the men were finally back in place, ready to resume action. Lee began his pursuit of McClellan (with Ewell in the lead) the next day, a march that failed to find the elusive, hard-running enemy.

Ewell awoke the morning of July 3rd suffering from both chills and a fever, an attack of malaria (not surprising considering his recent exposure to swamps and mosquitoes). His body ached in every joint. Sure that McClellan's forces had eluded the Confederates, Ewell felt that he could afford to stay in bed for another hour or so. He was lying on his cot when Jackson stormed into his tent. Stonewall was on a rampage, infuriated by the general laxity within his force, and Ewell was just one stop on his tour. Jackson was there and gone before Ewell could explain that he was really sick.

Continuing to march eastward on July 4th, Ewell finally established contact with the Yankees late that hot and humid morning. McClellan had dug in by Harrison's Landing, a port on the James River. Lee immediately issued orders, "Prepare to attack!"[51] Although Ewell obediently formed his men, he did so reluctantly. He had little hope of a great victory. His division was depleted. In addition to his wounded, over 3,000 men had been lost because of illness or straggling during the campaign, and few among those remaining had stomach left for combat. They were tired and they were afraid of the Union gunboats. Colonel James Walker reported that his Thirteenth Virginia would not fight.[52] Fortunately, Jackson sensed the men's mood and convinced Lee to call off his plan for battle.

For the next four days, the two adversaries remained in position. Neither made an aggressive move. Forced to admit the futility of confronting McClellan in his entrenched post, Lee withdrew his army on July 8th. While the battles fought had been drawn, the Confederates had maneuvered the Federals away from their capital. Richmond had been saved.

* * * *

Ewell took his division to Strawberry Hill, a site near the Meadow Bridge, north of Richmond. Choosing to stay with his troops in the field, he spent his time writing letters to Lizinka and his niece, Lizzie. He reviewed the campaign, then described his revulsion to war. "For my part, I would be satisfied to never see another field. What pleasure can there be in seeing thousands of dead and dying in every agony . . . ?" he questioned. "So many times . . . wounded are left without help for hours . . . ."[53]

Strange words from the tough old fighter whom people knew was always eager to go into battle. But seeing D.H. Hill's disaster at Malvern Hill had shaken Ewell, and where he once talked of the road to glory, now he was beginning to understand the toll that road extracted. And there was no end in sight.

Second Manassas

"I have come to you from the West, where we have always seen the backs of our enemy . . . ." Major General John Pope boasted to his new Northern army.[1] Composed of troops drawn from McDowell, Major General Franz Sigel (who had taken over Fremont's command) and Banks—Jackson's old enemies from the Valley—the Union Army of Virginia was organized on June 26, 1862. While McClellan's exhausted men recuperated at Harrison's Landing on the James River, this new force moved south in early July to cut the Rebel's supply line between Richmond and the Shenandoah Valley.

"They say this new general claims my attention," Stonewall noted. "Well, please God, he shall have it!"[2]

Ewell's response was typical. Instead of offering grim commentary, he chose to make a joke. "Pope would not want to see the backs of my men," he offered. "Their pantaloons are out at the rear . . . ."[3]

Lee was also thinking about Pope. Charged with holding McClellan and his 100,000 men (still clinging to a toehold on the Peninsula) at bay, he also had to find a way to deal with Pope's army of 47,000 who were advancing from the north. Lee seemed more concerned with his new adversary's program for feeding his troops than with Pope's threats of attack. The Union general had declared his intention to live off the land, confiscating food he needed for his men from the families living in his path. He also declared a policy of requiring that all Southern males dwelling behind his lines take an oath of Federal allegiance. Those refusing would be banished from their homes, and if they returned without proof of having sworn to uphold the Union, they would be shot.[4]

Lee, the perfect gentleman, was enraged by Pope's flouting of the rules of "civilized warfare." With the concurrence of President Davis, he sent an angry dispatch to the Federal government in Washington, saying that he would withhold prisoner of war status for Northern officers captured in the

Nathaniel Banks

John C. Fremont

John Pope

George McClellan

Photographs from the Library of Congress Collection

upcoming campaign. And if Pope shot any civilians, he would retaliate with his own executions.[5] Lincoln would not "accept" the note (he could not acknowledge correspondence from a nation he did not recognize), but the obnoxious decrees were soon modified. It was too late for General Pope. Determined to suppress the "miscreant," Lee ordered Stonewall to head north on July 13th to confront the new Yankee army.

Ewell led the way. His troops traveled by train, moving first to Louisa, a small village halfway to Gordonsville, where they switched to different gauge tracks for the rest of their journey. Ewell and his staff rode on horseback, accompanying the caissons and supply wagons. The division met at Gordonsville on July 20th, then went further north to Liberty Mills near the Rapidan River. Ewell immediately put his men to work with a rigorous drilling schedule to reestablish discipline. Although their dislike for marching had not abated, the regiments responded well. They were happy to be back in the mountains and away from the heat and insect-laden swamps of the Peninsula. Clear water, fresh air, and crisp evenings for sleeping made the hard training bearable.

Despite the peaceful conditions, the troops were keenly aware that the war lurked nearby. Pope, positioned somewhere across the Rapidan, kept tabs on Ewell's activities by having his cavalry ride every day to the river's edge. Most always, they just eyed the Rebels glaring back from across the water, but now and then a flurry of shots would ring out to remind everyone that existence was perilous.

On August 2nd a chaplain just assigned to the Louisiana regiments came to visit Ewell. The Reverend James B. Sheeran, only five feet tall, weighing about one hundred pounds, and looking more like a leprechaun than a priest, walked erectly through the flaps into Ewell's tent, disdaining to stoop as most were forced to do. His opening words astonished Ewell. Instead of uttering devout comments about his having come to save souls, the tiny father laced into the Union army, describing the Yankees as "Lincoln's bandits" and "abolitionist robbers."[6] Sheeran was a feisty patriot for the Southern Cause, and his unexpected fervor caught Ewell off guard. He usually harassed new chaplains with profane expressions of his disbeliefs, but it seemed inappropriate with Sheeran. Ewell liked this man and chose not to insult him. As they talked, Ewell discovered that Sheeran had neither a horse nor enough money to buy one.

"Tell the boys," Ewell suggested slyly, "to capture one [for you] at the next battle."

Sheeran thought that a wonderful idea, and their interview ended on that larcenous note.[7]

Winder's Division followed Ewell to Gordonsville in the press to confront Pope, and when A.P. Hill also arrived with his troops, Stonewall had 24,000 at hand, more than enough to launch his campaign. He remained in camp, however, to await just the right opportunity.

In the interim, Jackson took up a postponed but not forgotten matter, the court martial of Brigadier General Richard Garnett. Stonewall had relieved the former subordinate from command after the March 23rd Battle of Kernstown for failing to obey his orders during the fray. Ewell sat on the judges' board, an uneasy seat for him because he had studied the evidence and considered Garnett innocent of the indictment.[8] He escaped having to rule against Stonewall, however, because in the midst of the trial, a courier interrupted the proceedings to report that Pope had split his army in half. Banks, leading the forward element, was reported near Culpeper. Jackson had been waiting for just such a moment, and he again called off the court martial by directing all brigades to start preparing to move out.

Ewell's instructions were to hurry east to Orange Court House where he would meet the rest of the army marching north from Gordonsville. The rendezvous would take place the next night. As Ewell gathered up his men, he received new orders. Stonewall wanted him to divide his division, sending a force across the Rapidan River as if to attack Pope's right wing at Madison Court House. With the enemy pinned in place because of this maneuver, Ewell would then backtrack above the river, joining Winder and Hill at Barnett's Ford for the assault on Banks and the isolated Union left wing.[9]

Ewell sent a brigade across the river that night. They headed west until daybreak, then turned about to begin coming back east. The rest of the division plodded below the water, parallel to their movement. Progress was slow. Not only was the day extremely hot, but also there were no roads on either side of the stream; the troops trampled through corn fields. About 2:00 p.m., Jackson rode up. Ewell expected a reprimand because of his laggard advance, but Stonewall had not come to criticize him. Both Winder and Hill had done worse, so much so that Stonewall had brought his whole army to a halt. The men could rest until dusk, then resume their trek in the cool of evening.[10]

After sunset Ewell put his troops back in line, moving east. They reached Barnett's Ford about midnight, wheeled to the north, and promptly encountered bluecoat cavalry. Unsure whether he should push past the enemy horsemen, Ewell sent an aide back to Jackson for orders. Stonewall advised Ewell to stop and camp for the night. There was no point in his rushing ahead, as Winder and Hill continued to lag behind (Hill had yet to clear Orange Court House).

Ewell was up early on August 9th and soon had his brigades started for Culpeper. His mood was surly because up to now, other than advancing toward Banks, Ewell had no inkling of Stonewall's plans, where he was going or what he should do when he finally came upon the Federals. "General Jackson . . . ordered me to [be] . . . ready to move at . . . dawn," he complained to anyone who would listen. "[I] have had no further intimation of [his] plans. And that is . . . all I ever know . . ." [11]

As Ewell pushed his men slowly up the pike, he suddenly heard shots ring out ahead. It was 10:00 a.m. Assuming that the skirmish was just another delaying tactic by the Federal cavalry, he was surprised when Beverly Robertson (leading the Rebel horsemen at the fore) sent back a different report. A large detachment of bluecoats had been spotted to the right, holding a position in a valley. Ewell quickly ordered Early, leading his front brigade, to switch from column into battle line, with pickets posted along both sides of the road. When everyone was in place, the regiments crept cautiously ahead. The air was still, as if nature itself was breathless, awaiting combat. Ewell, riding at the van, silently signaled the troops behind him to halt as he reached the crest of a slope. He could see into the coming arena. The highway ahead split in two—one fork going toward Madison Court House, the second arm in the direction of Culpeper. A dense woods lay west of the pike. To the east, a solitary mountain (Slaughter's) sat like a giant turtle enjoying the sun.[12]

To the right center, fields of green corn and just-cut, yellow wheat were bisected by an unpretentious rivulet (Cedar Run). A low ridge hovered beyond the grain. And as Robertson had reported, a long line of Federal cavalry stood poised atop that hill. Ewell could see that with most of his force still in column, he was in no position to confront the Union. To buy time, he ordered Early to take his troops ahead to the fork in the road, set up a defensive line, then fire several rounds of artillery to discourage any thought of the Yankees charging him.

Early quickly posted his men, placing most of his regiments in the grove of trees above the intersection. After he was settled, his guns lobbed a few rounds at the Yankees, who at first remained as motionless as a wooden rail fence, then slowly backed out of sight. As the Federal horsemen vanished from view, cannons roared from beyond the ridge, replying to Early's feeble salvo. Ewell had found Banks' entire corps.

Knowing that he should do no more until Jackson reached the front, Ewell quickly set up an interim position. He sent an aide ahead to tell Early to hold his post. Another scout was dispatched to the rear to halt Trimble and Forno, in command of Taylor's Louisiana regiments, in place, then continue on to find Stonewall. Ewell himself rode east, toward a home at the base of Slaughter's Mountain, to await Jackson's coming. When he reached the dwelling, a ramshackled cottage with a long, narrow porch facing the valley, Ewell dismounted and climbed the steps to the veranda. As he scanned the horizon before him, looking for the Yankees, a whispered noise behind him caused Ewell to whirl about to stare into the dirty faces of several frightened children, peering out through a screen door. To avoid further startling the tykes, Ewell stooped to their height, offered a warm smile, and beckoned them to join him on the porch. The youngsters returned his grin and after opening the door, came outside for a closer look at their unexpected caller. Ewell began talking to the children, and he became so absorbed in the discussion, he failed to hear the heavy thump of boots until Stonewall had reached his side.[13]

Jumping to his feet, Ewell was chagrined at being caught playing with children while the enemy threatened combat. But

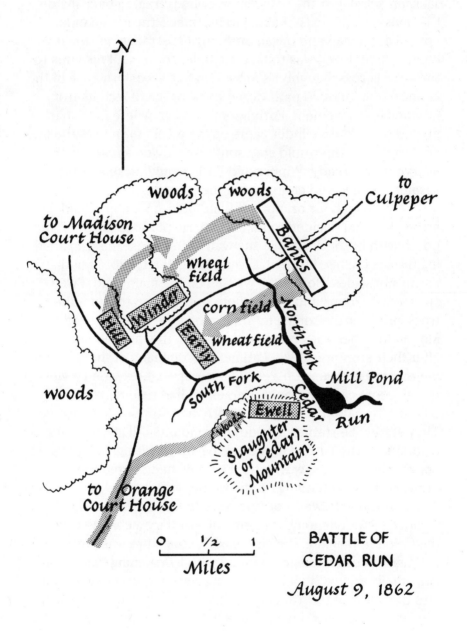

N

to Madison
Court House

woods

woods

to
Culpeper

Banks

wheat
field

Winder

corn field

North Fork

Early

wheat field

woods

South Fork

Mill Pond

Ewell

Cedar

Run

woods

Slaughter
(or Cedar)
Mountain

to Orange
Court House

0   1/2   1

Miles

BATTLE OF
CEDAR RUN

August 9, 1862

Jackson acted as if the youngsters (who retreated back inside the house) didn't exist. Falling to his knees, the commander spread out a map and began outlining his strategy for the on-coming fight. Ewell was to take Trimble, Forno, and his guns to the right across Slaughter's Mountain to the eastern base of the eminence. A forested path would prevent the bluecoats from noticing his movement. Early was to remain where Ewell had posted him. When Winder came up, he would form in battle line on Early's left. Hill would stay south to provide a reserve. When everyone was ready, Winder and Early would make a frontal assault; Ewell would charge from the flank.[14]

With an hour or more at hand before Winder would arrive, Jackson decided to take a nap. He plopped down on the porch with his back against the wall of the house, his cap shad-ing his eyes. While he slept, Ewell went after Trimble's and Forno's brigades. Both were waiting on the main road. Ewell started the troops and the artillery to the right, through the trees and over the rolling foothills along the base of Slaughter's Mountain. When they reached their goal, the men fell out to rest after their strenuous hike. Latimer, in command of the cannons, unlimbered two guns on a rocky outcrop that provided a view of the bluecoat cavalry. Banks' horsemen had resumed their forward formation shortly after Early had stopped his barrage. They stood like statues astride their mounts. All at once, the troopers on the far end of the line began wavering, falling back. Looking left, Ewell saw why the Federals had started to with-draw. Early was charging up the Culpeper Road.[15]

Although Ewell's orders were to join the attack, he decided to wait a moment to give his artillery a chance to rout the Union horseman. The command to open fire was given, and Latimer's two cannons responded with a deafening blast. The twin shells arched high into the air before swooping downward into the midst of the Yankee cavalry, which scattered to escape the flying fragments. Enemy guns hiding in the rear answered Ewell by sending a flurry of rounds into Early's force, stemming his assault. "I ordered the men to retire a few steps," Early recalled, "and lie down to avoid the effects of the enemy artil-lery."[16] As his troops huddled in their shallow depressions throughout the open ground, subjected to the furor of the

Federal bombardment, other Southern cannons to Ewell's left entered the fray, their noise blending with the roar of the Yankee guns, shattering what had been up to now, a peaceful summer afternoon.

With the infantry attack obviously stalled and Early in dire straits, Ewell looked for an advantage, a better site to emplace his guns. He glanced up the towering mountain slope and saw the perfect spot—the front yard of an ornate mansion that crowned the peak. The house was virtually inaccessible; horses could never pull a cannon up to the crest. But human hands might do the job, so Ewell summoned a squad of "volunteers", the division's scouts.[17] It was a prodigious task. The guns were heavy and cumbersome; the slope was both steep and covered by trees and brush; and the stony ground caused a slip or two. But in just minutes, Latimer was unlimbering on Dr. Slaughter's grassy lawn. Ewell ordered the barrage to begin. From the summit, the Confederate cannons gained extra range, easily reaching the now visible area where their foes had placed their weapons. The Federals tried to answer, but the mountain was too tall, out of their range. Only a few Yankee rounds came even close to Ewell's elevated position.

Ewell was elated with his advantage. He became jovial, turning his attention during this hiatus in combat to a quartermaster who had climbed the mountain to watch the artillery exchange. The officer happened to wear his dress uniform that day. "I say, you, man, with the fine clothes on," Ewell cried when he spotted the resplendent soldier. "Who are you? . . . Where do you belong?"[18]

The quartermaster, not knowing the volatile temperament of the commander who had accosted him, answered with an exaggerated display of dignity as he revealed both his organization and occupation.

"Good heavens!" Ewell exclaimed, grabbing his bald head in mock wonderment. "A quartermaster on a battlefield. Who ever heard of such a thing?"

If the quartermaster thought he would escape Ewell with just this jest, he was sadly mistaken. He was quickly given an assignment. "As long as you're here," Ewell declared, "I will make you useful as well as ornamental." He ordered the officer downhill, through the heavy fire, to carry a message to Jackson.

The quartermaster hurried off, delivered the note, then returned with Stonewall's answer. Mumbling he had "necessary business about his wagons," the now sweaty and disheveled officer then fled before Ewell could think of another duty.

About 5:00 p.m., both adversaries began to reduce their rapid cannon fire. Anticipating that Jackson was planning to charge, Ewell came down from the heights to form his brigades — putting Trimble up front with Forno to follow. As the men fell into line, Banks, commanding the Federal force, attacked the Rebel left. His assault, cleverly organized to lash the Confederates from two directions (east and north), was a huge success, mostly because the Southerners attacked were leaderless. Winder, responsible for the men under storm, had just been killed, struck by a Union artillery shell.[19]

When he saw Winder's line break, Ewell urged Trimble to start his troops forward. The Fifteenth Alabama stepped out, but their advance soon came to a halt. "We had expected to move . . . straight to our front," Campbell Brown recalled, "but were prevented by a mill pond . . . which our skirmishers reported to be impassable."[20] If the troops swung right, they would not only proceed away from the battle but also isolate themselves from the rest of the army. Left was their only alternative, but in that direction, Ewell's cannons were raking the ground with grape and canister. Latimer had seen Winder's men retreat, and he was using his guns to protect Early. Ewell saw he could not move until his own artillery stopped firing. An aide was dispatched to order Latimer to halt his barrage; a second messenger was sent to tell Stonewall why Ewell had not entered the fray.[21]

Waiting, watching the main arena, Ewell saw that while the fighting was frenzied, the Rebel line had stabilized, and Early's brigade still held their ground. Latimer's shelling had had a marked effect in stemming the Yankees' attack. All at once a line of gray swept up from the left and drove into to the billowing clouds of white smoke enveloping the battlefield. A.P. Hill's troops had arrived on the scene. As they charged into the southwestern end of the melee, the Federals emerged from the opposite side, running up Culpeper Road. And Latimer's cannons suddenly stopped firing. The path had finally opened for Ewell to join in the fray. He quickly ordered his men forward.

When Ewell's men reached Culpeper Road, they merged in disarray with Early's and A.P. Hill's combined ranks, coming up from the southwest. Jackson had to check his pursuit of the enemy to sort out his lines. The sun had dipped below the horizon before the realignment was completed, but Stonewall was not about to give up the chase. He went after Banks in the dark. After creeping cautiously for about a mile, the Rebels spotted campfires burning in the brush to their left. Jackson decided to halt and bring his guns forward. A series of rounds were sent screaming into the trees, and in answer, the Confederates heard loud yelping and panicked thrashing in the thickets. The enemy had restarted their retreat.

Knowing that Banks was running to hook up with the rest of Pope's army (who far outnumbered the Confederates), Stonewall proceeded with care. He sent just a single brigade, one of A.P. Hill's, and an artillery battery off the road to pursue the bluecoats. Once through the woods and into a meadow, the Rebels stopped to shoot another series of rounds into the forest ahead. They received a blistering answer from Yankee guns. The enemy had dug in for battle.

Fortunately for Stonewall, his pursuit of Banks had produced a prisoner, a negro servant of one of Sigel's officers, who told Jackson what he needed to know. Banks had just been reinforced, probably by Pope's whole army. "Believing it imprudent to continue to move forward," Jackson wrote later, "I ordered a halt for the night."[22] The Southerners quietly retired, moving back to Slaughter's Mountain.

The next day, August 10th, was hot and sultry. Defiant as ever, Stonewall waited for Pope and his men to come to him. At the same time, he sent his troops onto the battlefield to retrieve the wounded (of both North and South), to bury their own dead, and to gather up the arms and other gear left behind by the Yankees in their haste to escape from yesterday's fierce charge by the Rebels. Dark clouds formed that afternoon, and a hard rain followed. The downpour discouraged any Northern offensive plans, but it did not stop Jeb Stuart. He had come up with his troopers at noon, and proceeded to scout the Federals' encampment. When he reported that night, he confirmed Jackson's conclusion: the Union's numbers were overwhelming.

Shortly after sunrise on August 11th, a Federal detachment waving a white flag galloped into view. They rode up to request a truce. Stonewall had left the Union dead lying on the field, and the Yankees wanted to bury their fallen compatriots. Jackson eagerly agreed to a ceasefire. Having decided to withdraw, he saw the peaceful interval as a means to mask his retreat. Pope's men took all day to complete their grisly assignment. At dusk, when the Northerners had finally left the field, the Confederates built campfires across their entire front. When it was dark, they slipped away after the wagons that had departed during the day. Stonewall retreated all the way back to the Rapidan River and Gordonsville where he waited for Lee and the rest of the army to come.

The mystique of Ewell as a salty, eccentric, but highly competent leader was enhanced after the Battle of Cedar Creek by a story that swept through the camp. During the Confederate withdrawal from Slaughter's Mountain, he had ordered one of his scouts, Frank Myers, to set up a series of couriers.

Myers failed to carry out his assignment, and when Ewell got back to Liberty Mills, he went looking for the young lieutenant. "Why didn't you send the detail?" he demanded.[23]

Myers made an error by offering an excuse. "I supposed . . . " he began.

"You supposed!" Ewell shrieked with indignation. "What right had you to suppose anything? Do as I say, Sir!" From that moment on, whenever the word "supposed" crept into one's vocabulary, Ewell's quote was used in reply.

Ewell also gained fame for his role in the battle. The *Baltimore American* heaped praise on him, saying that Ewell's guns had paved the way for the Southern victory. Ewell protested, "Where these . . . accounts speak of [me], Jackson's [name] ought to be substituted."[24] Although he shunned publicity for himself, Ewell was not averse to promoting his subordinates. After Early complained that Jackson's official report slighted his battle exploits in favor of Winder, Ewell quickly asked Stonewall to amend the record. "It was not my design to speak of surviving officers," Jackson revealed, but he did modify his report, adding Early's achievements to his account.[25]

Amidst all the talk of Ewell, no one mentioned the mistake he had made that could have caused the South to fail at Slaughter's Mountain. He had assumed his post on the flank early in the afternoon. With over three hours to get ready for an assault he knew would come, Ewell failed to survey his front, did not discover the large mill pond that delayed his charge into the fight. He would repeat this error at Gettysburg to the Confederacy's ultimate dismay.

Robert E. Lee arrived at Gordonsville with Longstreet's Corps on August 14th. He had a strategy in mind, born out of necessity, because of a move made by the Federals. McClellan —hopelessly bottled up below Richmond—had been ordered to leave his haven at Harrison's Landing, evacuating his men by water to the north to join with Pope. This would pit 150,000 men, twice Lee's numbers, against the Rebels. But if Lee engaged Pope now, before the Army of the Potomac arrived at the front, he could rout the "miscreant" Pope and then deal with McClellan on more even terms.

The opportunity was all the greater because of a tactical blunder Pope had made. He had moved his army forward to the shores of the Rapidan, west of the "V" formed where this stream joined the Rappahannock. If Lee sent his cavalry behind Pope's bivouac to torch the bridges spanning the Rappahannock, Pope's line of escape would be severed, and he would be trapped between the two rivers. Lee could possibly annihilate the entire Union Army of Virginia.

Lee put his plan into motion on August 16th. Stonewall started his corps toward Clark Mountain, only six miles from Pope's position, where he would sit, hidden from view, until Stuart's cavalry had burned the bridges. Jackson would then launch the opening attack.

Ewell's Division brought up the rear on the rapid march to Clark's Mountain. Sensing the need for speed, he was incensed when a guide waved his van off the roadway, around an obstinate skunk who was sleeping on the path ahead. Ewell's oaths were cut short, however, when the sentry noted that the polecat was "[Probably] one of Pope's scouts."[26] Ewell could appreciate a good joke, particularly when it was directed at the enemy. It was dark when Jackson's corps finally reached their destination.

The next morning, Stonewall climbed Clark's Mountain to spy on Pope's extensive encampment. He was happy to see that the Federals were relaxing, lounging about with no idea they were about to be assailed. Jackson eagerly anticipated Lee's order to attack. He waited throughout the day in vain. The instructions, which were finally received that evening, were to hold in place. The cavalry was late in getting into position to burn the bridges. The delay lasted for two days, giving Pope the time he needed to recognize his peril and withdraw across the Rappahannock, out of danger.

Lee quickly organized a pursuit, fording the Rapidan to confront Pope, who was based on the north shore of the Rappahannock. He found the Yankees standing firm on higher ground, easily able to dispute any attempt by the Rebels to cross and bring them to battle. To prove it, Pope opened his artillery on Jackson, camped just above a repaired railroad bridge. It was the same one Ewell had destroyed, to Taylor's consternation, only seven months ago.

Lee's dilemma was clear. He had to force an engagement with Pope before McClellan and his reinforcements reached the front, but with the river as a barrier, the Federals were inaccessible. They could remain in place for days in their impregnable position. The only Confederate alternative was a flanking movement.

Stonewall was given the assignment to move around Pope, and on the afternoon of August 21st, he began by starting an artillery bombardment of the enemy's entrenchments. His salvos were meant to distract the Yankees, to keep them from seeing Longstreet's men slip around behind Jackson. That night, as Stonewall's troops evacuated their post and headed northwest to sprint around Pope, Longstreet's men advanced into the vacant entrenchments. His guns opened in the morning as if nothing had changed.

After fording the shallow Hazel River, Stonewall headed east for Sulpher Springs on the Rappahannock. He reached the tiny village late that afternoon. There he found Jeb Stuart's cavalry dueling with a small bluecoat force across the river.

Jackson, looking to slip by the Federals, followed the water
north to Warrentown Springs, where the way was clear to cross
unobserved into Pope's rear. The bridge at this location had
been destroyed, but the river was shallow. Troops could wade
to the other side. Lawton's Brigade (just assigned to Ewell)
started into the stream. Knowing that he had to move his men to
the far shore quickly, Stonewall looked downstream for another
avenue he could use to parallel Lawton's crossing. An old, shaky
dam offered the best possibility, even though rain had started to
fall and the river was already rising, lapping the top of the aged
bulwark. Jackson instructed Ewell to send first Early and then
Forno over this dubious viaduct.

"What should [I] do," Ewell asked, pointing to the fast
flowing stream, "if the river gets past fording?"[27]

"Oh, [the water] won't get up," Stonewall assured him.
"And if it does, I'll take care of it."

Early began to cross, starting with his artillery, then his
troops. The footing was treacherous as the dam's smooth
surface was now awash. All at once, the sky turned black and a
howling wind blew in from the west. A storm exploded overhead, coming "with a fury unsurpassed," Charles Blackford, a
cavalryman, remembered. "I [had] never seen such lightning,
heard such thunder, or felt such rain."[28]

As the last of Early's troops stepped onto the opposite
shore, Forno (next in line) brought his regiments up to cross the
dam. Ewell stopped them. Drenched by the driving rain, shouting to be heard above the roaring wind, he nodded toward the
rising water, explaining that the stream would be flooded before
all the Louisiana soldiers could get across. Forno would have to
remain on this side of the river that night. Ewell then went over
by himself to confer with Early, telling him to hide his men in a
pine woods, as he would be isolated from most of the corps
until morning. After this brief discussion, Ewell returned to the
western bank.

When a bright sun announced the dawn, Ewell woke to
see the Rappahannock raging over its banks. Even worse, he
found that Lawton had not forded his whole brigade across the
river last night. Only one regiment had actually waded to the far
shore. Early was more alone than he had been told. Hurrying

north to where the old bridge had stood, Ewell found Jackson attempting to construct a new span. His pioneers were chopping down the lofty pines bordering the stream, trimming their sparse branches, then hurling the trunks into the swirling water, hoping to snare the fresh cut logs on pillars that rose like stepping stones for a giant out of the river. The columns were all that remained of the former span. Jackson's effort seemed a waste, as none of the ponderous timbers caught on the masonry supports. Each was quickly flipped aside and sent downstream by the fast-running current.[29]

Early watched anxiously from the opposite bank. During the night, bluecoats had approached his camp, and he had sent word to Ewell that "If the enemy advanced upon [me] in force, the whole of [my] troops . . . must be captured."[30] He had moved his brigade north that morning to join with Lawton's stranded regiment to await rescue.

About noon, the Rebels had a stroke of luck. A mass of flotsam, carried downstream from another span washed free by the storm, crashed into the center pillar and caught on. The next log thrust into the current latched onto this bit of debris. When a second, then a third, and finally a fourth tree trunk were similarly established, a new passage began to take form. It was none too soon. From Early's camp, a cannon exploded, and it was answered by enemy guns close by. A banging artillery fight had begun, which continued for an hour before dying down.

The troops worked feverishly toward finishing the span. The stream had fortunately begun to recede and by late afternoon, it finally dropped to a level that allowed the men to wade into the waters. And as darkness fell (hastened by a rolling fog, rising from the soggy earth), the bridge neared completion. All at once, the stillness of the gloom was shattered by the chatter of muskets. This was followed by three cheers, then a "Yankee Tiger," signifying a Union threat to Early.[31]

Jackson responded aggressively, sending Lawton with the rest of his regiments over the just-finished bridge to assist Early in defending his beachhead through the night. At first light, if the enemy force proved overwhelming, both brigades could withdraw to the west bank. When Early learned of Jackson's plan, he protested vehemently. "The enemy was in heavy force," he remembered, "and if I was to be withdrawn, it had better be done that night without waiting for daylight, as . . . the enemy could post artillery . . . and prevent my being . . . withdrawn [at all]."[32] Doubting the validity of Early's conjecture, Ewell went over the bridge about 3:00 a.m. to take his own look at the situation. He found Early so insistent about being in peril that Ewell felt he had no choice but to issue orders for the two brigades to retire back over the stream.

Dawn was breaking when the last infantryman stepped off the makeshift bridge to the safety of the far shore. The retreat had been completed without molestation by the Federals. Ewell and Early remained alone on the enemy side, and in the silence of a peaceful morning, Ewell chided Early for falsely predicting that the enemy planned to attack him. The Yankees answered for Jubal. A barrage of rifle and cannon fire came flying toward the two officers, "making it prudent for us to retire," Early wrote.[33]

They probably vied to see who would be first to gallop over the shaky logs to the haven of Jackson's camp.

Stonewall soon heard that Pope had easily discerned his flanking movement, and had sent three corps, Sigel's, Reno's, and Banks' to prevent its success.[34]

Jackson was enraged because of his failure to elude the enemy, and he vented his wrath on the men. He filed charges against five officers from Gregg's Brigade because their regiments had burned fence rails on the march north, berated his quartermasters because breakfast for the troops was served late the morning of August 24th, and ordered three soldiers shot for attempting desertion.

Ignoring Stonewall's rampage, Ewell concentrated on his own problems. He had not slept for twenty-four hours, and he was still soaking from the rain, his clothes covered with mud from head to boot. He had a clean, dry uniform in his wagon, but when he went to get it, he learned that all the trains had been dispatched to the rear. Campbell was sent after the missing outfit.

Soon after Campbell left camp, the Union (Sigel's corps) started an artillery barrage, laying a pattern of shells that reached as far rearward as Jeffersonton. To protect his men,

Ewell posted them behind a series of low hills that lay near the stream. He was huddled there when Campbell returned.

"What's going on?" the young aide asked as he hurriedly leaped off his horse.[35]

"Nothing particularly," Ewell grunted in reply. "Where are my clothes?"

Campbell did not have them. When he heard the guns, he thought a battle had started, and had galloped back to pitch into the fight.

"No harm done," Ewell said with a sigh. Then, his face lit and he asked, "Have you a towel you can lend me?"

Campbell dug a white terry cloth out of his saddle bag. Ewell grabbed it from the lad and strode purposefully toward the creek that flowed below the knoll. In full view of his men and the Federals (and their cannons), he stripped, jumped into the water, and took a bath.

While Ewell was cleaning up, Stonewall was meeting with Lee in Jeffersonton. The two decided on a new strategy. The corps would start out as if headed for the Valley, but after marching to the brink of the Blue Ridge, Stonewall would turn and drive deep into Banks' rear to capture the enemy's supply base at Manassas. Jackson was so excited by the prospects of Lee's plan, he cried, "I will be moving within the hour!"[36] He even skipped services that Sunday morning to start to prepare for the move. As usual, he told no one in the corps of their destination. Ewell only knew that he was to fix three days rations and be ready to march by first light.

The troops were on the road before dawn on August 25th. Leading Jackson's column northwest, Ewell had Forno up front with Trimble, Lawton, and then Early trailing behind.The men marched rapidly, thinking they were heading for their homes and their loved ones in the Valley. Their pace slowed a bit from disappointment, however, when they arrived at Amissville. The van wheeled northeast, away from the Shenandoah. Jackson led them past Orleans, through the shallow waters of the Hedgman River, and on to Salem, keeping out of sight of the enemy by using back lanes, farm paths, and "no roads," as Campbell described the out-of-the-way route.[37]

Ewell bivouacked at Salem that night, hiding his troops

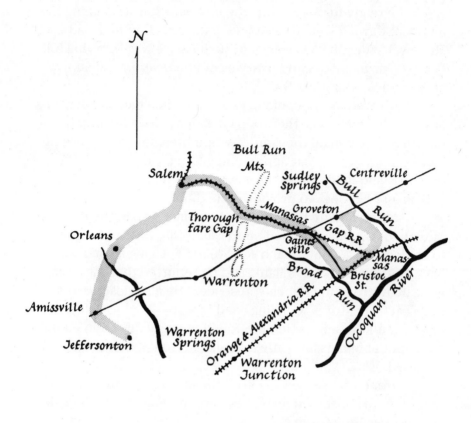

EWELL'S MOVEMENTS
August 25-28, 1862

behind a clump of low knolls where no one could see them. No
fires were permitted. The men slept in brigade formation so all
would be ready for a fast start the next morning. Resuming the
march at dawn, Ewell followed the Manassas Gap Railroad east.
Stonewall's destination was now obvious. He was hurrying for
Pope's rear to cut his adversary's communication and supply
lines from Washington, D.C.

Spurred by thoughts of capturing bluecoat wagon trains
laden with provisions, the troops began to move faster. Most
had already eaten all their rations, and breakfast that morning
had been limited to just apples and green corn, scavenged from
orchards and fields along the way. The men looked ahead to
"Commissary Pope" to provide them dinner.

After winding through Thoroughfare Gap in the Bull Run
Mountains, Ewell continued on to Gainesville, where he halted
to confer with Stonewall and Jeb Stuart. The cavalryman had
been covering Jackson's flank, and he reported that the enemy
were unaware of the Rebels' presence.[38] He also described a
huge cache of stores, buildings and boxcars filled with food,
clothing, and weapons that stretched in every direction out of
the depot at Manassas. Only a small garrison of bluecoats was
on guard.

Stonewall wanted to corral those supplies, but he knew
that time was needed if he was to sort and load as much as he
could carry, then torch the rest. He decided to divert south to
Bristoe Station, capture the village, and burn the Orange and
Alexandria Railroad bridge across Broad Run. This would keep
Pope from using the tracks to advance reinforcements to
Manassas and disturb the Rebels' pillaging.

It was almost dark when Ewell, leading the army, neared
Bristoe Station. He met Jackson there, and the two agreed on a
plan of action: Munford's cavalry would form in the woods one
hundred yards from the train station; Forno would put his
troops behind the horsemen; when everyone was in place, the
Confederates would charge the depot. But before the men were
set, the Yankees saw the threat and sounded an alarm. The
attack started prematurely with a disjointed rush, but Ewell's
troops dispersed the few Union defenders. Most of the enemy
soldiers ran to hide in the buildings adjacent to the tracks where

they were captured within minutes.

As the rest of Ewell's force advanced into the village, a lonely whistle rose from the south. The familiar rumble of a train approaching could be heard. A frantic scramble broke out. Some troops lined up alongside the tracks, prepared to shoot the oncoming engine to a halt. Others threw loose ties onto the rails to block the path of the locomotive. From out of the darkness, a speck of light glowed, growing ever larger and brighter as the Federal express bore down on the waiting Rebels. The Union engineer, when he spotted the Confederates gathered up ahead, added steam and roared through the gauntlet, surviving a splatter of bullets and easily pushing aside the wooden ties strewn on the track.[39]

Ewell's troops were not too disappointed, because while it was dark, they had noted that the train was running empty. No booty had been lost. Jackson, however, was upset. The engineer would certainly report the Confederate presence to the garrison at Manassas. He could not allow another train to go by. Locating a switch connecting the main rails to a siding, Stonewall had it set half-open/half-closed, a position that would derail any following engines. He then posted troops on both sides of the embankment, telling them not to fire at the trains but to save their ammunition for any Federal soldiers embarking after the engine left the tracks.

After laying their trap, the Confederates waited in the dark. They were soon rewarded when another ghostly whistle, blowing from the south, split the night air. The locomotive, its single headlight making it look like a giant Cyclops, roared toward its unsuspecting fate. It thundered past the eagerly watching Rebels, who despite Jackson's adamant orders, fired frantically into its iron flanks. When the engine struck the misset switch, a screeching howl rose above the general din. The monstrous locomotive—smoking and steaming—flew off the track, rolled down the embankment, and slithered to a stop on its side. A few of the cars followed the engine. The others remained on the rail, bunched together with the center coach actually hoisted into the air, giving the train the semblance of a caterpillar in mid-crawl.

Ewell's men descended on the stricken engine. Those

who were first on the scene raised a joyous cry. "It's Old Abe!"[40] The front of the cab was decorated by a huge portrait of Lincoln's face, gazing morosely at the gathered Rebels.

This train, too, was not carrying cargo. A few minutes later, yet another whistle was heard from the south. While most of the Rebels stood idle, assuming the oncoming locomotive would just plow into the wreckage on the rails, one man knew better. He grabbed a splintered board loosened by the previous accident, ran to the last car, and smashed both glowing red lanterns on the rear railing. Denied these warning lights, a third train roared out of the darkness and crashed into the cars blocking the track.

Hasty searching revealed that this train, too, held no cargo. Its only load was a shaken crew and a few frightened passengers, seated on narrow benches that only hours ago had been filled with Union troops being transported to Pope. As the Confederates sorted out their prisoners, another whistle shrieked from the south. A fourth train was approaching.

The Southerners scurried off the tracks to await their next quarry. But in the quiet that followed, the dark night remained unlit by an approaching headlight. "Evidently they suspected something," Campbell Brown wrote, "[even] tho' one of the Louisianians had mounted the captured engine and was blowing all right."[41] The train stopped far short of the Rebels. Several minutes passed by. Then, the "whoosh" of a locomotive backing up could be heard, growing ever more distant. The train was retreating, returning south to warn Pope of an enemy at his rear.

"[I was] inspired with sudden ambition to capture it," Campbell recalled the moment. "[My] plan as to shoot the engineer and if there were troops on board, to disappear rapidly . . . . [I] set off full tilt through the fierce woods . . . .A limb knocked off my hat, and I never saw it again . . . [When] I got alongside the engine, [I] shouted to the driver to stop, but he only went the faster. I fired at him three shots . . . but had the mortification to see him get off unhurt. It was the only time during the war that I fired on the enemy."[42]

The engine racing to the rear would soon inform Pope that he was being flanked, and the Northern leader would surely hurry north to confront Jackson. At the same time, the train that earlier rode through the Rebels' gauntlet was by now at Manassas, alerting the authorities to the Confederates' presence at Bristoe Station. Washington no doubt would rush McClellan and his army to the scene, looking to catch Jackson in a pincer between the two Union forces, ruining Lee's strategy for engaging Pope before McClellan reached the front with his reinforcements. And that battle could not take place until Lee and the rest of the army, coming north, united with Jackson. Stonewall's only option was to maneuver, moving about, drawing Pope toward him and away from McClellan. He would do so, but first there was the subject of Manassas and its plethora of provisions. Jackson was determined to bag those spoils.

Trimble's brigade, accompanied by Stuart's cavalry, was ordered to leave for Manassas that evening. Stonewall would follow in the morning with the divisions under A.P. Hill and Brigadier General William B. Taliaferro, who had assumed command of the fallen Winder's troops. Ewell would stay behind with Lawton's, Forno's, and Early's brigades to protect the rear.

After burning the railroad bridge over Broad Run at daybreak, Ewell set up a defensive line just south of the water. Lawton was posted east of the tracks, Forno west of the railroad, and Early on a low hill further to the right. Cannons emplaced on each flank completed the front. Each element was hidden inside woods that dotted the area like checkers on a board.

Satisfied that he was ready to receive the enemy, Ewell next turned to further obstructing Pope's way north. He sent Forno and four of his regiments plus one of Lawton's south to destroy the railroad bridge over Kettle Run. After torching the wooden span, they would then hurry back to camp, tearing up tracks on their way.

At noon Forno rode up to report that the Federals were bringing up troops by train. Nine cars of infantry had already been unloaded south of Kettle Run. The Sixth Louisiana was skirmishing, disputing the Union advance, while the Eighth Louisiana ripped up track between Ewell and the oncoming Yankees. Battle was imminent, but Ewell had no idea how hard or how long he was supposed to fight. He sent Campbell back to

Jackson for instructions, while at the same time alerting his men to be ready for action.

Shortly after Campbell's departure, Forno's pickets appeared. Behind them a cloud of dust billowing from the south announced the advance of the enemy. As the Rebel skirmishers melted into the thickly-wooded glen which hid their brigade, the bluecoats, marching in two long columns, came into view. The warm, summer air was still except for a steady buzz, like bees in a hive, coming from the Yankee ranks. When the Union soldiers came to within sixty yards of the Confederate front, Colonel Strong sent his Sixth Louisiana out from under their trees to fire as one into the oncoming enemy's ranks. "Many were killed or wounded," an observer recorded, "[while] the rest ran like turkeys."[43]

Major General Joseph Hooker, commanding the Union force, quickly regained control of his men, putting them in position for a second attack. Additional numbers were brought forward so that the Federals' line lapped Ewell's front from flank to flank. Then, under the covering fire of their cannons, the Yankees charged again, bearing left, a tentative advance that was quickly blunted by just one salvo from the Rebels.

Despite having repulsed the Union twice in a row, Ewell was in trouble. He was out-manned, and the enemy was sure to recognize their advantage. Hooker's next assault would probably overwhelm him. Retreat was Ewell's only option, but he could not retire without Jackson's permission. Fortunately, Campbell soon rode up with new orders. "Feel [the Federals'] strength," Stonewall had ordered. "If they are in force . . . fall back on Manassas . . . don't . . . become entangled."[44]

Jackson's orders were more easily given than fulfilled. At any point that Ewell pulled back, he opened a path for the enemy to exploit. Quickly analyzing the problem, Ewell came up with a clever plan. He would withdraw by echelon: as one brigade retreated, the other two would safeguard its movement. And nothing would be left behind! All casualties were to be carried off; every piece of artillery was to be driven rearward; even the harnesses of dead horses were to be retrieved. Ewell was resolved to show the enemy that he was retiring at his leisure, not because the Federals had forced him to withdraw.

He would not allow his enemy any reason to claim this affair as a victory.[45]

The withdrawal went smoothly, more like a camp exercise than a movement under duress. Lawton left first, followed by Forno and then Early. After the men had safely crossed Broad Run, Forno and Lawton started for Manassas, but Early stayed behind, forming his brigade on a series of knolls in sight of the enemy. Ewell had ordered him to open fire, to flaunt his position as if the Rebels remained in full strength. When it became dark (assuming the Yankees stayed at bay), Early would retire to catch up with the rest of the division.

Ewell rode with Lawton to Manassas. The sun had set by the time they reached the village, and as they cantered along the street brightly lit by torches, their eyes widened at the incredible display of supplies the Union had assembled there. Wooden buildings, each several stories high and crammed wall-to-wall with provisions, lined both sides of the muddy, main road. Loaded railroad cars stretched endlessly into the dark night. Sutlers' white tents, bulging with long forgotten delicacies, had sprouted like toadstools in every vacant corner. The stores, however, were disappearing fast, as Jackson's men, like sparrows raiding a cherry tree, darted in and out of the larders gathering loot. Word passed quickly through Ewell's ranks that the stealing was legal, that Jackson was allowing all to take whatever they wished. In seconds, Ewell's troops broke formation and scattered to get their share. "There was no great variety," Campbell recollected." . . . "Coffee and sugar, coats, shirts, pantaloons . . . blue, of course."[46]

While his men were stuffing their haversacks, Ewell met with Jackson to discuss their next move. Hill and Taliaferro would leave now, but Ewell would remain behind to burn whatever supplies were left after the troops had had their fill. Come morning, he would rendezvous with the rest of the corps. Stonewall, however, could not tell Ewell where that might be. He would have to send a guide back to Ewell after sunrise to lead the division to its next destination.

Just before dawn on August 28, 1862, the sky above Manassas glowed with an eerie, orange hue. "The scene [was] as wild and grand as I ever imagined," Campbell wrote. "Many of the men were gathered around the burning cars and buildings, examining their contents, throwing back into the flames what they did not want, looking dark and strange against the fiery background from which tall columns of flame leaped up as the fire spread to each new car or storehouse."[47] The conflagration provided light for the troops as they assembled for the coming march.

After being up most of the night, Ewell was exhausted, but that was not the reason for his surly mood. Trimble, acting on his own, was missing. He and his brigade had started out after Stonewall without the rest of the division. Ewell was so exasperated, he made the men (including Early's, who were just now arriving after successfully restraining the Federals at Broad Run) stand in formation while his aides went looking for the errant Trimble. In the midst of all this confusion, Stonewall's guide reported, asking if anyone knew where they were supposed to go. Ewell of course shared the frustration. Jackson's penchant for secrecy had reached new heights of nonsense— not even his guides were taken into his confidence.

Ewell was both worried and angry because of Stonewall's foolish reticence. He was in a most vulnerable position, being separated from the rest of the corps and expecting to be assailed at any moment from either of two foes, Pope from the south or McClellan approaching from the east. Ewell decided to leave at once, heading for Centreville as the most likely place to find Stonewall. And even if Jackson were not there, Ewell would at least be on familiar ground just fifteen miles from his boyhood home.

After two hours of fruitless searching, marching to and fro, Ewell finally found Trimble and his troops at Blackford's Ford and Bull Run. His obstinate subordinate had good news. Stonewall was nearby at Sudley. Ewell set out at once toward the northwest, to reunite with the corps. He arrived at the rendezvous point about 10:00 a.m. and met with Jackson and Taliaferro (Hill was absent, lost without directions just as Ewell had been) in an ankle-deep field of clover adjacent to the road.

Stonewall reviewed their situation. Pope had split his army into separate marching units to avoid clogging the roads and thus speed his progress north. He was closing on Manassas from a number of different directions. While the Federal leader might be looking to attack the Rebels at the Junction, (unaware that Stonewall had moved on that morning), there was the chance that he was headed back toward Washington to join McClellan, advancing out from the Federal capital. An adroit combining of the two enemy armies before committing to combat made good sense. Stonewall could not take that risk. He had to bring the Union to battle at once by attacking any one of Pope's scattered units, drawing the rest toward him and away from McClellan. While he could not hope to win that fight on his own, Lee with Longstreet's troops was now coming through Thoroughfare Gap in the Blue Ridge only fifty miles away, and if he arrived before McClellan did, the Rebels (per Lee's original plan) would win the victory.

After finishing his briefing, Jackson plopped down by a worm fence and closed his eyes. One of Pope's marching units was sure to come within striking range soon, but until then, he would catch up on lost sleep. Ewell and Taliaferro napped in the soft grass beside Stonewall. About noon, a messenger woke the three generals to report a Union column approaching, coming east out of Gainesville along the Warrenton Turnpike. Jackson leaped to his feet. "Move your division," he snapped to Taliaferro. " . . . Attack the enemy!" Turning to Ewell, he added, "Support the attack!"[48]

All three officers hurried to their troops. When Ewell reached his division, he found Campbell struggling to control a strapping, excited mare just captured that morning. Ewell had asked the lad to find him a new horse; his usual mount, Rifle, was "used up" from the ongoing activities of the past few days. Ewell swung aboard the high-strung animal to wave his brigades forward after Stonewall, who was leading the way through the fields paralleling the highway. When he reached a gully, an unfinished railroad cut, which ran at an acute angle to the road, Jackson stopped to guide the oncoming troops into position. Taliaferro's regiments slipped into the trees back of the ditch, facing the pike. Ewell took up a post to Taliaferro's rear. Hill, who had finally rejoined the corps, placed his division to the east, completing a line two miles long. Everyone was in place by 3:00 p.m., waiting resolutely for the enemy and battle.

Several hours passed without incident. Frustrated with his idleness, Ewell went looking for Jackson. His search led him to the front where he found some cavalry officers taking turns drinking from a canteen. Forgetting all about the Federals who were expected at any moment, Ewell concentrated on the flask.

"What [do you] have [there]?" he demanded.[49]

"Buttermilk," answered William Blackford, a lieutenant colonel serving under Jeb Stuart.

Ewell's eyes sparkled at the mention of the rich elixir—so soothing to his ever taut and suffering stomach. "For God's sake, give me some."

Blackford turned the canteen over, showing that it was empty. "Sorry . . . ," the colonel stated with a grin. "But if you will send your orderly with me, I will show him where he could get some more."

Ewell nodded eagerly. Sensing that his craving was too obvious, he said lamely, "Buttermilk is a delicacy not to be despised by [Jackson] himself . . . . "

A party of six volunteers mounted and rode off to fetch buttermilk for Ewell. They soon returned, bringing not only refreshments but also five bluecoats they had captured at the farmer's house. Interrogation of the prisoners revealed that they were an advance guard for a large Union force coming up the highway.

While this was critical information, Ewell had a higher priority in mind. He asked for his buttermilk. After taking a huge gulp from the flask, Ewell turned to his benefactors. "Trust a cavalryman for foraging," he said.[50]

While Ewell drank his buttermilk, Stonewall reacted to the report of the approaching enemy. He guided his horse to the crest of a small ridge that overlooked the road to await the Yankees. They came in column, their rhythmic step timed by an unseen band playing to their rear. The Union soldiers were dressed in dark blue coats that hung below their knees, pale blue trousers, and tall, black hats, shaped like stovepipes. Each left brim was turned upward, pinned in place by a feather.[51] As the bluecoats passed by, Stonewall rode to and fro atop the hill, the lone Rebel in view. Suddenly, he ended his inspection and galloped down the ridge, halting in front of Ewell and the other out-of-sight Southern officers. He ordered, "Bring up your men!"[52]

Ewell raced to his spirited horse, mounted, and spurred the unruly animal toward the forest hiding his division. But before he reached the trees, a cannon bellowed, starting the Battle of Groveton. Ewell was not late. Stonewall's plan of assault, discussed earlier that afternoon, called for Taliaferro to begin the charge one regiment at a time, a "swinging gate" from right to left, with Ewell's men starting after the last of Taliaferro's men were committed. When he reached his camp site, Ewell sent only Trimble and Lawton forward, holding Early in reserve. Ewell then galloped back to the ridge, expecting to find the Federals in flight. A surprise assault from the flank should have scattered the bluecoats. But the Yankees were not retreating. They had turned left to make a stand, using a drainage ditch along the road as an entrenchment. The low gully offered little protection. But instead of falling back under the hail of lead fired by Ewell's brigades atop the crest of the hill, the enemy soldiers rose to advance on the Rebels.

Sensing a hellish duel, Ewell made some snap decisions. He sent Campbell back to the rear (and out of danger) to tell Early to hurry the reserves forward; and he ordered all his officers to dismount. A man on horseback offered too easy a target on open ground.[53]

By this time, the enemy troops had closed to within one hundred yards of Ewell's array. The opposing lines stood shoulder-to-shoulder, firing salvos into the tightly compressed ranks of the other. Men dropped by the score with every blast, and it seemed that in time, none of the combatants would be left untouched. White, acrid smoke swirled about the field, offering an invisible but still penetrable shield. As the sun slowly dropped below the western horizon, it became even more difficult to see, but the steady shooting continued on and on.

All at once, the balance of the contest shifted ever so slightly. Glancing to his left from behind his troops, Ewell saw that the extreme end of his line was faltering, about to break from an unexpected assault on their flank. He hurried on foot to the threatened point to find a small group of Lawton's men contesting Yankees, hidden in a ravine filled with thick

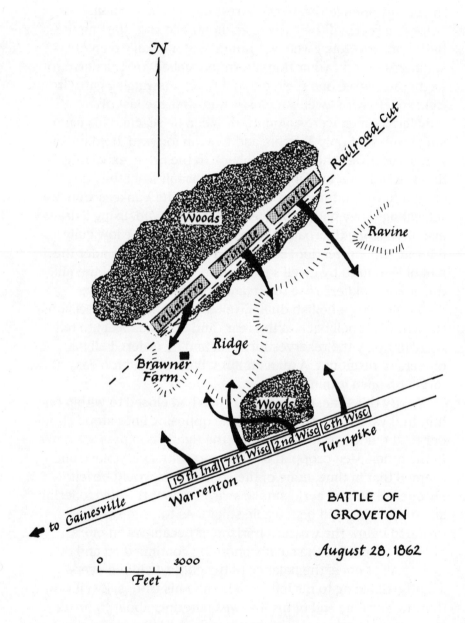

N

Railroad Cut

Woods

Ravine

Ridge

Brawner
Farm

Woods

19th Ind 7th Wisc 2nd Wisc 6th Wisc

Turnpike

Warrenton

to Gainesville

BATTLE OF
GROVETON

August 28, 1862

0   3000
Feet

brambles. Recognizing the bony officer who was joining their skirmish, they raised a yell, "Hurrah! Here's General Ewell."[54] Spurred by the greeting, Ewell boldly charged down into the brush-filled gully, leading the Georgians who fired blindly ahead as they followed. The bluecoats fled. Having thwarted the enemy threat to their flank, Lawton's men turned and clambered out of the ravine to run back to their place in line. Ewell, however, lingered behind a moment to make sure that the Yankees had really retreated. Unable to see because of the gathering dusk and the thick overgrowth, Ewell stooped low, cocking his head to get a better view. He saw a flash, heard the flurry of shots, and then a bullet smashed into his right knee. Ewell collapsed to the ground.[55]

As night fell, Ewell lay where he had dropped. He felt utterly alone, the combat having shifted to the west, far away from this part of the field, and he was suffering—the pain from his shattered, bleeding, throbbing knee was excruciating. Ewell's thoughts concentrated on one, irrational point. Amputation![56] Neither death nor being maimed were a concern. He looked only for relief, to end the agony by cutting off his aching limb.

The combat finally stopped. In the following quiet, an unearthly scream suddenly pierced the air.[57] A second, then a third cry replied. These howls must have brought Ewell to full consciousness because those were Union cheers! Had they won the battle? Awake and now concentrating on his surroundings, Ewell turned his head and spotted two wounded Rebel privates lying nearby. When he called out, identifying himself, they started to shout for help—not for themselves but for Ewell. Their yelps brought a team of litter bearers to the scene.

The rescuers answered anxious questions about the fight (the South had won, driving the Yankees from the field), then moved to carry the privates to a nearby hospital. The common soldiers refused attention, insisting that Ewell be attended to first. Ewell countered by ordering that the privates receive priority, explaining that his injury was so severe, his leg had to be amputated there in the field.[58] Both sides refused to yield, and as the argument continued, Campbell Brown, who had been searching for Ewell for several hours, arrived. He pleaded with Ewell to let the litter bearers carry him to the surgeons where they could better study the extent of his wound, but Ewell remained adamant. He demanded that Campbell go find a doctor and bring him back. Ewell then obstinately shut his eyes to take a nap while waiting his aide's return.

Given Ewell's unyielding insistence, the litter bearers moved off with the privates, and Campbell, too, left to find a surgeon. Ewell did fall asleep, but his uneasy slumber was soon interrupted by loud curses. Early had heard of Ewell's being wounded, and he had come to take charge of toting his superior to the rear. Ignoring Ewell's protests that his limb had to be amputated there and then, Early ordered the aides that he had brought with him to put the general onto their stretcher. When they approached Ewell, he began swearing, demanding that they leave him alone. They held back, causing Early to shout in thundering tones that they disregard Ewell and just do as he had told them. Faced with the choice of obeying a healthy Early or the enfeebled Ewell, the bearers recognized that it was better to side with Early, and they hoisted the infuriated Ewell onto their litter.[59]

The episode with Early exhausted Ewell. He fell asleep before those gently carrying him climbed up out of the ravine. A few minutes later, Campbell and a surgeon he had brought to the front met Ewell's party, and they accompanied the troupe to a field hospital. After a quick look at Ewell's leg, the doctor ordered him moved to more comfortable quarters, a tiny house across Bull Run near Sudley.[60]

The home was crammed with wounded men from the Groveton battle. Leaving these charges, three surgeons, Dr. McGuire, Dr. Laume, and Dr. Robertson, came to Ewell's side to look at his leg. Although Dr. Laume thought the limb might be saved, both Robertson and McGuire recommended amputation, and their conviction prevailed.[61] But the operation was delayed until morning to give Ewell time to gather strength for the ordeal.

Shortly after sunrise on August 29th, as the physicians prepared to start their grisly work, the roar of cannons rose outside the house. Drawn by Jackson's attack late yesterday, Pope had concentrated his army and come to open the Battle of Second Manassas. Fighting swirled around the makeshift hospital and bullets actually thudded against the house. Feeling it was too risky to operate under those conditions, the surgeons decided to move to safer quarters. They put Ewell on a litter and wound their way through the combat to the Buckner House, about four miles away.[62]

Finally, at 2:00 p.m., everything was ready. While one doctor pressed a cloth soaked with chloroform against Ewell's nose, Hunter McGuire wielded his scalpel. He cut through the flesh around the shattered knee—a deep, circular incision to the bone. After tying off the gushing arteries and bleeding veins, he picked up a saw.

Ewell was semi-conscious throughout the initial part of the operation, but showed no signs of pain, just muttering to himself, giving orders to his men, and remembering past movements. His words were spiced with the usual profanity. But when McGuire's blade started to rasp against the bone, Ewell cried out, throwing both arms to the sky.

"Oh my Lord!" he screamed.[63]

More chloroform was hurriedly splashed on the rag under his nose, strong hands pinned Ewell tightly to the table, and McGuire sawed determinedly away.

When the amputation was completed, Dr. Robertson opened the severed limb. "We found the knee cap split in half, the head of the tibia knocked into several pieces," Campbell remembered. "The ball had followed the marrow of the bone for six inches, breaking the bone itself into small splinters."[64] The operation had been unavoidable.

Robertson suggested that Campbell bury the leg, but the aide was too shaken to perform such an appalling assignment. John Frame, a litter bearer who had helped carry Ewell to the Buckner House, volunteered for the task. He gently wrapped the limb in an oil cloth, and placed it in a shallow grave in the garden behind the cottage.[65]

The fight to save Ewell's life had just begun. Fearful that the patient might die from exhaustion, Dr. McGuire prescribed a powerful stimulant—brandy. "I was to give [Ewell] a little mixed with water every fifteen minutes," Campbell recalled, "taking care to avoid nauseating him, and to wake him if asleep."[66] Hour after hour, Campbell and Dr. Morrison fed Ewell his dose of

liquor. Nothing happened. Ewell remained wan and scarcely
breathing. Finally, about midnight, he began to respond. Ewell's
pulse rate quickened. At 2:00 a.m., Campbell noticed an ominous
change in Ewell's condition. He thought the general was losing
ground, and called to Dr. Morrison to come look. The physician
rushed to Ewell's bedside, made a quick examination and
breathed a sigh of relief. The crisis was over.[67] Ewell, although in
a drunken stupor, was recovering. He would live.

* * * *

All through Ewell's operation and into the following day,
the Battle of Second Manassas was being fought. On August
29th, Pope assailed Jackson in his position along the railroad
cut. Despite an advantage in numbers plus a resolute effort by
his troops, the Yankee general could not dislodge Stonewall.
The next afternoon, Pope, unaware that Lee had reached the
front, renewed his attacks on Jackson. He charged repeatedly,
exposing his army to a devastating blow on the flank from
Longstreet late that day. Pope's men scattered, retiring in
desperation all the way to Washington, where they finally found
McClellan and his troops sitting idly outside the capital. The
joining of the Union armies had come too late. Lee's plan to
isolate Pope and attack him in detail had succeeded, resulting in
a great victory.

While Ewell did not participate in this final battle of the
campaign, his record prior to Second Manassas blazed with
glory. Stonewall, in a rare display of commendation, made a
number of favorable references to his subordinate's notable
performance. "Ewell . . . reached the northwest termination of
Slaughter Mountain," Jackson recorded in his official report of
that fray, "and upon an elevated spot . . . planted Latimer's guns,
which opened with marked effect upon the enemy's batteries."[68]
Northern newspapers (e.g., *The Baltimore American*) also admired Ewell's feat.[69] Writing about Bristoe Station, Stonewall
recalled Ewell's adroit retreat from Broad Creek. "A portion of
the troops were actively engaged and the enemy advancing,"
Jackson praised, "yet the withdrawal of the infantry and artillery

was conducted with perfect order."[70]

Ominous portents of Ewell's future also evolved during the campaign. His failure to fully reconnoiter his front at Slaughter's Mountain was a critical error, one that would be repeated at Gettysburg. Even more sinister, Early, by complaining that Jackson had not credited him for his performance during the battle, revealed his greed for high rank, actually for the position held by Ewell. While Early offered no evidence of "backbiting" or the urge to shove Ewell aside, that time would come, and the Southern Cause would suffer when loyalty lost to ambition. In addition, Ewell's health was now an issue, one that would rise again and again until the end of the War.

Ewell's wound also raised a most personal question. He had to wonder while suffering the pain and mental torment accompanying his amputation whether Lizinka would still want to marry a one-legged man.

Recuperation

Ewell spent a week in bed at the Buckner House after his operation, gathering strength for a move to more comfortable quarters for further recuperation. By September 5, 1862, he was strong enough for the trip, and he was placed on a litter and carried west toward the house of his cousin, Dr. Jesse Ewell. Campbell Brown, Dr. Morrison, and twelve scouts were included in the entourage who trudged for the home (called Dunblane) nestled at the base of the Bull Run Mountains.[1]

One wonders about Ewell's thoughts as he lay flat on his back, staring up at the blue sky in the first horror of awareness of his maiming. He no doubt was despondent thinking that he was no longer virile. Psychologists who deal with male amputees report that they often "view the amputation as castration,"[2] seeing the loss of a limb as being no different from losing their manhood, and this perception is almost unbearable in the first day after amputation.*

When Ewell finally reached his destination, the first to greet him was Dr. Jesse's youngest daughter. "I remember well the maimed figure on the litter, covered with a sheet, and the pale, haggard face upon the pillow," Alice Maude wrote. "The keen, blue eyes were, however, wide open. He spoke not a word, but one had the impression that nothing escaped him."[3]

---

*Edwin Jones, Head of the Department for Artificial Limbs for the Veterans Administration Hospital, Indianapolis, Indiana, says, "An amputee feels that it is the end of the world, that he cannot do anything as he did before. He feels that he is doomed to fail, that others, especially women, view him with disgust. In time this despair will turn into anger, and the amputee grows bitter, looking illogically to gain revenge against those he blames for his loss of limb."

"Grief, self-pity, and despair are almost inevitable [in an amputee]," agrees Dr. Lawrence W. Friedmann, professor for Rehabilitation Medicine, State University of New York, Stony Brook, New York. "Fear for the future and panic with compensatory rage and anger are frequent later."

While these feelings may soften over time, the amputee's psychological insecurity never goes away. "The feeling of loss is persistent," Friedmann says, "and remains throughout life." Future events would seem to show that Ewell was no exception to this amputation syndrome.

Jesse Ewell's family was ready for the arrival of their famous cousin. All the furniture in their parlor (located in the center of the home) had been removed to open the way for a four-poster bed that sat like a fat castle almost touching each of the four walls. But when the litter bearers tried to maneuver Ewell to his quarters, they found that the stretcher was too long for them to turn in the narrow hall leading into the parlor. Only a small bedroom at the rear of the house proved to be accessible. Leaving Ewell on his stretcher in the corridor, the bearers dismantled the large bed, then reassembled it in the chosen chamber. This effort also proved to be impractical as the fourposter was too tall. Ewell was finally placed on a simple army cot.[4]

Soon after Ewell's arrival at Dunblane, two of his brothers joined the entourage that had assembled at Dr. Jesse's estate. Colonel Benjamin Ewell (age 52) obtained a furlough from his post as Chief of Staff for General Joe Johnston (who was himself still recovering from wounds he had suffered during the Battle of Seven Pines), and "Parson" William Stoddert Ewell (age 38) took a sabbatical from the church where he was minister. In spite of their concern, they were no doubt amused by the way Ewell took charge of his own convalescence. His earlier, death-like taciturnity gave way to cranky officiousness, and Ewell now insisted on a diet of fruit and wine for himself. Grapes were picked from a nearby vineyard; the madeira came from Richmond. The wine had originally been stored in the cellar of Dr. Cunningham's mansion, where Ewell spent the winter of 1861/1862. After the Louisiana Tigers discovered the cache, they started to deplete the stock by "buying" bottles at one dollar apiece from the overseer. Ewell stepped in to rescue what remained, boxing and shipping the madeira to Dr. Hancock (a friend living in the Southern capital).[5] In the tradition of the Tigers, Ewell was now appropriating Dr. Cunningham's wine for himself. It was, at least, an indication that he was improving.

On the morning of September 17th, the muffled thunder of artillery rose to the north, and Ewell's depression returned. A battle had started, and as it continued on and on without a pause throughout that day, Ewell grew ever more despondent. He knew that Lee's army was engaged in a furious fight, and in an odd stroke of prescience, worried that Jackson would be killed. "If [Stonewall] falls," Ewell asserted, "the Confederacy might fall with him."[6]

Ewell had good reason to be concerned. After trouncing Pope at Second Manassas, Lee had marched his force into Maryland to carry the war to Northern soil and keep the Union out of Virginia during the harvest season. McClellan, once more in charge of the Army of the Potomac, followed Lee, and they met in battle at Sharpsburg, a small village located on Antietam Creek. Although outnumbered two to one, Lee managed a stalemate in the savage fray that resulted in combined casualties for North and South of over 25,000 in just one day of fighting. That night Lee learned that his ammunition was too low to continue the combat, and he abandoned the field to McClellan. He fell back across the Potomac River to Virginia the next day.

Stonewall survived the conflict, but news of his safety failed to restore Ewell's flagging spirits. Over three weeks had passed since his wounding, and he had yet to hear a word from Lizinka. If he followed the typical pattern, as an amputee he must have been tortured by fears that she would no longer consider marrying him. And then her letter arrived.

> *My Dear Richard, [I] . . . learned from a Tuscaloosa paper of the 10th . . . that General Ewell is getting well. You cannot realize my anxiety . . . . I do not know whether you wish for me [to come to you] or not, but I know your limb has been amputated . . . . Will [you] be able to travel in a railroad car . . . . If so, cannot you come to Nashville . . . and let me . . . nurse you there where I think you could have more comfort than elsewhere? If not, I will go to you as soon as I know you desire it.*
>
> *Dear Richard—while I sympathize with your terrible suffering and loss, it is only womanly to [note] that one of its consequences will be to oblige you to remain at home and make me more necessary to you, and another is that where I thought before you ought to marry and could well marry a younger woman—now I will suit you better than anyone else if only because I will love you better. The truth is I have grown old very rapidly*

*during the last six months—my eyesight is not good and
my hair is turning gray besides being thin and sallow, but
you will care more than less for me on that account when
anxiety had so much to do with it.*[7]

Lizinka was a very clever lady, raising Ewell's spirits in
two ways: expressing her love for him, and by disparaging
herself, making him feel less a cripple. His thoughts turned from
despair to the hopes for the future he had been dreaming of for
over twenty years. Ewell wrote asking her to come to his side at
once.

Lizinka left Alabama immediately to hurry to Ewell. As it
happened, she was not the only one seeking him. The enemy
had learned of Ewell's whereabouts and were coming to capture
the now famous Rebel officer. Those with Ewell heard of the
danger from a visiting neighbor, who reported Federal cavalry in
the area, asking about the general. Benjamin Ewell admonished
the general not to remain at Dunblane a minute longer, but he
refused to move until Lizinka arrived. The two argued long and
loud before Ben finally convinced Ewell that he had to go. About
October 1st, just before sunrise, sixteen men—Ewell, his twelve
scouts, Campbell, "Parson" Stoddert, and Dr. Morrison—started
toward a gap in the Bull Run Mountains.

"There was no time for final leave-takings," Alice Maude
Ewell remembered. "Only my mother followed the litter a few
steps from the door . . . ."[8]

Using a shaded, country lane, the contingent arrived at
the crest of the mountain about noon, stopping there to rest.
Ewell quickly noticed that his wine had been left behind, and
continuing to act with petulance, he insisted that one of the
scouts return to Dunblane to get the madeira. Private Fox volunteered to go. After waiting for several hours with no sign of Fox's
return, the party concluded that he had been captured by the
enemy, and that they had better move on. They started down
the slopes, arriving at Ned Turner's house (Kinlock) by sun-
down, where they spent an anxious night.[9]

They headed for Salem early the next morning. Turning
south at that village, they traveled without incident for the next
three days, reaching Culpeper, where Ewell was put aboard a

train for Charlottesville. He was now out of danger of capture by his pursuers, so Ewell halted there to wait for Lizinka's coming. He spent several days with Mrs. Thomas Farrish before settling at Millboro Springs, a large house owned by the Dickenson family. Lizinka soon arrived and took charge of his care.[10]

The flight from Dunblane exhausted Ewell, so much so he remained for four weeks in Charlottesville before he regained the strength to travel. On November 6, 1862, he and Lizinka started for Richmond. A raging blizzard greeted them as they approached the Confederate capital, but they made it through the snow to their borrowed residence at 306 East Main Street, the home of Dr. Hancock, the keeper of the wine.[11]

Campbell accompanied Ewell and his mother to Richmond, but he soon left for Nashville. Lizinka required "things"— horses, two carriages, and servants—to maintain a "genteel" household.

Shortly after Campbell departed, the Union Army of the Potomac, now led by Major General Ambrose Burnside, gathered north of Fredericksburg, across the stream from where Robert E. Lee had posted his forces. The Federals forced a passage over the Rappahannock on December 13th to engage the Rebels. Working their way through the town, they attacked Lee's men, entrenched on the hills above Fredericksburg. Six times the enemy massed and charged the impregnable heights. Six times Lee's troops repelled them. And although the Rebels suffered over 6,000 casualties in the fearsome battle, the North left 12,000 lying dead or wounded on the frozen slopes.

Ewell, of course, was intensely interested in the fray, and followed it closely, thanks to on-the-scene letters from Major General Lafayette McLaws to Ewell's niece, Lizzie. He was delighted by the Confederate success and looked ahead to discussing the battle with Campbell, expected to return from Nashville in time for Christmas. The holidays started gaily with the aide's arrival, but soon turned to disaster because Ewell, forgetting he had only one leg, tried to take a step. He toppled and landed on his stump, tearing open the sutures which began to hemorrhage.[12] Ewell went into shock. His recovery, thought to be almost complete, regressed to where it had begun in September.

Six weeks later, Ewell was still bedridden. If he sat up or

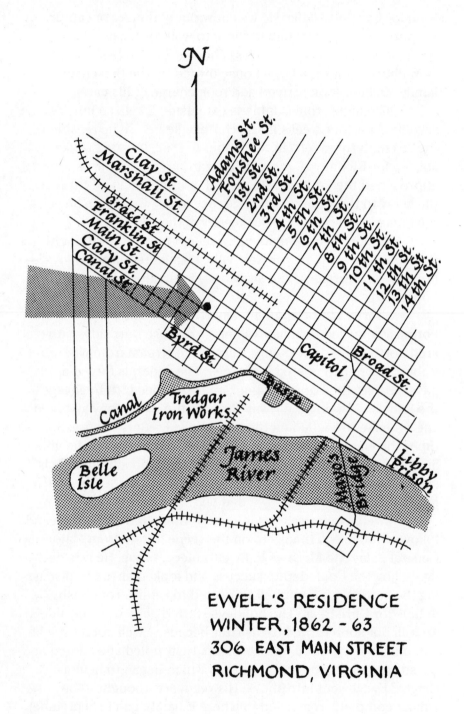

EWELL'S RESIDENCE
WINTER, 1862 - 63
306 EAST MAIN STREET
RICHMOND, VIRGINIA

let the stump hang vertically, he became dizzy and his missing foot felt "pinched . . . twisted, and cramped."[13]

Although physically disabled, Ewell had passed through the initial psychological shock from the amputation. His mental capacities had revived, and he displayed a keen awareness of current events in a letter to Jubal Early. Referring to the constant harping by Early on not being promoted, Ewell wrote that "I intend to go to work to have [your case] corrected."[14] Assuming Early would achieve division rank and expecting his own return to command, Ewell also showed his wry wit when he admonished his former subordinate not to improve his staff by stealing Ewell's people in exchange for "your bad bargains." And he showed an interest beyond the Virginia scene, writing "I am more anxious about Vicksburg . . . than any other [area]."

Through February and into March, Ewell saw little signs of improvement in his physical condition. His continued confinement became discouraging, and he showed this by lowering his sights on eventual assignment to active status. "I won't ask for any particular duty . . . ," he said in a letter to Early. "Let them do as they see proper for me."[15] As Ewell's mood soured, his obstinance grew. He refused treatment. Lizinka, becoming desperate, wrote to his brother Ben for advice. He offered a novel solution, that she ask her overseer in Spring Hill to send a black servant named Emmeline east to Richmond to manage Ewell's convalescence. "She is a good and respectable wet nurse," Ben observed, "who is in the habit of having her own way."[16] Lizinka did not have to resort to this step, as just the threat of Emmeline's presence was enough to bring Ewell back in line.

While Ewell was now taking his medicine, he still swore with regularity, a practice Lizinka was determined to break. She enlisted the aid of Reverend Moses Hogg, who spent hours with Ewell, chiding him for every oath.[17]

Ewell had other callers, too. Constance Cary, the pert lass who had made a sensational visit to his headquarters at Sangster's Crossroads in the fall of 1861, brought word from Union General William Hays, a West Point classmate of Ewell. "Give my best to good Old Dick," Hays had related, "and tell him I wish it [his amputation] had been his head!"[18] While Ewell enjoyed the quip and laughed heartily, Lizinka frowned with disapproval. Hays' banter did not bother her; she was jealous of Ewell's attentions to another lady (according to Connie, who saw Lizinka assuming the role of "guardian of his health and spirits").

Toward the end of March, Ewell finally started to make real progress in his recuperation. His early despondence over the shock of maiming had dissipated and his recovery was so rapid that he was able to use a wooden leg (a makeshift contraption that was unsightly but serviceable),[19] and start riding his horse again. By galloping recklessly through the fields outside of Richmond, he proved that he was still an exceptional cavalier, despite his missing limb. Ewell was about ready to return to duty.

The South was facing a determined Union army on every front and needed the exceptional talents of men such as Ewell. To the north, Major General Joseph Hooker, who had succeeded the inept Burnside, had assembled 135,000 men at Fredericksburg, across the Rappahannock from Robert E. Lee; Grant was doggedly stalking Lieutenant General John Pemberton, defending Vicksburg, the main Southern bastion on the Mississippi; and Major General William Rosecrans confronted the Rebels in Tennessee, led by Major General Braxton Bragg.

Problems brought on by the war were also faced at home, and Ewell could see them firsthand. Inflation had soared. Corn meal cost $17.00 per bushel, up from just $6.00 only a few weeks ago, and because their wages had not kept up with rising prices, many people in the Southern capital were actually starving. Frustrations exploded on April 2, 1863, when hundreds rioted, breaking into the stores at the intersection of Cary and Ninth Streets to loot for shoes, flour, rice, anything. Only the impassioned pleas of President Davis, standing atop a dray, stayed the mob.[20]

Ewell reacted to these pressures by mounting a campaign for an assignment, hounding the War Department daily, asking for "just a little division."[21] The young clerks ignored his appeals and his opinions on the war, causing him to complain, "There are enough [administrators] and their clerks here to form a regiment, and it would puzzle a wiser man than myself to say what a good one-half of them do."[22]

On April 29th Hooker attacked Lee. Dividing his army, he left 60,000 men at Fredericksburg to confront the Confederates across the river while marching 75,000 troops to the right to flank the Rebel position. Lee countered, splitting his smaller force. Early guarded the front; Jackson hurried west to meet the Federal threat there. The two foes clashed in the tangled forest surrounding Chancellorsville. Lee was the aggressor. Having already divided his army once, he did it again, sending Stonewall around Hooker to assault the enemy rear. The early evening attack resulted in a rout of the Yankees, but as they fell backward, clawing their way through the thick brush, one salvo of Rebel muskets spelled disaster for the South. Jackson, reconnoitering the shifting front in the dark of night, was shot, his left arm smashed by bullets fired by his own troops. His wounds were critical, requiring amputation. The grim news was tempered by reports that Jackson would recover, but several days later, word came to Richmond that Stonewall had contracted pneumonia.

Visiting the War Department for information about Jackson's condition, Ewell found himself the center of attention. Gossips reported that Stonewall was not expected to recover, and that Ewell would be named to replace the departed idol.[23] While Ewell despaired for his former superior's life, he probably worried more about taking Jackson's place. He had never sought advancement beyond brigadier general, which was enough to win Lizinka's betrothal, so Ewell wanted no more rank. And self-doubt, the psychological insecurity induced by his amputation, certainly contributed to his stated belief that he was incapable of the lofty position. He described promotion as "painful" because of the added responsibility.

Acting in desperation, Ewell apparently attempted to bargain with God. In exchange for Jackson's recovery, he forsook atheism by taking the vow of the Episcopalian faith (administered by Bishop Johns) on May 8th, 1863.[24] And just in case Providence did not accept this sacrifice, Ewell looked for another candidate to dispute his claim to Jackson's position. He chose P.G.T. Beauregard, stationed in Charleston, South Carolina, writing him a letter the same day Ewell joined the church.

"I have heard from everyone such strong expressions of feelings in regard to yourself," Ewell opened (knowing that flattery would attract the vain Creole), "and hope that something may be done to bring you to this scene of operations.   .. .. After the glorious results of Charleston, hardly less important than Fredericksburg, it . . . [is] to be hoped that you will again be in the field . . . . Troops are going on to General Lee, and some speak of a forward movement. Your name with the army [of Northern Virginia] would be a tower of strength . . . . "[25]. Ewell further revealed that "Jackson's life is despaired," and he disqualified himself as a possible successor to Stonewall through a droll reference to his "shortcomings in the way of legs."

Two days later, on May 10th, 1863, Stonewall died. Ewell took part in the funeral proceedings, hobbling on his wooden leg behind the horse-drawn hearse as it moved slowly through downtown Richmond on its way to the Capitol for the public viewing. He accompanied the immortal Jackson's body to Lexington, Virginia, for the final services and burial, then returned to Richmond on May 17th to await his fate. He stayed out of sight in the quiet of his home, hoping for a reply to his letter to Beauregard. Ewell's lonely vigil ended on May 23rd when he received word that he had been promoted to lieutenant general, in command of Jackson's former corps.[26]

Given Ewell's abhorrence for assuming Jackson's prestigious berth, one has to wonder why he accepted it. Duty was a significant factor, but subsequent events suggest that Lizinka was the driving force. Her fierce support and defense of Ewell throughout his time in corps command showed how impressed she was with his high rank, and she no doubt pressed Ewell to accept the promotion. Her feelings were so strong, Lizinka may have even suggested an immediate marriage to induce Ewell to undertake Jackson's command. While there is no record to substantiate this conjecture, the sequence of events intriguingly suggests it.

Richard Ewell and Lizinka Brown were united in marriage on Sunday, May 24th, 1863, by Reverend Charles Minnegerode, Rector of St. Paul's Church. Because the vows took place on the spur of the moment, few of the friends and relatives who would have wanted to attend were asked. President Davis was there. Colonel Ben Ewell, by chance on leave from his staff position with Joe Johnston, was best man; Lizzie Ewell, the groom's niece, was Lizinka's only attendant.[27]

On Monday Ewell received his orders to prepare to come north and assume command. He and Lizinka boarded a train for Fredericksburg on Friday, May 29th. As they approached Hamilton's Crossing, the last stop on the line, the engine began to slow. Ewell, glancing out the window of his car, was both surprised and gratified to see row after row of Confederate soldiers at attention along the tracks. He recognized some of the figures, the most prominent being a stooped, bedraggled officer who was scowling from the station platform. Jubal Early had assembled Ewell's old division to hail their newly-appointed corps chief.[28] This kindly tribute was only the first in a series of festivities sponsored for Ewell and his bride. But the gaiety, a bit forced due to both the impoverished local economy and the surrounding war, soon ended. Six days after arriving in Fredericksburg, Lizinka was seated on a train headed back to Richmond, and Ewell was leading his corps north toward Pennsylvania.

* * * *

When Ewell was wounded, the question a rose as to whether Lizinka could love a one-legged man. Her response was positive, viewing Ewell not as a cripple but as a gallant hero, worthy of her full devotion. Status was inextricably interwoven into their romance and marriage; Lizinka loved Ewell not only as a man but also as a lieutenant general, and she would fight to keep her husband in his position of power.

While Lizinka's attitude toward Ewell's rank was worrisome, his view was even more disturbing. In spite of having accepted the position, he obviously did not relish leading a corps. If modesty was the real reason behind Ewell's reluctance, there was no problem. He had resisted being promoted to division command, yet had performed remarkably well under

fire. But if deep down he was afraid of the responsibility, thinking that a one-legged man was doomed to fail, then promoting
Ewell was a mistake. The South needed another "Jackson" in the
field in 1863, a leader who was audacious, quick and confident
with his decisions.

Even if Ewell's resolve was all that it should be, this
meant nothing in the heat of battle where both the emotional
and physical energy to act was everything. Had he recovered
sufficiently to endure an arduous campaign?

Robert E. Lee asked himself these same questions,
which, of course, are still debated today. Lee, however, considered not only the facts he knew but also other intangibles, about
which we can only guess. And Lee certainly knew better than
anyone—then or now—who should lead the Second Corps.
There were good men he no doubt considered, but Lee selected
Ewell, a significant decision. That choice serves as the prelude
to the rest of this narrative.

Pennsylvania

Robert E. Lee called his top three generals to a briefing on June 2, 1863. Ewell and Longstreet both attended the session, but A.P. Hill, also just promoted to corps command, missed the parley (the first of many occasions when illness would keep him from duty). Lee's reason for bringing his leaders together was to reveal his plans for invading the North. He had a number of objectives in mind for the coming campaign. First, he needed provisions. Two years of Yankee and Confederate forces' foraging the countryside for supplies had exhausted Virginia's larder. If Lee was to feed his hungry troops, he had to move his army to more plentiful ground, and the lush farms of Pennsylvania were like a beacon calling him north.

A second reason for crossing into Federal territory was the strategic advantage to be gained from invasion. Lee knew that Jackson's Valley Campaign in 1862 had posed a threat to Washington, causing Lincoln to hold troops close to the Union capital, denying their use to McClellan. He hoped a similar move now would force the Northern President to recall some of Grant's men who were besieging Vicksburg, the main Rebel bastion on the Mississippi River.

Lee also reasoned that the frightening sight of Confederate troops amassed in their midst would bring the realities of war to the Union people, that a taste of Virginia's sorry experience might bring them to demand a peace initiative from their politicians.

Most of all, Lee was looking to whip the Federal Army of the Potomac. He envisioned slipping past Hooker, forcing the bluecoats to follow him as he hurried north. After entering Pennsylvania, Lee would suddenly concentrate his army, turning and pouncing on the trailing enemy while they were still marching in column. Wave after wave of Rebel soldiers would smash into the melee, driving one Union corps back on the other until the Northern army was annihilated.

Robert E. Lee

Photograph from the Library of Congress Collection

Jubal Early

John B. Gordon

Robert Rodes

Edward Johnson

Photograph from the Library of Congress Collection

Ewell's role was to lead the advance, crossing the Blue Ridge into the Shenandoah Valley, then marching north to ford the Potomac River into Maryland. He would hurry through the former slave state and on into the Cumberland Valley of Pennsylvania. Along the way, his men would forage, sending food back to the corps of Longstreet and Hill trailing behind him. The campaign was scheduled to begin in two days, June 4th. Shortly after receiving his orders, Ewell drove Lizinka to the railroad station to catch a train for Charlottesville. She would stay there with relatives while he fought the war. "[I've] served as long as Jacob for a wife,"[1] he noted sadly, feeling entitled to have more time with his bride. But after less than two weeks of married bliss, Ewell had to resume the lonely life of a bachelor.

Ewell sought solace in his work, preparing for the campaign, calling his three division leaders to a meeting at his headquarters, a tent pitched on a high hill overlooking John Yerby's farm. Jubal Early, Edward Johnson, and Robert Rodes attended the session. As the three generals, each acquainted with Jackson's secretive ways, listened to Ewell's presentation, they quickly saw that their new superior was emulating Stonewall, revealing only the barest details of his strategy. Ewell described only the opening leg of the impending march, a trek to Culpeper.

At dawn on June 4th, Rodes, the young officer who led a regiment under Ewell at First Manassas, took his division out of its encampment close by Fredericksburg and marched southwest toward Spotsylvania. The roundabout path was chosen to mask his real destination, Culpeper, from the Yankees. Rodes was responsible for five brigades: three from North Carolina and one each from Georgia and Alabama, led by Junius Daniel, Stephen D. Ramseur, Alfred Iverson, George Doles, and Edward O'Neal.[2]

Early followed Rodes later in the day, using a parallel trail to avoid congestion. His four brigades, from Virginia, North Carolina, Louisiana, and Georgia, were headed by "Extra Billy" Smith, Isaac Avery, Harry Hayes, and John B. Gordon.[3]

Edward Johnson waited until the following morning, June 5th, before leaving the Fredericksburg area. He followed the same road as Early. His division, two Virginia brigades plus one

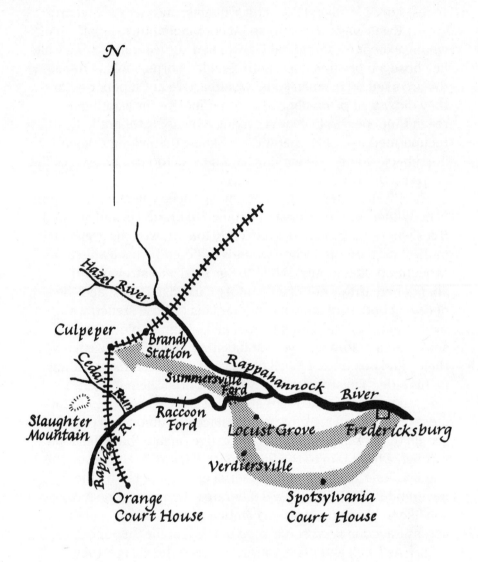

EWELL'S ROUTE
TO CULPEPER

June 4-7, 1863

each from Maryland and Louisiana, were commanded by John Jones, James Walker, Colonel J. Williams, and George Steuart.[4]

Ewell was the last to go. Accompanied by his staff, all of whom, except for Campbell Brown, had served under Stonewall, he chose a more northerly path than his corps, looking to cut the arc used by his men so he would arrive at Culpeper before they did. Ewell probably had another motive for wanting to reach Culpeper first. He was driving a buggy.[5] Still not fully recuperated from his operation, he knew that a long ride on horseback would be wearying, and he was too proud to have the corps see him appearing enfeebled.

Ewell soon forgot about appearances when he drove into "The Wilderness," the area of entangling brambles and stunted trees where Jackson had so recently fought, won his greatest battle, and then died when wounds inflicted by his own troops brought on pneumonia. While the ground was strewn with abandoned army equipment, empty cartridge boxes, and the decaying bodies of animals and humans (whose stench was overwhelming), the Union lines that Jackson's soldiers had shattered a month ago were still distinguishable. "The enemy [held] fine positions," Ewell observed to Jed Hotchkiss, riding by his side. "I'm surprised they did not hold them longer."[6]

Ewell spent the night at Locust Grove, stayed there for most of the following day, held in place by rumors of Federal scouts threatening his flank, then drove on late that afternoon through a hard rain to the banks of the Rapidan. He began Sunday, June 7th, with sunrise services, conducted by the Reverend Lacy (probably a deliberate attempt to appear Jackson-like to his staff). He then climbed into his buggy and drove across Raccoon Ford and turned northwest for Culpeper.

As Ewell and his entourage neared the village, they encountered Rodes' Division, plodding in column to their right. The men recognized Ewell and started to cheer, giving him an accolade they usually reserved only for Stonewall. Ewell was trapped, exposed as impotent in his buggy when he would have rather been astride his mount. He reacted instinctively, snapping the reins to cause his horse to gallop. As he sped alongside the columns, Ewell doffed his hat, showing his bald pate.[7] The soldiers, not expecting this display of virile bravado, responded with delight, shouting all the louder. Ewell, still waving his cap, raced past Rodes' van and on into Culpeper.

The next morning, as Ewell waited in place, Lee arrived in town, and Jeb Stuart, whose cavalry had ridden as a shield between Ewell and the enemy, greeted his coming by holding a grand review of his troops. Ewell declined an invitation to attend the festivities, electing instead to get his men ready to cross the Blue Ridge into the Shenandoah Valley. Knowing that he had to appear stalwart, he was determined to ditch his buggy and spend the entire day on horseback as he personally visited every unit in his command. His strenuous effort produced the desired impact. "The more I see of General Ewell, the more I am pleased with him," Sandie Pendleton, the corps' chief of staff, wrote. "Yesterday he rode 20 miles on horseback, often at full speed, and exhibited no sign of fatigue."[8]

The morning of June 9th, sounds of musketry rose to the northeast. The Yankee cavalry which had followed Stuart out of Fredericksburg had decided to attack. As Ewell listened anxiously to the battle exploding around Brandy Station, orders arrived from Lee, asking Ewell to rush some infantry forward. Rodes was camped closest to the conflict; his division drew the assignment. Ewell accompanied the troops, following the Orange and Alexandria Railroad tracks toward the fight. Two miles below Brandy Station, he halted the columns. He wanted to confer with Lee before committing his men. Looking for an expedient place to bivouac, Ewell spotted a good location, a house with a spacious front yard, perched high on a hill that overlooked the area. He ordered Rodes to take his troops up the slope. As they neared the mansion, the angry owner burst out the front door and began shouting.

"[I'm] a neutral," John Minor Botts howled, "and I'll have no fighting around my house."[9]

Ewell had no use for neutrals, particularly those from the South. But before he could tend to Mr. Botts, Rodes had already done so. "Make that damned fool go back," the young general called to an aide, "and [make him] behave himself."

Botts quickly disappeared; Ewell and Rodes rode ahead to look for Lee. They found him on the porch of the Barbour House, an elegant mansion located on the top of a low ridge. The site was very familiar to Ewell, as he had headquartered there during the winter of 1862, prior to joining Jackson in the Valley.

After dismounting in the yard, Ewell and Rodes climbed the steps to the veranda only to see a line of Union cavalry riding hard, headed straight for the house. Lee and his aides were glued in their tracks to the porch, watching the oncoming horsemen.

"Gather in the house," Ewell cried. "[We'll] defend it to the last!"[10]

Ewell's proposition was highly implausible, but fortunately for the Confederate commanders, that dire stand proved unnecessary when a group of Southern riders swooped down from the north and drove into the enemy flank. The Federals, almost on top of the Barbour House, were forced to veer away from their target.

That charge was the last of the battle, a close victory but an embarrassment for Stuart. The Yankee cavalry had surprised his men, posted along the Rappahannock, by assaulting from two directions. The Rebels had to draw back from along the stream, and only the alert firing by a battery, which unlimbered one cannon atop Fleetwood Hill, prevented the Union from winning the fray. Both sides charged each other for hours. Neither gave ground in the hand-to-hand fighting. The South's superior numbers proved decisive, but even then, the enemy's retreat had been deliberate and disdainful. The Confederate cavalry, so pretentious in their review yesterday, was proven no longer invincible.

Ewell met with his division commanders the next morning to lay out their path to the Valley. Rodes would lead, using the Old Richmond Road to head north through Gourd Vine Church to Newby's. He would turn left at that point, and go to Washington where he would hold while Early and Johnson, coming up the turnpike through Sperryville, marched past on their way to Flint Hill, Chester Gap, and Front Royal. He would then fall in at the tail of the column. The men were ready to move out at once, but Lee held them in place to see if Hooker would renew his cavalry attacks of yesterday. Throughout the hot and sunny day, however, the front remained quiet. Lee finally released Ewell's advance late that afternoon.

Ewell stayed behind to review with Lee a plan he was especially eager to implement. The Federals under Major General Robert Milroy had been most obnoxious to the loyal citizens of Winchester, and Ewell wanted to free them from this Yankee despot. Lee refused the plea. While he, too, felt that Milroy deserved a good thrashing, Lee noted that his troops were desperate for food, and that Ewell's higher priority was to reach the Potomac, go into Maryland, and start sending provisions to the rear. When Ewell slyly suggested that Milroy might attack his rear, giving him an excuse to offer battle, Lee insisted that he only "leave a division [behind] . . . then advance to the Potomac."[11]

Ewell still would not give up his plan, and he continued to argue until Lee finally conceded that if Ewell could drive Milroy from Winchester without slowing his northward progress, he could make the attack. Ewell silently accepted this option as his only course, and as soon as he left Lee, Ewell started to execute a plan. He secretly ordered that pontoons for crossing the Shenandoah River at Front Royal be sent ahead.

Ewell left Culpeper the next morning, following Early's route toward Sperryville. He caught up with Jubal about noon, finding his columns bogged down in mud and far short of their objective of meeting Rodes at Washington. Early asked that he be allowed to take an alternative, better road to the village. After approving Jubal's request, Ewell drove his buggy ahead to tell Rodes about the change. He found him north of Newby, also following a different path than planned. "[The] road [to Washington]," Rodes reported, "was the worst I have ever seen."[12] While he was with Rodes, Ewell learned that Johnson, too, had switched roads to avoid the mire, passing Early in the process. To restore some semblance of order, Ewell sent Rodes to Flint Hill, had Johnson fall in behind Rodes, and informed Early that he was now bringing up the rear. That night, Ewell would meet with the division leaders at Early's encampment to give them their instructions for the morrow.

At his briefing that evening, Ewell revealed his intention to attack Milroy at Winchester. Surprise was essential. He would tolerate no more delays. The men had to be up and on the road before daybreak.

181

Rising at 2:00 a.m. on June 12th, Ewell began the march with Johnson, but the slow pace of the trudging troops soon exhausted Ewell's limited patience. He galloped ahead to the van of Rodes' column, where he invited the Virginian to join him in his buggy. As they drove up Chester Gap, the sun rose behind them to shine down on a spectacular countryside. The green grass was lush and sparkling with morning dew. Soaring mountains crowded both sides of the narrow way, their rocky, gray slopes like two arms of a "V" with Ewell's tiny rig at its apex. The view was a high contrast to the flat, brown ground around Fredericksburg. Even the air was better, cool and invigorating. Ewell must have felt a rush of exuberance as he drove over the summit and began to wind down the undulating path into the Valley.

The tiny village of Front Royal soon came in view. Its few streets were jammed with people, watching (it turned out) for Ewell. When they saw his buggy leading columns of gray-clad troops out of Chester Gap, they started to cheer. Ewell was aghast. Obviously, the townsfolk anticipated him, and if they expected his coming, then Milroy, too, was aware of the Rebels' imminent arrival and knew that he was in peril. The Union commander was probably preparing his defenses, and even one day's resistance would save him. Ewell could not wait to lay siege. His dream of freeing Winchester seemed lost.

Scowling as he drove through Front Royal, never pausing to acknowledge the frenzied, vocal crowd, Ewell soon knew why his appearance was expected. West of the town, on the shore of the Shenandoah River, he saw the pontoons that he had sent ahead when back in Culpeper "conspicuously . . . displayed along the bank as if . . . [we] were not outside our lines."[13] Lieutenant Douglas, their arrayer, proudly reported, saying that he was ready to deploy.

Infuriated by the breach of security, Ewell launched an awesome stream of insults at the startled and no longer smug officer. Ewell then turned to Rodes. There was no time to build the pontoon bridge; when his men arrived, they had to ford the river. Rodes' troops soon came up and started to file into the knee-deep, fast-running stream. As they waded through the flowing waters, Ewell, thinking furiously all the while, devised a

new plan. Rodes would march his division to Cedarville; Johnson would trail Rodes; Early would halt at Front Royal. They
would all get together that evening to develop a strategy for
routing Milroy the next day.

Ewell waited at the river until Johnson's men began the
crossing, then drove on to Cedarville where he met with Rodes
and Brigadier General Albert Jenkins, chief of a cavalry command just assigned to the Valley (and Ewell) by Lee. Ewell's first
glance at Jenkins must have caused him surprise. The man's
dour expression and thinning hair were not unusual for one
thirty-three years old, but his beard was extraordinary, so long
that Jenkins had it tucked under his belt.[14] Evidently being well-
groomed was not a requirement for Confederate officers these
days. Ewell himself had proven that.

Jenkins had wonderful news. No Union soldiers had been
in this immediate area for days, and he was certain that Milroy
had no idea that over 20,000 Rebels were nearby, about to
pounce on him.

Based on Jenkins' report, Ewell called his division commanders to an immediate meeting to lay out plans for capturing
Winchester. They decided that Johnson would open their attack
by charging up the Front Royal Road to intimidate Milroy from
the south and east. He would make contact with the bluecoats,
shove them back into the town, then stop as if stymied by the
enemy's defense. While Milroy was absorbed with keeping
Johnson at bay, Early would advance on Winchester along the
Valley Pike, shift left just below the village, and then attack from
the west. Two formidable entrenchments guarded this way into
Winchester, but Ewell assumed that if Johnson provided enough
entertainment for the bluecoats, Milroy would deploy most of
his troops to the east, leaving the western forts undermanned
and vulnerable to a surprise from Early.

Ewell recognized that by attacking Winchester, he risked
being charged with disobedience of orders. Lee had explicitly
said not to tarry there. A quick, one-day victory would keep
Ewell out of trouble, but if Milroy held him off, delaying his
advance into Pennsylvania, Ewell would certainly face a court
martial. To protect against that event, Ewell kept Rodes from the
battle, sending his division and Jenkins' cavalry forward toward

the Potomac. He was "halfway" following instructions. After clearing Berryville and Martinsburg of Federals, the two would cross the river into Maryland. Jenkins and his troopers would ride on into Pennsylvania to start foraging; Rodes and his infantry would lay low in Maryland to await the arrival of Ewell with the other divisions after their conquest of Milroy.

Riding as usual in his rig, Ewell accompanied Johnson as he moved ahead early the following morning, June 13th. He remained with the van until they encountered Union pickets five miles outside of Winchester. Guiding his buggy off the road, Ewell watched as the men, their eyes aglow with determination, pressed onward to meet the enemy. As the columns hurried past Ewell, an officer on horseback rode up and asked for any last minute instructions.

"You're the operator now," Ewell replied to Johnson. "I am only a looker on."[15]

Johnson rode ahead, but Ewell changed his mind. Instead of "looking on," he decided to join the advance. He called for his horse; he would not ride into battle in a buggy. Rifle, his favorite mount, was brought forward, and Ewell was helped into the saddle. Taking a practice trot, he guided the gray into a nearby meadow, pranced to and fro, then galloped back for the road. A fence, bordering the path, stood in the way. Without thinking, forgetting that he was disabled, Ewell tried to jump the barricade. The feat proved impossible for the one-legged Ewell. Rifle leaped over the fence, but Ewell left his mount, crashing with a sickening thud to the hard ground. Aides ran to Ewell, who lay stunned, gasping for breath. Despite feeble protests by Ewell, they lifted him up and helped him into his buggy where he rested a few minutes, then drove on toward Winchester.[16]

He seemed weak and uncertain throughout the rest of the march. Most thought that he hurt himself in the fall, but those more observant knew that Ewell's health had already started to deteriorate before his attempt to jump the fence. Just a few days ago, Sandie Pendleton had reported that "Ewell walks with only a stick, and mounts his horse easily . . . ."[17] Now he used crutches to get about because his stump had been rubbed raw by his makeshift leg. Ewell had punished himself mercilessly to fulfill the image of the strong officer and worries about whether he could meet the demands of a strenuous campaign were being answered early and ominously.*

As Ewell approached the outskirts of Winchester, he saw that Johnson had deployed exactly as planned. Both Stewart's and Walkers' troops were posted in a ravine east of the village; Nichols' and Jones' men were stationed in the woods to the south. The Rebels were exchanging languid shots with the enemy. There was no sign of Early.

Scanning the area, looking for a site for a field headquarters, Ewell spotted a low hill just short of the Millroad Road. He climbed out of his buggy, and with the help of his aides, headed toward the top. Just as he reached the peak, a chatter of muskets exploded to the southwest, along the pike by Kernstown. Early had been discovered by the Federals, who were disputing his path to Winchester. The skirmishing continued in place until 4:00 p.m., when the noisy exchange grew louder, indicating that the Rebels were finally driving their adversary. The bluecoats, withdrawing up the road, were the first to come into view. The retreat was deliberate, but when Johnson entered the fray, firing his cannons with devastating accuracy into the midst of the slow-moving Union troops, the enemy soldiers scattered, every man for himself, in a desperate race for the safe environs of Winchester.

When Early came in sight, he moved off the trail to the left, where he brought his division to a halt. The stage for the assault Ewell had planned was set, but the sun was going down. It was too late to attack that day. And surprise, the element Ewell had counted on to speed his routing of Milroy, was unfortunately lost.

At that point, Ewell should have given up his plans for taking Winchester and moved on toward Pennsylvania. But when a lone horseman waving a white flag of truce rode out of Winchester toward Ewell and his entourage on the hill, he

---

*In his study of amputees, Dr. Lawrence W. Friedmann saw three general attitudes toward recovery. "The more intelligent amputee realizes that while his goals . . . remain the same, he must take different means to achieve (them)." Those less well-adjusted will "withdraw . . . almost to the point of becoming hermits," or overcompensate as if "to deny that any disability exists." Clearly Ewell belonged to the latter body, and his trying to do too much would harm the Rebel cause.

waited to see if Milroy was surrendering. The Federal officer came up the slope, stopped in front of Ewell, and delivered an ultimatum. If the Rebels attacked the town, Milroy would burn every home in Winchester.

"If [you do]," Ewell replied angrily, "I will raise the black flag, and put the [Northern] garrison to sword without mercy."[18] He had committed to routing Milroy.

The Federal envoy nodded, wheeled, and rode back toward the town. As he disappeared into the distance, the sky above grew dark with black clouds, rolling from the west, rumbling with thunder. It was 6:00 p.m. Looking to confer with Early before the rain came, Ewell called for his buggy and started down the hill to Jubal's encampment.

When Ewell reached Early's camp, he found his subordinate boiling with frustration, not only because his attack had been put off by the enemy's unexpected defense along the pike, but also because he was not sure if he could charge tomorrow. Bowers' Hill, an eminence below Winchester held by the Union, blocked his view of the forts west of the village. With the bastions hidden from sight, Early could neither determine their strength nor offer a strategy for taking them.

Ewell ruefully revealed that Bowers' Hill lay between his headquarters knoll and the forts, too. Early would have to capture the obstruction at first light, then decide on tactics to rout the enemy out of their forts.

Their brief conference was ended by a sudden splatter of raindrops in advance of the coming storm. Ewell gambled on getting back to his headquarters before the heavens opened, but only halfway there, the rain fell in sheets, and he was drenched. When he arrived at camp, Ewell did not bother his aides with raising his tent. He spun out of the buggy, crawled beneath, and spent a cold, wet, sleepless night on the ground.[19]

Toward the morning of June 14th, the storm blew by, and as the stars began to glow, Milroy suddenly opened the battle by unleashing his artillery against Ewell's line. The noisy shelling proved more irritating than damaging, but it did delay Early's preparations to attack Bowers' Hill. His charge, with two regiments, one from each of Hays' and Gordon's brigades, did not start until 7:30 a.m. An hour and a half later, the Rebels occupied the summit, and Ewell rushed there to consult with Early.

The two generals peered through their binoculars toward the northwest. They saw with dismay that the two forts they had to capture in order to drive Milroy from Winchester were protected by a third citadel, located on a higher ridge, left of their objective. While a flanking movement was still likely to succeed in overwhelming the bluecoat bulwarks, Early would have to form his troops further west than they had originally planned. And to reach this position would take hours; Early would not be ready to charge until almost sunset. Ewell had no choice. He had gone too far now to call off his assault, so he ordered the turning maneuver. Johnson was told to occupy Milroy with feints to keep him from seeing Early's force gathering to the west and reinforcing his forts against this threat.

Johnson's men crept forward at 11:00 a.m. Although the assault was not designed to enter Winchester, the Rebels were so pugnacious that they roused a vigorous defense from their adversary. Hand-to-hand fighting raged throughout the sultry afternoon. About 4:00 p.m., noting the failure of the Rebels to break his line, Milroy concluded that he was about to win the affair, and he decided to counterattack, reinforcing his ranks with men drawn from the forts. At first, Ewell was delighted by Milroy's error of weakening the point where Early was about to attack, but when the Confederate ranks began to bend under the Federals' charge, he became worried. His concern soon ended, as Johnson regained control of the front.

Early made his move at 5:00 p.m. Opening with a twenty cannon barrage on the westernmost fort, he blistered the Federal entrenchment for an hour before committing Hays and his gritty Louisianians to the attack. They charged down into a gully, up the slope toward the Union breastwork, and over the top into the bastion.

Ewell, surrounded by aides sharing his hill, watched the battle through his field glasses. As he hopped to and fro on his crutches to get a better view, he gave a running commentary of the fighting. "Hurrah for the Louisiana boys," Ewell cried as they drove into the Federal fort. "There's Early!" he shouted as a hunched figure on horseback galloped into the fray. "I hope the

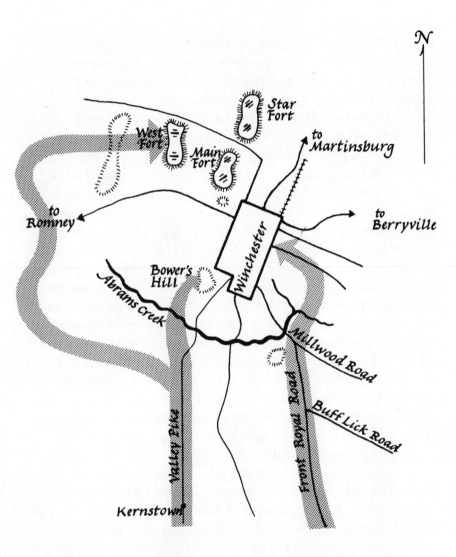

BATTLE OF WINCHESTER — JUNE 14, 1863

old fellow won't be hurt."[20]

The words were barely out of Ewell's mouth when a spent ball, whizzing through the air, bounced with a "thud" off his chest. Staggered by the blow, Ewell said that he was not injured, but Dr. Hunter McGuire insisted on an examination. He unbuttoned Ewell's shirt to find a huge welt already turning black and blue. Deciding that his patient should rest a bit, the doctor confiscated Ewell's crutches, saying, "Let those sticks alone for the present."[21] Ewell meekly sat down, but as soon as McGuire's head was turned, he got up to resume his view of the battle.

Hays' Louisianians drove the Union from the outer fort, a feat which sealed Milroy's fate. His other two breastworks stood lower than the one just lost, rendering them untenable. Recognizing they were doomed, the enemy troops abandoned the bastions and ran for Winchester, leaving the town defenseless against an attack from the west. Early wanted to follow, but by now the sun had set, and again, maddeningly, the town was wrapped in darkness. He could not risk a blind assault; he would have to wait until morning before resuming his offense. Watching from atop his knoll, Ewell thought that Milroy would not dare a fight to the finish, and would flee in the night. To prevent the enemy from escaping, he had Johnson rush north to block the road out of Winchester to Martinsburg. If Milroy decided to hold and make a stand, Johnson could come from above the town to join Early's sunrise attack.

Before dawn on June 15th, Ewell knew that his guess had been correct. Musketry and cannon fire exploded north of the town, announcing that Johnson had intercepted the Federal retreat. The bluecoats, rocked by the unexpected Rebel ambush, surrendered over 4,000 prisoners, 300 drays loaded with much needed supplies, 23 artillery weapons, and 300 horses.[22] The casualty cost for the South was only 47 killed, 219 wounded, and three missing during the two day fight. The only flaw in Ewell's success was that during the night, Milroy, along with a few of his aides, had slipped through Johnson's snare.

While the victory was impressive (the newspapers called Ewell "The New Jackson"), its effect went far beyond the capture of men and materials. Ewell was personally transformed by the conflict. Recently lacking in confidence due to the loss of his limb, which had caused him to fear promotion, he now seemed personally reinforced, and eagerly looking forward to even greater conquests ahead. All at once, rank and position, as future events would reveal, took on new importance for Ewell, especially since they would bring approbation from his prestige-minded wife.

The next day, the people of Winchester celebrated their release from Federal rule by raising the Rebel flag atop Fort Jackson—the name chosen by the Confederates for the largest of the three breastworks last occupied by Milroy and his men. Ewell and Early came to watch the joyful rites. Thinking he would only be a spectator, Ewell was shocked when a group of tittering females swarmed him, begging him to make a speech.

"I can't make a speech to ladies," he sputtered. "I've made a speech to but one lady in my life."[23]

Early smiled broadly at Ewell's dilemma. His wide grin caught Ewell's eye, presenting a solution to the awkward situation. Ewell pointed to Early and said, "My friend . . . will address you ladies."

It was Jubal's turn to squirm. "I could never find the courage to address [even] one of you," the confirmed bachelor protested. "Of course, I can't speak to a hundred."

Cries of "Please" rose, but Early would not bend to the demands. He sat on his horse, his lips pursed tight with irritation at Ewell's cunning trick. Fortunately, a cannonade (part of the ceremonies) suddenly roared, drawing the women's attention away from the generals, allowing Ewell and Early to ride away hurriedly from their admirers.

With his corps scattered, Jenkins's cavalry in Pennsylvania, Rodes' Division at Martinsburg, and both Johnson's and Early's troops in Winchester, Ewell was eager to consolidate across the Potomac. Lee, however, restrained him with orders to hold in place until Longstreet and Hill caught up from below. Before Lee had wanted Ewell to hurry northward; now he thought that if Ewell advanced above the Potomac without support nearby, he risked being isolated, attacked, and defeated by the enemy's superior numbers. Lee also sent his congratulations for the capture of Winchester, making no mention of the fact that Ewell's losing two days out of a strict schedule to do so had been a blatant disobedience of his orders. Lee would not reprimand a winner.

Ewell did not wait in Winchester. To position his corps for the coming advance, he sent Johnson ahead to the Potomac. Early moved his men north to Bunker Hill, and Ewell rode with him. After establishing his headquarters in the Boyd House, Ewell issued a Stonewall-like statement that complimented the troops for their Winchester effort. "The Lieutenant General . . . asks the men and officers of the corps to unite with him on returning thanks to our Heavenly Father for the . . . success which has crowned the valor of this command," he proclaimed.[24] Quite a declamation by the former atheist! However, when he was reminded by his aides that Jackson would have set aside a day for thanksgiving and prayer, Ewell qualified his just-found zeal. "Hold religious services," he said, "[but only] at such times as may be . . . convenient."

On June 19th, finally authorized by Lee to move ahead as far as Hagerstown, Maryland, Ewell began advancing northward. Rodes led the way, taking a circular path that threatened the Federal depot at Harper's Ferry, thus dissuading the Yankees posted there from any ideas they might have had for sniping at Ewell's left flank. Johnson was next in line; Early's men brought up the rear. Heavy rains that day caused the Potomac to flood, temporarily isolating Jubal below the stream, but by June 22nd, the water had receded, and Early, too, crossed the river. Ewell, accompanied by his staff, came over last, gloating with his new orders from Lee. Not only had Lee approved going on into Pennsylvania, but also he had offered, "If Harrisburg comes within your means, capture it."[25]

Ewell's good spirits were broadly based. Obviously Lee was happy with his recent past performance. Moreover, he was giving Ewell independence, choosing to travel with A.P. Hill, who probably bore watching. And he had just given Ewell the "plum" of the campaign, the chance to capture the capital of Pennsylvania, an extraordinary opportunity for glory. Ewell would make sure that Harrisburg came within his means.

That evening Ewell met with Rodes, Early, and Johnson at Boonsboro, where he revealed his plans for the move into

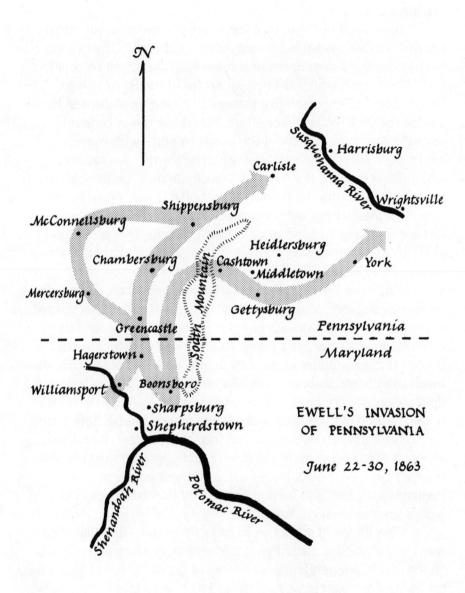

EWELL'S INVASION
OF PENNSYLVANIA

June 22-30, 1863

Pennslyvania. He proposed advancing along a broad front: Early to the right where Federal attack was most likely, Rodes in the center, and Steuart's Brigade (Johnson's Division) alone defending the left, the flank least liable to be assaulted by the enemy. The rest of Johnson's troops would follow Rodes. The corps progress would be slow because the men would need to forage as they moved into Federal territory. When gathering provisions, everyone had to follow Lee's stringent rules: "No private property shall be destroyed; Requisitions . . . for necessary supplies . . . shall be paid the market price [Confederate dollars]; and [only] if the inhabitants refuse to comply with such requisitions will supplies be taken."[26]

Ewell's subordinates voiced their objections to obeying Lee's strict policy, pointing to the atrocities that the Federals had committed on Southern soil. They argued that they should be permitted to retaliate, to match the cruel deeds of the enemy. Ewell, however, insisted that they support Lee's program. "Plundering by individuals," he warned, "[will see] the severest penalties known to the service."[27]

The march north into Pennsylvania began at dawn on June 23rd. Pausing at Greencastle that night, the troops moved on toward Chambersburg the following morning. Ewell personally took charge of Rodes' Division that day. He had every confidence in his subordinate, but Ewell felt the urge to command, and he was more comfortable with the smaller unit. Reaching Chambersburg at noon, Ewell ate lunch in the town, then drove his rig about three miles north where he set up headquarters in a Mennonite church. He spent the rest of the day planning his strategy to "harvest" Harrisburg.

While Ewell plotted away, his troops dispersed to "purchase" supplies from the local farmers. Steuart on the west, Jenkins to the north, and Early on the east gathered up provisions in wagons and sent them south to Lee and his oncoming forces. A prodigious haul was realized. Ewell described it best when he chortled that Pennsylvania was "like a hole full of blubber to a Greenlander."[28]

His plans set, Ewell again met with his generals to lay out his Harrisburg campaign. The corps would be divided into two halves: Early would march east, over South Mountain and through Gettysburg and York to Wrightsville. After demolishing the bridge over the Susquehanna River at Wrightsville, to prevent Yankee reinforcements from the south crossing the water to interfere with Ewell's chess-like moves, Early would turn northwest and march for Carlisle where Jenkins, Johnson, and Rodes would be waiting after coming up from Chambersburg.

When all had reassembled, Ewell would launch his attack on Harrisburg. Jenkins' horsemen would lead the way, trailed by Rodes and Johnson, taking separate but parallel routes on their way east. Early would hold as a reserve. The briefing ended with Ewell passing out maps and reminding everyone the advance would start at first light.

Although Ewell had been most serious when revealing his plans that evening, the mood of the meeting was hardly sober. His subordinates nodded their agreement as he described each move, their excitement growing with Ewell's every word. When he wrote his niece the following morning, Ewell reflected the jubilant outlook by referring to distant relatives living in York. "[I'll] let [them] off tolerably easy," he joked, "not taking more than a few forks and spoons . . . no houseburning or anything like that."[29]

A soft rain began late that evening and continued falling throughout the next day. Plodding steadily ahead, every step an effort because of mud, the troops headed for Carlisle and were thoroughly soaked by 2:00 p.m. Ewell took pity, coming to an early halt at Shippensburg to let the men seek shelter. He and his staff sought refuge from the cold, steady drizzle in a nearby farmhouse. Their host, a stout Dutchman, was unnerved by the unexpected appearance of Confederate officers, and he acted as if his guests were about to "eat or . . . torture him."[30] Nevertheless, he asked them to supper, served by his spouse and two daughters. Campbell found the scene disgusting. He remembered that although the farmer "owned 150 acres of land, a large, fine barn, and a tolerably good house, [he] kept no house servant . . . his wife and daughters did the cooking, washing, etc." Life without slaves was unbearable to a Southern boy, biased as to what constitutes a gentleman.

After staying the night in the farmhouse, Ewell had his men on the road by 6:00 a.m. The rain continued to fall, but despite the inclement weather, the troops made good time, arriving in Carlisle at 1:00 p.m. They were greeted by sullen citizens and (at last) a bright, shining sun. Rodes occupied the village. Ewell drove his carriage north to the U.S. Barracks, the cavalry center where he had served upon graduating from West Point. He set up headquarters in the commandant's office. Shortly after he was established, Ewell received an unexpected visitor. Isaac Trimble, recovered from the wounds he had suffered at Groveton (the same bitter encounter where Ewell had lost his limb), had come seeking assignment. Ewell was elated. Trimble was good at officering and familiar with the local geography. Prior to the war, he had worked as a civil engineer for the Baltimore and Ohio Railroad and had surveyed the Harrisburg area. Ewell added the irascible brigadier to his staff at once.

Later in the day, Ewell called Jenkins to his office to assign the bearded trooper an important mission. He was told to take his men on to Harrisburg to find out how many Federal troops were stationed there, their experience (army regulars or local militia), and the strength of the capital's defense. Jenkins was to report as soon as possible, as Ewell meant to attack within two days.

Ewell was still working at his desk that evening when a committee of local citizens arrived to ask a favor. Would he object if a local mill kept operating? The mill ground flour for the poor.

"It isn't my mill", Ewell growled. "If any of my people interfere, come and tell me. Is that all?"[31]

"No . . . we are Lutherans and we've got a church."

"Glad to hear it."

"Can we open it next Sunday?"

"Certainly . . . I'll attend myself if I'm here."

The group seemed shocked by the prospect of Ewell being at their services. After a lengthy silence, the spokesman for the citizens finally raised the real reason for coming to see Ewell. "We hope you won't get mad. In our service, we pray for the President of the United States . . . Can we pray for him?"

"Who do you mean, Lincoln?" Ewell barked. They nodded. He began to smile, revealing the high spirits he had enjoyed ever since Lee had authorized an attack on Harrisburg. "Cer-

tainly, pray . . . I don't know anybody that stands more in need
of prayer."

Instead of attending church in town the next day, Ewell
chose to remain at the barracks to attend a special ceremony,
the raising of the new Confederate flag recently sanctioned by
the legislature. Lee had given the Second Corps the honor of
being the first to fly the banner, the familiar blue cross on a red
background in the upper left corner of an all-white field.

"It was a grand occasion," Private Henry London vividly
remembered.[32]

Jed Hotchkiss, Ewell's mapmaker, was less enthusiastic,
describing the ritual as an "animating scene."[33] The ceremonies
were not at all what the officials in Richmond had so fondly
envisioned.

It was a hot, sultry day. When the new flag, carefully
sewn by the women of Richmond, was unveiled, Ewell refused to
raise it because the banner was too small to impress the people
from Carlisle. Tailors were summoned from the ranks and told
to stitch a new ensign, using the full-sized battle flag of the
Thirty-Second North Carolina. While they worked away, a keg of
lager beer was tapped by the Rebel officers who were scheduled
to speak that day. "It was the strongest [brew] I ever saw,"
Campbell Brown wrote later as an excuse. "I never saw Rodes
intoxicated before."[34]

About 4:00 p.m., the improvised banner was finally
completed. Ewell said a few words to the 8,000 men gathered on
the lawn in front of his headquarters, then retreated inside to
his office. Rodes and Daniel struggled through their remarks
without a mishap. But when Trimble stepped up to make his
speech, decorum departed. Campbell described him as being
"quite jolly" and his oration "not too neat."[35] The men loved it,
and they called for more. Major Ben Greene seized the podium,
smiled, waved his hands, and began to talk. "He was utterly
incoherent," Campbell ruefully remembered.[36] As the troops
laughed and jeered, someone reached out and yanked Major
Greene by the coattails from view.

Loud boos greeted Greene's sudden departure, and as
the soldiers began crying for still more speeches, consternation
swept the stage. No one wanted to step up and face the jeering

mob. Finally, a volunteer surged to the front and began to babble. It was Greene again, offering a "worse exhibition than before."[37] At that moment, thankfully for the propriety of Lee's Army of Northern Virginia, the heavens intervened. The skies darkened and rain, accompanied by loud thunder and flashes of lightning, fell in sheets. The ceremony abruptly ended with everyone running for shelter.

The next morning, June 29th, Ewell received a note from Jenkins saying that Harrisburg was defended by untrained militia who manned two forts, one west of the Susquehanna River, the second across the stream next to a railroad bridge. The water was easily forded up and down along the shore. Twenty-five cannons were emplaced, but because they were of varying calibers, Jenkins concluded that the enemy was probably short of ammunition. The report convinced Ewell that he could capture the city with just a token force, so he decided to send only Rodes forward. Johnson would remain at Carlisle. Early would hold to the south, between Wrightsville and York. The move to take Harrisburg would begin today!

As Rodes' long lines formed on the road eastward out of Carlisle about 1:00 p.m., a cold drizzle began to fall. The gloomy weather seemed an omen, shadowing the dismal news that did come at 3:00 p.m. A courier rode up to Ewell and handed him a dispatch from Lee. "General Hooker has crossed the Potomac," the letter read. "[His army] is advancing by way of Middletown. Move your force back to Chambersburg at once."[38]

Ewell was dumfounded. But no matter how hard he tried to read a different meaning into Lee's note, the words stayed straightforward and irrevocable. The assault against Harrisburg was cancelled. Ewell's road to glory, only moments ago so close, so achievable, had been detoured.

Ewell woodenly called Rodes back to Carlisle. Johnson and the corps' wagons started for Chambersburg, and word was sent to Early to tell him of the change in plans. Ewell was so stunned by Lee's change in strategy that he forgot to let Jenkins know that the attack had been cancelled, that the cavalry should leave Harrisburg and come west.

After issuing his orders, Ewell went into his office to get out of the rain. He soon received a second dispatch from Lee, who had changed his mind about where to rendezvous. Instead of Chambersburg, Lee had decided to mass his troops at Cashtown, just east of South Mountain. "We're going to fight at Cashtown . . . " Ewell moaned. "I may get killed."[39]

"You're in the habit of taking that chance," one of the aides quietly replied.

"It isn't that I mind getting killed," Ewell noted with an unhappy smile. "It's the idea that my name may go down in history as being killed at a place called Cashtown."

If Ewell had glanced more closely at Lee's dispatch, he could have saved himself a bit of misery. The order gave him a choice. He could march his corps to either Cashtown or to another nondescript village known as Gettysburg.

* * * *

When Jackson died, Lee bemoaned, "I know not how to replace him."[40] This feeling, common throughout the Confederacy, placed an awesome burden on Stonewall's successor. How could anyone be as audacious, as quick to seize advantage of every opportunity as the legendary Jackson? Ewell was given this dubious assignment, and his peers wondered and worried. They did not doubt Ewell's leadership abilities; they were concerned with his strength. Brigadier General William Pendleton, Lee's Chief of Artillery, spoke for many when at the time of Ewell's promotion he questioned whether the General had recovered where he could be "sufficiently active to exercise field command."[41]

These doubts seemed to have been put to rest by Ewell's movement north from the Rappahannock camps. He did a masterful job in marching his 20,000 troops from Fredericksburg to Carlisle without a misstep. On the way, he whipped Milroy at Winchester. In doing so, Ewell disobeyed Lee's explicit instructions to avoid battle, but he escaped censure because he won while holding to his schedule. Crushing an enemy who enjoyed greater numbers in an entrenched position was a triumph over both the Union and Jackson's ghost. The victory earned Ewell the respect of his men, particularly Sandie Pendleton, who noted, "He resembles General Jackson and I look for great things from him."[42]

Robert E. Lee, watching from afar, agreed with Sandie's observations. "I am much gratified at the success which has attended your movements," he commended in a message to Ewell, "and [I] feel assured . . . it will continue."[43]

Had Lee been close to the scene, he would not have been so confident. Ewell's energy was fading. The spill from his horse prior to the battle of Winchester was only one of many falls, and as Jed Hotchkiss mentioned, "each . . . seemed to take something out of Old Dick."[44] He was driving himself in true post-amputation psychological frenzy, if the experts are correct, spending nights developing strategy, then rising before sunrise to move on to his next stop. Sandie Pendleton wrote that Ewell "disregarded his own personal comforts."[45] With the key confrontation of the war approaching, Ewell had used up much of his precious vigor. Would he break down? The fact that the South had to ask such a question cast a deep shadow on the Confederate odds at Gettysburg.

Gettysburg: Day One

Ewell was not the only one depressed at seeing his plan for capturing Harrisburg cancelled. Robert E. Lee, too, was most disheartened by having to issue that fateful order. He thought that his strategy to race into Pennsylvania, drawing the Yankees in column after him, exposing their forces to an attack in detail, was succeeding. Now, however, he suddenly found himself in the dark, knowing only that the enemy stood uncomfortably close by with uncertain numbers.

Lee had relied on Jeb Stuart, shielding his right flank, to keep him informed of Hooker's position, to give him ample warning when it was time to concentrate for the attack. But Stuart had failed him, riding off in a vain attempt to circle the Union army, to regain the personal prestige he considered lost at Brandy Station. Halfway around the Federals, east of their encampment, Stuart was suddenly shocked to find Hooker heading north. Jeb was cut off, unable to communicate to Lee the critical news that the enemy was closing on the Confederates, that a confrontation loomed.

Because Stuart had not reported the enemy's move north, Lee wrongly assumed that he was secure, that Hooker's troops were still camped south of the Potomac River. Late at night on June 28th, he finally learned that the Union had not only closed to within thirty miles of the strung out Confederates, but also that the unstable Hooker had been replaced by Major General George G. Meade, a conservative but competent leader.[1] Lee had to concentrate his army immediately, preferably east of South Mountain, at Cashtown or Gettysburg, where he could better protect his line of supply back to Virginia.

Ewell's own corps were scattered. Johnson was moving west for Chambersburg, Rodes was returning to Carlisle, and Early was near York. The general faced an ominous task in gathering his three divisions, then moving on to Cashtown or Gettysburg. He was operating in an area infested with unfriendly people, likely to report his vulnerability to the Northern army.

The enemy might assault him at any moment. Ewell made his plans. Rodes would march south, Early would hurry west, and the two would join at Heidlersburg the night of June 30th. The next morning, they would head south to merge with Johnson, coming east out of Chambersburg through a gap in South Mountain.

While Ewell was well aware of the valid reasons causing Lee to call off the assault on Harrisburg, he could not bring himself to accept the decision with good grace. So when his men left at dawn the next morning, Ewell hid his deep disappointment by driving his buggy at the rear of Rodes' column.

Ewell carried a passenger beside him, John Cabell Early, a young nephew of Jubal's. The fifteen-year-old John and his father had just arrived from Lynchburg, both intending to enlist in the Confederate Army. Ewell considered the times too perilous for a young boy to be wandering loose on his own, so he took personal charge of John to keep him from harm's way.

As his buggy bounced slowly down the country lane, Ewell eyed the red cherries ripening in orchards that lay alongside the path. He had been coveting the sweet fruit for days, but had been unable to indulge his desires because his wooden leg precluded climbing trees. The boy at his side offered a solution to the quandary. Ewell made repeated stops to send the lad into the boughs to gather cherries. When Ewell halted at noon for lunch, young John wearily climbed out of the rig and dropped to the ground to rest. As a result of his many trips into the trees, his face was dirty and his elegant clothes (a tailored gray uniform and white shirt of "tucks, interspersed with puffs,")[2] were stained with sweat. "How could so small a man," he groaned to himself, "hold so many cherries?"

The afternoon leg of the march to Heidlersburg was hard on the troops. The road was like a caterpillar's back, hill and dale, hill and dale, and the marchers found it difficult to breath because of the dust raised by their own pounding feet. Ewell tried to ease the men's suffering by ordering frequent halts, one of which was at Papertown, Pennsylvania, the site of a stationery plant. Taking advantage of the break, Ewell toured the factory. The owner, Mr. Mullin, led the way past cribs full of clean rags, rows of well-oiled machinery, and vats of foaming pulp into the large storeroom. Shelves, sagging under their stacks of ledgers, forms, and notepaper, stretched from floor to ceiling. Mullin had assumed that he was entertaining a tourist, but he soon found that Ewell was a customer.

"I wish to [make a] purchase," Ewell suddenly stated, "Five thousand dollars worth of forms and paper."[3]

Mullin was both astonished and delighted by Ewell's unexpected order. Assigning his workers to load boxes into the Rebels' wagons parked in front of the factory, Mullin quickly completed the requisition. He then received payment for the purchase.

"Here is a receipt voucher on which you may claim reimbursement," Ewell said to his host as he handed him a scrap of paper. "The Confederate Government will be very glad to get these needed supplies."

Mullin's face turned white with shock. Knowing that he could never journey to Richmond to collect the money, worthless Rebel dollars at that, he staggered at the size of his loss. He bid a sad farewell to Ewell, who was no doubt grinning broadly over the unusual transaction.

The sun was setting when Ewell arrived at Heidlersburg. The men fell out to set up camp; shortly thereafter, Early's division came up. Jubal joined Rodes and Trimble to discuss with Ewell two messages just received. The first was from A. P. Hill, advising that the Union Eleventh Corps had been spotted near Gettysburg. The second note was from Lee. "Proceed to Cashtown or Gettysburg," he ordered, "as circumstances might dictate."[4]

After reading Lee's letter out loud to the group, Ewell sarcastically asked if anyone knew where they were supposed to go. He left no doubt that he was frustrated by Lee's continuing ambiguity. Early agreed that Lee's directions were unsettling, that it was impossible to concentrate in two places seven miles apart at the same time. Spurred by Early's sharing his view, Ewell caustically reread the order.

"Lee . . . plans to attack the advance of the enemy," Isaac Trimble noted, "and as it . . . is [toward] Gettysburg, we should march to that place."[5]

Perhaps Trimble spoke too smugly. The others dissented

with his contention, and the argument continued late into the night without a resolution. Ewell finally sent his generals to bed while he stayed up to wrestle with the riddle. As the sun rose, Ewell, who had not slept at all, made his decision. He would compromise, heading toward Middletown, a crossroads halfway between Cashtown and Gettysburg, where he could wheel to either village without losing time. He hoped that before he had to commit himself to one town or the other, Lee would finally make up his mind.

The July 1st move toward Middletown would not be just a Sunday stroll. The Federals were close by, in large numbers, and Ewell could not risk being attacked while in column. The cavalry usually rode along the flanks to deal with any enemy assault, but Jenkins, finally recalled from Harrisburg after being noticed as missing, was not yet at hand. Ewell decided to split his force, putting Early's Division, his most experienced troops, on the left where the Yankees were most likely to attack. Rodes would advance to the right, ahead of Early. If the Union threatened either flank, each could quickly turn to rush to the aid of the other. Ewell himself would travel with Rodes, in the center of the corps (assuming that Johnson would soon come up from the west), closer to his line of communications with Lee.[6]

About 8:00 a.m., just as Rodes' van was entering Middletown, a worried courier came looking for Ewell, who was still sulking at the tail of the column. He had shocking news: A.P. Hill, moving on Gettysburg, had collided with the enemy west of the town and become engaged. Ewell must come at once to his aid.

Ewell's lethargy vanished. Barking out orders, he sent Rodes ahead to Gettysburg. Early was to continue on his path down the Heidlersburg Road, which led to the crossroads town. Campbell was dispatched to tell Lee that Ewell was rushing to reinforce Hill. Ewell then called for his horse. He was determined to ride his mount, not that humiliating buggy, into battle.

Galloping to the van of Rodes' columns, Ewell took command, hurrying the division south on the Middletown Road. He was on edge, often thinking he could hear rifles shooting up ahead. Every time Ewell halted the lines, however, to listen closely, the only sounds were the footsteps of the troops to his rear. The sinister silence ended about 9:00 a.m., when the boom of cannons roared and reverberated to the front.

With a battle obviously underway ahead, Ewell knew that Rodes had to resume command of his troops, so he relinquished the leadership he had assumed. Ewell did, however, stay with the van advancing toward the fighting. A mile above Gettysburg, Rodes turned his force off the highway and onto a ridge that paralleled their path. The slope was thick with trees, concealing the Confederates' approach to the front. Once under the cover of the woods, Rodes changed alignment, putting a brigade up front in line as skirmishers. His remaining men were kept in column.[7]

Suddenly, the chatter of muskets broke out ahead. Rodes ordered a halt, and sent a scout forward to determine who was firing the flurry of balls that zipped overhead. The soldier soon returned to report that Northern cavalry had blocked their path, fired a few shots, then retreated south.[8]

Anticipating imminent action, Rodes prepared for battle. He deployed three brigades in line, Doles' on the left, O'Neal's in the center, Iverson's to the right, while the remaining two brigades (Ramseur's and Daniel's) were kept in column in reserve. Rodes, riding at the van with Ewell, advanced his troops.

It was close to noon, and the fighting ahead had slowed to a desultory artillery exchange, as Rodes' troops poured out from under the trees to climb a small rise that peaked atop a bare hill. Below and to their right were two ridges in a "V" formation. The left leg was a continuation of the knoll (Oak Hill) they occupied; the right fork (McPherson's Ridge) ran southwest. The latter was covered with Yankees, facing west, fronting Hill's men on yet a third rise. A meandering stream ran between the two adversaries.

Ewell saw at once that he had stumbled onto the enemy's flank, and that he was in perfect position to attack and roll up the Union's defenseless line. He ordered Rodes to charge immediately. His subordinate, however, asked for a short delay so he could shift his line west and improve his angle of assault. Approving the maneuver, Ewell took advantage of the pause to bring his artillery forward, to fire on the Yankees, to hold them in place. Carter's guns opened on the Federals, who finally

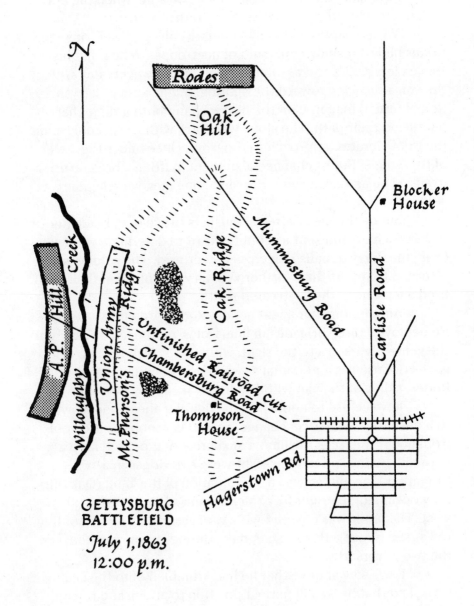

GETTYSBURG
BATTLEFIELD
July 1, 1863
12:00 p.m.

recognized they were in great peril.

The Union's response was surprisingly quick. A portion of the troops fronting Hill whirled about and raced into some woods below a railroad cut just beneath Oak Hill to take a position facing Ewell. On the left, a host of bluecoats poured out of Gettysburg, coming up the Mummasburg Road to assume a north-south line protecting the town. And Northern artillery answered Ewell's guns, blistering not only Oak Hill but also the woods to the west where Rodes was gathering his brigades. Ewell watched with growing anxiety. His momentous chance to strike a vulnerable enemy was slipping away.

At that moment, Campbell galloped up from the rear, returning from seeing Lee. He brought shocking orders: Ewell could not attack; he was to avoid a general engagement until the rest of the army came up. Seeing the unparalleled opportunity before him, Ewell protested "It [is] too late."[9] He could not obey such instructions. Campbell answered that Ewell had to follow his orders, that Lee was boiling mad, showing "a querulous impatience . . . never [seen] in him before" because others had disregarded his directives.[10] He went on to explain that Lee had asked, "Have [you] heard anything from . . . Jeb Stuart? I have heard nothing from him for three days and . . . Stuart has not complied with his instructions. I told him to cross one of the upper fords of the Potomac, keeping along the eastern base of the ridge and constantly in communication with me . . . but he has gone off clear around [the Federal army] and I see by a Baltimore paper that he is near Washington. A scout reports Meade's whole army marching this way but that is all I know . . . . "

Pausing to catch his breath, Campbell then finished his astonishing report. "You're to send out to your left and try to open communication with General Stuart. Firing was heard last night by Hanover Junction, and that may be his command."

Ewell must have remembered how a year ago, Jeb had said that Lee's orders were not binding, that he allowed subordinates to use discretion based on local conditions. Ewell had attacked Milroy at Winchester on that premise. Now, however, he knew that Jeb had been wrong. Lee expected his orders to be obeyed, and those who failed to follow instructions risked censure. Ewell had to comply with Lee's wishes, even if doing so cost the Confederates an unparalleled opportunity for whipping their enemy.

Agonized by his dilemma, Ewell finally decided he could not just blindly obey Lee. It made no sense to leave Gettysburg to go looking for the rambling Stuart. He had to seize the opportunity at hand. Ewell elected to compromise, to go ahead with his attack, but after driving the Yankees from the field, calling off all pursuit. A courier was sent to Rodes with this order; Campbell left to intercept Early and give him these same instructions. Each was told to emphasize Lee's furious mood, that they risked his censure if they prolonged the engagement.[11]

If Ewell had any second thoughts about his decision, he soon saw it made no difference. The bluecoats were preparing to attack him. Directly below Oak Hill, a skirmish line was charging out of the woods to front the brigade which had come over from A.P. Hill's front. The Yankees to the east (those who had rushed from Gettysburg to set up a defensive position along the Mummasburg Road) had opened fire, encouraged by the sight of even more reinforcements pouring from the town, extending their line to the right beyond the Carlisle Road.

As Ewell watched the developing scene, Rodes came up to report that he was ready to charge. Doles would hold to deal with the Northern troops who had rushed out from Gettysburg; O'Neal and Iverson would assault the enemy advancing from below Oak Hill. To the right, Daniel would trail O'Neal's and Iverson's attack, protecting their flank until they had overwhelmed their opponents. Daniel would then turn west to roll up the Union line on McPherson's Ridge. Ramseur would be in reserve. Ewell approved the battle plan, but again reminded Rodes that he must break off the engagement once the Federals were sent reeling in defeat. Rodes agreed to this condition, then hurried off to direct his division. Ewell stayed on Oak Hill. His expectations turned to horror through the next half hour, as Rodes' carefully conceived strategy disintegrated.

O'Neal led off at 2:00 p.m. but, perhaps too anxious to close with the enemy, he advanced with only three of his five regiments. He was lacking the Fifth Alabama, which ran left to join Doles in fronting the Yankees emerging out of Gettysburg.

The Third Alabama, also misunderstanding their orders, held their ground to the west. O'Neal's support was also insufficient because Iverson's brigade, scheduled to charge on his right, found their path to the front blocked by Carter's guns, firing at the oncoming Yankees. Iverson held in place, waiting for the way to clear. With only a token force available, O'Neal was no match for the bluecoats. His charge was shattered, and his men staggered backward.[12]

As O'Neal retreated, Iverson finally moved forward. His men, massed in formation with no skirmishers leading the way, crossed the Mummasburg Road about 2:30 p.m., then wheeled to the southeast. They pressed ahead, unmindful of a stone wall paralleling their path to the left. All at once, a horde of Federals rose from behind the barrier to send a hail of flame into the flank of Iverson's compact ranks. In less than one minute, over five hundred Rebels lay dead or wounded like toy stick lines in a row on the rolling ground. The remnants of the brigade scrambled for cover, re-formed, then charged the now-seen enemy. Their assault was feeble, futile, and easily repelled. And as Iverson's North Carolinians faltered backward, Yankee soldiers clambered over the wall to capture most of what remained of a once proud organization.[13]

As the disaster unfolded, Ewell looked right to see why Daniel had not come to Iverson's aid. He saw that the Rebels had lost touch with each other. As Iverson turned southeast, Daniel had continued to advance straight ahead. Even worse, when Iverson's men were attacked, three of Daniel's regiments broke off from their formation to rush left to their support. Seeing they were too late, the errant troops stopped short of the carnage, isolated on the field. Daniel, heading for the railroad cut that fronted the open Union flank, never noticed he was missing over half his force. The enemy, however, was quick to recognize his dilemma, and they charged, driving him backward. Only the accurate bombardment of a vigilant Rebel artillery battery saved Daniel's troops from also being taken prisoner.[14]

Three consecutive repulses against an open enemy flank! Ewell must have been dismayed at the inept performance of his troops. At that moment, Major Andrew Venable, the inspector general for Stuart's cavalry, rode up to Ewell's headquarters area to report that Jeb was at Carlisle, about to come south to join Ewell.[15] Venable knew nothing of Lee's exasperation with Stuart, and Ewell was not about to divert his attention from the battle to pass on the bad news. He sent Venable to Lee so he could personally tell him of Jeb's whereabouts, to learn for himself how upset Lee was with Stuart.

With the front on his right quiet for the moment, Ewell decided he had better check on Doles. He rode east where he found the situation as desperate as the west. Doles was being assailed by large numbers of bluecoats, so many they were overlapping each of his flanks. Reinforcements were needed, and only Ramseur's brigade was available. Ewell wheeled his mount and headed back for Oak Hill to rush troops to Doles' aid. He never saw the shell until it was upon him. With extraordinary luck, a Federal battery intercepted Ewell's path and scored a direct hit, their ball smashing into his horse's head.[16] The detonation scattered deadly shell fragments throughout the area, wounding several soldiers but miraculously missing Ewell. Sitting stoically in the saddle while his mutilated mare crumpled to her knees, Ewell waited until his only foot touched ground, then stepped neatly aside and quietly asked for a spare horse. Numbed,of course, by the incident, his third experience during the war of having his mount shot out from under him, Ewell nevertheless found himself still capable of showing exceptional courage. The men watching noted his calm, military manner, and the display deeply impressed them, just as it had earlier affected Ewell's compatriots in the Shenandoah Valley, at Gaines' Mills, and at Groveton.

Soon astride again, Ewell galloped back toward Oak Hill to find Ramseur and hurry his troops east to reinforce Doles. When he arrived at his headquarters, Ewell was greeted by astonishing news. During Ewell's brief "distraction," the tide of battle had shifted dramatically. The South as winning on all fronts!

On the west, Daniel had managed to reassemble his force, and at 3:30 p.m., had gone forward again. The Yankees, using the railroad cut as an entrenchment, had blistered his front, inflicting multiple casualties. But Daniel had cleverly sent only three of his five regiments against the man-made trench.

The other two regiments had circled the Union flanks, arriving in position just as the bluecoats were being reinforced, men jumping into the gully to join their engaged comrades. Rushing up to the lip of the cut, Daniel's outer regiments opened a murderous fire, like shooting fish in a barrel. The volley brought a Union retreat, which was met in the rear by A.P. Hill's men, who were finally entering the fray. Most of the retiring enemy soldiers were captured; the few who escaped sped east for the haven of Gettysburg.[17]

While Daniel was driving the Federals on the right, Ramseur had joined with O'Neal in charging the enemy holding the center ground, taking the identical path that had earlier led Iverson to disaster. There was, however, a marked difference in leadership. Iverson was a political general; Ramseur was a trained military man who knew better than to wander into an ambush. When he saw the stone wall hiding the enemy, Ramseur swung left behind the barrier to attack the bluecoats' flank. His charge at 4:15 p.m. dislodged the Yankees from their protected lair, sending them scurrying for Gettysburg.[18]

Seeing his forces victorious on the west, Ewell hurried back to where Doles had been in peril to the east. He arrived just as Doles, contested on both front and flanks, was mounting an assault! After allowing the enemy to his right to slip by, Doles charged them, neatly trapping the bluecoats between himself and Ramseur, pursuing the Federals he had flushed from behind the stone wall. Caught in the vise, harassed by Doles' onslaught, the Yankees had no choice but to turn back to join the growing flight for Gettysburg.[19]

Doles seemingly took a huge risk, turning right to face one adversary, leaving his rear exposed to the other Federals attacking him. His daring was not suicidal. Doles saw that rein-forcements were at hand to repel the threat to his eastern flank. Early had finally arrived at Gettysburg! He had been there, hidden from view in a woods northeast of the town, for about thirty minutes, giving his men a chance to catch their breath from their race to the village.

After unlimbering his cannons and aligning his brigades, Early delivered a stunning blow to the Federals. His artillery opened first, spreading a rain of shells over the unsuspecting

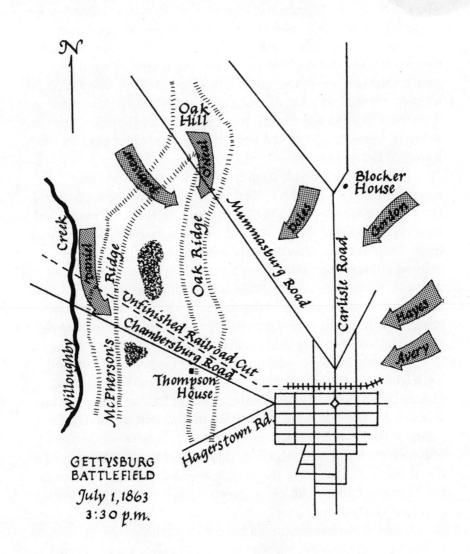

GETTYSBURG
BATTLEFIELD
July 1, 1863
3:30 p.m.

enemy. Then his infantry charged the Yankees, enveloping Doles' left. Gordon's regiments came running through a field of yellow wheat ripening under the July sun to shatter the enemy's front. "Gordon was the most glorious and inspiring thing I ever [remember]," Robert Stiles said. "Standing in stirrups, bare-headed, hat in hand, arms extended, and in a voice like a trumpet, exhorting his men."[20] As the enemy withdrew, still holding their alignment, Hays' and Avery's troops exploded on their right. The retreat became a rout, as every Federal not captured or killed fled for Gettysburg.[21]

In complete control of his force, Early, obeying orders from Ewell, ended his assault. Gordon stopped above the village, Avery circled east to front the heights below the town, and Hays went into Gettysburg to gather prisoners. Doles and Ramseur joined Hays in town, but Rodes' other three brigades, exhausted from the cruel fight, all organization lost, stayed scattered west of the village.[22]

As the tide of victory swept the Rebels into Gettysburg, Ewell and his staff left Oak Hill about 5:00 p.m. to join the jubilant southern troops. Ewell's thoughts as he rode down the slope must have been mixed, a blend of highs and lows. Although he was gratified about having routed a determined and sizeable foe, Ewell mourned the price. The Rebel losses approached 2,900 killed, maimed, or captured—20% of the force Ewell had sent into the fray.[23] Dead and dying men, blue and gray, lay scattered in his path. Ewell was also worried that Lee would be angry because he had disobeyed orders by becoming "engaged before the rest of the army came up." Most of all, however, he felt exhausted. Ewell had not slept in over thirty-six hours.

After traveling only a short distance, Ewell turned his party left off the Mummasburg Road to cut through the fields to the Carlisle Road north of town. Small groups of combatants continued to skirmish west of Gettysburg, blocking a direct entry into the village. As he rode through the low meadow where Doles' brigade had fought so well, Ewell looked up to study Cemetery Hill, the heights south of Gettysburg. The crest was crowned with cannons, lined wheel to wheel. Close by the guns were thousands of seemingly fresh Federal troops, shouting encouragement to comrades who were running to escape the Confederate onslaught. They were calling to their compatriots to climb up to the haven of the hill. A red brick, twin-towered gate on the peak offered a beacon to the fleeing men.

Should he try to organize an operation to deny the high ground to the Federals? With no idea that his decision would be the most controversial of his career, Ewell quickly opted against an attack. Lee's orders forbade it, and while he had disobeyed his superior once today, he was not about to do so again. As Ewell would say later when others urged him to assault, "I will wait for [Lee's] orders."[24]

As Ewell neared the village, Trimble, then John Gordon, and finally Kyd Douglas fell in with his entourage. "[Johnson] is marching on Gettysburg," Douglas reported. "He will be ready to put [his troops] in as soon as he gets here."[25]

"I can join in with my brigade," Gordon offered. Pointing to the heights below Gettysburg, he added, "We can carry that hill."

"General Lee told me to come to Gettysburg, and he gave me no orders to go further," Ewell snapped at Gordon. "I do not feel like . . . making an attack without orders from him . . . "

Ewell's response was out of character. While he usually sought others' opinions, now he refused to listen to Gordon's proposal. Ewell's curtness showed that he looked to Lee for his next move, that he was determined not to attack the enemy on his own.

Immediately after his comment, Ewell must have realized he had made an unpopular decision. The silence that followed his words said more than any expressions of protest. And if the quiet was not enough, a resonant whisper by Sandie Pendleton cinched the disgust of the group with Ewell's view. "Oh, for the presence and inspiration of Old Jack . . . . " Sandie said too loudly. Ewell ignored the insult.

As he entered the northern outskirts of the town, Ewell became exposed to skirmishing, the dying embers of the battle for Gettysburg. The "crack" of muskets still barked, adversaries ducked in and out of doorways to dodge the balls fired in their direction, and an occasional shell exploded noisily overhead. Impervious to the danger, Ewell led his procession slowly up the street. Suddenly, a flurry of bullets whizzed by. Ewell spun in his saddle at the same instant an ominous "thud" was heard.

"Are you hurt, Sir?" Gordon asked anxiously as he urged his mount up beside Ewell.[26]

"I'm not hurt," Ewell said with a sly smile. "But suppose the ball had struck you? We would have had the trouble of carrying you off the field." When Gordon, puzzled by the reply, frowned, Ewell nodded toward his right leg. "You see how much better fixed for a fight I am . . . it don't hurt a bit to be shot in a wooden leg."

Stopping in the town square (actually a diamond), Ewell was quickly besieged as both officers and men crowded against him. A lieutenant offered him a toast from a bottle of wine he had filched from a nearby cellar. While Ewell should have scolded the officer for pillaging, he saw that the times made a little booty acceptable. Ewell demurred without mention of Lee's policies against foraging.[27]

The pleasantries were interrupted by Harry Hays, one of Early's brigade commanders. Forcing his way through the mass of people surrounding the General, he asked loudly why Ewell had not ordered an assault on the enemy occupying the heights south of town.

"Won't you Louisianans ever get your bellyful of fighting?" Ewell answered, trying to turn Hays' query into a joke. "Can't you wait a day?"[28]

"I want to attack now!" Hays snapped. "That'll prevent the slaughter of my men tomorrow."

Ewell refused to debate his responsibilities with Hays, and as he turned away, Sandie Pendleton came through the mob to Ewell's side. The aide had found a good site for a field headquarters, and he urged Ewell to go there now as Gettysburg was too dangerous a place for a corps commander. Ewell agreed, and he followed Sandie north out of the village to a stone house, located 100 yards beyond where the Carlisle Road split into two forks. The home was owned by Mrs. Blocher, a kindly German lady, who had taken in wounded Rebels but still had room for Ewell and his officers.[29]

As Ewell dismounted, Trimble, who had accompanied Ewell in and out of Gettysburg without comment, walked up and said, "We've had a grand success, but aren't you going to follow it up and push our advantage?"[30]

"Lee has instructed me not to bring on a general engagement without orders," Ewell replied dourly, showing his growing irritation at being badgered to make an assault. "I will wait for those orders," he stubbornly concluded.

"That hardly applies to the present state," Trimble protested. "We've fought a hard battle already and should secure the advantage gained."

Ewell, tight-lipped with mulish annoyance, would not discuss Trimble's contention.

"It's a critical moment for us," his assistant insisted.

Ewell remained silent, glaring. Seeing he would get no reply, Trimble turned to mount his horse. "I will reconnoiter the area," he cried before riding south.

Entering the Blocher House, Ewell found it crammed with wounded Rebels. He moved from man to man, giving each a word of encouragement. His tour seemed endless, for just when he thought he had tended to the last injured soldier, additional casualties would be carried into the home. When he had finally finished his sad duties, Ewell prepared to rest himself, only to be called outside. Trimble was waiting to see him.

"There," the old brigadier shouted, pointing south, "is an eminence of commanding position . . . it ought to be occupied by us or the enemy soon. I advise you to send a brigade and hold it if we are to remain here."[31]

"Are you sure it commands the town?"

"Certainly . . . and it ought to be held by us at once."

Ewell weakened for a moment, thinking of sending troops to occupy vacant Culp's Hill, close by Cemetery Hill held by the Yankees. But his stubborn streak prevailed, and he held back, refusing further comment.

"Give me a brigade," Trimble urged "and I'll engage to take that hill."

Ewell still sullenly declined to answer.

"Give me a good regiment and I'll do it."

Ewell shook his head, causing Trimble to turn and storm to his horse. He mounted, but before galloping away, he eyed Ewell with an angry glare. "I will not serve, even as a volunteer aide, for such an officer as you!"

The unpleasant scene must have bothered Ewell. Trimble was an old friend, and his outburst against Ewell had to have hurt the General's feelings. And soon after, Ewell probably felt guilty because Early sent him a note confirming that the hill above the heights held by the Federals was vacant, that it commanded the Yankee position, and when Johnson arrived at the front, his troops should be sent to seize the eminence.[32] To gain advantage he had to act at once.

Ewell called for his horse and started the ride back to Gettysburg to find Early and start preparations for occupying Culp's Hill. On the way, Ewell met Campbell and James Smith, a former aide to Jackson, just now returning to duty to serve on Ewell's staff. Smith had interesting news. Since yesterday morning he had been with Lee, who came to Gettysburg upon hearing the opening sounds of A.P. Hill's encounter with the Yankees. Lee had been on the field for hours, had seen Ewell enter the fray, and had watched as the Rebels drove the enemy to their present lodgement on top of Cemetery Hill.[33]

Ewell must have been encouraged by Smith's report. Lee was nearby, had seen the battle, yet had neither reproach for Ewell because he had become engaged nor orders for him to assault the enemy entrenched on the heights. Lee must be in agreement with all of Ewell's actions.

Ewell had expected to discuss climbing Culp's Hill when he found Early in Gettysburg, but when they met, Jubal introduced a plan for driving the Yankees from Cemetery Hill. He admitted lacking the force necessary for charging the slopes, but said that he had already sent a request to A.P. Hill for reinforcements. Ewell opposed the attack. Lee, who was here on the field, had not ordered it; the knoll was teeming with Union troops; and they were supported by an impressive array of cannons. Recalling Malvern Hill and how the Yankee guns had slaughtered the Rebels when they tried to climb the rise, Ewell added that in his opinion, they had no suitable site to emplace their artillery so they could neutralize the enemy's weapons.[34] Early still insisted on making an assault. Ewell finally accepted Early's plea, provided that Lee approved the strike and A.P. Hill sent additional men.[35]

Since Early had already dispatched a courier to Hill to ask for assistance, only Lee's assent was needed, and Smith, who had just left the army's command post, was picked to go see Lee. As Smith galloped away, Ewell, energized by the imminent assault, began discussing tactics. His talk with Early was interrupted by Freddy Smith, the son of the brigade commander, posted east on the York Road. He rode up to report that his father was threatened by an approaching enemy force.

"I don't believe this," Early snorted, "but I prefer to suspend my movements until I can send and inquire into it."[36]

Ewell no doubt eyed Early with surprise. Where was the ardor for battle so strongly stated only minutes ago? In an instant reversal of roles, Ewell became the aggressor. "You do so," he snapped. "Meanwhile, I'll [go and] get Rodes into position."

After riding back into the village square, Ewell turned west to head toward Oak Hill and Rodes. He was flagged to a halt just west of Gettysburg by a small, dark-skinned officer with a thin, black mustache. Colonel Walter Taylor, an aide to Lee, hurried up to say, "The enemy's retreating over that hill (Cemetery) in great confusion. [You need] only to press those people to secure possession of the heights . . . . " Taylor then added with great importance, "General Lee wishes you to do this, if possible."[37]

Ewell nodded, meaning that he understood Lee's message. Perhaps because the order was ambiguous, more likely because Taylor had acted so smugly, Ewell did not think to note that Smith was already with Lee, asking approval to assault Cemetery Hill, nor that Hill's assistance was required. Ewell's omissions gave the mistaken impression that he was committed to an attack on his own.

Soon after Taylor left, Ewell learned that Rodes was in Gettysburg, and he returned to the village, where he again met Early. Jubal related that while he did not consider Smith's troops in any peril, to be safe he had sent Gordon's brigade east to bolster the numbers along York Road. Ewell realized at once that Early had only Avery's men available for an assault (Hays was occupied with 4,000 Yankee prisoners), and at best, Rodes could marshall only two brigades, Doles' and Ramseur's. And both of their ranks had been depleted during the afternoon fighting. If Ewell was to drive the Federals off Cemetery Hill, more than ever, he needed troops from A.P. Hill.

That assistance was not available. Shortly after Ewell re-met Early, Smith rode up to report that Lee "regretted his people were not up to support [Ewell's proposed attack], but . . . he wished him to take Cemetery Hill if possible." He then added that Ewell must "avoid a general engagement."[38] It was a para-doxical order, impossible to execute. Attack Cemetery Hill without reinforcements? And avoid a general engagement? What else would an assault on the heights be? Ewell, disgusted with Lee's continuing ambiguity, abandoned all plans for Cemetery Hill, deciding instead to go back to the Blocher House to await Johnson, to direct him to Culp's Hill.

Riding with Early, heading north out of town, Ewell finally ran into Rodes. Ewell reviewed their evolving situation, and Rodes emphatically agreed with the decision not to attack Cemetery Hill. Seeing that Rodes was flushed with fever, Ewell suggested that he lay down to rest a bit, but Rodes insisted on accompanying Ewell and Early to Mrs. Blocher house. As he entered the home, Ewell was met by scouts from Stuart's cav-alry, who reported spotting Northern horsemen approaching Gettysburg on York Road, headed for Smith's position.

"Those troopers," Early scoffed, "are waifs . . . . "[39]

Maybe so, but Ewell was through making decisions on second-hand information. He would ride out to see for himself. Ewell remounted, and together with Early, Rodes, and most of his staff, he headed east to the bluff above Rock Creek where an open vista was available. All three generals began scanning the far horizon with their field glasses.

"There they are!" Rodes suddenly cried, pointing toward shadowy figures creeping through the fields one hundred yards in the distance.[40] Early saw the same men, but unlike Rodes, he did not think they were Federals. He reasoned that if the nearby troops were hostile, they would not be skulking in the meadow, they would be shooting at Ewell's party. He insisted the soldiers were from Gordon's brigade.

While the others were jumping to conclusions, Ewell was thinking ahead. If the troops in doubt were in fact Northern soldiers, they blocked Johnson's path to Culp's Hill. Ewell could not take that chance. He had to know if they were Yankees so he could alert Johnson to expect enemy opposition to his occupation of the slopes. A scout, Tom Turner, was sent forward to determine if the unknown troops were friends or foes, then report his findings back to Ewell at Mrs. Blocher's house. Early, miffed because his suppositions had not been accepted, requested that one of his aides accompany Turner, implying that he did not trust Ewell's man with the mission. It was an invitation to argue, but by waving his hand, Ewell agreed to Early's intrusion. He was both too tired and too troubled to debate small matters. Mounting up, Ewell began to ride toward Blocher's. Rodes and the other members of his staff went with him, but Early, still sulking, headed for Gettysburg to check on Hays.

As he entered the Blocher House, Ewell was gratified to see Trimble among those waiting to see him. The bold officer had returned to duty. While he no doubt felt badly about his outburst against Ewell that afternoon, Trimble continued to smolder with proud defiance. Neither mentioned their earlier encounter.

Ewell was told that Johnson had finally reached Gettysburg and was halted west of the village, where he was waiting for orders. Culp's Hill was still the mission Ewell planned for Johnson, but he saw no reason for him to move there until Turner determined who was friend and who was foe along the eastern flank. He would hold Johnson in place for awhile.[41]

As others clamored for Ewell's attention, one voice rose above the crowd. Lee was dismounting out front!

Ewell hurried to the entry, invited Lee inside, and led him through the house, then outside to the backyard where a grape arbor offered privacy. Rodes accompanied Lee and Ewell. An aide was sent to bring Early to the meeting.

Lee sat in a swing, quietly observing his hosts. Ewell was probably just as silent. He had not slept in over forty hours, and he must have been dragging. Still suffering with a fever, Rodes, too, was languid and nodding.

When Lee finally opened serious discussions, he made no mention of either Ewell's engagement or the enemy on Cemetery Hill. Instead, using cold and formal tones, he asked for details on the situation facing the Second Corps. Ewell gave a short summary of the location of his divisions, the condition of his men (including an estimate of casualties suffered during the day's battle), and the strength of the enemy position to his front. He had just completed his briefing when Early burst on the scene. Jubal was in an arrogant mood, and when Lee next inquired if an assault was advisable from this flank tomorrow, he answered for the corps.

"I don't believe an attack should be made [from] south [of] Gettysburg against Cemetery Hill," he proclaimed firmly. "Deployment and ascent would be difficult in the face of any enemy who evidently is concentrating and fortifying." Calling Lee's attention to the Round Tops, two hills on the Rebel right, Jubal suggested the assault "be made from that side."[42]

"I doubt the wisdom of any advance," Lee replied. "Our men have made a fatiguing march and gone through a battle . . . Meade's men are fresh. I don't know whether Meade is already occupying those hills or, if so, in what force. I can't tell what resistance I might encounter. And if I take possession of those hills, I might be surrounded . . . the escape of my army would be difficult . . . . The loss of my army would mean the loss of the Southern cause."[43]

Still sure of himself, Early insisted that an attack on the Round Tops, from the west, was the correct strategy.

"Then . . . I had better draw you around toward my right," Lee countered. "Our line [is] very long and thin if you remain here, and the enemy may come down and break it."[44]

"You need not fear that [Meade] will break through our line," Early snorted. "We can repulse any [size] force that he sends against us."

Early's strong stance convinced Lee to accept his plan. "[I will] attack . . . from the right at daylight . . . " he decided. "A diversion should be made on your flank to favor it . . . making that diversion a real attack (if you see) any disorder or . . . giving way on the enemy's part."

Although Lee had made an aggressive decision, he began to offer disclaimers. "I may decide to draw off by my right flank to get between the enemy and Washington, to force them to attack us in position," he noted. Turning to Ewell, Lee advised, "Do not become so much involved as to be unable to readily extricate (your) troops."[45]

Ewell's heart no doubt sank when Lee presented this condition. Was Ewell expected to decide if and when to go into battle, become irrevocably committed to combat (a decision as much the enemy's as his), then be told to disengage within a moment's notice? Failure to carry out this illogical assignment could cost the Confederates the battle, even the war. It was "Cashtown or Gettysburg" all over again.

After Lee's departure, Ewell heard from Tom Turner that the force seen east of town had been a group of Southern skirmishers (as Jubal had claimed so vehemently). The scout also reported that he had crept up Culp's Hill and found it still empty. Ewell immediately ordered Johnson to rush to the foot of the slope, but to hold there until he received further instructions. Ewell's reluctance to have Johnson climb Culp's Hill was based on two factors. He was concerned that Johnson might find the Yankees dug in by the time he reached his destination and he would need to reconnoiter before finally scaling the heights; and he was unsure whether Johnson should camp on Culp's Hill. He might find it difficult to evacuate this position, should Lee decide to maneuver.[46]

Having dealt with Johnson, Ewell next turned to finding a new headquarters. His current lodgings were both too small and too far from the front. Mrs. Blocher, serving a meal of sandwiches and tea to her guests, heard Ewell discussing various alternatives, and she suggested a red barn, owned by the Lady family, located two miles to the southeast. It sounded perfect. But before leaving for the site, Ewell rewarded the hospitality shown by his Union hostess by placing a guard by her home and removing his wounded.[47]

Shortly after arriving at his new command post, a large barn, pungent with the smell of fresh hay, Ewell lay down to sleep. He needed rest. He had been up for over forty hours, his head ached, and his stump was bleeding. The tender skin had been rubbed painfully raw by his ill-fitting wooden limb. After only a few nods, Ewell was awakened by Colonel Charles Marshall's arrival with new orders from Lee.

"In case your corps cannot be used to advantage (here), you're to draw (it) to the right," Marshall announced. "The nature of the ground . . . is good on that side."[48]

Lee's new instructions seemed more like a question than orders. After Marshall left, Ewell called Rodes and Early to his side. What should he do? No one wanted to retreat from the ground bought so dearly that day, but it seemed that they had no choice. As they discussed their options, Turner came into the barn to announce that Johnson's men were in position by Culp's Hill, and he had just come down from the still unoccupied summit. Early urged Ewell to capture the knoll now. Rodes, however, felt that he should wait until morning since Johnson's troops had marched twenty-five miles that day. The men were probably too tired for a steep and stealthy clamber in the dark.

Ewell was beset with uncertainty. While holding Culp's Hill would turn the Yankees' position atop Cemetery Hill, Lee had just suggested he come right. Obviously, the plans laid earlier that evening with Lee in the grape arbor had changed, but Ewell was not privy to the new strategy. If Lee knew of the Culp's Hill opportunity, would he still want Ewell to relinquish his post? The only way to answer this question was for Ewell to go to Lee. He called for his horse.

Riding west and then south, Ewell soon arrived at Lee's headquarters, which were located in the Thompson House, only a few yards south of Cashtown Road, across the far slope of Seminary Ridge. A few sleeping tents were raised next to the highway, but Lee had not yet gone to bed. He was in the back room of the small cottage, studying maps spread out on a pine table, lit by candlelight.[49]

Ewell quickly presented his story. As he completed his case, Lee slowly nodded in agreement. The plans drawn up in the grape arbor behind Mrs. Blocher's house would stay in effect. Longstreet would attack on the right at dawn; Ewell would demonstrate on the left.

Hurrying back to the red barn, Ewell wasted little time in sending word to Johnson to occupy Culp's Hill at once. It was past 1:00 a.m. With dawn fast approaching, Johnson's men had to be on the slope before the bluecoats spotted them and moved to ruin the Rebels' plans. Ewell was in desperate need of sleep, but he decided to stay up until he heard from Johnson that he had executed his mission.

A courier arrived, but he came not from Johnson but from Lee. Fearful of yet another change in orders, Ewell read the message tremulously. The news was not bad. Lee was touching base, letting him know that Longstreet was not sure just when he could place his troops into position. The attack might be delayed. Ewell was to hold until he heard Rebel guns open on the right.[50]

About 2:00 a.m., John Gordon stormed into the barn. He had returned from York Road to see the Yankees digging in atop Cemetery Hill. "A line of heavy earthworks, with [guns] and ranks of infantry behind them, will frown upon us at daylight," Gordon declared. "[But] a concentrated and vigorous night assault . . . can carry those heights."[51] He asked that he be allowed to make that attack. Ewell was well aware of the Union's fortification, but he was also certain that when the enemy saw Johnson on Culp's Hill come morning, they would know their efforts had been in vain. The bluecoats would withdraw without a fight. There was no reason to attempt a dangerous charge in the dark. He shook his head, "No."

"If we wait until morning," Gordon badgered, "it [will] cost us ten thousand men . . . . "

Not about to argue his decisions with a brash subordinate, Ewell looked to Early, who had joined the vigil awaiting news from Johnson. Jubal offered conciliatory words but like Ewell, did not explain the current situation. Gordon, deeply disappointed with his superiors, returned to his troops.

At 3:00 a.m., Tom Turner appeared to report devastating news. Johnson had arrayed his men below Culp's Hill, but before starting to climb, had sent scouts up the slope to check out the heights. They found bluecoats in strength on top of the peak. Instead of proceeding to drive the Yankees off the hill, Johnson had elected to wait below for further orders.[52]

Ewell, of course, was livid. Johnson had been sent to climb Culp's Hill. Why had he disobeyed orders? Turner provided the reason, a note captured from a Union courier. Sykes, commander of the Federal Fifth Corps, reported he was within four miles of Gettysburg, moving to join Slocum's Twelfth Corps already occupying Culp's Hill. Their combined numbers were too many for one Rebel division to contest. Johnson thought it better to stay below the heights.

Although Ewell disapproved of Johnson's timid determination not to contest the slope, swearing to those nearby that he would "hold that officer accountable,"[53] there was little he could do now. The chance to flank the enemy's breastworks on Cemetery Hill was gone. All that was left was to include Johnson in the demonstration when Longstreet began his attack come morning. Turner was sent back to Johnson with these instructions.

The night was now fading, and darkness was replaced by the gray mist that preceded dawn. Deciding to put all trifles behind before the day's demands were upon him, Ewell took Early, Rodes, and his aides back to Mrs. Blocher's small house to beg some breakfast.

* * * *

After the war, Early, Trimble, and Gordon each asserted that the South had lost Gettysburg due to Ewell's failure to drive the bluecoats from Cemetery Hill late the afternoon of July 1, 1863. All of Ewell's former subordinates wrote that they had urged the assault that would have captured the high ground, but that Ewell would not listen to their advice. He could not bring himself to make that crucial decision.

While these accusations were made after Ewell died, when he could not defend himself, it is doubtful whether they would have bothered him. "Yes, I know I have been blamed for not having pressed my advantage the first day at Gettysburg," he acknowledged afterwards, "but then, I cannot see why I should be censured. General Lee came upon the ground before I could have possibly done anything; and after surveying the enemy position, he did not deem it advisable to attack until reenforced."[54] Ewell would not fight without orders, and to his mind, they never came from Lee.

Was Ewell (or Lee) right or wrong in not attacking Cemetery Hill? The answer most reasonably lies in practical facts —

the true chances for success.

At the time that the Yankee line broke and their troops began streaming toward Cemetery Hill, the enemy already had a significant force in place atop the heights. Colonel Orland Smith's 2,000-man brigade had been posted there as a reserve, bolstered by Buford's 1,600 cavalry troops. Over forty guns were entrenched. And the lead elements from Slocum's Twelfth Corps, General Stannard's 2,100 soldiers, were just now filing into position. Added to the remnants of the Eleventh and First Corps, about 10,000 men, the Union presented a formidable front to contest any attempt by the Rebels to drive them from their elevation.[55]

The Federals' defense, of course, was not passive. "We formed a line of battle in town," Lieutenant Warren Jackson, Eighth Louisiana, Hays' Brigade, recalled, "and Company I had to go out as skirmishers. The enemy were posted on Cemetery Hill about 600 yards from town and had command of every place . . . around it . . . . We were subjected to a galling fire . . . I spent about two hours as miserably as I ever did in my life."[56]

What could Ewell muster against this force? Just 4,500 men. From Rodes' Division, only Ramseur and Doles were still in formation; Iverson, O'Neal, and Daniel were west of town, their troops disorganized and exhausted. And Early had only Avery available. Smith was posted out on York Road, protecting the Confederate flank; Hays was in Gettysburg guarding about 4,000 Federal prisoners; and Gordon was above the town and out of ammunition.

Ewell's scanty numbers were not his only problem. He had no suitable site to emplace his artillery to bear against the enemy guns. And so when Lee refused to send him reinforcement, Ewell quite obviously could not afford to charge.

In the face of this overwhelming evidence, why the disparagement of Ewell? The answer must lie in political and personal reasons, not military causes. One must study the emotional climate of the South to understand the problem. Early, Trimble, and Gordon hoped to enhance their own images by advancing the reputation of Robert E. Lee. They gained acceptance of their vitriolic assaults on Ewell because the embittered people of the South wanted an idol, a leader of the

Lost Cause, one who had done no wrong. Since Lee could not be blamed for losing Gettysburg, someone else had to be held accountable and that someone was Ewell. The result has been a manipulation of the facts. So much for the first day of Gettysburg.

As the sun rose on July 2, 1863, the South found itself in a poor position to carry on the conflict. Lee's hopes for intercepting the Yankees in column had failed, and now the enemy was entrenched on higher ground. The Rebels had few supplies at hand, and since foraging was impossible with the Federals nearby, they had to fight or flee. There was no time to maneuver, to seek a more advantageous field. Lee attempted to develop a plan, but he was uncertain of what he should do. He had changed his mind three times over the past few hours.

Much would be asked of Ewell that day, but he had little left to give. Already weak because of the continuing strain of an incomplete recovery from his amputation, he was further sapped by having not slept during the past forty-eight hours. Yet, by necessity, Ewell must face a time as tense as any he would encounter throughout the war. He was totally exhausted when the hour demanded fresh, vigorous leadership. Disaster loomed.

Day Two and After

Mrs. Blocher had been expecting Ewell and his entourage. After greeting the Rebels at her door, she took them into the dining room where a table sat heaped with fresh biscuits and hot coffee. The officers mumbled a hasty "thanks," then went for the food. Ewell, less ravenous than the others, was the first to note that Mrs. Blocher was distressed. He asked why she was troubled.

"[I'm] frightened," she answered.[1] She knew the battle would soon re-start, and she was worried whether both she and her daughters would be safe.

Showing Southern chivalry, Ewell quickly arranged for a wagon to take the women to the rear. He helped them into the cart, then ordered an aide to accompany the ladies, to find a safe place for them to stay for the next few days.

The sun was now above the horizon. As Early and Rodes left to join their troops, Ewell returned to the red barn to wait for Longstreet to start his assault. For over an hour, Ewell listened in vain for the Rebel cannons to roar from his right. Exasperated by the delay, Ewell summoned Campbell and sent him to Lee. "Tell him," he ordered, "I am ready and waiting."[2] Ewell should have also mentioned that Culp's Hill remained in enemy hands, but he evidently decided against beginning Lee's day with bad news.

About 7:00 a.m., two riders galloped up the road out of the west to approach Ewell, observing from the doorway of the red barn. After dismounting, Colonel Charles Venable reported that Longstreet was delayed in getting organized. His charge against the Union left would not start until 9:00 a.m. Venable then asked a question from Lee. "Can you attack from your position?"[3]

Twice Ewell had argued Lee out of that proposition, and now he had to do so again. Grimly determined to prove he was not able to mount an offense, Ewell insisted that Venable accompany him to the front where he would see for himself that

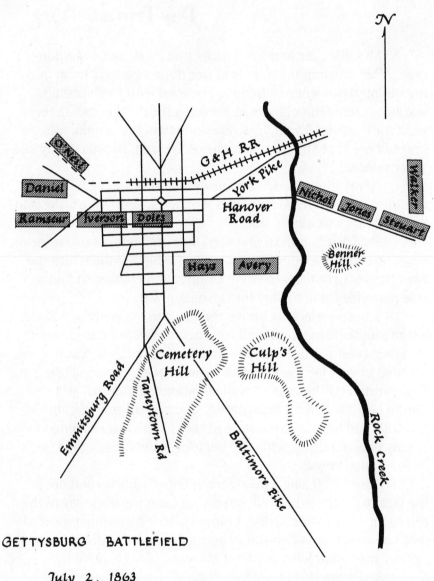

GETTYSBURG BATTLEFIELD

July 2, 1863

7:00 a.m.

the enemy's entrenchments were impregnable to an assault from the north.[4] Ewell mounted his horse and led Venable west of Gettysburg, where Rodes had deployed his men. Ramseur, Iverson, and Doles were arrayed west to east along the Hagerstown Road; Daniel and O'Neal were located above Ramseur. Noting that all five of the brigades were a good distance from Cemetery Hill, Ewell explained that they could not get any closer without falling within range of the Federal guns high on the heights.

Ewell's next stop was at Early's bivouac, below Gettysburg in front of Cemetery Hill. Only two brigades, Hays' and Avery's, were under the cover of the woods there. Smith and Gordon were still posted far out on York Road, protecting against a possible flank attack by the Yankees. Venable saw that while Early had access for charging the slope, he lacked the numbers for a successful assault.

Retracing his steps back into Gettysburg, Ewell turned right on Hanover Road, leading Venable east for Johnson's post. Three brigades, Nichols', Jones', and Steuart's, were in a line behind the road fronting Culp's Hill. Walker's men were entrenched at a right angle to the other troops, facing east, guarding against a Federal movement against the Rebel's left flank. A meandering brook, Rock Creek, bubbled between Johnson and his adversary on the knoll, protecting his troops from assault, but making any offense on his part difficult.

Venable was convinced that Ewell was right. An offense by the Second Corps made no sense; its position was suitable only for a defense. His concurrence pleased Ewell, who then led the way back to his headquarters. As the pair approached the red barn, they saw two Rebel officers, Trimble and Lee, standing outside. Ewell hurriedly dismounted to greet his superior. Lee responded with an icy stare, refusing to speak, forcing Trimble to open the conversation. He noted, with evident satisfaction, that he and Lee had just come from the cupola atop the Alms House where they had been observing the front. The Union occupation of Culp's Hill had been very evident. Trimble's comment caused Lee to erupt with anger.

"We did not . . . pursue our advantage of yesterday," he alleged. "Now the enemy are in a good position. They have the advantage [of] . . . a short and inside line while we are too much extended."[5]

Ewell could have laid the blame on Johnson, but he knew that any failure by his subordinates was his, and he took the rebuke without comment.

Just then, Early rode up. He was in a jaunty mood, but when Lee quickly repeated his accusations, Early's banter was stilled. He looked up at Culp's Hill (obviously the point of Lee's displeasure), then to Ewell. Whereas last night Early had been eager to portray that he was in charge of the corps, today he was perfectly content to let Ewell assume his right. Lee's presence seemed to offer a magnet to Ewell's subordinates. Rodes soon appeared, and Lee again noted, "We did not . . . pursue our advantage of yesterday . . . . " Given the acid atmosphere, no one spoke for some time. Lee ignored those by his side to scan the horizon with his binoculars, peering to the southwest, looking for Longstreet to initiate his charge. All was quiet for an hour. Growing ever more exasperated by the delay, Lee finally called for his horse. He would return to the right to find out why Longstreet was not moving. But before he left, Lee reminded Ewell that he was to demonstrate at the sound of Longstreet's guns, to attack only if the enemy weakened his front, but to avoid becoming so entangled he could not extricate himself if necessary.

As Lee rode off, Early approached Ewell to whisper they were not ready to fight. They had not yet emplaced their artillery.[6] He had been hesitant to reveal this while Lee was there. The two generals hurriedly mounted and headed east to tend to the guns.

While Lee rode west and Ewell went east, the Union army was completing its dispositions. They had over 65,000 men at hand: Slocum's Twelfth Corps were up on Culp's Hill, backed by Sykes' Fifth Corps to their rear, below the rise; Howard's Eleventh Corps and Hancock's Second Corps were west on Cemetery Hill, with Doubleday's First Corps in reserve behind the heights; and Sickles' Third Corps extended the Federal line southward along Cemetery Ridge. The only troops yet to reach the scene were Sedgwick's Sixth Corps, 13,000 in all, hurrying to Gettysburg, expected that afternoon.

When Ewell arrived east of Gettysburg, he found that he had been right in his observations yesterday. There were few if any suitable sites for posting his cannons. Just a treeless rise called "Brenner's Hill" showed promise. The slight elevation lay halfway between Johnson's camp and Culp's Hill, near Ewell's red barn headquarters. Offering no cover, and so small there was room for only about twenty weapons (to oppose more than a hundred Yankee guns), the slope was a death trap.[7] Most would have protested at being sent to occupy such an exposed position, but Latimer, the "Boy Major," moved without a murmur and unlimbered his pieces.

Having attended to his artillery, Ewell started back to Gettysburg to complete preparations for the coming fight. He followed Hanover Road west into the village, then stopped in front of a church with a tall steeple. The belfry seemed an ideal spot for observing a battle. Ewell dismounted, went into the chapel, and decided to stay. He would establish his command headquarters there.[8] Minutes later, a messenger from Lee arrived to inform Ewell that Longstreet had postponed his attack until 4:00 p.m. Since it was only noon and four more hours were available for dispositions, Ewell felt no need to hurry. He called Gordon in from the flank to form a reserve for Hays and Avery, then he relaxed. Suffering from both physical and mental exhaustion, he probably was overcome by the need to sleep. At any rate, when Longstreet finally opened "on schedule," Ewell was no more prepared for action than he had been at noon. It was the first of a series of blunders and inadequacies that should have never happened.

Longstreet's guns announced his charge against Sickles, defending the Union left. Ewell's artillery provided support as Latimer bombarded the enemy right on Cemetery Hill. With their few weapons in the open, the Rebel cannons presented an inviting target to over one hundred Union guns, who answered Ewell's barrage with a terrible vengeance. Despite his being at such a disadvantage, Latimer held his position, giving as good as he took for over two hours.

At first, Ewell watched the exchange from his post high in the church belfry. He soon grew tired of the clamor, however, a seeming waste of both shells and soldiers, and left his cupola to join Early, stationed below Cemetery Hill. At 6:00 p.m., Rodes suddenly appeared with compelling news: the enemy was drawing men from Ewell's front, shifting them left to reinforce Sickles, who had failed to stem Longstreet's onslaught. The opportunity to launch a successful assault, as Lee had anticipated, lay open to Ewell.[9]

Still smarting from Lee's rebuke delivered that morning, Ewell saw a chance to redeem himself in his superior's eyes. He ordered an attack in echelon. Johnson would begin the assault by charging Culp's Hill; Early would approach Cemetery Hill from the east, using the saddle between the two heights; and finally Rodes would rush that elevation from the west.

The plan was sound, but no one was ready. Rodes was the first to request more time, noting that his western flank was in the air, that he needed to ask A.P. Hill's nearest troops to close the gap to his right before he could move out. When Ewell questioned how long that would take, Rodes was forced to admit that he did not know, that he had no idea which unit lay next to him, nor where they were posted.[10] He would send a messenger west to an unknown destination to find an unnamed commander who was both able to act and willing to cooperate.

Assuming that Rodes' courier would find Hill's adjacent brigade and convince them to cover his flank, Ewell still looked to send Johnson ahead at once. He found this impossible. Smith, picketing York Road east of Gettysburg, reported a Yankee force approaching Johnson's position. If the account was accurate, Johnson would be forced to hold in place to defend his post. He could not launch his assault. Turning to Early for advice, Ewell was reminded that Smith had submitted a false report of Federals in his area yesterday. Jubal suggested sending a reliable man to check out the scene, and if he found the way clear, to then go on to Johnson and tell him to charge. Ewell accepted Early's recommendation, and Gordon was selected to ride east.[11] As daylight slowly faded, Ewell waited anxiously, his frustration rising as he wondered if and when he would ever attack.

At 7:30 p.m., rifles barked to the east. Johnson's men were advancing! Early had guessed right; there were no enemy troops threatening Ewell's left flank. The battle had begun! Through the gathering gloom, Ewell could see Johnson's lines creeping slowly ahead, their progress marked by the red flare of muskets firing. Answering bursts identified the Northern position at the base of Culp's Hill. When the Rebels reached Rock Creek, several hundred yards short of the enemy breastworks, they came to an abrupt halt. No one had reconnoitered the ground earlier in the day, and only now did they discover that the water separating them from the Yankees was too deep to ford. The only shallow point for crossing was upstream, a spot so narrow that Johnson was forced to switch from line to column in order to get over the creek.[12]

As Johnson herded his confused men into the murky water of Rock Creek, the courier sent to locate A.P. Hill's closest force returned to report that he had talked to General James Lane, in command of Pender's Division. While he was eager to engage the enemy, Lane said that his actions would be guided by conditions on his front, not those faced by Ewell's corps.

"Go back," Ewell snapped to his scout. "Tell [Lane] that I am attacking . . . and ask his cooperation."[13] As his courier rode west to re-contact Lane, Ewell hurried south to see Early, to commit his troops into battle as soon as Johnson had crossed Rock Creek. Ewell meant to fight, whether Lane joined him or not.

It was dark before Johnson finally formed his men below Culp's Hill. His troops, frustrated by their long delay, ran recklessly forward. Their fire, and the reply by the enemy, roared as one explosive crackle that was so loud the awesome Rebel yell could not be heard above the din. Initially, the flash of rifles revealed two distinct lines shooting at each other, but they soon merged into a single whirl of red. This was the critical moment that Ewell had been waiting for, and turning to Early, he ordered him ahead.

Hays advanced on the right. Avery who was astride his mount, and was the only officer on horseback,[14] urged his men forward on the left. The Federals, firing from three positions, the base of Cemetery Hill, halfway up the elevation, and from the peak, expected the Confederates to charge directly at them, but Early's troops ran instead for the saddle east of the eminence. In the dark, hidden by the shadows from the heights, the bulk of the two Southern brigades poured into the chasm, then turned

235

right to climb the slope. Their vantage flanked the Yankee soldiers below Cemetery Hill, forcing a retreat up the rise. As the Union first line scrambled for cover, Hays' and Avery's troops followed them in close pursuit. The bluecoats posted halfway up the slope saw their comrades coming, but instead of grimly holding in place to contest the Rebel's charge, they, too, elected to run. The panic was contagious. When both Federal lines surged in disorder over the crest of Cemetery Hill, they carried those atop the peak with them as they raced south along Cemetery Ridge. Early's men found the summit virtually empty. Only a handful of Federals remained willing to fight, and the enemy cannons stood silent, waiting for Confederate hands to put them to use.

Ewell saw it all and cheered Early's success. But when he looked for his reinforcements to join with Hays and Avery, to solidify their just-won ground, no one was in sight. Left of Cemetery Hill, Johnson was engaged in a fierce but futile battle to dislodge his adversary from their breastworks below Culp's Hill. In the center, Early had sent all his available troops into the charge. His only reserves, Gordon's brigade, were still north of Gettysburg while their leader was absent, not yet returned from his mission to see Smith, then Johnson. Rodes should have been attacking from the right, supported by Lane, but there was no sign of either division.

The men who had folded under Early's onslaught on Cemetery Hill belonged to the Eleventh Corps, the same troops who were routed by Stonewall at Chancellorsville and by Ewell yesterday. Only two of the six brigades, however, (Harris' and von Gilsa's) bore the shame this time. Howard's remaining units, along with Carroll's troops from the Second Corps, rushed to the scene to counterattack, driving the Confederates off the peak. Early's men came to a halt halfway down the slope as if to make a stand, but the Federal pressure was too much. Almost as fast as Early's charge had materialized, it disintegrated and dissolved into the black of the night.

The only remaining activity was on the left, where Johnson fought toe-to-toe with the enemy. Neither side advanced, neither retreated. But as the minutes ticked by, the combat ebbed, then died. The Yankees held. Ewell's assault had failed.

Distraught by the bumbling performance of his subordinates, Ewell rode back to his church quarters to await reports on
the battle. He was prepared to lash out in anger because of the
ineptness. When Early arrived, Ewell bitterly berated him for
failing to send in his reserves. Jubal defended his holding
Gordon's men at bay. "The attempt would have been a useless
sacrifice," he blustered, conveniently forgetting the fact that the
troops were leaderless, as Gordon had been sent to York Road
to check out Smith's report of Union threats to his flank.[15] He
blamed Rodes for not supporting him from the right. Adding to
Ewell's black mood was the news that Avery had been killed,
shot from the saddle during the opening charge. The officer's
foolish insistence on appearances—riding into battle—had cost
him his life.

Rodes was the next to report. When Ewell belabored him
for not assaulting on the right, the Virginian offered a lame
excuse. He was delayed because Lane had refused to join him in
the attack, holding back because A.P. Hill (his commander) had
not ordered it. Rodes had finally gone ahead, but since his flank
was exposed, he came slowly and carefully, marching around
Gettysburg, taking the long way to the front. By the time he got
there, Early was already falling back, and it was too late to enter
the fight.

Ewell was so disgusted by Rodes' timidity, that months
later, when he wrote his battle report on Gettysburg, he avoided
the details of his subordinate's behavior. "Major General Rodes
did not advance," he said, "for reasons given in his report."[16]
This was the closest Ewell ever came to censuring a man under
his command.

Rodes did offer a faint hope of better things to come.
When his troops finally reached the front, they had found a
swale below the heights that protected them from the enemy
cannons on the peak. The hollow offered a perfect point for
launching a charge, should Ewell want to continue his assaults
come daybreak. His men were entrenched and ready to advance
at a moment's notice.

While Ewell considered the potential of Rodes' position,
he received word from Johnson that offered yet another option
for renewing his attacks on the enemy. After a savage fight of

over four hours, Johnson had finally driven the Union from their breastworks halfway up Culp's Hill. He was arrayed on their flank and believed that one more strong assault would push his men over the top, forcing the enemy from the high ground. Ewell quickly relayed his alternatives to Lee, who soon sent his response. Ewell was to advance on Culp's Hill come dawn. At the same time that he started his charge, Longstreet (who had also gained a vantage on the right) would send his troops forward.

Determined to succeed, Ewell strengthened his left. He took Daniel and O'Neal from Rodes and moved them east to join Johnson's command. Smith was withdrawn from his post on York Road and added to the assaulting force. And Walker, who had been in reserve during the charge that had penetrated the enemy right flank, rejoined the division. Hays' and Avery's troops were placed within striking distance along Hanover Road.[17] The attack, however, would not be supported by Rebel artillery. During the late afternoon exchange with the enemy, Latimer had held until his guns were literally blown off Benner's Hill. He was down to just four cannons when he was hit by a Yankee shell fragment that almost severed his arm. Despite his wounds, the "Boy Major" had safely extracted his weapons, but he could no longer occupy the only available site within range of Culp's Hill.[18]

In order to be close to the morrow's action, Ewell once again moved his headquarters, shifting to a house on the Hanover Road, 150 yards short of Rock Creek. As he lay down to to get desperately needed sleep, Ewell was heartened by further assurance of a probable victory in the morning. The Yankees were making lots of noise, the sound emanating from the Baltimore Pike, a sign that a withdrawal was taking place.[19]

Scarcely three hours after Ewell put his weary head to the pillow, he was rudely awakened by the loud roar of cannons. The shelling was too close to be Longstreet's pieces, and since his own guns were not scheduled to fire, the sounds had to be Federal artillery, opening on Johnson. No matter. Because the Southern attack was supposed to start at dawn, it made little difference if the bluecoats initiated the action. Ewell's stoical acceptance of battle soon changed to despair. He received word from Lee, telling him that Longstreet would be delayed, that the

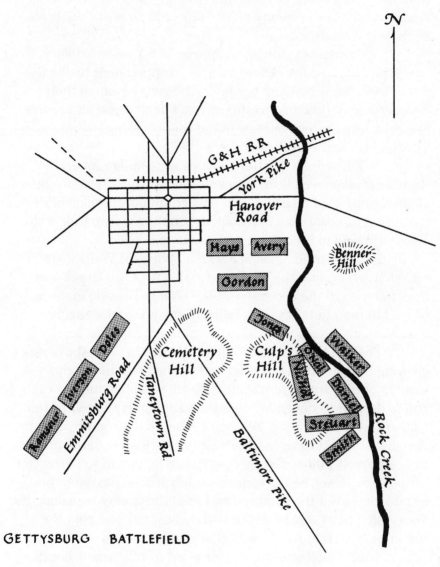

GETTYSBURG BATTLEFIELD

July 3 , 1863

4:00 a.m.

charge from the right had been postponed until 10:00 a.m.[20] Without a coordinating assault to occupy the Yankee's attention, the Union could concentrate their men against Ewell. His odds for driving the enemy off of Culp's Hill were suddenly and decisively diminished.

The battle was fought in spurts. The Yankee artillery, which had opened fire before sunrise, stopped their fusillade about 5:00 a.m. A half an hour later, the guns resumed their bombardment, this time to support an infantry assault against Steuart's brigade, entrenched in the Union's former bastions. The Rebels fought off the charge.[21]

At 7:00 a.m., while the Yankees were still recuperating from their offensive effort, Johnson sent Walker's men up the slope. Ewell could hear the charge, a continuing crackle of rifles that failed to fluster the bluecoats he could see atop Culp's Hill. The rattle died in less than thirty minutes.[22]

Johnson tried again at 8:00 a.m. Whereas Walker's men had charged against the Union right, this time the attack was directed toward the Federal center. O'Neal's Brigade made a brave attempt, but they, too, failed to penetrate the enemy line.[23]

The sun had risen, and this third day of Gettysburg was growing hot and humid. Already concerned that his troops would not bear up under the heat, Ewell soon had further reason to despair. A courier rode into headquarters to report that soldiers were infiltrating Johnson's rear.[24] If the rumor was true, then Ewell would have to withdraw his troops. He dared not risk the capture of Johnson's whole division. Reluctant to surrender his position, Ewell sent a request to Jeb Stuart (posted to his left) to check out the rumor. If he found the enemy menacing the Rebel left, Stuart was to attack with his cavalry and rout the Union, leaving Johnson free to continue his battle.

While Ewell was waiting for word from Stuart, a courier arrived with new orders. At exactly 1:00 p.m. Lee planned to open a massive artillery bombardment on the center of the enemy line. Ewell's cannons were to join in the barrage. Once the Yankees' ranks had been softened and their guns silenced, Longstreet would finally make his charge.[25]

Ewell had been counting on Longstreet to attack within

minutes, but now with the advance postponed for over four
hours, the enemy was free to rush men from their left to the
right at will to stem his attempt to seize Culp's Hill. Johnson's
chances for carrying the eminence had been dealt a fatal blow.

Bearing the bad tidings gracefully, Ewell issued instructions to have the guns unlimbered and ready for the coming
fusillade. As his aides were contacting the batteries, passing on
Ewell's orders, Lee heard from Johnson that he had sent
Walker's troops in yet another dash against the heights. The
Rebels had been repelled for the third time that morning, and
resorting to desperation, Johnson would now try one, last
attack. Daniel's and Steuart's well-tested troops would charge at
10:00 a.m.

The Rebels advanced with fury, but just as Ewell had anticipated, the enemy's numbers were too great. Hidden behind
huge boulders and tall oaks, they opened a withering blast of
musketry that slowed, then stopped Ewell's determined troops.
As the Confederates retired, the Yankees counterattacked, driving not only their oncoming adversary but also the other Confederates still on Culp's Hill off the rise and back across Rock
Creek.[26] Ewell's defeat was total, and except for his artillery
support of Longstreet's grand attack against the Federal center,
his role at Gettysburg had ended.

The sun burned brightly in a cloudless sky. The summer
day was sultry, dreamy, even peaceful following the finish of
Ewell's furious fight. The calm belied the carnage to come.

A little past 1:00 p.m., the curt bray of two cannons
echoed from Longstreet's front. This timid demonstration was
the cue to start the artillery extravaganza that Lee had envisioned. With a mighty bellow, every Southern piece at hand
(thirty-two belonging to Ewell) exploded as one. The Yankees
replied in kind, and soon both fronts were blinded by clouds of
thick, acrid smoke. The earsplitting thunder of cannons grew
until even shouted commands could not be heard above the
booming tumult. For over an hour, both sides sustained their
barrage. While spectacular at the start, the duel grew ever more
sinister as it persisted. How much longer could it continue?
What damage was being done to the Northern emplacements?
Would the Yankee line be sufficiently softened to allow a suc-

cessful Rebel attack? These answers could only come from testing the Federals' position, by executing Lee's planned charge.

The enemy was the first to slacken their fire. Then Lee followed suit. As the billowing white smoke lifted to drift eastward over the Union line, all eyes turned to the west, to look for Longstreet's advance. Ewell's post, north of Cemetery and Culp's Hills, was blocked by the heights. He could not see the front, but the quiet that followed the end of the artillery clash told him that again, Longstreet was delayed. Seconds ticked away, the minutes accumulated, but the assault did not start. Finally, as if rising out of the ground, fifteen thousand Rebel soldiers suddenly appeared atop Seminary Ridge, marching down the slope, heading for the center of the Union line. Pickett's Charge was underway.

The advance was divided into two lines, separated by an interval of 600 yards. The troops stepped with the precise unanimity of a military drill, their ranks perfectly aligned, elbow to elbow. At first the Federals only watched, fascinated by the audacity of the oncoming Southerners. But as the Rebels began closing on the Yankee position, the bluecoats opened fire with rifles and cannon, ripping gaping holes in the closely knit Confederate array. Paying little heed to their losses, Pickett's men closed ranks and continued their charge in formation. The wave of gray reached and broke through the Union line. Wreathed in the swirling smoke from the guns that had failed to thwart them, the triumphant Southerners looked back for the reinforcements thought to be trailing closely behind them. They saw only the enemy, pouring from every direction, surrounding them. Standing in an eddy of blue, the Confederates were soon inundated, every man on his own. Some fought and died, many dropped their weapons and surrendered, only a few turned to retreat to the safety of their own lines. Less than half of those who began the charge reached the haven of Seminary Ridge. The Yankees could not pursue, as the will to fight had drained from everyone. By 4:00 p.m., the field was still.

"We knew of Longstreet's failure," Campbell Brown wrote in his memoirs, "[so] we were not unprepared for the order to retreat."[27]

Ewell received his instructions in person. Shortly before sunset, he was called by Lee to A.P. Hill's headquarters along the Cashtown Road. Ewell rode west through the gathering darkness, spotted the command tent, and dismounted. When he entered the canvas shelter, he found Lee and Hill studying a map spread on a narrow table, lit by a single candle. Lee had nothing to say. He simply handed Ewell written orders to pull his corps back to Oak Ridge (the point where the battle had begun), put his troops in a defensive line, then start to move his wounded back to Virginia, crossing the mountains at Cashtown before turning south for Williamsport. Once the injured men were safely gone, the rest of the army would use a more direct route to the Potomac, marching south to Fairfield where they would cross the heights through a gap at Monterey Springs.

When Lee reached Waynesboro, he would turn left for Leitersburg, Hagerstown, and then Williamsport. Longstreet's corps would lead the retreat; A.P. Hill's men would follow; Ewell's divisions would be last in line. Lee's instructions were so clear and concise that there was no need for verbal additions. And Lee's mood was so somber, his face revealing "an expression of sadness . . . never [seen] before,"[28] Ewell did not bother asking for commentaries. He nodded his acquiescence, left the tent, and mounted his horse to ride back to his men. After arriving at his headquarters on Hanover Road, Ewell issued his own orders for retiring from the area around Gettysburg. Each of the divisions was to begin pulling back at 2:00 a.m., meeting by sunrise along Oak Ridge. They were to move in secret, as quietly as possible. Ewell next called Major John Harmon, his quartermaster, to his side. He wanted the corps' wagons started south for Fairfield at once. "Get that train safely across the Potomac," Ewell thundered, "or I never want to see your face no more!"[29] Harmon had been intimidated often in the past by Stonewall, and he was usually immune to his superiors' threats. Ewell, however, was so vehement, his words had their desired effect. The wagons were moving by 3:00 a.m.

The night was black with the moon hidden behind a cover of thickening clouds, so the withdrawal was conducted without benefit of light. After moving to a new command post on Cashtown Road, Ewell waited for his divisions to come. Rodes reported first about 4:00 a.m., positioning his troops along the railroad cut on Oak Ridge. Early arrived next, emplacing his men north of Rodes' location. Johnson failed to appear.

To complicate the situation, a dense white mist suddenly settled over the ground, obscuring the sun's rise. Ewell was concerned that Johnson had been intercepted by the bluecoats, that his men had all been captured. But later that morning, bedraggled lines of gray came out of the fog to file into the camp. Johnson ruefully admitted that he had been lost, that when he attempted to circle the village instead of coming through Gettysburg, he had drifted astray. He had spent the last six hours wandering about the countryside.[30] Ewell ruefully accepted the explanation. Even in retreat, nothing was going right. Ewell put Johnson into line alongside Rodes, then had Sandie Pendleton ride to Lee to say that the Second Corps was assembled, ready for action.

When Sandie returned after seeing Lee, he was red-faced with chagrin. He had given Ewell's report, then offered this commentary, "I hope . . . the other two corps are in as good condition . . . as ours." Lee replied icily, "What reason have you to suppose they are not?"[31] While Pendleton was embarrassed by his encounter with Lee, Ewell was encouraged. He recalled how taciturn Lee had been last night, and it was a relief to know that his superior had regained his usual cold aplomb.

The ground Ewell occupied was the site of the First Day's battle. Dead Yankee soldiers from the encounter were strewn about the area, their corpses decaying under the hot sun. The bodies were so bloated that "buttons were broken from the loose blouses . . . and the baggy pantaloons fitted like a skin—so blackened that the head looked like a cannonball."[32] A hideous smell filled the air, causing many of the troops to become sick to their stomachs. Ewell wanted to move his men to a less rancid position, but was reluctant to do so, afraid of a Union attack. But when the soft drizzle that began about 1:00 p.m. intensified into a raging thunderstorm, Ewell felt it safe to relocate. Later that afternoon, he took his troops west, away from the battleground. The rain continued to pour into the night, causing Ewell to violate one of Lee's strictest rules. He told the men to dismantle a nearby fence and use the rails to build warming fires.

Scheduled to start the trek south at dawn, Ewell roused his corps at 2:00 a.m. The men stood in place in the continuing rain for ten hours, held up by Longstreet, who again was slow to move. The mood of the troops as they waited in line was not that of a beaten army. "The fight wasn't out of the troops by any means," Campbell noted. "They felt that the position and not the enemy had outdone us."[33] Almost all of them looked forward to renewing the fray on more equal terms.

Ewell finally moved out at noon. Rodes led the parade, Johnson was next in line, and Early brought up the rear. The men plodded through thickening mud one step at a time, fending off repeated nips at their heels by Union cavalry. About 4:00 p.m., after arriving in Fairfield, Ewell sent the corps into camp while he rode into the tiny village to look for Lee and report his position. Upon reaching the command post, he was told that Yankees had attacked Harmon's wagons last night and that his entire train had been destroyed. Ewell was outraged by the news, by another example of a cowardly enemy who hid behind impregnable breastworks, only attacking when they found defenseless people. He stormed into the house that Lee was occupying, and demanded permission to go after the Union horsemen to avenge his loss. "We must let those people alone for the present," Lee replied. "We will try them again some other time."[34] But Ewell would not accept Lee's advice. He was too angry to listen to reason, and continued to rage that he be allowed to punish the Yankees. Lee was finally forced to order Ewell, still raving, to return to his men.

The next morning, Ewell had his troops up at dawn, moving toward the pass over South Mountain. Their progress came to a halt after they had marched only two miles. Those at the front of the advance had found that the gap was too narrow for both men and wagons to go through at the same time. While delayed, Ewell's rear was attacked by Union cavalry, a thrust weakly made and easily repelled by Rodes' Division. Ewell's columns reached the peak about noon, then descended, arriving at Waynesboro at dusk. As his troops set up camp, Ewell sent Jed Hotchkiss to report to Lee. He was probably reluctant to go himself because he was embarrassed by his "performance" of yesterday. Hotchkiss brought back the good news that Ewell

had not lost all of his wagons after all. The train had been am-
bushed by the enemy cavalry, but before many had been captured, Brigadier General John Imboden's Confederate horsemen
arrived to drive the Yankees away. Even more important, when
Hotchkiss mentioned the Union attack on Ewell's rear earlier
that day, Lee had suggested the retaliation that Ewell had so
vehemently requested last night. "If these people keep coming
on," Hotchkiss quoted Lee, "turn back and thrash them."[35]

"By the blessing of Providence," Ewell shouted, "I will do
it!" He immediately went to Rodes and ordered him to take his
men back to the pass to ferret out and punish their pursuers.
Ewell personally led the search, but he was unable to find the
Federals and bring them to bay. The enemy troopers had disappeared into the dark. Well past midnight, Ewell's and Rodes'
disappointed soldiers trudged back into Waynesboro.

The Second Corps marched to Hagerstown on July 8th.
As the troops set up camp, Ewell and the other Rebel leaders
began to reconnoiter, looking for suitable ground for building a
strong defensive position. They surveyed for two full days
before deciding on their alignments, days that were free from
enemy harassment. When the Yankees finally appeared on July
10th, the Rebel entrenchments were in place, and now the
Federals had to take the time to study the ground. They probed
the Southern line, looking for weaknesses, making their plans to
attack. Meade was ready by July 12th, but just as he was set to
launch his assaults, the skies darkened and it started to rain.
Thunder and lightning accompanied the steady downpour,
which lasted throughout the night and into the morning. As the
rain fell, the Potomac, at Lee's back, rose, flooding its banks,
jeopardizing the Rebels' escape across the stream. Lee was
short of supplies. He could not afford a battle. He had to ford
the water now while he still had the chance. His order was
dispatched to Ewell and the other corps.

After dark on July 13th, Ewell quietly took his men out of
their lines one division at a time. Rodes left first, and Johnson
followed. Early's troops were the last to withdraw. Ewell assumed that Lee's arrangements for crossing the stream were
working well, and so he did not abandon the front until his last
man had left the entrenchments. He then mounted his horse and

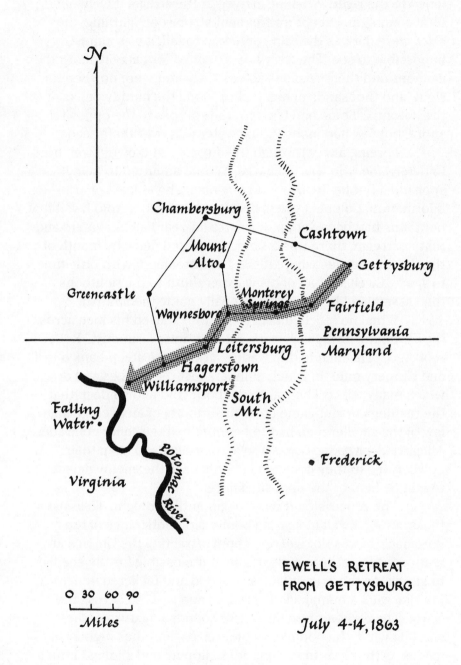

N

Chambersburg

Cashtown

Mount
Alto

Gettysburg

Greencastle

Monterey
Springs

Waynesboro

Fairfield

Pennsylvania

Leitersburg

Maryland

Hagerstown

Williamsport

South
Mt.

Falling
Water

Potomac River

Frederick

Virginia

0 30 60 90

Miles

EWELL'S RETREAT
FROM GETTYSBURG

July 4-14, 1863

loped to the river. When he arrived at the stream, Ewell found total confusion. Except for frequent strobes of lightning, the skies were dark as the rain continued to fall. It was almost impossible to see. The ferry boats needed for carrying both the cannons and their caissons across the water were nowhere in sight, and thousands of men milled along the muddy banks of the Potomac. Some had tried to wade across to the opposite shore, but few had made it. The water was over their heads.

Forcing a way through the disordered crowd, Ewell tried to determine who was in charge. No one admitted to being responsible, but he finally found one man who at least offered information. Colonel Corley, Lee's quartermaster, told Ewell that pontoons had been set up downstream near Falling Waters and that upstream, there was a sandbar located near the mouth of the Comocoheague where it met the Potomac.[36] With little time to spare, Ewell sent all of his wagons south to the pontoons, then assembled his men to personally guide them north.

When he reached the river, Ewell started his men across the sandbar. "It was very dark, raining, and . . . muddy," Rodes reported. "The men had to wade . . . down the steep bank of soft and slippery mud, in which numbers lost their shoes and down which many fell."[37] The water was both cold and so deep that the rushing current came up to the armpits of an average man. A few of the smaller men had to be toted by their taller comrades. All carried cartridge boxes above their heads to keep their powder dry so they could still fight in case the enemy decided to follow them to the opposite shore.

The procession did not begin until midnight. To assist the crossing, Ewell lit roaring bonfires on both sides of the Potomac. He was not worried about attracting the Union's attention, as the storm made it almost impossible for the enemy to attack. As the bright flames crackled and flickered under the pouring rain, a human chain bobbed and weaved across the water. The night air was filled with sound, a mixture of the snarling wind, the boom of thunderclaps, and the laughter of the troops as they saw their comrades slipping and sliding in the water. Dawn broke, and while the sun was hidden by gray, floating rain clouds, it became light enough to see that the crossing was progressing satisfactorily. By 8:00 a.m., every man of Ewell's command was on Virginia soil. The Gettysburg campaign was finished. While it covered only five weeks out of Ewell's lifetime, it was a period that neither he nor history would ever forget.

* * * *

Ewell is commonly portrayed as the "Goat of Gettysburg" because he did not attempt to capture Cemetery Hill the first day of battle. As noted earlier, that charge is unfair. Ewell can however, be considered a "goat" for his failure of the second day. With the Union right weakened by Meade's hurrying reinforcements south to rescue Sickles from Longstreet's onslaught, the door swung open to finally seize the heights. Ewell watched as his subordinates stumbled and fell instead of marching triumphantly through the portal.

On the left, Johnson found out too late that Rock Creek was deeper than he had expected. Johnson had to shuffle from line to column to line to get his troops across, slowing his charge, losing precious daylight the Rebels could not afford. Early did well, but not well enough. By limiting his risks, moving to the attack with only two brigades, he was unable to capitalize on his penetration of the Federal front. And Rodes' performance can only be considered pitiful. When the time came for him to enter the fight, he was not there. His troops were still north of Gettysburg, far from the enemy line, and he never did coordinate his actions with Hill's adjacent division. When he finally did advance, he was late because he had not accounted for having to circle the village.

Ultimately, Ewell must shoulder the blame for his subordinates' failures. Told to be ready for action by first light, he received twelve extra hours to prepare to fight because of Longstreet's almost predictable delays. Ewell squandered this reprieve by sitting still instead of reconnoitering his front. It was a repeat of Cedar Mountain, where Ewell spent the afternoon of August 9th, 1862, in relaxation, only to find a mill pond blocking his path to the front when finally called to attack.

Ewell openly acknowledged his mistakes. "It took a dozen

blunders to lose . . . Gettysburg," he admitted, "and [I] committed a good many of them."[38] Privately, however, he held Johnson and Rodes accountable. He was disappointed with Johnson, who refused to obey Ewell's orders to attack Culp's Hill on the first night of the battle, then was slow to mount a charge the second day because he had not reconnoitered his front. And Ewell was so disenchanted with Rodes' performance that same day that he could not bring himself to discuss the subject in his official report.

While it is easy to be critical of Ewell, one must concede he had good reasons for his substandard performance. He had gone without sleep for forty-eight straight hours by sunrise on July 2nd. Before his leg was amputated, Ewell was known as "the toughest . . . most enduring man in the army." Now he could no longer rely on nervous energy to compensate for a lack of sleep. And during those twelve, critical hours, when Ewell might have perfected his plans, he showed himself to be too drained to do all he had to do.

In addition to his physical problems, Ewell no doubt had mental strain to deal with, too. He was posted on the Confederate left, apart from the rest of Lee's army, left to wonder why others (Longstreet) were not meeting agreed-upon schedules. And Lee had imposed an impossible condition on Ewell, "not to become so involved he could not readily extricate his troops." Lee's repeated ambiguity probably raised questions in Ewell's view as to what Lee meant or whether he would again change his mind. Most important, Ewell's confidence was no doubt shaken. His feelings of inadequacy because of his amputation had been alleviated by his triumph at Winchester, but the complexity of Gettysburg no doubt brought a return of self doubt.

Ewell seemed to recover his strength during the retreat from Gettysburg, but there were signs that his emotional control was slipping away. His threat to Major Harmon, his unreasonable response to the capture of his wagon train, and his obsessional outbursts about attacking the enemy nipping at his heels showed him close to breaking under the strain. The road to glory had turned uphill.

Virginia

How did Ewell view the results of Gettysburg? Did he see the contest as a turning point, a faltering step backward toward ultimate defeat for the South? Ewell left no comment, but he certainly knew of the importance of the battle and his own place in it—and history. The Army of Northern Virginia lost over 20,000 troops killed, wounded, or captured in the battle, almost one-fourth of their force—men they could no longer replace. Able-bodied males, willing to enlist to fill the decimated ranks, were just not available.

Perhaps more important, Lee and his ragged troops suffered more than a depreciating defeat at Gettysburg. Their cloak of invincibility was stripped away. The Federal Army of the Potomac entered future encounters with a new, vital confidence in themselves.

Most disheartening, the Confederates' failure at Gettysburg was matched at Vicksburg, where Grant captured the main Rebel fortress on the Mississippi River. The Federal victory in the west gave them control of this mighty stream, severing the South in two, isolating their western troops from much needed supplies.[1] The burden of winning independence from the Union lay ever more heavily up on Lee's shoulders.

The morning of July 14th, 1863, Ewell was concerned about problems of a more immediate nature. His men were soaked and dead tired from their all night effort of crossing the river, but they could not stay along the shores of the Potomac. The Yankees could see them from across the water and were likely to open fire with their cannons at any moment. After calling his troops into line, Ewell marched them south for an hour before coming to a halt. As the men collapsed in column, Ewell saw that they had stopped in familiar surroundings. Jackson had camped in this same location in 1862 after routing Banks at Winchester. The site was on dry ground and fresh water was plentiful nearby, so Ewell decided to bivouac there. "The day was quite pleasant," Jed Hotchkiss recalled, "and we all dried ourselves."[2]

On the morning of July 15th, Lee began moving his force south. Longstreet took the lead, followed by A.P. Hill, then Ewell. When the Second Corps broke camp that afternoon, the order of march had Johnson up front, with Rodes next in line. Early was supposed to trail Rodes, but the progress ahead was so slow, he did not leave his bivouac until the next morning. He headed for Darksville, where Ewell was holding Johnson and Rodes.

As Early's men trudged into camp that night, they found the mood hushed with sadness. Latimer, the "Boy Major" loved by all the corps, lay dying from his Gettysburg wounds. Although the surgeons had amputated his right arm, gangrene had developed, and the doctors gave Latimer no chance of recovering.[3] Ewell was shattered by the doleful news. While he had never hesitated to order troops to probable death in combat, seeing them die was almost more than he could bear. He tried to cope with these occasions by exposing himself to the same risks he asked of his men, and while this usually helped, the danger had little meaning in the case of the twenty-year-old Latimer. The young man's death demanded revenge. Despite the late hour, Ewell sent Johnson's division back to Martinsburg that night to tear up the B & O Railroad tracks. It was a fruitless gesture, but Ewell could think of no other way to ease his bitterness.

Over the next few days, the rest of the Second Corps remained in camp. Ewell attended church services on July 17th, then rode south to Bunker Hill to confer with Lee. Hill and Longstreet also attended the briefing to discuss options open to the Rebels. Lee at first favored climbing the Blue Ridge into Loudoun County, following the Potomac River toward Washington to threaten the Union capital. While the thought was appealing, reports from scouts proved the scheme impractical. Fording the Shenandoah River, swollen from the recent rains, would be too difficult, and even if the crossing could be accomplished, Meade had positioned his cavalry in the mountain gaps. Forcing a passage would bring the Northern army to the scene, provoking a useless battle.[4]

Moving either north or west made no sense, and Lee knew, too, that he could not stay in place. The Rebels were out of food, and attempts to forage had confirmed that the local area was totally lacking in provisions. The only course left was to return to the environs of Richmond. With great reluctance, Lee ordered the retreat. Longstreet would go first, A.P. Hill would follow, and Ewell would bring up the rear.

Because he would be the last to leave the Valley, Ewell had several days to prepare for the march. He took advantage of the time by having Hotchkiss draw detailed sketches of the path that each division would take, but before he could pass the results on to his subordinates, the opportunity to attack the enemy arose. Johnson, ripping up railroad tracks to the north, reported that the Federals had incautiously dispatched a force south of the Potomac River. The bluecoats, 6,000 in all, were posted near Hedgesville and beyond being reinforced by their compatriots.[5] Ewell sent a hurried note to Lee asking permission to attack the isolated Yankees, and he quickly received the requested approval. Calling Rodes and Early to his side, Ewell offered his plan. Rodes would hurry to unite with Johnson to face the enemy, being careful not to "spook" the Union detachment from their exposed position. Meanwhile, Early would hurry his men northwest through Mill's Gap, then follow Back Creek into the enemy's rear. When Ewell's pincer was in place, the Rebels would pounce on the unsuspecting adversary.

Both Rodes and Early left that afternoon. Ewell, rushing forward to Johnson, halted that evening near Martinsburg, then drove his rig on to his subordinate's bivouac. When he arrived about midmorning, Ewell received discouraging news. Local Union loyalists had alerted the Yankees to their peril, and the enemy troops had scurried to safety over the Potomac. Ewell was disgusted. His running north to strike a blow had been in vain, and now his corps was isolated from the rest of the army. Lee moved both Longstreet and A.P. Hill south while Ewell went after the enemy in the opposite direction. Ewell now had to move quickly to close the breach. Rodes was told to turn about and head up the Valley. Johnson would fall in behind him, and Early, approaching the vacated bluecoat post from the north, would then pick up the rear.

Ewell drove at the van of the corps, which reached Winchester the night of July 22nd. The next morning he started

his long, winding columns left toward Front Royal, intending to
wheel there and continue south along the eastern slopes of the
Massanutton. About 4:00 p.m. that afternoon, the sounds of
combat arose faintly up front. As they grew louder, Ewell
pushed his men forward at a faster pace. They were marching at
double-step when a breathless rider intercepted them. He had
been sent to find and bring help to Captain C.H. Andrews' men
from Walker's Brigade, Anderson's Division, Hill's Corps, who
were engaged at Manassas Gap with an overwhelming enemy
force.[6] Ewell had to come at once.

    With Rodes beside him in the buggy, Ewell drove forward
to see a line of Rebel infantry, only 600 in all, astride the railroad
tracks, running east to west in the gap between two towering
peaks of the Blue Ridge. They were trying to slow a horde of
Union troops, four times their number, advancing at a deliberate
pace. Behind the Federal van, the gorge swarmed with
bluecoats, over 10,000 men, moving to throw their weight into
an already uneven fray. If the enemy broke through the thin
Confederate ranks, they would cut Lee's army in two, exposing
the Southerners to an assault in detail, a contest the Rebels
could not hope to win. Ewell had to find some way to stem this
tide.

    There was no time for him to form lines. Looking back,
Ewell spotted Major Eugene Blackford's elite band of riflemen at
the van, and he called the two hundred plus sharpshooters
forward to join with Andrew's besieged troops. They ran into
the gap and fired a deadly accurate fusillade toward the oncoming enemy. "These troops . . . showed great gallantry," Ewell
praised, "and though intended merely to make a show, held the
enemy back . . . . "[7] During the stalemate, O'Neal guided his men
into position behind a rise 300 yards from the front. He had an
artillery battery (Carter's) with him, and they unlimbered to the
rear of the slope. Just when the Union unleashed what they
thought would be a finishing charge, Carter opened fire, lobbing
his shells into the narrow gorge. The rounds landed with devastating effect, exploding in the crux of the Federal ranks, turning
the enemy assault into a panicked withdrawal. Through dusk
and into nightfall, the two adversaries remained at bay. Ewell
completed his dispositions, filling his front with the rest of

Rodes' division and posting Johnson's troops along the Shenandoah River. He could have saved himself the trouble. The Yankees (Major General William French with his entire Third Corps) were so timid that Ewell was able to keep the bluecoats in place by throwing a few rounds of artillery per hour in their direction.

While the Union presented no offensive threat, they did occupy the pass, ready to spring on Ewell as he marched by in column. He had to get past the Yankees, and he had to hurry before French discovered that he held an advantage in numbers. After studying his maps, Ewell came up with a novel strategy. Rodes and Johnson would withdraw to Front Royal that evening, then march south for Luray, east of the Massanuttons, in the morning. Early's troops (still above Winchester) would come west of the mountains to New Market, then cross to unite with the rest of the corps, exiting the Valley via Thornton's Gap.[8] Ewell's orders were issued and the plan executed. Everything went smoothly until the last of Johnson's troops were leaving Front Royal about 10:00 a.m. on July 24th. Northern cavalry suddenly threatened the Confederate rear. A few rounds of artillery chased them away, and both divisions arrived in Luray that afternoon. Since the Federals had elected not to follow him, Ewell halted in place for two days, to allow the troops to rest until Early appeared. His division reached the area on July 27th, and Ewell then took his corps through the gap and out of the Valley.

The weather was hot and the roads, deeply rutted by the recent rains, were execrable. Because conditions were adverse (and the bluecoats were nowhere in sight), Ewell did not force the march. He stopped in Sperryville that evening, then made an equally short trek the next day. The corps completed the retreat on July 30th, joining Lee with the rest of the army at Madison Court House.

While the men set up camp, Ewell called on his superior at Culpeper for new orders. He learned that Meade was swinging down toward Fredericksburg, looking to position his army between the Rebels and Richmond. Lee's plan to establish his defenses along the Rappahannock had to be changed; he had to hurry south to assume a position on the Rapidan River. Ewell

also found out that the Confederates' coming had been anticipated by the ladies of the South, and that many wives of the
officers were rushing north to greet their husbands. Lizinka was
among the entourage headed for Orange Court House. When he
heard the good news, Ewell quickly asked for (and received
Lee's permission) to go on leave to spend a few days with his
spouse. He put his troops on the road, then drove his buggy
ahead to be reunited with Lizinka on August 1st.[9]

Ewell's joy at seeing his wife was more than matched by
Lizinka's response when she spotted him. Unknown to Ewell, a
Boston newspaper had reported that he was killed during the
battle at Gettysburg, and she was, of course, relieved to find him
both alive and well.[10] Lizinka showered Ewell with affection, and
he reacted like a frisky puppy. He was, then, totally shocked
when she suddenly decided to go to Richmond for a few days.
Their separation brought out the worst in Ewell. He reverted to
acting the tyrant his men recalled from the early days of the
war.

The most memorable of Ewell's rages in this period came
on August 8th, the day after Lizinka had gone. When he arrived
at his headquarters (located at the base of a hill topped by Mr.
Shaw's mansion), he found that aides had taken his tent up the
peak, pitching it in front of the home. Screaming that he had not
approved any changes, Ewell refused to listen to reason, that
the new site was not only cooled by the breeze but also provided him a better view of his camp. "General Ewell," Hotchkiss
observed, "got into a towering fashion about the move."[11] His
anger reflected a need to lash out at someone.

Ewell moped until August 14th, when Lizinka returned to
his side. While he was happy that she had come back so soon,
Ewell also felt guilty because he had been so churlish while she
was away. He tried to make amends. On August 19th, Ewell
treated his staff to a picnic on top of Clark's Mountain, a peak
that overlooked the entire area. A few days later, he found
another opportunity to display his good will. Elliott Johnson,
one of his aides, had fallen off his horse while delivering a
dispatch to Lee's headquarters. Ewell went to see the chubby
captain, laid up in his tent.

"I'm sorry to see you so much hurt," Ewell offered.[12]

Johnson opened one eye and groaned inwardly when he saw Ewell. He was battered, but while he appreciated the concern that his superior was showing by visiting him, Johnson could not reveal that while on his mission, he had toppled from his horse a number of times because he had been drinking.

"You must have had a pretty bad fall," Ewell exclaimed, "but how in the world did you manage to hurt one and the opposite side of your head?'

"I don't know, Sir," Johnson mumbled, thinking rapidly as to how he would explain his many bruises. Then he had an inspiration. "[I must have] ricocheted."

The August days and evenings were hot and sticky, often interrupted by thundershowers. The men grew despondent. Not only was the weather unpleasant, but also they lacked suitable shelter, food, and clothing. Many were absent without leave. Others, like Captain Johnson, drank too much. Luckily, there was little chance that the enemy would attack Lee's position. Meade's force had been depleted when troops were sent to New York City to quell the draft riots that started on July 13th. Order had since been restored up north, but those dispatched had not yet been returned to duty.[13]

Ewell was oblivious to it all. Having Lizinka at hand, he experienced only the unfamiliar bliss of being a husband, enjoying his role to the fullest. Ewell especially liked the parties, held every evening, when he would strap on his wooden leg and dance with Lizinka. As the corps commander's wife, she was the center of attention and she seemed to revel in his rank. Naturally, when a committee of Protestant chaplains called on Ewell to demand that he stop the nightly balls, arguing that dancing was a mortal sin, he was in no hurry to comply with their wishes. He dallied with the decision until his friend, the Catholic priest, Father Sheeran, startled Ewell by agreeing with the prudish preachers.

"[Dancing] is no sin in itself," Sheeran retorted after Ewell raised the subject by making fun of the ministers, "but it might be very sinful under some circumstances."[14]

"What do you mean?"

"Parties now are entirely out of place, and have a very demoralizing effect upon your men," Sheeran explained. "How do you think our soldiers must feel, confined in their camp, living on [meager] rations . . . whilst they see their officers . . . gallanting ladies, indulging in luxuries . . . ? I tell you, General, these parties must be stopped [before] they do much injury to your men."

Sheeran's blunt advice convinced Ewell to put an end to the nightly balls, and he began to pay more attention to military duties. In early September, while he was riding along the front, carrying out a revitalized interest in his troops, Ewell came upon a band of soldiers hiding in the brush along the banks of the Rapidan. He asked them why they were assembled at this particular spot. Private Casler, pointing to a house on the opposite shore, explained that the home was an enemy picket post. After dark, they planned to go across the water to capture both the men inside and "some good, genuine coffee."[15] Did the General object?

"You'd be running a risk that is not at all necessary," Ewell admonished. "If a soldier does his duty in the ranks, that is enough without his volunteering to do any more."

While the Rebel enlisted men were disappointed because Ewell would not approve their excursion, Casler was "pleased to think that he would not rush us into danger unless it was necessary."

At that time, Lee was in Richmond conferring with President Davis about sending Longstreet's troops to Tennessee to bolster Bragg's army. With Meade in no mind to come forward and challenge the Rebels, Lee's force was essentially without an enemy. Since his army was unemployed, Lee agreed to reinforce Bragg against an oncoming Northern force led by Major General William S. Rosecrans. The decision was made to start the First Corps west. Worried that the soldiers left behind would grow lazy because they had so little to do, Lee planned a series of reviews, starting with Ewell's troops on September 9th.[16]

The first parade began at noon on a broad, open field a mile east of Orange Court House. Standing on a tall podium, watching his corps march by, Ewell could well have recalled the time two years ago when Lizinka had first come to visit him. She was here now, but today there was no "buggy tipping" incident to spoil the festivities. Lizinka saw Ewell's regiments perform flawlessly, saw him as their fearless commander, and those who observed could see her pride.

Longstreet left for Tennessee that same day, riding the rails south through North Carolina, taking a circuitous route to the Chattanooga front. Coincident with his departure, the Federal soldiers sent to New York City returned to Virginia, and Meade was quick to exploit his advantage in numbers. He led his army across the Rappahannock River toward Lee's position astride the Rapidan.[17] But just as Meade was about to strike the Rebels, a dramatic message arrived from the west. Bragg, reinforced by Longstreet, had attacked the Yankees at Chickamauga Creek on September 19th.[18] Rosecrans was routed, sent reeling back into Chattanooga, where he lay under siege. Lincoln reacted by immediately replacing Rosecrans with Major General George Thomas, hurrying Grant to the scene to assume overall command. He took two corps from Meade, sending the men to Tennessee to bolster the bluecoats invested by Bragg. The roles in Virginia were reversed. Meade was the one short of troops, and as he began to retreat, Lee saw his chance to take the offense.

On October 9th Ewell led the advance toward the Yankee encampment, now back on the Rappahannock. Heading northwest, he reached Madison Court House that evening, then started for Culpeper the next morning. Meade, however, had no intention of waiting in place to take a blow. He began a run for Washington, using the road parallel to the Orange and Alexandria railroad tracks. Lee ordered Ewell to stay on the bluecoats' heels while A.P. Hill swung left to circle Meade's army. His strategy was similar to that used by Jackson against Pope.

Ewell closed on the Federals on October 11th, skirmishing with their cavalry about ten miles north of Culpeper. He continued to pressure Meade's retreating columns the next day, following them beyond Warrenton Springs. Resuming the chase at dawn on October 13th, Ewell rode northeast with the corps' van. He soon spotted a small, shivering figure on horseback by the side of the road. Father Sheeran, Ewell's old friend, was wrapped in a blue Union blanket, trying to stay warm.

"Father," Ewell piped loudly, "were you in battle yesterday?"[19]

259

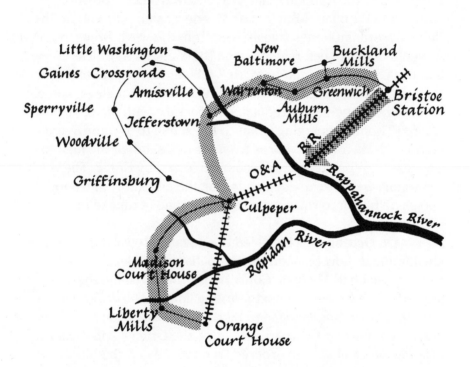

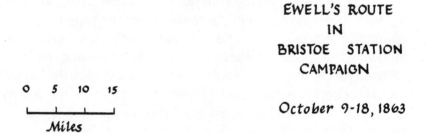

EWELL'S ROUTE
IN
BRISTOE STATION
CAMPAIGN

October 9-18, 1863

0   5   10   15
Miles

260

"Why do you ask?" Sheeran growled, obviously in a sour mood.

"I see you have a Yankee blanket, and I thought you captured it."

Sheeran's face turned tomato red as he rose to stand in his stirrups. "I was at the battle, General," he roared, "but I captured nothing. One of your good boys stole my overcoat so I have to wear my blanket."

Those riding with Ewell chortled over Sheeran's misery, but his discomfort was no laughing matter. His plight showed the pressing shortage of warm clothing in Lee's army, a need the Confederacy could not fill, a need that had led a soldier to steal from a representative of the Church.

Lee's two corps converged that night in Warrenton. The plan for Hill to reach Meade's rear had gone awry as the Yankees had retreated too quickly, but still there was cause for celebration. By driving the enemy northward, the Rebels had freed the local people from Union occupation, and they showed their gratitude by preparing a feast for the Southern troops. All manner of cakes, pies, breads, meats, and vegetables were laid out on tables along the main street when Ewell rode into town. As he stepped out of his carriage, a woman ran up from behind to embrace him, giving Ewell a loud kiss on his cheek. When the embarrassed general turned to admonish his accoster, he recognized the eighty-year-old Mrs. Semmes, a lady he had known since childhood.[20]

The festivities in Warrenton were soon over. Late that night, Lee learned that Jeb Stuart, out in front of the army, had taken his cavalry between two Yankee forces, and was now trapped. Lee ordered Ewell to rush to the troopers' rescue at first light. Up at 5:00 a.m., Ewell took his men forward toward Bristoe Station where he would feign an assault to free Stuart. He soon found the Federals, deployed his artillery, and fired a few rounds that scattered the bluecoats. A route opened for Jeb's men to ride to safety.[21]

Ewell then continued his advance northeast. About noon the sounds of musketry broke out to the left where Hill's men were known to be pressing the Federal rear. The "old" Ewell, always anxious to be the first under fire, would have wheeled and rushed to join the fray. But instead of moving to Hill's support, Ewell ignored the combat. He continued to plod forward as if Hill's encounter had nothing to do with him or his men. Those who had served under Ewell since the start of the war were aghast over his seeming indifference. Had he become conservative, perhaps even timid? Ewell was not indifferent to Hill's engagement; he was just tired again, or perhaps still incapable of extending himself beyond his psychologically and physically limited capacities. Although the campaign had not been extremely strenuous, it had robbed Ewell of an energy supply that was already dangerously low.

When the Second Corps arrived at Bristoe Station, Ewell was distressed to learn that his listless advance had deprived Lee of his force in the crucial battle of the campaign. Hill had caught up with the Yankees and foolishly charged into an ambush. Heth's division, his leading element, bore the brunt of the Federals' fire, delivered from behind a railroad cut. Before he could extricate his troops out of the snare, Hill lost the better part of two brigades. When Lee saw the dead strewn about the field, he delivered a solemn rebuke. "Well, well, General," he said to Hill, "bury these poor men and let us say no more about it."[22]

Encouraged by his victory, Meade stopped running and set up an impregnable line along Bull Run. Lee remained at Bristoe Station, sending Stuart's cavalry ahead to probe Meade's encampment, to seek an opening that the Rebels might exploit. Jeb spent all of October 15th exploring the Yankees' line, but found no avenues vulnerable to attack. The next morning low clouds formed overhead, portending rain. The skies opened at noon, and the downpour lasted for two days. As Bull Run rose over its banks (putting Meade's army on the far shore beyond the Rebels' reach), Lee knew that he had no choice but to retreat. Ewell was sent south during the storm to tear up the railroad track, and when the rain finally ended October 18th, Hill started after the Second Corps. He marched twenty miles that day, catching up with Ewell, bivouacked along the Rappahannock River.[23]

Lee decided to set up winter quarters along the stream. Ewell's post was centered on a ruined railroad span, the same bridge he had destroyed (to Taylor's consternation) in 1862.

Arraying his divisions in a triangle, Ewell emplaced Early at the crossing with most of his troops stationed in a fort or *tete du pont* that the Yankees had erected on the north bank of the river. Rodes was located east at Kelly's Ford and Johnson was positioned in the rear.

As the men dug in, Ewell began to search for a place where he and Lizinka could live. She was expected to arrive in a few weeks, and Ewell knew she would demand a comfortable house. He found a large mansion, situated well back of the Rappahannock River. The residence, however, had been recently ravaged by vandals. The glass in the multi-framed windows was broken, the plastered walls had gaping holes that looked into adjacent rooms, and most of the fine furniture had been smashed or stolen.[24] Ewell sent some privates into the home to make repairs before moving in himself on October 21st.

Those not involved in fixing up Ewell's house were busy recovering the iron rails the troops had torn up during their withdrawal from Bristoe Station. During one of the trips to the north, Captain George Williamson discovered a large cache of tin, and asked Ewell if he should bring the metal back to camp.

"A very good idea," Ewell agreed. "[My wife's] bathtub needs mending."[25]

Williamson had planned to use the tin for repairing the men's canteens. When he saw that Ewell was selfishly considering only his wife's personal needs, the captain angrily left the tin in the field. Lizinka would suffer with a leaky tub when she finally arrived at the front.

The excursions for iron along the Orange and Alexandria tracks resulted in an occasional skirmish between the Confederates and the Yankees (now venturing back south again), but no one expected anything more from Meade's army. With colder weather rapidly approaching, the Rebels looked for a seasonal lapse in action. They were engrossed, building their winter huts, when the Federals attacked about noon on November 7th. Their initial thrust was at Kelly's Ford. Beginning with an artillery barrage, the enemy caused Rodes to hurriedly set up his line of defense along the southern shore. It was a trap. As the Confederates assumed their defensive position, a Union brigade that had earlier crossed upstream charged out of the east to roll up the

Southern line. Within minutes, they captured over 300 men, and Kelly's Ford was compromised.[26]

As Rodes fell back, the Federals laid pontoons over the Rappahannock and sent wave after wave of their men across the river. When Ewell heard of the attack, he ordered Johnson's reserves to Kelly's Ford, then he galloped to Rodes' position to take charge of the defense. While he was en route, Ewell received word from Early that the Federals were forming above his line, too. Ewell could have split his reserves, sending a portion of Johnson's force to bolster Early, but he decided that since Rodes was already under attack, he had better concentrate his troops with the Virginian.

When Ewell reached Rodes' position about 3:00 p.m., he found that the situation at Kelly's Ford had stabilized. The Union assaults had ended, and while they held a line along the shore, they seemed no threat to penetrate any deeper into Rebel-held territory. Although the fighting was over, Ewell decided to stay with Rodes for awhile. He had no idea he was playing into Meade's hands, that the attack on Rodes' troops had been a feint, that Early's position was the key objective of the enemy's campaign that day.

Through the rest of that afternoon, the enemy gradually increased their pressure on Early, causing him to concentrate more and more men in the fort north of the river. He parried the Yankees' frequent but feeble attacks, and by sunset, when the shooting ebbed, Early thought he had won the engagement. Soon after dark, however, the bluecoats finally mounted their real advance, a bayonet assault by troops from Major General John Sedgwick's corps. The charge overwhelmed Early's ranks, sending his force reeling back across the water, and leaving 1,600 of his soldiers in Union hands.[27] Meade, with uncharacteristic aggressiveness, followed up his victory. He came across the water to push Early south. Rodes' flank was turned, forcing him to retire that night, too. Ewell's embarrassing retreat exposed A.P. Hill's corps, and by morning, Lee found that he had to take his entire army back to the Rapidan, the position the Army had left on October 9th when Lee started his campaign.

Ewell's performance in the fight along the Rappahannock can best be described as "absent." Ewell missed the climactic

attack because he was with Rodes when Sedgwick's men
charged out of the dark to smash Early. But although Ewell's
earlier failures could be attributed to fatigue, this time he was ill
—seriously so. His stump was red and raw with the tell-tale
signs of blood poisoning creeping up his thigh.[28] And as the
Rebels ran south on November 8th, his aides had to carry him.
They put him to bed in the Morton House by the Rapidan.

Lizinka arrived two days later. Finding her husband so ill
was shock enough, but she was even more unsettled to hear
from his physician, Dr. Hunter McGuire, that Ewell was refusing
treatment. He required rest, but would not accept a furlough.
Driven by whatever demons compelled him in these post-
Gettysburg days, Ewell raved that he would not forsake his
troops, even temporarily, during such perilous times. Lizinka
immediately took charge. After obtaining Lee's approval for
Ewell to take three weeks' sick leave, she made arrangements
for them to stay in Charlottesville, where he could relax under
her care. Lizinka even convinced Dr. McGuire to accompany
them. Ewell was prepared to go on November 15th, but that
morning, the enemy was reported gathering at Raccoon Ford.
Insisting against all reason that the threat was an emergency, he
stubbornly refused to leave the front. When the ominous assembly proved to be just Yankee cavalry probing the Rebels' defenses, Ewell lost his excuse for remaining on duty, and he went
with Lizinka to Charlottesville.

Ewell's enforced vacation lasted only thirteen days.
When he learned on November 29th that Meade was mounting a
new offensive, Ewell hurried back to rejoin the army.

The Yankees had moved east on November 26th, looking
to turn the Rebels' flank. Lee, assuming that Meade was heading
for Richmond, countered by hurrying to his right. He proceeded
parallel to the bluecoats' columns to block their path to the
capital. Ewell's corps under Early led the march, with Jubal's
division up front, Rodes' next in line, and Johnson's in the rear.
Hill's troops followed the Second Corps.

On November 27th, Meade assumed that he had successfully turned the Southern flank, and he suddenly whirled and
headed south. He was unaware that Lee, too, had abandoned his
line, and was shocked when his men collided with the center of

the winding, strung-out Rebel columns. Lee was just as surprised by the unexpected meeting as was Meade, and as a
result, the vicious fighting that followed was so confused that by
nightfall, neither side had gained an advantage. Under the cover
of darkness, Lee withdrew south to a stronger position along
Mine Run to began building entrenchments. Meade dug in where
he stood, and by noon the next day, each had completed their
fortifications and were ready to receive the other's assault. They
remained at bay for four days, spending ninety-six miserable
hours under a cold, icy rain.[29]

On December 1st, Lee's patience gave out and he ordered a charge against the Federal line. But when the Confederates reached Meade's entrenchments, they found him gone,
returned to his former encampment above the Rapidan River.
Lee had no choice but to return to his original position.

Ewell resumed command of his corps on December 4th,
replacing Early, who had been sent to the Valley on a temporary
assignment to track down and expel a Union raiding party led by
Brigadier General William Averell. Losing Early's companionship
added to Ewell's many problems: the only food available to his
hungry men was corn meal and stale potatoes; the troops could
not practice drill in cold weather because their clothes were
tattered, with new patches covering old patches; and worst of
all considering Ewell's precarious emotional health, Lizinka
hated her home at Morton Hall.

The house had once been an elegant mansion. All of the
rooms were huge. Ewell's headquarters office measured twenty-
six feet by twenty-six feet with deep bay windows. Each of the
many fireplaces were lined with beautiful Italian marble. Large
mirrors hung on almost every wall. But despite its opulence,
Morton's residence was just plain uncomfortable. The oak
floors, once covered by plush rugs, were now bare, allowing
cold air to seep in through cracks between the thick planks.
Northern vandals had smashed or stolen most of the furniture,
leaving open spaces for the damp winter winds to wander from
room to room.[30]

The home was not only inhospitable but also remote.
Ewell jokingly called it his "outpost," far removed from society's
track. Lizinka's days were devoid of visitors, leaving her too

much alone, too free to pester Ewell with her complaints.

Lizinka was most upset with their cook. Despite repeated instructions, the black slave could not prepare rice, their daily fare, as Lizinka like it. The grains, she noted to Ewell, were always soggy, not "dry, [with] each . . . separate from the other."[31] In an attempt to mollify his disconsolate spouse, Ewell gave her a most unusual Christmas gift: two new cooks, negro girls he bought in Richmond. These blacks, however, proved just as inept at cooking rice as the female that they replaced.

Shortly after the New Year, Ewell was offered an escape from his problems. Bragg's siege of Chattanooga had ended in a devastating defeat when the Federals under Grant drove him from his breastworks on top of Missionary Ridge. As the Confederates retreated into Georgia, President Davis saw that he could no longer ignore the repeated protests by Bragg's subordinates that their leader was incompetent. Davis felt that he had to reorganize the Army of Tennessee. After replacing Bragg with Joe Johnston, Davis suggested that Ewell move west to assume a corps command under his old friend. Lee was probably a factor in the proposed change. His reports to Davis about Ewell's fragile health induced the President to note to Ewell that this new assignment would be less arduous for one who was disabled.

As Lee conspired to send Ewell west, Lizinka plotted to keep her husband with the Army of Northern Virginia. She saw the change as a demotion, and Lizinka was not about to accept the loss of Ewell's prestigious post. She convinced him to reject the transfer, but he felt bound to review his decision with Lee before sending it on to Davis in Richmond. "[I] experience no inconvenience from [my] injury," he wrote to Lee. "Do you agree?"[32]

Lee's reply was more diplomatic than direct. "You are the proper person . . . to best judge . . . your ability to endure," he replied, "but I fear we cannot anticipate less labor than formerly."[33]

With the decision still open because of Lee's typically ambiguous answer, Lizinka resorted to a most unusual arrangement. While Ewell rested as much as possible that winter to regain his strength, she would "pitch in" by assuming many of his chores in running the corps. The concept was absurd but Ewell, "worse in love," according to Brigadier General James Conner, "than any eighteen-year-old . . . you ever saw,"[34] bought her idea without qualms. He sent his letter, refusing corps command in the west, to Davis.

Lizinka began at once to act in Ewell's stead. When he had a bad spill several days later (riding a new horse across fields covered by fresh snow), she put him to bed, then threw herself into the center of a controversy. She proposed that Sandie Pendleton be assigned as brigade commander, paving the way for her son, Campbell, to assume his position as Ewell's chief-of-staff. While her suggestion was presented as a promotion for Pendleton, her intent to advance Campbell was too obvious. Ewell's advisors not only refused her plan but also were put on guard against any other schemes Lizinka chose to tender. She had many in mind. "She manages everything," one officer moaned, "from [Ewell's] affairs down to the couriers who carry his dispatches."[35]

Ewell returned to duty on February 6th, the day the enemy elected to turn the Rebel right flank. Slipping over the Rapidan at 10:30 a.m., a brigade of infantry overwhelmed the Confederates on the southern shore, then moved inland, headed for a prominent ridge one mile away. A mansion, Morton Hall, (Ewell's home), loomed just below their target.

As the Yankees crept silently forward, they saw the men defending the hill leave their posts. The Confederates, four regiments, two each from Doles' and Ramseur's commands, were changing guard. An equal force of troops from Stewart's brigade had come to assume their place. The vacant breastworks lured the Federals into the clear, where they were spotted by a vigilant Southern battery which opened fire on the attackers. Aroused by the cannons, Ewell came hobbling out of his home, gaped at the bluecoats forming in his front yard, and reacted with a vigor and decisiveness not often seen of late. Ewell limped up the slope to take personal charge, sending couriers to the rear to rush reinforcements to the scene, then posting all eight regiments (double the usual force at hand) back into the emplacements.

While most Confederates assumed position with prac- ·

ticed skill, one group seemed unable to maneuver into place. Their leader, an old Georgian colonel, shouted orders that marched them left, right, then left again, but never ahead. Watching with growing impatience, Ewell finally turned to an artillery captain, mounted nearby, and appealed to him for help.

"Mr. Stiles," he thundered, "for Lord's sake, take that regiment and put it into the works!"[36]

"Do you really mean that, General?" Stiles asked.

"Of course I do!"

"Right face!" Stiles cried out, urging his horse ahead. "Forward, run—march!" The regiment slid into position.

The old colonel was humiliated. Dismounting, he walked up to Ewell, withdrew his sword, and offered the blade as his way of resigning his rank. Ewell, showing a compassion that his comrades from the Valley would not have thought possible, refused the saber. After assuring the elderly Georgian that he was not incompetent, just temporarily excited, Ewell asked him to return to his troops.

With his line in place, Ewell turned to his guns, which were holding the Yankees at bay. He moved among the weapons, selecting targets for them, changing their alignment, showing himself to the Federal artillery answering his salvos. Ewell remained at the front until dusk when reinforcements arrived to force the enemy to withdraw back across the Rapidan.

Lizinka was enraged with Ewell for taking what she considered unnecessary risks during the fight. She badgered him continuously, and on the cold winter night of February 17th, while they were entertaining Father Sheeran, her fury reached its peak. "Do you think a general is justified in carelessly exposing himself on the battlefield?" she asked the priest.[37]

"No ma'm!" Sheeran replied emphatically. "I think he is not. A general is the soul of the army, and his fall always causes despondency and sometimes greater disaster to his command. A general in my opinion should keep himself as far as possible out of danger . . . ."

"There, now," Lizinka shrilled, turning on Ewell. "You see that the Father is just of my opinion."

Taken back by her outburst, Sheeran, too, looked to his host, who indicated that Lizinka was referring to his recent experience with the enemy. She no doubt provided more details. Over five thousand Federals had approached Ewell's front, but he had foolishly disputed the Union's advance with just a few troops plus his artillery.

The priest sought neutral ground. "There may arise circumstances," he said, "which would require even a general to expose himself to every danger."

It was too late. Lizinka, triumphant in her proving of Ewell's irresponsibility, refused any further comment on that subject. Would the good father like to stay for supper? He thought not, choosing instead to escape before Lizinka began other uncomfortable discussions.

Several days later, Lee rode to Richmond to review with President Davis his plans for the spring campaign. Ewell, as the senior officer under Lee, assumed command of the Army of Northern Virginia during his superior's absence. While Ewell could have presided at Lee's headquarters during the interim, which Lizinka would have preferred, Ewell decided to stay at Morton Hall where he would be consulted if "matters of importance" arose. Lee's staff could handle their usual routines by themselves. Ewell's odd, distracted indifference during this period was evident the night of February 24th when Sandie Pendleton arrived with a pile of papers for Ewell to sign. After scribbling his autograph on each, he cajoled Sandie into staying to be the fourth hand at whist. Cards were shuffled and dealt until past midnight.[38]

Lee resumed command by the end of February. A few days later, another Rebel general returned to duty. Early, having completed his mission in the Shenandoah Valley, rejoined the Second Corps. Jubal was a changed man, not only in his dress (he wore a new, tailored uniform, topped by a beaver hat with a fluttering black plume) but also in his demeanor. "He had never been more ambitious . . . " Douglas S. Freeman concluded, "or more intolerant of others."[39] Early had first tasted primacy when he was named to replace Ewell back in November, and his thirst for power had been further magnified by leading an independent command in the Valley. Lizinka was quick to sense this threat to Ewell's post, and the two were soon at sword's point.

The personality conflicts rising in early 1864 in the

Confederate army were highly reminiscent of those that had plagued the Yankees from the onset of the war. Just as the South's leadership problems were coming to a head, however, the enemy's were lessening. Lincoln promoted Ulysses S. Grant to commander-in-chief of all Federal armies, and his selection brought a halt to most of the petty bickering for rank by the Northern generals. The key to Union harmony lay in Grant's strategy for the war: to put everyone to work (leaving no time for conspiracies) by pressing the South from all directions, using the North's superiority in numbers and weapons. No longer would the Rebels be capable of crushing a Rosecrans by shifting inactive troops from one front to another. Lee's army would be the primary target for the coming campaign, with Grant personally directing the effort from the field.[40] To accomplish this end, an enormous buildup of men and material took place along the Rapidan, clearly visible to the Confederates.

Lee made his own preparations. He started by asking for the return of Longstreet's corps from Tennessee, and President Davis quickly approved the request. As the First Corps began their trek to Virginia on April 11th, Lee turned to the troops at hand, stepping up their training for the expected Northern onslaught, sure to come as soon as the roads dried. All "distractions" were to be removed. Wives at the front were ordered back to Richmond.

At first Lizinka ignored Lee's directive. But on April 22nd, when the suspense of an imminent Federal assault became unbearable, she finally yielded and started back to Richmond. Her leaving distressed Ewell so much that when Early took that moment to utter one of his now typically caustic comments, (possibly about Lizinka), Ewell arrested his unruly subordinate, citing Early with "conduct subversive of good order and military discipline."[41] After reviewing the accusations, Lee agreed with Ewell but asked him to drop his complaint, noting that "now is not the time for internal strife." With evident reluctance, Ewell set aside his order.

On the morning of May 2nd, Lee met with his three corps commanders on top of Clark's Mountain, above the Yankee encampment. They had overlooked this scene before; little had changed. The ground was dotted with thousands of white tents, men wandered about under the warm sun, and loaded wagons moved to and fro across the landscape. While the visible scene was green from Fredericksburg on the east to the foothills of the Blue Ridge on the west, it was patchy, not arrayed in neat squares as would be expected in springtime. A once symmetrical network of planted fields was now a scrubby waste of weeds.

While Lee surveyed the scene through field glasses, the others kept a respectful silence. They remained quiet until Lee finally spoke. "The enemy's crossing," he predicted, "[will] by at Ely's or Germanna . . . . "[42] Both fords led into the area called "The Wilderness," a dense arena of scrub oaks, hanging vines, and tightly woven brambles. Jackson had been mortally wounded here during Lee's decisive defeat of Hooker, and many of those who had died in that battle around Chancellorsville remained unburied a year later. It was poignantly ironic that destiny had decreed this field of horror for another great contest. Lee warned his generals to be ready to march at a moment's notice, then added that he would issue his orders by signal from this mountain top.

The next night Ewell was roaming his line, checking on his alignments, when he saw lights flashing from atop Clark's Mountain. The coded dispatch read: "General...Ewell...have... your...command...ready...to...move...at...daylight."[43]

* * * *

And so he must move out. If he allowed himself to consider his present military and personal situation it must have given him pause. During his early recuperation, Ewell had known only tenderness and compassion from Lizinka, and he probably expected more of the same during the winter of 1863/ 64. Her complaints, domineering ways, and intrusion into his affairs must have come as a shock. Ewell submitted willingly to Lizinka's sway, however, not only because he was in love with her, but also because he possibly feared that Lizinka might leave if he did not comply with her every whim. Weak, ill and insecure in his hastily-contracted marriage, he was quite aware by now that Lizinka's interest in him was inextricably bound up with his rank. She certainly gave him reason to assume so by the strong emphasis she placed on his retaining command.

The tie between his marriage and the Second Corps was crucial to Ewell by this time, and he had to defend his position not only from his enemies in the field, but also the envious in his camp. Jubal Early was his chief threat, and whereas Early had spent a lifetime conniving, Ewell was only beginning that loathsome game. He was particularly vulnerable since Lizinka, who could have matched Early's guile, was no longer there when he needed her most.

And then there was Sam Grant. He was different from the bumbling generals Lee had bested before, and he would present a supreme test for the Rebels who were dangerously undermanned and militarily pressed on all fronts.

Both physically and emotionally handicapped by his missing limb, his attention divided between the war and his wife, facing challenges both in his camp as well as the field, Ewell must have viewed the coming campaign with dread.

Robert Milroy

Philip Sheridan

Photographs from the Library of Congress Collection

The Wilderness

The dawn of May 4th, 1864, was gray and cool. As the sun started to rise in the east, its rays were blocked from view by a damp fog hovering above the ground, enveloping the men, seeping into their clothing to chill their bones. Ewell had assembled his corps in column by Lee's order, received via lantern light the previous evening. The troops shivered as they waited word to march east to intercept the Yankees. But no orders came. Finally, after the sun had penetrated the mist to dry the dew, a Southern flagman showed on top of Clark's Mountain. He began waving his banners, sending his message. Ewell, squinting as he studied the far off figure, read the intricate code.

"The enemy...seems...to...be...moving...to...the...right ...on...Germanna...and...Ely's...Roads....[Only]...cavalry...to...our...front."[1]

The message, sent about 9:00 a.m., was informative but did not include the eagerly awaited order to advance. A second false alarm came soon after when a courier rode up to Ewell and dismounted. He handed him a note, sent by Major W.W. Cowles, leader of the First North Carolina Cavalry. Grant's army was crossing the river at Germanna Ford, moving south in heavy force. Their van was already two miles into the Wilderness. From the sounds that accompanied the Yankee parade, Cowles concluded the enemy columns held many wagons.[2] This report demanded that Ewell hurry his men east to intercept the Federals. He was about eighteen miles away, and if he hoped to meet Grant in the Wilderness, Ewell had to start now. But without instructions from Lee, Ewell was locked in place.

As he waited with growing frustration, peering into the morass ahead, Ewell must have understood why the area merited its forbidding title, "the Wilderness." The ground had once been the realm of spiral hardwood trees. Cleared for fuel to smelt the iron ore deep below the forest floor, the land had been abandoned once the mineral deposits were exhausted. The scarred earth had returned to life, not in its prior sublime form

Ulysses S. Grant

George Meade

Photographs from the Library of Congress Collection

but as scrub saplings, briers, and vines that sprang up, then wound together into a giant web of greenery. Only dirt paths and an occasional glen interrupted the dense growth.

Suddenly, the flagman on Clark's Mountain began pumping his arms, but again his signals relayed only unimportant news and not Lee's orders for Ewell. His frustration did not end until after 11:00 a.m. when a messenger from Lee finally rode up with instructions. Ewell was to leave some troops by the Rapidan to picket while the rest of his force marched east on the Old Stone Road. When he reached Locust Grove, Ewell was to halt and set up camp for the evening.[3] Lee was willing to allow Grant to slip past him, gambling that when he attacked the center of the Yankee columns tomorrow morning, they would be forced to call their van back into the Wilderness.

Ewell assigned Ramseur's brigade as his pickets, adding six regiments (three each from Rodes and Johnson) to buttress the guard. The deployment delayed Ewell's start for an hour. When he was ready to go, Ewell handed his crutches to an aide and called for his horse. He would not drive a buggy toward this battle.

There was a marked difference in the numbers that Ewell led into the Wilderness from those he had marched to Pennsylvania. The large losses from the Gettysburg Campaign had never been restored, and whereas Ewell's corps totaled 20,000 in 1863, he had only 13,500 at hand now.[4] But despite having fewer men, he still would field a strong fighting force, due mostly to an improved officer cadre. Those who had stumbled at Gettysburg, Williams, Iverson, O'Neal, and Smith, had all been replaced by more competent leaders: Stafford, R.D. Johnston, Battle, and Pegram.[5]

Another advantage was the mood of the troops. In prior days they had laughed and joked while tending to their duties, but now they were somber, showing a grim determination and understanding that they faced perhaps their last chance to trample the Yankees. They were ready to give the extra measure that Ewell would ask from them.[6]

Ewell reached Locust Grove about sunset. He posted his force in line: Early in the village, Johnson two miles to the south, and Rodes below Johnson. While the men set up their camp,

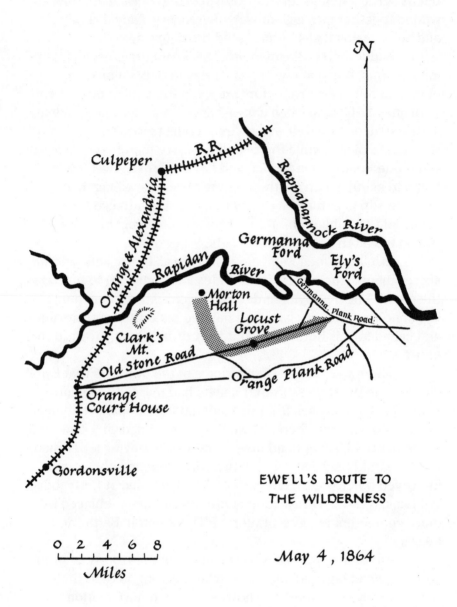

EWELL'S ROUTE TO
THE WILDERNESS

May 4, 1864

Ewell sat anxiously awaiting the messenger Lee had promised to send with orders for the morning. The courier rode up about 8:00 p.m. and gave Ewell instructions that must have caused him satisfaction. For once, Lee was succinct, offering no discretion: "If the enemy moves down the river," the order read, "push after him . . . bring him to battle as soon as possible."[7]

Elated with the chance to fight without having to guess at Lee's intentions, Ewell left his tent and moved toward the front, east of Locust Grove, where he plopped into a pile of dry leaves nestled against a fallen log. He slept there, the first in line, eagerly anticipating the coming combat. Reinvigorated by the prospect of battle again, Ewell was up before dawn, absorbed with building a fire to boil his morning coffee, stumping around on his wooden leg. One of his favorite people—Captain Robert Stiles—approached from out of the dark. The young officer had impressed Ewell during the Yankee attack on Morton's Ford, and ever since that affair, he had been trying to lure Stiles out of the artillery, into the infantry.

"Dismount," Ewell called out, "and take a cup of coffee with me."[8]

Stiles obliged, and sat next to Ewell, who handed him a steaming mug. As he gingerly sipped the boiling brew, Stiles dared asking a confidential question. "Any objection to your telling me your orders?"

"None at all," Ewell barked with obvious relish. "Just the orders I like . . . go right down the Plank Road [and] strike the enemy wherever I find him."

After Stiles left, Ewell assembled his troops in column with Johnson in front, next Rodes, and finally Early. He led the long parade through wispy clouds of fog that would clear, close, then open again to offer a fleeting glimpse of the way ahead. The line moved slowly forward. The quiet sound of the forest, a mixture of calling birds, deer plunging through the thickets, and breezes stirring among the tops of trees, were deadened by the dull, steady thumps of thousands of Confederate feet.

Suddenly, about 8:00 a.m., as Ewell rode around a curve in the road, he came on a band of cavalry, clad in butternut, milling at the intersection fifty yards ahead. Ewell raised his hand to halt the ranks behind him, then spurred his mount forward to greet the troopers from the First North Carolina. They reported that the enemy was two miles away, going south. The Federal columns were so strung out that some of their men had yet to cross Germanna Ford. Several alternatives were available for intersecting the Yankees: continuing along the Old Stone Road or turning left to rush up Culpeper Mine Road. Both paths terminated on Germanna Plank, the route the bluecoats were travelling.

Ewell considered the situation, settled on a plan, then issued his orders. Campbell was sent to Lee (and out of danger) to report the corps' position; the cavalry would guide Walker's brigade up Culpeper Road where they could defend the flank; the remaining troops would continue along the Old Stone Road with Jones' brigade in front as skirmishers.[9]

When his dispositions were set, Ewell led his men ahead at a slow, careful walk. They had gone only a short distance when Campbell galloped up with changed instructions from Lee. "Regulate your march [with that of] General A.P. Hill," the young man reported, pointing to the south where the Third Corps was marching in parallel along Orange Plank Road below Ewell. "[Avoid] a general engagement."[10]

Ewell's heart no doubt sank when he heard Lee's orders. Here was Gettysburg all over again. How could Lee expect him to approach the flank of the enemy, the best position for an assault, and not take advantage of the opportunity? And what if the Yankees saw their vulnerability and whirled to charge him? Should he refuse battle to run away like a coward? The morning's ardor must have cooled for Ewell. Nevertheless, he remained a good soldier and obeyed Lee's instructions. He sent word to Jones to avoid combat, then started the march forward again.

It took almost three hours for the men to move the last two miles to the Germanna Plank. While his progress was slowed by A.P. Hill, whose position was most evident due to the continuing bark of muskets to the south, Ewell's advance was also checked by Federal pickets, hidden behind the brush along the road. They harassed his columns by firing and then fleeing before they could be answered. Ewell plodded ahead. About 11:00 a.m., just as he approached Germanna Plank Road, Ewell heard a Yankee band providing marching rhythms to the trains and troops passing only steps from his front. To avoid imminent confrontation, Ewell halted in place.

Knowing he could not remain in line along the Old Stone Road, Ewell started to array his corps. Jones was positioned south of the lane, behind a small opening; Steuart was told to assume a post above the road; Stafford, still well to the rear of the column, was also sent north, to join Walker in a line facing the east, alongside Steuart. Ewell cautioned his leaders to avoid battle. If the Yankees attacked, they were to fall back and not offer resistance. We can assume Ewell was frustrated about his inability to engage the enemy because he tried to get Lee to change his mind. While waiting for Rodes to reach the front, he sent Sandie Pendleton to Lee to ask for permission to take the offense.[11]

Sandie returned about noon to report that Lee would still not allow them to initiate battle. As he presented the bad news, a burst of musket fire sputtered in front of Jones' position below the road. Grant had finally discovered that the Rebels were on his flank, and he had dispatched a probe to feel his adversary's strength. As Ewell anxiously watched, waiting to see if a charge would follow, forcing him to withdraw, Rodes arrived on the scene. His strung-out columns could not be left standing on the road. Ewell had to either send them back or put them into position. When the firing to the right died away, Ewell decided to post the brigades. Battle moved in behind Jones; Doles went south to extend the line started by Battle; Daniel formed on Doles' right.[12]

About an hour later, Early's Division came up and Ewell ordered them into reserve. Gordon moved south behind Rodes; Hays assembled his men in the thick brush alongside the road; Pegram, still several miles away, would move north in back of Johnson when he reached the front.[13]

Ewell, posted in the rear with Rodes, found that he was sweating profusely and gasping for a breath. The stunted trees gave him no protection from the blazing sun and the thickets covering the ground blocked the breeze. He waited in anticipation.

The quiet was shattered at 1:15 p.m. Without any warn-

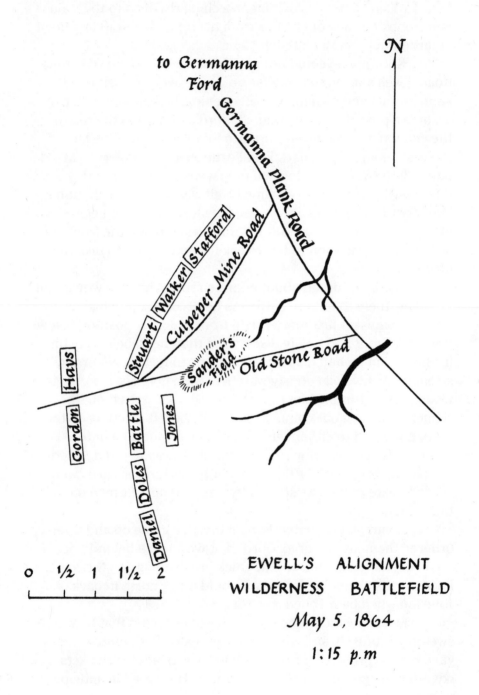

to Germanna
Ford

N

Germanna Plank Road

Stuart Walker Stafford

Culpeper Mine Road

Sander's Field

Old Stone Road

Gordon Hays

Battle Jones

Daniel Doles

0   ½   1   1½   2

EWELL'S ALIGNMENT
WILDERNESS BATTLEFIELD
May 5, 1864
1:15 p.m

ing, the enemy attacked in full force along both sides of the Old Stone Road. Ewell had no chance to retire to avoid the engagement. Steuart and the other brigades to the north held an advantage of angle, and their fire into the Union's right flank shattered the charge above the road. But to the south Jones' post was quickly overrun, and as his troops scrambled to the rear to escape the onslaught, they mixed with Battle's line, taking his men with them in frantic retreat. Doles and Daniel on the far right, seeing that they were shut off from the rest of the corps, fell back, too.[14]

Ewell was on the road when the disaster started. While he could not actually see the rout unfolding, mobs of fleeing Rebels scurrying out of the brush and onto the path, their quickest route to safety, clearly told him that calamity was at hand. He whirled and galloped for the rear to call up his reserves. When Ewell spotted John Gordon and his aides in a small clearing just south of the road, he veered toward them. "The fate of the day," he shouted to Gordon, "depends on you, Sir."[15]

Gordon knew nothing of the breakthrough, nor did he ask for details. Accepting Ewell's challenge without question, he replied, "These men will save it . . . . "

As Gordon brought his troops into line, they came under fire from the enemy, who were advancing toward him, unseen because of the heavy growth. Several men in his front ranks were hit and toppled to the ground. Ignoring the danger, the rest of Gordon's seasoned troops calmly filed into formation and held their place to await word to attack. When Gordon ordered the charge, his brigade stormed into the thickets and crashed into the first wave of Union infantry. The combat was hand-to-hand as the Confederates wielded bayonets and musket butts to bludgeon the bluecoats into a frantic retreat. Gordon pushed the pursuit, but soon called a halt. To the north and south, Yankees were advancing in a direction opposite to his. He had pierced the heart of the enemy's attack, but their flanks had enveloped him. Gordon resolved his dilemma brilliantly. Dividing his force in half, he sent one group right, the other left. Roaring like lions, their shouts as loud as a legion, each charged into the midst of the adversary. Staggered by the unexpected blow from an improbable direction, and unable to judge the impotency of the numbers against them because of the thick growth, the Yankee soldiers to the north and south broke ranks and began to run back to their lines.[16]

On the left, Battle, who had reformed his brigade in the interim, saw the Union withdrawal start. He immediately sent his men after the retreating enemy. Doles was just as alert to the south. He had held formation while retiring, and once he recognized that the bluecoats had lost their organization and were falling back, he brought his brigade into the chase. Daniel, too, joined the pursuit, and as the Rebels closed on the enemy, they captured hundreds of prisoners. The counterattack ended at the original Confederate line.[17]

Ewell followed Gordon's drive on the right, and when he saw victory, he thought of Lee and his orders not to bring on an engagement. His superior would be angry. Looking for an excuse to avoid Lee's wrath, Ewell quickly sent Campbell back to Lee to report that while he had had no choice in fighting because the Yankees had attacked before he could withdraw, he had held his ground. He was now preparing to fall back to a position along Mine Run if the enemy came forward again.[18]

Despite his message to Lee, Ewell was planning just the opposite strategy. Knowing that Grant would never quit after just one try and that his former comrade was sure to mount a second attack, Ewell did not ready his men to retire. He had them entrench. Ewell's disobedience of Lee's orders did not last long, however, because when Campbell came back from seeing Lee, he reported that the army commander was pleased with Ewell for standing firm. His instructions had been misunderstood; retreat was only an option to be taken if Ewell found it impossible to hold his line.[19]

Delighted with this interpretation, Ewell moved quickly to follow Lee's now positive instructions. He ordered Rodes to strengthen his defenses, then mounted up to visit Johnson. As Ewell galloped north along the Culpeper Mine Road, he could take satisfaction in the present position. Rodes was now in good shape and the brigades under Johnson had never been in trouble. Wave after wave of enemy infantry had advanced against their lines, but each had been repelled. The key to

Johnson's success was the brilliant maneuver by Walker, who had gained the Union flank to pour a deadly fire into the Northern ranks.[20]

When Ewell reached Johnson's post at 2:00 p.m., a singular, unnerving sight greeted his eyes. Sander's Field, a narrow ravine covered with only dry grass, was blazing with fire. Confederate and Federal soldiers were working in concert to put out the flames. Their common concern was a host of wounded troops (mostly bluecoats) lying helplessly in the path of the fire. When the red flames engulfed a fallen soldier, paper cartridges in the poor unfortunate's pockets exploded like popcorn in a covered pan. Many were being burned alive.[21]

The blaze suddenly died. Adversaries, mingled together on the field, united in the joint cause of squelching the flame, all seemed to notice at the same time that their reason for a temporary peace had vanished like the smoke from the fire. The men scattered for the safety of their own lines, and an odd and poignant moment in the Civil War passed. The battle resumed.

Ewell soon found Johnson, who wore a worried expression on his face. He had just heard that a sizeable Yankee column was bearing down from the north, approaching on Culpeper Mine Road. While Stafford's and Walker's brigades were ready to contest the advance, Johnson doubted if their numbers were enough to fend off the probable assault. Ewell sent for two of Early's brigades (Hays' and Pegram's) to strengthen the line, but he knew that since the enemy was almost upon them, these added troops would never arrive in time. He needed to take a drastic step. He would charge the Union front.[22]

By mounting his assault, Ewell hoped to catch the enemy off guard, perhaps causing them to divide their force to send men east to meet the charge. This would weaken their threat to his flank. Steuart's troops eagerly accepted the mission, and they swarmed out of their entrenchments to race down the slopes of Sander's Field, then up the rise toward the Federal line. The Yankees fired furiously, trying to stem the Rebel advance, but while their salvos kept the Confederates at bay, they could not force a retreat. Lying behind swales for protection, Steuart's dogged troops held their ground for thirty minutes before scampering back to their breastworks.[23]

The Union strategy had been to mount a charge from both front and flank, but Ewell's unexpected attack had so enraged the enemy that before their troops up north were in position, the infantry to the east launched a fierce counterattack. Steuart, after returning to his entrenchments, turned to meet the charge, and he managed to hold the Federals at bay until Walker, brought south by Ewell, entered the fight. His added weight was enough to force the Union from the field, back to their line. And by the time the Yankee flankers were finally unleashed to the north, Hays had arrived with his troops. He put his men along a ridge where they easily withstood the enemy assault.[24]

The shooting stopped about 5:00 p.m. A ghostly silence followed, but the quiet proved just an illusion. As both the Rebels and the Yankees grew accustomed to the lack of rifles popping, they heard a now familiar crackle. The dry land between their lines, littered with the bodies of both dead and injured men, was once again aflame. The grass, the brambles, and even the scrubby trees were on fire, and under billowing clouds of thick smoke, the wounded cried out in terror as the relentless flames bore down on them. Earlier, common compassion had evoked a truce to save the doomed soldiers, but the barbarity of the recent fray had destroyed such trust. North and South watched the holocaust with the numbed indifference that prolonged fighting eventually brings. The inferno burned for an hour. Then, as if someone had blown out a candle, the flames ebbed and died. The shrieks stopped.

Ready to resume battle, Grant committed his whole force above the Old Stone Road to a third assault against the Rebel line. In the midst of the fight, a courier approached Ewell with new orders from Lee. "The enemy have made no headway in their attack [here]," he wrote. " . . . Get General Ramseur and be ready to act early in the morning . . . . The enemy is all moving up to our right . . . . I suggest to you the practicability of moving over and taking [Wilderness Tavern Ridge], thus severing the enemy from his base, but if this cannot be done . . . you must be prepared to reinforce our right . . . . "[25]

Lee's assumptions were obviously in error. The Yankees

were not all moving to the right, and most (it seemed to Ewell) were massed and attacking his front. No wonder A.P. Hill was doing so well to the south! And as long as the Federals persisted in charging his front, Ewell had no chance to advance and "sever the enemy from their base." Faced with these uncertainties, Ewell decided to wait before sending the messenger back to Lee with his answer.

Through the next hour, the Rebels continued to hold off the determined enemy, who were charging without pause against Ewell's equally resolute men. Even after the sun had dropped below the low trees to the west, the Federals continued their attacks. In the following darkness, another courier from Lee arrived. "Be ready to support our right," Lee repeated. "If the opportunity [opens], cut the enemy off from the river."[26]

Ewell still did not know what was possible. The firing was even more fierce on his front; Grant had just launched a last, desperate assault. But if his line could repulse this final charge, Ewell would win the day. And come daylight, he would move to cut the Yankees' supply line to the river. He would not serve as A.P. Hill's reserve.

Despite their almost inhuman efforts, the enemy did not break Ewell's lines that May 5th. "Dear, glorious, old, one-legged Ewell," Porter Alexander wrote. "[He] sat back and not only whipped everything that attacked him but he even sallied out on some rash ones [of his own] . . . During the night he entrenched himself nicely. That was the first [time] that General Grant ever saw the fighting of Lee's Army of Northern Virginia, and, good soldier as he was, I am sure he must have admired it mightily."[27]

Ewell's performance had been outstanding, but A.P. Hill had problems to the south. He had come up Orange Plank Road that morning with a force about the same size as Ewell's, was attacked at 4:15 p.m. by Federal infantry equal in number to those charging the Second Corps, and while he threw back that single assault, nightfall found "his men . . . exhausted, his ammunition low, and his line disarranged and ragged."[28] Grant had camped in place, ready to renew his attacks come sunrise. Lee feared the Third Corps would break, and since he had given Ewell the option to act on his own, he could look only to Longstreet, who was rushing toward the front from

Gordonsville, thirty miles away, to arrive in time to shore up Hill.

Late that evening, Ewell began to plot his strategy for severing the enemy from the supply lines. First he reviewed the casualty reports from the brigades. His losses that day had been heavy, especially in key officers: Jones was killed during the first Federal assault, Stafford had been mortally wounded that afternoon, and Pegram was down, shot in the leg.[29] Each had been replaced by a less experienced man. Looking for a capable commander to lead the morning attack, Ewell chose John Gordon. He pulled the Georgian and his men out of line and sent them north to take a starting position on the flank. Jones' regiments were assigned to Johnson's brigades, posted north of the Old Stone Road, to replenish their numbers. And Ramseur, still picketing along the Rapidan, was ordered forward to provide a reserve. Unlike at Gettysburg, where he had left depositions up to his subordinates, Ewell took personal charge of these changes. He made sure that the men moved into their assigned locations, then rode toward the rear to intercept Ramseur and guide him to his position.[30]

Upon meeting Ramseur about 3:00 a.m. near Locust Grove, Ewell led his troops toward the front. At 4:30 a.m., just as they arrived, Rebel cannons roared, the signal for Gordon to launch his attack. His regiments poured over their entrenchments toward the bluecoat line, only to be met halfway there by the Yankees, bent on their own assault. Grant was following a plan that was timed and executed coincident to Ewell's. The two foes grappled in the soggy field between their lines, neither gaining an advantage. Seeing that he was stalemated, Gordon decided to retire behind his breastworks and carry on the battle from a protected position. The bluecoats followed closely on his heels.[31]

Gordon was not alone in combat. Grant was now charging Ewell's whole front, throwing wave after wave against his emplacements both above and below the Old Stone Road. Johnson and Early faced a serious challenge, but south of the winding pike, those assaulting Rodes were not so daring. The Yankee skirmishers there crept forward to the Confederate line, made contact, then fell to the ground, content to show their presence but not their nerve.[32]

Although he was successfully withstanding the Federal assaults, Ewell was greatly frustrated by the unexpected turn of events. Lee had given him two options: turn the Union's right or reinforce Hill, and he was doing neither. Pinned in place, he found his situation was soon further complicated. A courier rode up about 6:30 a.m. to report an enemy force approaching the gap between Ewell and Hill. Only Ramseur was on hand to meet the threat, and his men were rushed to the sector. They arrived just in time to thwart the Union thrust.[33]

As this crisis passed, another loomed. Union infantry were spotted to the north, heading toward Ewell's upper flank. Fortunately, R.D. Johnston's troops had just arrived, breathless from a sixty-six mile hike from Hanover Junction. Showing no mercy for their exhausted condition, Ewell sent these welcome reinforcements north, where they met and repelled the oncoming Yankees.[34] The fighting waned. With his position stabilized, Ewell reported his situation to Lee, then awaited further orders.

About 9:00 a.m., John Gordon galloped into Ewell's camp. As he leaped off his horse, he shouted that the enemy's right flank was in the air, the Yankees had no guard, no entrenchments, no way of defending themselves against a quick attack. When Ewell expressed doubts, Gordon offered proof of his claim. His scouts had gone north of the Federal line before dawn, and they had seen the opportunity.

"I was so impressed with the importance of this report," Gordon said, "I sent others to make [an] examination . . . to proceed, if possible, to the rear of Grant's right and ascertain if the exposed flank were supported by troops held in reserve behind it."[35]

These men not only confirmed the earlier report but also found that the enemy had no supporting troops within miles of the exposed Union position. Still not satisfied, Gordon went forward to look for himself. "I found the reports correct in every particular," he exclaimed. "There was no line guarding this flank."

Ewell was still not convinced, noting that the Federals stood on his flank. If Gordon left his post to carry out the assault, would not the Yankees quickly move forward into the

vacated ground to roll up the Rebel's line? "No!" Gordon insisted. The earlier enemy movement from the north had been a
feint. These bluecoats had fallen back and were too far away
now to present a threat.[36]

Ewell asked how Gordon would organize the movement,
and Gordon suggested an echelon attack in which he would
charge from the north, while Pegram's troops advanced from
the west. Caught in a pincer, the Yankees would run, allowing
Pegram to turn south to unite with Gordon in driving the
Federals. Hays' brigade, next in line to Pegram, would then
advance, routing the foes to their front, and so on down the line.
Grant's entire army would be destroyed.[37]

The vision Gordon offered was so attractive that Ewell
put aside his misgivings. He agreed to the scheme, provided that
Early, Gordon's superior, who was expected to arrive at headquarters any moment, also concurred.[38] Jubal rode up at 9:30
a.m. He listened to Gordon's plan, then raised the same danger
that Ewell had mentioned, that the Yankees were poised in
strength above the Confederate flank to the north. When Gordon
hotly protested that those soldiers were no longer there, Early
exploded with anger. "We have no reserves," he thundered as he
shifted his argument to a new basis. "If your plan fails and the
enemy shows . . . enterprise, a serious disaster would befall not
only our [troops] but . . . Lee's whole army."[39]

"I'll assume all responsibility . . . ," Gordon flared with
equal ire, "should any occur."

At this point, Ewell stepped between the two. He noted
that Early's points were valid, but that the reward was worth the
risk. He supported Gordon's proposed assault.[40]

Early would not give up his position. Aware of Ewell's
respect for military protocol, he asked permission to conduct
his own reconnaissance of the front before making the attack.[41]
He judged his superior correctly. Ewell reluctantly accepted that
a division commander had this right, that he should make a
personal study of the ground before embarking on a mission as
risky as that proposed. He agreed to postpone the assault until
Early had examined the enemy lines.

Before Early could head for the front, a messenger from
Lee arrived with orders for Ewell to attend a meeting at army

headquarters, which were located with Hill's Corps.[42] Since Early was next in seniority to Ewell, he took over command of the corps during his superior's absence. He had to postpone his reconnaissance until Ewell returned.

Ewell reached Lee's headquarters about 10:30 a.m. At that point he was brought up to date on the situation to the Confederate right. The enemy had attacked at dawn there, too. A.P. Hill was driven from his entrenchments, but as his men ran for the rear, Longstreet suddenly appeared on the scene. His troops had spent the night marching toward the front, and while they were exhausted from the effort, they immediately entered the fray by charging the Federals, sending Grant's troops reeling back to their line.[43] In the quiet that followed, Longstreet sent his scouts ahead into Union territory, and they had just returned with a report that the Yankee left flank was in the air. Lee was busy planning a turning maneuver to exploit Grant's defensive lapse. Could Ewell bring his corps to the south to act as the reserve?[44]

While no record exists to prove the point, Ewell certainly reported that the Federal right flank was also open, and that he, too, was preparing to attack. Early was waiting for his return so he could reconnoiter the ground to find the best point to launch his charge. Lee's decision is obvious. He left Ewell's troops to the north rather than bringing them into reserve behind Hill and Longstreet, and he approved of Early's personal scouting mission because he did not order an immediate assault in coordination with Longstreet's effort.

As Ewell rode back to his line, he no doubt heard Longstreet open his assault on the Northern left flank. He would not know until much later that while the charge began with a rout of the Federal troops, it ended in tragedy. Longstreet, supervising the pursuit of the shocked and shattered Yankees, was shot in the neck by his own men, who mistook his party for enemy officers in retreat.[45] When Longstreet went down, the Confederate attack ground to an untimely halt.

Early left for the Federal right flank as soon as Ewell arrived back at his command post. Ewell anxiously waited for his return. One, two, three, then four hours passed without a sign of the obstinate officer. Finally, at 5:00 p.m., both Early and

Gordon rode into camp. Jubal loudly announced (as if he had just discovered new information) that the Federals' flank was open to the left, that the enemy lay vulnerable to an assault, that they had no reserves in sight.[46] Ewell immediately ordered the charge. Although Gordon must have been seething over Early's arrogant assumption of credit for finding the opportunity, darkness was less than three hours away, and he had no time to claim his due. If he was to defeat the enemy, Gordon had to move now, so he hurried to gather up his men.

In planning his attack, Gordon made a small change in the strategy he had proposed earlier. The assault would come from three directions: his troops would begin the battle by swooping down from the north; when the Union turned to face this threat, Pegram's men would charge from the west to smash into the abandoned front; and as the enemy fled in disarray, R.D. Johnston's troops, veering east, trailing Gordon, would explode in the Yankee rear to block all avenues of escape.

The initial Confederate charge at 6:00 p.m. brought all that Gordon had promised. His blow scattered the Yankee brigades on the flank. But as the sun slowly slipped below the western horizon, the assault began to unravel. Pegram's men swerved right, and instead of engaging the force that Gordon had disrupted, they ran up against a stable Federal front below their intended target. They were easily repelled, taken out of the clash.[47]

R.D. Johnston's brigade also faltered in their mission. Assigned to swing around Gordon's troops, they lost their way in the tangled brush and growing darkness. When they finally charged, they collided with Gordon's soldiers. The confused and intermingled Rebel ranks quickly came to a halt, allowing most of the fleeing enemy to escape. Unable to re-form their men in the inky depths of the Union's encampment, Gordon and Johnston were forced to end the assault, taking 600 prisoners (including two Yankee generals, Truman Seymour and Alexander Shafer) with them as they stumbled through the stunted forest back to their original line.[48]

Early the next morning, Ewell decided to feel his front to find out what effect Gordon's night attack had made on the Yankees. Brigadier General Armistead Long, the Chief of the

Second Corps Artillery, led the patrol. In less than an hour he returned to report that the Federals had vanished from their entrenchments across from Culpeper Mine Road. Gordon's assault had allowed Ewell to achieve Lee's hopes of severing the Union supply line through Germanna Ford.[49]

While the enemy was cut off from retracing their steps north, they remained in place, fronting the Rebels south of Old Stone Road. Grant held three options: he could retreat by heading east to Fredericksburg, then returning to the north via the sea; he could continue his assaults on Lee's line; or he could march south, seeking to renew his campaign on more favorable ground. Lee chose to wait for Grant to make his move. In the meantime, Ewell was to entrench troops above the Federals' position to strengthen his stand between the enemy and Germanna Ford. Over 1,500 Yankee dead lay scattered throughout the area, and in addition to raising emplacements, Ewell had to dig graves for the rapidly decaying bodies.[50]

As the hours passed, Ewell peered often into the still, dark forest to his front, but he saw only blackened trees, still smoldering from flames ignited by Gordon's assault the previous night. The quiet ended about 5:00 p.m. when cheers rose out of the depths of the seemingly empty woods facing the Rebel troops. The joyous Union shouts reverberated left and right as regiment after regiment repeated cries.[51] Expecting to be attacked at any moment, Ewell's pickets fired blindly into the growth to their front, but no rifles replied to their blistering barrage. The dusk returned to stillness.

Late that night, Ewell finally learned why the Federals had been so vocal. Grant was not going to retreat. His army was headed south, and the Yankee soldiers were cheering the knowledge that the drawn battle would not result in once more returning north in defeat. Renewed fighting would open on different ground tomorrow.

* * * *

Forty years after the Civil War, John Gordon recorded a fascinating story. He said that late in the afternoon of May 6th, 1864, Lee came to Ewell's headquarters. "Can't something be done on this flank," he asked impatiently, "to relieve the pressure upon our right?"[52] He was offered options by Ewell and Early, but neither mentioned the enemy's open right flank. Gordon wrote that he felt compelled to interrupt the evasive discussion to reveal that the opportunity to turn the Yankees' line had been available all day, and he proceeded to lay out the plan he had presented to his superiors, the strategy they had rejected. Early objected again according to the Gordon story, and repeated the points he had made earlier. Ewell, the corps commander, had nothing to say. Lee listened with a cold silence according to this version of the incident. After Early had completed his riposte, Lee turned to Gordon (ignoring Ewell and Early—an extraordinary rebuff), and told him to attack.

It is a remarkable tale, so much so that ever since his memoirs were published, Gordon's story has been included with almost every account written on the Battle of the Wilderness. Ewell's reputation is scarred by Gordon's accusations because they picture him as irresolute and timid, a slave to Early's strong personality. The charges are totally false.

First of all, Gordon claims that Lee did not know prior to his visit that the enemy's flank was exposed. This cannot be true since Ewell was called to Lee's side that morning after Gordon had reported finding Grant's right unprotected. And since Ewell favored a charge as soon as possible, he certainly gave this news to Lee, along with Early's objections against taking what he considered an unreasonable risk. By not ordering Ewell south to reinforce Longstreet or to attack the Union's flank that morning, Lee obviously agreed that Early was right in insisting on additional reconnaissance.

Edward Steere, the foremost authority on the Wilderness Battle, writes that Gordon's tale that Lee ordered the attack is simply unbelievable. He points out that Lee (like Ewell) was too devoted to following army protocol to ignore the input of a senior officer.[54] He also documents that none of the other battle reports support Gordon's assertions. Lee, in fact, makes no reference to the late afternoon attack in his record, and both Early and Ewell are in concert that Early suggested the assault and Ewell ordered it.

Lastly, given the many inaccuracies throughout Gordon's

1903 memoirs, there is little reason to accept this particular incident as being true. Almost forty years had gone by, but the rancors of the lost war had not diminished. In trying to enhance his own reputation, Gordon elected to degrade Early—a man whom he openly hated for charging him with dereliction of duty during the Battle of Cedar Creek.[54] Gordon's target was Early, but his arrow found Ewell, who in a rare burst of the old, decisive energy, was the most exemplary performer in the Battle of the Wilderness.

Spotsylvania

Grant was not just "moving" south. His army was racing toward Spotsylvania to seize the ground between the Confederates and Richmond. Lee countered that same evening, May 7th, by sending the First Corps, now led by Major General Richard Anderson, on a route to intercept the Federals and foil their plan. While A.P. Hill held his ground, facing the enemy and guarding the Rebel flank, Ewell started to slide to his right toward Hill. Lee had told him that if he found no bluecoats posted to his front, Ewell should slip around and behind Hill to follow Anderson toward Spotsylvania. A new road was being hacked through the woods by Rebel pioneers for this march.[1]

Ewell began to sidle to his right at once, and by sunup on May 8th, he confirmed that the bluecoats had abandoned the front to the east. He called his corps into column and started for Spotsylvania. The trek proved arduous. The road that had been carved through the Wilderness was no more than a rough clearing whose stumps and stubble seemed to leap out of the weeds to trip even the most careful of plodders. And while the billowing, yellow dust raised by thousands of Rebel footsteps made it hard enough to breathe, the problem was compounded by hovering smoke from fires set by the prior combat. The men gasped and coughed as they stumbled ahead.[2]

As he rode at the van, zigzagging the many obstacles in his way, Ewell was intercepted by a courier bringing a letter from Lee. Marse Robert had ordered changes in Ewell's command: Early was assigned as temporary head of the Third Corps in place of A.P. Hill, who had been taken ill. Gordon was promoted to assume Early's post; and consolidations in the corps were necessary because of losses incurred during the recent fighting. Hays would absorb the slain Stafford's depleted regiments into his brigade, which was reassigned from Early's to Johnson's division; and R.D. Johnston's brigade was shifted from Rodes to Early.[3] These changes were complicated, but

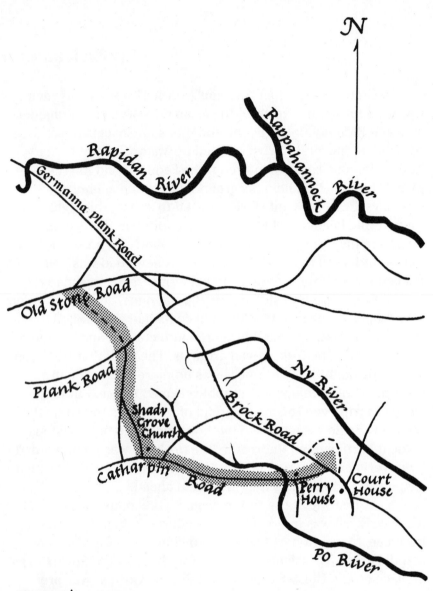

EWELL'S ROUTE
TO SPOTSYLVANIA
COURT HOUSE

May 8, 1864

Ewell managed to reorganize without missing a step on the trail.

About noon, Ewell's columns broke out of the Wilderness onto a "real" road, where he ordered the men to pick up their pace. Lee had said in his note that he expected Anderson to become engaged when he intercepted the Yankees, and Ewell was certain that the First Corps would need his support. When he reached the Catharpin Road, Ewell turned his lines east on a direct route toward Spotsylvania. He had gone about one mile along the highway and had arrived at Shady Grove Church, when Lee suddenly rode up. He told Ewell that Anderson had won the race south, that the Federals had tried to break through the Confederates' hastily formed lines, but they had failed in their attack.[4] All was quiet now, but Lee was nervous. He feared that the enemy would soon mount a second charge, and he urged Ewell to get his corps to the scene as soon as possible.

Ewell asked his troops to further speed their step, and they shifted into double-time. They ran to the Po River (a narrow, shallow stream), forded the waters, then moved hurriedly down the road past the Perry House, a bizarre structure built with squared-off logs.

The bark of rifles suddenly exploded to their left. As Ewell looked in the direction of the firing, he saw a soldier riding south on the path that intersected the Catharpin Road at the Perry House. The horseman was waving, trying to catch Ewell's attention. He galloped up to gasp that Anderson was under assault, but unlike his earlier encounter, this time the Federals were charging with superior numbers. Help was obviously needed immediately.

Ewell whirled in the saddle and called to Rodes to rush his columns north into the fray. Ramseur's brigade, the unit at the van, started forward at once, spreading out in battle line as they advanced. Daniel's troops followed Ramseur. As the two approached the front, they saw that Anderson's Corps was formed behind a makeshift breastwork of fence rails. They had just staved off an enemy attack, but a wave of bluecoats was about to turn their flank. Ewell's men swerved toward the on-coming Yankees and charged recklessly into the wide-spread line.[5] Fighting hand-to-hand, they smashed the adversary's formation, forcing a disorganized retreat. Both Ramseur and

Daniel chased after the enemy soldiers, but found the bluecoats running too fast to be caught. When the Rebels reached a hill overlooking open ground, bounded east and west by a thick growth of oaks, they halted and began to entrench.

The position that Ewell's men occupied was ahead of the ridge held by Anderson, with a line that followed the contour of the slope, shaped like a mule shoe. And "digging in" was not a casual effort. The troops burrowed five feet down into the soil, throwing the red clay up front. Additional protection came from hewing logs, then embedding them into the dirt piles. Cannons were strategically emplaced so that each field piece had a clear field of fire to the front.[6]

Ewell brought his whole corps into the salient: Rodes' four brigades (Ramseur's, Battle's, Daniel's, and Doles') entrenched in a north to south line along the western edge; the troops under Johnson (Steuart's, Jones', Hays', and Walker's) built fortifications on the eastern rim; and Gordon's regiments (Evans', Johnston's, and Pegram's) were posted in the rear as the reserve. Early took his men (A.P. Hill's Corps) east, below Ewell, on the same line as Anderson's.[7]

Although his position was well fortified, Ewell quickly saw that the site offered serious disadvantages. The forests nearby were so close that an enemy attack could not be discerned until the foe was almost on top of the line. Northern sharpshooters, protected by the trees, proved the point by harassing the Rebels as they built their entrenchments.[8] Casualties were light, but included an irreplaceable leader, Harry Hays, wounded as he directed his men in digging their emplacements. But while Ewell may have wanted to pull back out of the salient, his troops would not hear of it. This was ground fairly won, and they were not about to retreat.

By the afternoon of May 10th, the Rebels were ready for the enemy to test their works, and the Federals were quick to oblige. They started by probing Anderson's line, mounting a timid thrust to the west that was easily repelled. The enemy then turned to Ewell's more promising position. Their guns, posted far to the rear, fired salvos into the salient for one hour to soften the way for an infantry charge against Doles' entrenchments late that afternoon. Despite a blistering hail of bullets

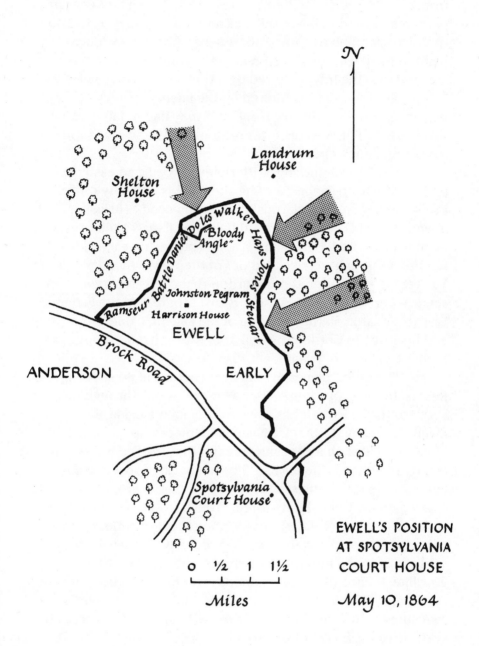

N

Landrum House

Shelton House

Walker
Doles
Daniel "Bloody Angle"
Battle Hays
Ramseur Jones
Johnston Pegram Steuart
Harrison House

EWELL

ANDERSON
Brock Road
EARLY

Spotsylvania Court House

0   ½   1   1½

Miles

EWELL'S POSITION
AT SPOTSYLVANIA
COURT HOUSE

May 10, 1864

from the Rebel line, the Yankees roared up to the Confederates' parapets, scrambled over the logs and mounds of dirt blocking their path, and poured into the trenches where they fought hand-to-hand with their adversary. A second Federal wave charged into the fray, followed by a third, then a fourth. Doles' troops were soon outnumbered by the enemy infantry concentrated against their narrow front, and they had to fall back into the salient. The Yankees, fanning out left and right, pursued the Georgians.

Ewell was infuriated with Doles for being so easily expelled from his trenches, and he showed his anger by ordering Doles to "Regain your skirmish line at any cost!"[9] He knew, however, that Doles would need help. Ewell marshalled every man he could find. Daniel and Walker (posted on each side of the breakthrough) were called out of their bastions to pinch the Yankee force between them; Gordon rushed his reserves to the scene where they blunted the forward progress of the Federals. Steuart, located on the east side of the salient, came across to add his force to Gordon's. Ewell, too, was at hand. "Charge them!" he shouted, "Damn 'em, charge 'em!"[10]

The Union plan was to take advantage of penetrating the Rebels' front by pushing more and more troops through the gap and into the salient. But as the reinforcements came ahead, Ewell was ready for them. His guns, emplaced up and down his lines, opened such a concentrated fire that the Federal soldiers could not weather the blasts. They fell back, exposing their compatriots inside the salient to a ferocious, ever-growing, soon overwhelming Confederate force. Ewell's troops assailed the Federals from three sides, bludgeoning them relentlessly toward the vacant trenches that Doles had abdicated. The enemy soldiers dropped into the excavations, but stopped there, unwilling to face the Rebel cannons awaiting their dash into the open field. They huddled in their holes until nightfall, when the remaining able bodied bluecoats arose to sneak back across the clearing to the haven of their own lines.[11]

The affair continued to sputter long after the foes had separated. Guided by the flash of musket fire, sharpshooters from both sides poured shot after shot at each other. About midnight, the sparring ended when military bands took command of the contest. The Rebel musicians began by playing "Nearer My God to Thee." The Federals replied with the "Dead March." After several more tuneful duels, the Confederates ended the melodious challenge with "Home Sweet Home." The song brought tears to many eyes and quiet to the field.[12]

The Union attack, conceived by Colonel Emory Upton, had been a close call. And although Ewell had skillfully parried the thrust, the cost had been dear. His casualties exceeded 650 men. Ewell was particularly grieved that Tom Turner, one of his aides, had been slightly wounded. The young man, who was engaged to Lizinka's daughter, Hattie, had been hit by an enemy shell fragment while wrestling a gun away from a Federal.[13] Unlike Campbell (as usual, sent safely to the rear by Ewell), poor Tom had been "popped" into the hottest spot by his commander, and Ewell felt responsible for the boy's injury. His concern no doubt included how he would justify his action to Lizinka.

The next day was quiet, in part because the weather had grown worse. Ominous clouds that swirled overhead at sunup grew thicker throughout the morning, and by late afternoon, a cold rain began to fall. Toward evening, Lee came to Ewell's quarters to plan their strategy. He brought news that enemy wagons and columns of their infantry were hurrying east. Grant was obviously beginning another flanking maneuver, and Ewell must be ready to leave his position at any moment to intercept the Yankees. Because the rain had muddied the ground inside the salient, this would be particularly difficult for the cannons and their caissons. Lee insisted that Ewell limber his guns and send them to the rear immediately.[14] Ewell did not argue with Lee over this decision. He was too tired to question a superior's decision, so he issued the order to withdraw the guns and then climbed into bed.

About midnight, Major Hunter of Johnson's staff arrived at corps headquarters to ask that Ewell's aides wake him up. Still half asleep, Ewell listened as Hunter related that the Federals were massing at Johnson's front, preparing to attack at dawn. Johnson doubted if he could stem the assault without artillery. His cannons had to be returned at once.[15]

"General Lee," Ewell noted, "[has] positive information

that the enemy is moving . . . right."[16] He expected orders from Lee to follow the Yankees at first light, but if he sent the artillery back into the salient, he could not do so. The muddy ground would delay his departure. The weapons must remain in the rear.

After Hunter left to give this message to Johnson, Ewell put on his uniform. He was now wide awake, and perhaps a little worried over a possible threat to his eastern flank. As he paced the floor of his headquarters (the Harrison House), Ewell heard a Yankee band blaring in the distance. The faint music was flat and dispirited, revealing the weary condition of its players, but the cheerless notes droned on and on.[17]

About 1:00 a.m., Johnson arrived at the Harrison House to confront Ewell, insisting that the bluecoats were indeed preparing to assault his front at any moment. He demanded that his cannons be rushed into position at once. Impressed by Johnson's fervor, Ewell nevertheless repeated Lee's assurance that the enemy was planning to retreat. Johnson refused to accept the premise. The enemy was coming! He had to have those guns.[18]

Bowing to Johnson's tenacity, Ewell agreed to send most of the artillery back into the salient. He assured his upset subordinate that the weapons would be returned to their proper place within the hour, and an aide was rushed to the rear with orders to locate and move the cannons forward. Greatly relieved by Ewell's decision, Johnson promised that his force would not sleep that night. They would stay in the trenches, looking for the expected attack. The Yankees would not break his line!

Although Ewell had appeased Johnson, he did not believe the enemy would really attack, and he elected not to wake Lee to inform him of the change in plan. Ewell plopped into his chair, probably intending to wait up until the cannons passed his house. He fell asleep. When he awoke (about 3:00 a.m.), Ewell felt disconcerted. He could not recall hearing the artillery rumbling back to the front. He decided to go see for himself if his orders had been obeyed. Limping out the door, Ewell untied his horse, mounted, and started to ride for the rear.

The rain had stopped, but Ewell's clothes were soon wet from a thick, white fog that made it nearly impossible to see the way ahead. Almost an hour passed before Ewell completed the

short trip to the artillery park. He found that the guns had not
been moved forward, that Armistead Long, his Chief of Artillery,
was only now giving the order to rush the weapons back to
Johnson's front. When Ewell demanded an explanation, Long
noted that he had just learned of the impending assault, that the
aide carrying the instructions to return the cannons to the
salient had spent the last three hours wandering lost in the fog.[19]
Long went on to say that he would save time by dropping the
pieces into place without regard to their former post. Grumbling
to himself over the ineptitude of his staff, Ewell started the ride
back to his headquarters. The clouds parted for just a moment
when he arrived at the Harrison House, and the pale light of
dawn lit the area. As Ewell started to dismount, the mist returned, bringing with it the crackle of rifles from the northwest.
Grant had attacked at 4:30 a.m.

The initial Federal charge struck Steuart's line on the
lower right of the salient. Aided by two pieces that had not been
withdrawn from his front, the Marylander quickly parried the
Union's thrust. But ten minutes later the enemy charged again,
this time from the north, converging on a gap between Hays'
and Jones' brigades. " . . . About halfway to the [Rebel] line . . .
the men broke into a tremendous cheer," Union General
Winfield S. Hancock remembered, "and spontaneously taking the
double-quick, they rolled like an irresistible wave into the
[Southern] works."[20]

In minutes, the bluecoats overwhelmed their outnumbered adversary. Using the open breach like a funnel, thousands
of Federal soldiers poured into the salient, some turning right to
advance against Rodes' position along the western flank of the
salient, others charging south, down the eastern edge of the
Mule Shoe behind Johnson's line. Assaulted from the rear by
enemy hordes, Johnson's troops had no choice but to throw
down their weapons and surrender. Over 4,000 Rebels (including both Steuart and Johnson) were taken prisoner. The guns,
twenty pieces just now arriving at the front, also fell into Union hands.[21]

John Gordon, located southwest of the breakthrough
with the reserves, could not see the debacle unfold. He quickly
realized, however, that the enemy had entered the salient, that
he had to move at once to quash the tide. Gordon decided to

buy time by personally leading R.D. Johnston's troops (the only force at hand) on a daring assault northeast against almost certainly superior Yankee numbers. "The mist and fog were so heavy, it was impossible to see farther than a few rods," Gordon wrote later. " . . . [Being] concealed . . . the sheer audacity of [our] movement [was enough] to confuse and check the Union advance."[22] His charge delayed the Federal assault until Rebel reinforcements hurrying forward had reached the front, and as they arrived, Gordon sent them against the enemy coming down from the north. They bludgeoned the Federals backward into their own reserves pouring into the arena. The added numbers proved a handicap. The enemy formations dissolved into a panicked mob, an inviting target to the oncoming Southerners. Pelted by a steady hail of bullets, the bluecoats fled scrambling, every man for himself, hoping to escape the onslaught by sprinting for the safety of their initial lines. By 6:30 a.m., the whole right side of the salient was back in Rebel hands.

To the west, a different story was unfolding. When the Yankees broke through Johnson's line, they split their force. Half rushed south (where they were met and routed by Gordon); the rest hurried west and then south, following the contours of the salient. At the same time, Grant attacked Ewell's men entrenched along the western side of the Mule Shoe. His charge, clever in concept, proved disastrous to the Federals' cause. The attack was not only thrown back, but the Yankees also held the Confederates in place, preventing their rushing east to aid Gordon, leaving them in position to dispute the bluecoats approaching from the north.

Ramseur, not involved in defending the left flank, took his men behind the Southern line and pushed north to face the oncoming Yankees. "Keep your alignment," he cautioned his troops. "Move slowly until [you hear the] command 'charge' . . . . [Don't] pause until the lines of works are ours."[23]

While he stopped the Yankee advance, Ramseur found that he could not drive the enemy out of the salient. The fighting became fierce. Both adversaries rushed reinforcements into the fight, but neither could gain the advantage.

Finally, about 9:00 a.m., the pressure became too great for the Yankees, and they began falling back. They halted at the

Northern limit of the salient, occupying the breastworks built by the Confederates. From their protected lodgment, they struck back, firing with ruthless fury at the Rebels who had dug in within a few yards of the trenches. "So thickly lay the dead at this point," Hancock wrote, "the bodies were touching and piled upon each other."[24] The flying Minie balls were so many and continuous that a towering oak, measuring about twenty-two inches in diameter, was hacked in two by the deluge of lead. Overhead, gray clouds thickened, and amidst terrible thunder and lightning, the rain resumed. Those battling at the apogee, known ever after as "The Bloody Angle," remained unyielding, fighting on throughout the downpour.

At the first sound of battle, Ewell had mounted to ride directly toward the conflict. He soon encountered stragglers racing for the rear, and as the frightened men ran past him, Ewell saw that they came from different brigades. The Yankee breakthrough must be broadly based, a staggering blow. Perhaps looking for a miracle—that those troops still along the front had held their ground—Ewell continued to gallop ahead. Minutes later, he all but ran into Grant's first wave of infantry. Before the bluecoats could react to seeing a lone Confederate general bearing down on them, Ewell wheeled about and headed for his rear to try to counter the Federal onslaught.

When he arrived at his headquarters, Ewell's first order was to bring Campbell's Battery forward. Since the Yankees had obviously penetrated far beyond his front, the cannons there must have been captured. He had no artillery at hand. Campbell Brown was sent to the rear (out of danger) to gather reinforcements for Gordon. The remaining couriers were rushed to tell Rodes to stay in his entrenchments. Ewell anticipated that Grant would attack his left flank. With all available aides scattered in every direction, Ewell mounted and galloped east to look for additional messengers. He found John Gordon and his staff in the center of the salient, about to begin a charge against the Union.

"Lend [me] one of [your] staff!" Ewell cried as he rode up to Gordon. "[Mine have] all been dispatched . . . to different portions of the field."[25]

Gordon, busy arraying Johnston's Brigade, nodded

toward a nearby officer. Ewell rode up to the aide and began giving his customary in-the-heat-of-battle orders that made no sense. His frenzied words failed to keep pace with his anxious and rapid thoughts. Gordon and members of his staff took notice, turning from the battle to gape incredulously at Ewell's remarkable performance. They began to smile.

The unfortunate aide being addressed tried to translate Ewell's incoherent babble. "Let me see . . . " the officer began his questioning.

Realizing he had been spouting nonsense, Ewell suddenly halted his dialogue. "Who-oo-oot!" he wheezed, unable to explain himself. Despite being in peril (bullets were zipping throughout the area), the group around Ewell exploded with howling laughter. Ewell scowled, his face reddening with embarrassment, then wheeled and bolted off.

Back at his headquarters, Ewell met with Lee to discuss their options. Although Gordon had driven the enemy from the eastern side of the salient, the confrontation to the north, at the Bloody Angle, had settled into a savage impasse. The Mule Shoe had to be abandoned. But before the men could be withdrawn, a second line had to be built along the base of the node. Troops were put to work digging new entrenchments.

It was an awful job. Not only was the ground muddy and unyielding, but also the Union artillery harassed the workers by lobbing shells by the hundreds into the midst of the area. And whereas the previous breastworks had been built in a day and a half, only a few hours were available to duplicate this effort. The men toiled diligently all through the afternoon and into the night. To encourage their struggle, Ewell paced back and forth in front of the emplacement. "The fate of the army," he said again and again, "depends on having this line done by daylight."[26]

Lee shared Ewell's station in front of the slowly forming entrenchments. Late that night while he, too, encouraged the workers, a courier rode up with sad news. Union cavalry had made a dash for Richmond, and Jeb Stuart had followed to stop them. In a fierce skirmish at Yellow Tavern where Jeb's men had thwarted the enemy thrust, Stuart had been shot, a mortal wound. It was expected that he would die before morning.[27]

All the while, the battle at the Bloody Angle continued to

rage. Finally, twenty hours after combat had started, the new line was finished. The weary troops at the front began to withdraw. They fell back in small bands, and as each retired, those left facing the Federals spread their ranks to mask the Southern retreat. At dawn the last man slipped away.

Ewell's casualties from the fighting were staggering. Generals Johnson and Stuart had been captured by the Yankees, and their divisions were so decimated that those still at hand were consolidated into just a single brigade. Over five thousand troops had been killed, wounded, or taken prisoner, leaving Ewell with only eight thousand men in his corps. His loss in officers was equally bad. Daniel was dead. Walker, Ramseur, and Johnston had all been injured.[28]

When the realities of the calamity hit, Ewell sank into deep despair. He dropped all pretense of saving his strength and left his comfortable headquarters to share the rigors of the front with the men, as if his presence with the troops would recompense for the terrible losses to the corps. But while he was despondent, Ewell managed to show a positive face to his soldiers. On May 13th, a cold and rainy day, while touring the trenches, Ewell met Ramseur who, despite his wounds, was still with his men. "You were the hero of the day!" he told the brave officer.[29]

Later that afternoon, Ewell was handed a Northern newspaper with an article that lauded Lee's army. He decided to turn the article to his advantage, and rode to the lines of the Thirteenth Virginia where he read the commendatory piece to them. "The fighting of the Rebels," he recited, "was simply splendid."[30] When the soldiers good-naturedly agreed with the Federal press, Ewell played his card. "But boys," he said seriously, "you ought to hear what . . . Lee says about you." The men rose to the bait by clamoring for Ewell to pass on Lee's comments. He refused, shaking his head in mock dismay. "It would make you too vain," Ewell insisted with a laugh. He rode off with their pleas ringing in his ears.

When the rain continued through the next day, Grant saw he had little to gain by renewing his attacks against Ewell's front. He first fell back to his original lines, then began sliding left. To counter the Federals' changed position, Lee moved

Anderson's corps east, leaving Ewell with his depleted and weary ranks to cover the Rebels' left flank. Knowing he should have been at headquarters, Ewell still stayed at the front. He prowled the lines for three days, ignoring intermittent showers, shunning shelter, dropping to the cold, damp ground at night to sleep. Refusing to face the realities of both the horrible military defeat and his own damaged health, he immersed himself in the mindlessness of the front lines. It was the apogee of his physical and psychological deterioration.

On the morning of May 17th, the sun finally appeared to cast its bright rays toward the ground. Ewell welcomed the warmth, and because he was so exhausted that he no longer had the strength to plod the front, he stole away to take a nap. Out of the sight of his men, he plopped against a tree and shut his eyes.

Ewell woke to see an impeccably uniformed officer astride a gray horse looking down at him.[31]

Robert E. Lee glared at Ewell as he lay on the ground in his rumpled and dirty clothes. Ewell's face was white and drawn. He appeared mentally defeated, unfit to lead troops in these times of great danger. Lee turned his horse to gallop back to the rear. It must have been at this point that he was convinced that Ewell's days as the leader of the Second Corps were numbered. Shamefully aware of the poor impression he had given Lee, Ewell finally admitted to himself that he should be posted at his headquarters and not roaming the front like a common solder. He mounted up and hurried back to his staff.

Although the Yankees were still to Ewell's front, Grant was planning to slip past Lee's right flank as he had done in the Wilderness, looking to interpose his men between the Confederates and Richmond. He was so frustrated by Lee's dogged stand at Spotsylvania, however, he could not leave without a last attempt to break the Southern line. At 4:00 a.m. on May 18th, Grant sent his troops forward against Ewell's position.

But while Grant was willing to accept additional casualties, his men had seen too many of their comrades wounded and killed. They crept forward toward the Southern breastworks so cautiously that four hours passed before they came within range of a renewed and invigorated Ewell. He was waiting, ready for the confrontation. His guns opened with a terrible blast of shells and then canister as the Federals approached his emplacements. Their assault collapsed and the bluecoats scattered under the fusillade. The front was silent once more by 10:00 a.m.[32]

Convinced that further attacks were futile, Grant began his flanking maneuver the next day. He pulled his troops from in front of Ewell and started marching east. Lee asked Ewell to confirm the Northern movement by conducting a reconnaissance with his entire corps. Ewell led his 6,000 men forward at noon on May 20th. Campbell Brown, however, remained in camp. "[General Ewell] has insisted on my staying in the rear," he told his mother, "which is very repugnant to me until I think of . . . what your situation would be [should] we . . . both be killed at once."[33] Ewell's practice of keeping Campbell away from peril was now an open secret.

Marching through mud, Ewell's troops plodded west, then they turned north. Their pace was slow because the artillery—six guns from Braxton's Battalion—kept grinding to a halt in the boggy ground. When his force arrived at the Ny River, Ewell decided to abandon his cannons. He had to gain the enemy rear before dark, and he saw that if he continued moving ahead with the guns, he could not achieve that goal. He forded the river by 3:00 p.m. Half an hour later, the corps encountered a Federal force, which had not yet left its position. They had gone to the rear where they were waiting in troop formation, anticipating combat. Ewell appraised the situation, and saw that he had best retire. But before he could reverse his direction, the Yankees charged.

Stationed at the head of the corps, Ewell issued orders to turn around so the troops could withdraw instead of giving battle. Some obeyed his instructions; the rest insisted on contesting the Federal attack. The result was a milling mass of confusion. In the midst of the melee, a Northern soldier took careful aim at Ewell and fired. His shot struck Ewell's horse, and the general flew through the air, then crashed to the hard ground. Ewell was stunned, so shaken that he had to be carried to the rear.[34]

As the litter bearers hurried south with Ewell, Ramseur took charge, sending his brigade forward to stop the oncoming enemy. They stemmed the assault, but outnumbered, were soon threatened by Yankee soldiers on their left flank. Terry (in command of Johnston's brigade) moved up to cover the opening, but his men were also too few to handle the host of Federals. Hoffman, leading Pegram's brigade, rushed his troops into the breach, but even this added force was not enough to stem the oncoming tide of bluecoats. About to be encircled, the only chance the Confederates had was artillery, but their guns were gone—left behind when they had crossed the Ny River. Luckily, Wade Hampton's cavalry (assigned to screen the reconnaissance) came up, and they had four light weapons with them. The cannons were rushed into position, fired, and the Federals fell back, allowing the Rebels to escape the trap.[35]

Ewell left behind 900 men killed, wounded, or captured, an intolerable number of casualties for a reconnaissance. He had hoped to regain Lee's confidence by leading a successful mission, but these dreary results shattered that expectation. Ewell also suffered the ignominy of returning to his camp in an ambulance. His physical injuries were not serious, but he was terribly shaken, and even more depressed and discouraged by yet another setback.

Grant left the Spotsylvania area on May 20th, moving in a wide arc toward the southeast. Ewell led Lee's corresponding withdrawal down the Telegraph Road. He pushed his corps hard, keeping them on the trail for eleven hours before stopping at Steven's Mill. While it was critical that Ewell stay in front of Grant, the effort that he asked of his men was a bit severe. Well aware of Lee's concerns about his strength, Ewell probably seized this chance to demonstrate his fitness by pressing his troops almost beyond endurance. He even kept their breaks short. After only a few hours of rest, Ewell began the march again.[36]

The next morning, a bedraggled horseman trotted up from the rear and fell in alongside Ewell at the van. Jubal Early was finished with his assignment commanding A.P. Hill's Corps, and he had returned to Ewell. He found his division different from the one he had led only days ago. Hays' and Stafford's men had been consolidated into just one brigade, which Lee had transferred to a new division composed of this unit, the remnants of Johnson's force, and John Gordon's regiments. The

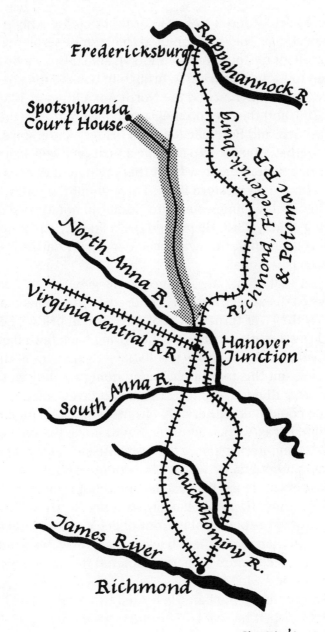

N

Fredericksburg

Rappahannock R.

Spotsylvania
Court House

Richmond, Fredericksburg & Potomac RR

North Anna R.

Virginia Central RR

Hanover
Junction

South Anna R.

Chickahominy R.

James River

Richmond

O   4   8   12   16
Miles

EWELL'S ROUTE
TO
HANOVER JUNCTION

May 21-22, 1864

shuffle had been ordered by Lee in order to create a higher post
for Gordon so he could be promoted to major general, rewarded
for his excellent performance at Spotsylvania.[37] Hoke's brigade
was added to Early's Division to bring him back to full strength.

Ewell's Corps reached the North Anna River at 1:00 p.m.
on May 22nd, and they set up their camp east of the Richmond,
Fredericksburg, and Potomac Railroad bridge. Anderson's men
arrived late that afternoon to assume a post on Ewell's left. A.P.
Hill's troops reached the new front that night, and they assumed
a position on the far western flank. Throughout the following
day, the Rebels lay unmolested and Grant did not appear until
the evening of May 23rd. He probed Lee's line with an immediate
attack on Hill, an affair that was a sad excuse for battle. Neither
side distinguished itself.

Later that night, Lee summoned his generals to a nearby
farmhouse to discuss strategy. He offered an ingenious plan.
Noting how the river turned west of the railroad bridge, Lee
proposed to strengthen that site, then bring back both flanks
into a "V" shape. The Federals would have to cross over the
stream to assault this formation, and in doing so, they would
find their army divided—split by the reinforced Confederate
center. Lee could hold either of his fronts with just a minimal
force behind breastworks, allowing him to move the bulk of his
troops along an interior line to the opposite side and gain the
advantage in numbers. He would then counterattack, and Grant
could not prevent defeat because he could not reinforce his
beleaguered army. He would have to ford the North Anna twice:
first to withdraw troops from in front of Lee's entrenchments,
then a second time to get them back across the water to where
they were needed. Before he had completed the maneuver, Lee
would charge and win the day.[38]

Grant refused the bait. He forded the river as Lee had
expected, but when he saw Lee's formations, he recognized the
impracticality of an assault. "We could do nothing where we
were unless Lee [took] the offensive," Grant recalled. "[When he
refused to charge], I determined . . . to make one more effort to
get between him and Richmond."[39]

Lee probably wanted to attack, to try to force Grant's
hand, but before he could order an assault, he came down with

indigestion. He would not fight unless he could orchestrate the action himself. Lee lay sick in his tent for three days. On the morning of the fourth day, May 21st, Grant started to withdraw from the front.

The Rebels also hurried south to counter Grant's move again. Lee, convulsed by stomach cramps, rode in an ambulance as he led his force along the Virginia Central Railroad tracks to the headwaters of the Chickahominy River. Ewell, too, used a buggy, but not because of his missing limb. He was writhing in agony, suffering from both scurvy and diarrhea.[40] When he arrived at Satterwaite's Farm that night, Ewell put Early in temporary charge of the corps, and then sent word to Lee that he was going on sick leave for a couple of days.

"I regret . . . that . . . your health renders it necessary for you to relinquish the command of your corps," Lee replied in a note he sent to Ewell that night. "I desire to assure you of my sincere sympathy for your suffering and recommend that you proceed to some place where you can enjoy repose and proper care of yourself, which I trust will speedily repair the trying you sustained from your late arduous services."[41]

Assuming that Lee's kind message meant that he would be returned to command just as soon as he felt better, Ewell decided to stay at Satterwaite's Farm while his corps moved on to Cold Harbor. After only two days of rest, he informed Lee that he was now recovered and was ready for duty. Ewell was shocked by Lee's cold and terse response.

"It will not be too well [for you] . . . to report for duty tomorrow," Lee answered on May 31st. "Your troops are now in line of battle under General Early . . . . Changes at the present time would [not] be beneficial . . . . I advise you . . . to move with safety to . . . endeavor to recuperate your health."[42]

Ewell was infuriated. Thinking that Early, eager to be corps commander, had stolen his position by convincing Lee he was feeble, Ewell sought to refute that charge by having Dr. Hunter McGuire confirm in writing that Ewell was "as able for duty . . . as at any time since the campaign commenced."[43]

Lee, however, was unimpressed by the physician's letter. "I am glad to hear that in the opinion of Dr. McGuire and yourself you are ready for duty," he wrote on June 1st. "It would be

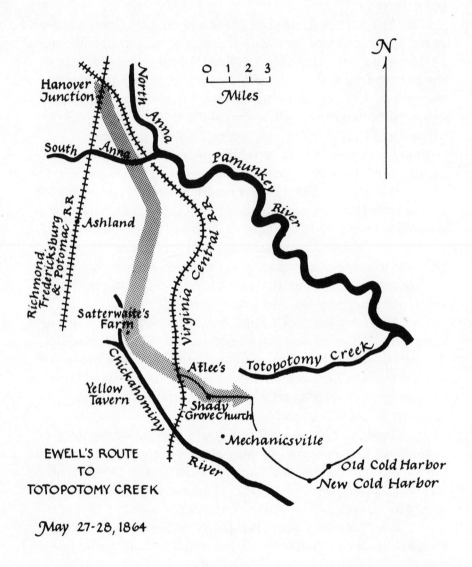

N

Hanover
Junction

North Anna

South Anna

Pamunkey River

0 1 2 3
Miles

Richmond, Fredericksburg & Potomac R.R.

Ashland

Virginia Central R.R.

Satterwaite's Farm

Totopotomy Creek

Atlee's

Chickahominy

Yellow
Tavern

Shady
Grove Church

Mechanicsville

EWELL'S ROUTE
TO
TOTOPOTOMY CREEK

River

Old Cold Harbor
New Cold Harbor

May 27-28, 1864

better for you to take the command of all the troops of Richmond than for me to disturb the present arrangement."[44]

The troops of Richmond? They were clerks, boys and old
men, not soldiers! Mounting his horse, Ewell rushed south to the
Shady Grove Church to confront Lee in person at his headquarters. He argued loudly against his removal from command, but
Lee held to his decision to replace Ewell with Early.

* * * *

In retrospect, Lee had good grounds for concluding that
Ewell's health was too precarious for him to remain in charge of
the Second Corps, and of course, it was only partly because of
the latest diarrhea episode. Lee could recall finding Ewell sleeping on the ground at Spotsylvania; Lee was aware of Ewell's fall
from his horse during the reconnaissance of a few days later; and
he had to have been worried about Ewell's recent illness. Early no
doubt reinforced Lee's case, offering evidence, promoting himself
as Ewell's replacement.

Ewell, however, would not admit to being enfeebled. "[I
have been] laid on the shelf," he complained in a note to Ben,
his older brother, "for what reason I cannot tell."[45] He refused to
accept that losing his leg had reduced his abilities, a poor but
typical psychological response to amputation. Ewell at this point
seems to have been adamant about regaining field duty. Soon
Linzinka would make equally fierce efforts to see Ewell returned to
his command, confirming the link between rank and his marriage,
and this would add desperation to his quest.

Richmond

When Grant withdrew from the North Anna River, marching east and then south in yet another attempt to get between Lee and Richmond, his route led toward Cold Harbor, the scene of the second of seven battles fought just outside the Confederate capital in June of 1862. Lee saw great peril in Grant's move.

A Federal army under Major General Benjamin Butler had come by sea to invade the ground below Richmond in early May. Butler had intended to attack the city from the south, but he was frustrated by troops led by P.G.T. Beauregard. His men were currently "bottled" on the Bermuda Hundred (the area between the James and the Appomattox Rivers), and Butler presented little threat to the capital from this position. But if Grant got past Lee's flank, he would open a way for Butler to come north and unite with the Army of the Potomac, giving the enemy overwhelming numbers.

To prevent the juncture of the two Northern armies, Lee took the offense. He sent the Second Corps (now under Early) against Grant's moving columns on May 30th. The assault was launched without adequate reconnaissance, and as a result, the Rebels suffered a bloody drubbing.[1] On June 1st, Lee threw Anderson's Corps upon Grant's strung-out troops. This attack was also easily repulsed, and Grant closed his ranks at Cold Harbor. Lee's only remaining option was to entrench in a defensive position.

Encouraged by his success in fending off Lee's thrusts, Grant assumed that Lee's army had been so weakened during the recent battles that one determined assault would shatter the Confederate lines. He thought he could take Richmond without the help of Butler, and on June 3rd, Grant mounted a massive attack up and down the entire Southern front. But instead of finding a feeble foe, Grant met unshakable resistance. Lee's men not only held their ground but also delivered a devastating blow. Within the first eight minutes of fighting, 7,000 Union soldiers were killed.[2] The morale of Grant's force was so crushed that he had to halt all operations. His troops rested while he made plans for uniting with Butler.

Ewell was at the front, observing the action, hoping he would regain his command after the crisis was over. But when the calm came, Lee held to his decision. Early would remain in charge of the Second Corps. Unsure what to do next, Ewell returned to Richmond to consult with Lizinka. She was as upset as Ewell over Lee's stubborn refusal to recognize that her husband was fit for duty, and it may have been her idea that Ewell go over Lee's head and appeal directly to President Davis to ask for his intercession. Ewell must have known that the Confederate chief would follow military protocol and support Lee's position, but nonetheless, on the morning of June 7th, he set out to see Davis.

The President's offices were located on the upper floor of the Customs House on Main Street. Ewell wasted no time in offering his case. "Has there been any dissatisfaction with my conduct?" he asked.[3]

"General Lee," Davis answered, "has been delighted with your services."

"Then place me in command of my corps!"

When Davis hesitated to answer the blunt request, Ewell changed tactics. He suggested a lesser role, perhaps leading a division.

Davis demurred. "Your rank is too high," he asserted.

"[I'll] resign," Ewell replied. "Appoint me a major general."

"No, I need you at the head of your corps."

How could Davis say such a thing when neither he nor Lee would grant him that very wish? The President, seeing that Ewell was not about to retire gracefully, beat a cowardly retreat.

"Report again to General Lee. [Tell him] . . . your health is recovered."

Ewell did just as President Davis had proposed. Riding back to the front, he approached Lee tremulously. Ewell began their meeting with the same plea he had offered Davis.

"Not wishing to trouble you, I am willing to resign and be placed on lower rank to go on duty."[4]

"There is no occasion for that. When these affairs are over, I expect to replace you in command."

"But General, I am in as good health now as I ever was. I

was up yesterday from 3 a.m. to 1 a.m., not fatigued or unwell, have worked as hard as anyone on the campaign. I was sick a little at Hanover Junction, but the instant . . . the necessity arose for increased exertion beyond my powers, I went on sick report, and was cured by two days rest."

"I have been constantly uneasy about you since last fall. You . . . go on exerting yourself, and I have been dreading every moment to hear that you have killed yourself by your exertions without good."

"My stump does not show the slightest injury . . . " Ewell snorted, showing his sensitivity to lacking a limb. Lee had been referring to Ewell's stamina, not his deformity. Ewell then introduced his suspicions that Early was behind Lee's ordering his exile. "I think highly of Early. If I thought you preferred him for other than . . . physical reasons, which I feel to be erroneous, I would not say a word . . . . "

"I do not prefer Early to you," Lee hastened to answer. "I think him stronger." To emphasize his point, Lee added, "I am unable to perform the duties of corps commander."

"Did I not perform them all?"

"Perfectly well, but remember how tired you were? You would sleep on the ground, liable to take cold."

"But I never did . . . . "

"I am glad to hear you give such an account of yourself, but I . . . have my fears . . . . The public interests are paramount to everything else . . . . At any moment you may give way, and in the most critical operation, confusion might occur . . . "

Looking to end the conversation, Lee added, "A few days may end all this and see you [reinstated] in command. You are now free from anxiety."

"These last few days are the most anxious I have [ever] spent!"

Stung by Ewell's sarcastic answer, Lee snapped, "It is due Early and the Corps that he receive the appointment just as Anderson has."

Ewell ignored Lee's assertion that Early was entitled to a turn in command. "Since the 4th of May, the Corps has been on the most desperate work . . . acquitting themselves to your expressed satisfaction . . . inflicting more than our share of loss on the enemy."

"Your best plan is to recover your health."

"It is recovered. But I will go somewhere to be out of the way."

While Lee probably did not understand that Ewell's need for field command was based on complicated insecurities, and that Ewell might have thought that his marriage was threatened by his losing that role, he could see how deeply his subordinate had been hurt by his removal from office. Lee was ashamed that he had lost his temper, and he tried to make amends. "You are not in the way," he declared, "but you better take care of yourself."

Ewell's dismissal from command was not popular with the Second Corps. "Everybody is disgusted," Campbell reported in a letter to Ewell.[5] Sandie Pendleton, the Stonewall devotee who had been openly critical of Ewell, described the decision as "outrageous."[6] And although Ewell had not yet been given new duty, many of his men said that when he obtained his next command, they would ask to be transferred to be with him.

Even Early showed signs of regret. Knowing that others thought him guilty of causing Ewell's removal, he declared in a letter to Ewell that "I have had no agency, directly or indirectly, in [being] given [your] . . . command." He added (with brazen insincerity, given his past politicking to oust Ewell), "I [will be] gratified . . . when you return."[7]

Early's actions did not match his expressed allegiance to Ewell. Instead of holding to Ewell's ways, he made a number of key changes, "kicking up a row in everything he does," according to Campbell. The young man added, "[And] he looks at me like a sheep-stealing dog."[8] Ewell was no doubt pleased over the many outbursts on his behalf, but if he anticipated that these dissents would lead to his return to command, his hopes were crushed on June 12th. Lee sent the Second Corps to the Valley to drive the Yankees out of the Shenandoah first, then to enter Maryland to threaten Washington, D.C. Ewell knew that once his men became actively engaged, his chances of regaining their command were gone.

Lee's strategy was to duplicate Stonewall's campaign of 1862. By advancing down the Valley, insinuating an attack on the Yankee capital, Jackson (and Ewell) had forced the Union to withdraw troops threatening Richmond, to move men north to protect Washington. The scheme had worked once, and perhaps it might do so again.

Ewell heard the discouraging news of the movement at Dr. Hancock's home on Main Street. He had left the front to come to Richmond to be with Lizinka while awaiting word as to his fate. He soon learned that he had been nominated by Lee to assume charge of the Department of Richmond. The post in which he replaced Major General Robert Ransom was a demotion, but, at last, duty. Having nothing better to do, he reluctantly accepted the assignment on June 13th, 1864.[9]

The Richmond duties that Ewell assumed included not only managing the military affairs for the city but also defending the capital, manning the defensive lines located on the outskirts. An interior trench circled the close-in perimeter of the town. Further out, an intermediate defense arch began along the James River (west of the city), running north, east, and then south, ending when it met the water again. A third exterior line, seven and a half miles from the capital, started at the Chickahominy River, flowed south to the New Market Road, and then turned west to terminate on the James at Chaffin's Bluff. The two outer entrenchments were connected by a line, running southwest. Fort Gilmor was located midway on this extension; Fort Harrison had been built where the ditch met the exterior works. A 'loop' continued on from Fort Harrison, running to the James, south of Chaffin's Bluff. Ewell's field headquarters were at Chaffin's farm, within this circle.[10]

Ewell's new command included about 6,000 men. His main unit, the Artillery Defense, was headed by Lieutenant Colonel John C. Pemberton, the defender of Vicksburg. Pemberton had surrendered the city to Grant, and as a result, found that he had to resign his commission as lieutenant general to obtain duty.[11] His 2,300 soldiers manned the heavy cannons emplaced along the exterior line from the river to the Darbytown Road.

Five regiments of cavalry (1,600 men) were available to Ewell. Three formed a brigade under Brigadier General Martin Gary; the other two (the First Battalion from Richmond and the Sixtieth Alabama) were unattached. Also unassigned were the

600 men of the Twenty-Fifth Virginia infantry.[12]

The rest of Ewell's force was composed of clerks, 1,400 in all, headed by Brigadier General C.W.C. Lee, the oldest son of Robert E. Lee. They were on temporary duty, manning their line only because an assault by the Union seemed imminent.[13]

Grant, however, did not attack the Confederate capital. After his devastating rout at Cold Harbor, he decided against waiting for Butler to come to him, and on June 13th, he took his force south to unite with the Army of the James in an assault on Petersburg. Lee, caught unaware by the sudden move, remained by Cold Harbor, and for three days, Richmond lay exposed to an approach by the enemy from below. Beauregard, defending Petersburg with meager numbers, managed to hold off the combined Yankee armies, and when Lee finally settled into position on June 18th, the stalemate became a siege.

To the north, above the James River, Ewell found he had little to do. Campbell, returned at Ewell's request to serve on his staff, issued his doleful orders: glean the oats and wheat growing below Chaffin's Bluff; protect the men ripping up the nearby railroad track for much needed iron; and keep watch over both Federal and Confederate prisoners, the latter being captured deserters. Ewell's front was so dull that on July 7th, President Davis asked Ewell to return the clerks to Richmond. Custis Lee assembled the citizen-soldiers and led them back to the city.[14]

Ewell soon lost more of his force when the Sixtieth Alabama was assigned to another field. The cavalry left immediately, but the arrival of Bushrod Johnson's infantry brigade, named to replace them, was postponed for the moment. Ewell saw the switch as yet another blow to his pride, a further threat to his regaining field command, and he looked for a way to prove his ability.

On the morning of July 9th, as Ewell watched the Yankee ships sailing with impunity on the James River, bringing provisions to Federal depots at the mouth of the stream, he saw his chance to gain recognition. He would disrupt the traffic with his cannons. Since his guns were emplaced out of range of the Union vessels, Ewell went to the river's shore to look for a site to locate his artillery. He found none available, as the ground was too muddy to move pieces in and out. Ewell did, however, see a way to harass the enemy. Torpedoes! If he could float a series of mines in the river, he could worry the Northern fleet without risk. Ewell proposed his idea to Lee, who liked it so much that he immediately sent an officer from Beauregard's staff, E. Pliney Bryan, to execute Ewell's plan.[15]

As Bryan began gathering materials for the escapade, he encountered problems. The Confederate Navy would not cooperate. They would not release any of their "ships" (rowboats) for Army use. When Ewell asked Lee to appeal to the Navy, he received a terse reply. "I hope you will be able to overcome [these] difficulties."[16]

Taking matters into his own hands, Ewell used his skills in intimidation (and probably his rank as lieutenant general) on the Navy, and two days later, July 13th, all that was needed (including "ships") was in place.

Approaching the stream that evening, Bryan and his crew were astonished to encounter another band of torpedo men, led by Dr. J.R. Fretwell, who were carrying out the same mission. The two argued over who had the authority for releasing mines into the river. Bryan cited his orders from Ewell; Fretwell revealed his contract with the Confederate government, which paid him half the value of what he could destroy.[17] Fretwell won out. Bryan retired without ever launching a missile.

Ewell was incensed with Bryan for giving up his mission, and sent him back to the river the night of July 15th. As he and his men pushed off from shore, a Union steamer bore down on Bryan. Enemy soldiers jumped off the ship into the water, waded to dry ground, and set up a picket line to cut off the Rebels' best avenue for escape. Trapped between the Northern boat and their troops along the shore, Bryan chose to abandon his "ship," and took his men through an open marsh to safety. When he reported later to Ewell, Bryan noted the Federals had anticipated his coming, that they were patrolling the stream day and night, and he recommended calling off the scheme to lay torpedoes in the James River.[18]

Ewell agreed, probably because he had just learned that he must return to Richmond. Lizinka had sent Ewell word that Leonidas Polk, a corps commander with Joe Johnston's Army of Tennessee, had been killed in Georgia when he was struck by a

Yankee cannon ball. While Lizinka's news was appalling, she also reported that Johnston, Ewell's old friend and 1862 commander, had asked that he replace Polk.

Arriving in Richmond, Ewell went first to Lizinka. She confessed to visiting the War Department to present his case to General Braxton Bragg, the official responsible for replacing Polk. Lizinka's attempt to ply Bragg with her womanly wiles had so offended the officer, he quickly dropped Ewell from consideration and gave the coveted post to Alexander Stewart.

"I regretted her going very much," Ewell said in a note to his brother. "I wanted the chance to give the authorities a plain statement of my case, and [if necessary], hand in my resignation .... I would be a captain under Johnston if he were a colonel ... . He is my only hope of regaining command."[19]

Ewell's despair over recovering a post in the field was no doubt fueled by Early's success with the Second Corps. He had swept the Yankees out of the Valley, defeated a Northern detachment under Major General Lew Wallace at Monocacy, Maryland, and by June 11th, stood on the outskirts of Washington, D.C.[20] He was basking in the glory that could have belonged to Ewell.

Early remained in place for just one day. He knew that he could not capture the city. Grant, as Lee had anticipated, had sent his Sixth Corps north, weakening the force fronting Richmond, to bolster the Federal capital's defenses. When Early marched leisurely back into the Valley, the enemy under Sigel and Hunter followed him. Early halted at Kernstown, waited for the Union to catch up, and then on July 18th, pounced with glee on his adversary. The Yankees were sent scurrying back over the Potomac River.

While Ewell was no doubt cheered by the exploits of his former corps, he could not help but compare their conspicuous success to his dreary existence outside Richmond. The glory that should have been his had gone unfairly to Early. He had to find action, and Grant gave him that chance.

Knowing that Lee fronted his superior numbers with only an extended, thinly-manned line, Grant was unleashing an inventive strategy. He would concentrate his army on a specific point along the Rebel entrenchments. If Lee moved to bolster

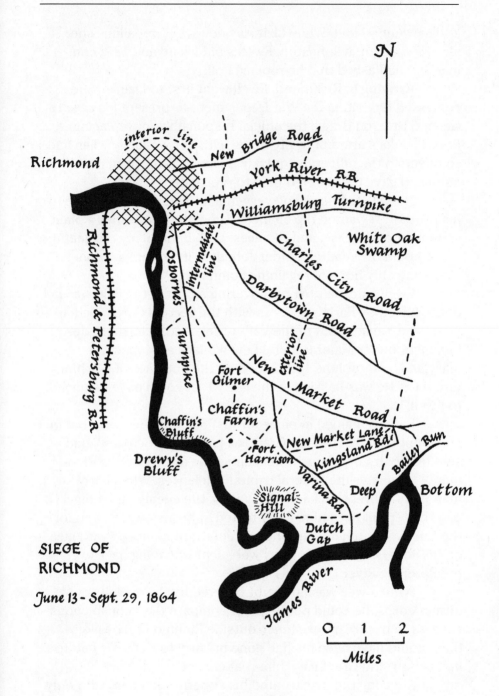

N

Richmond

interior line

New Bridge Road

York River R.R.

Williamsburg Turnpike

Richmond & Petersburg R.R.

Osborne's

intermediate line

White Oak Swamp

Charles City Road

Darbytown Road

Turnpike

Fort Gilmer

exterior line

New Market Road

Chaffin's Farm

Chaffin's Bluff

New Market Lane

Drewy's Bluff

Fort Harrison

Kingsland Rd.

Varina Rd.

Bailey Run

Deep

Bottom

Signal Hill

SIEGE OF RICHMOND

Dutch Gap

June 13 - Sept. 29, 1864

James River

0   1   2

Miles

that area, he would attack; but if the Confederates strengthened the imperiled site, emptying their trenches of men elsewhere, Grant would shift his force rapidly to attack another target. Sooner or later, by jumping from point to point, he expected to gain entry through the Southern shield to Richmond.

The initial test of the tactic was thrust against Ewell on July 25th. Federal cavalry began reconnoitering the ground around Deep Bottom, north of the James, about two miles from Ewell's front. He reported their actions to Lee, who replied stiffly, "I have thought it proper to call to your attention [that] a small body of [Northern] cavalry ought not to be allowed to traverse with impunity."[21] Although Ewell no doubt wanted to dispute the bluecoats' browsing at will, he was not equipped to do so. The only troopers Ewell had at hand were the 25th Virginia and Gary's horse brigade. Lee, despite his impolite note, recognized Ewell's dilemma, and he dispatched Kershaw's infantry brigade to the scene to drive the impudent Union back over the James.

Grant accepted the challenge by bringing more troops forward and having them build fortifications. When Lee learned about this new ploy, he wrote a second, brusque note to Ewell. "We cannot afford to sit down in front of the enemy," he groused, "and allow him to entrench . . . wherever he pleases."[22] Ewell, while he certainly agreed with Lee, was precluded from acting on the problem. Lee had relieved him of this responsibility by giving Kershaw the assignment of driving the Yankees away. Kershaw attacked on July 27th, taking his brigade between the New Market and Darbytown Roads in an attempt to turn the Northern flank. The Federals not only repelled Kershaw's assault, but also captured four of his cannons.[23]

Sensing a chance to break through the Confederate line, Grant rushed additional men (Ewell identified three different corps) to the front. Lee answered with Heth's Division plus the cavalry under Rooney Lee. Although these troops occupied Ewell's sector, they were not placed under his command. Lee sent Anderson north to take charge.

On July 28th, Ewell received word that Sheridan and his cavalry had arrived on the scene. He passed the report on to Lee, who responded with nervous irritation. "What is the enemy's force of cavalry?" Lee demanded. "What do you propose to do? Are you directing operations?"[24]

"As much as circumstances permit," Ewell replied dryly, choosing not to point out that Lee had put Anderson in charge of the situation.[25]

As conditions grew ever more tense, the Confederates committed all available resources. Ewell sent his artillerymen into the trenches, the clerks were recalled from behind their desks in Richmond to fill gaps in the line, Fitz Lee's cavalry arrived, and Field's division of infantry rushed up. Everyone was in place by 4:44 a.m. on July 30th when the Federals finally mounted their charge. Grant's attack, however, was not against Ewell's line. The assault was at Petersburg, far to the south, where Lee had weakened the front. The original Federal plan had been for Hancock's Second Corps and two divisions of cavalry to ford the James River at Deep Bottom. The infantry would assault the Rebels, holding them in place while the troopers galloped up the Charles City Road to turn their flank. When Lee countered by transferring men from his Petersburg line to the north, Grant aborted the attack above the James in favor of one against Lee's depleted force below the river.

The charge at Petersburg was based on the idea of a few ingenious ex-miners from Pennsylvania serving in the Northern army. They dug a tunnel that stretched 586 feet from their line to a point under the Southern breastworks, filled it with 8,000 pounds of explosives, and then detonated the powder to blow an enormous opening for their troops to exploit. The resulting crater (135 feet deep, 97 feet front to rear, and 35 feet wide) proved a death trap for the Yankee attackers. As they swarmed into the yawning chasm, their crowded mass offered an inviting target to Rebel cannoneers who, despite the shock of the explosion, stood their ground. The Union saw over 5,000 of their men killed, wounded, or captured before they escaped the snare their own cunning had created.[26]

Ewell's front grew quiet after the Battle of the Crater. When Grant relinquished his position above the James, all the clerks returned to their desks in Richmond. The rest of the reinforcements (excepting Field's Division) who had rushed to the north also went back to their original stations. Ewell's line,

from Chaffin's Bluff to the Charles City Road, was protected by
Gary's troopers to the north, Field's infantry in the center, and
the artillerymen (the only element still reporting to Ewell)
to the south.

The slack in action came because Grant had dispatched a
force to deal with Early in the Valley. Major General Philip
Sheridan was put in charge of two corps of infantry, the small
army of West Virginia, plus three divisions of cavalry, and
ordered to drive the Confederates out of the Shenandoah. While
Lee could not match the Union numbers, he did the best he
could by shipping both Fitz Lee's cavalry and Kershaw's infantry
to Early's support.[27]

On August 12th the enemy renewed their probes north of
the James River. They began digging a canal through Dutch Gap.
If Grant could bypass this bend in the river, Butler's army, still
entrapped within the Bermuda Hundred, could leave the bottle-
neck where the Rebels held them in place with just minimum
numbers. Lee would be forced to construct new lines which he
could not man. Ewell was ordered to try to impede the Union's
efforts, but before he could act, the Yankees approached his
line. Birney's corps came up the Varina Road, Hancock's infantry advanced between the Darbytown and New Market Roads,
and enemy cavalry closed on Richmond along the Charles City
Road. Recalling Grant's feint of two weeks ago, Lee chose not to
reinforce his position above the James. Ewell, Field, and Gary
would have to fend for themselves.

Grant's plan was the same one he had envisioned two
weeks ago. While his infantry threatened the Rebels' line to hold
them in place, his cavalry would turn Ewell's flank and ride into
Richmond. He opened his attack on August 14th when Birney
and Hancock crept up to the Confederate entrenchment and
stopped. The Union cavalry charged down the Charles City Road
on August 16th. Their advance was met by Gary, but the enemy's
superior numbers proved too much for the Rebel horsemen, who
retreated in disarray. The withdrawal left Field's flank along the
Darbytown Road open to assault. When Hancock saw the opportunity, he immediately threw his troops forward against Field's
weakened position. The Yankee infantry broke through, ripping
a huge hole in the Rebel line. The road to Richmond lay

undefended.

It was a desperate moment for the Rebels. Lee, who had come up to take command, called everywhere for reinforcements to rush up and close the gap. Ewell left his lines to bring the artillerymen north, Bushrod Johnson's brigade, consigned to Ewell earlier but just now reaching the front, pushed his men toward the breakthrough and the clerks came running out of Richmond. Before any of these added men arrived, however, Field closed his ranks and drove Hancock back down the Darbytown Road to his initial line.[28]

To the north, where Gary's cavalry had lost ground, the situation remained perilous. Wade Hampton, just starting for the Valley to support Early, heard of the emergency, wheeled his troopers around, and galloped to join in the fight. When he reached the scene, both his men and their animals were exhausted by the rush to the front, but they grimly charged the enemy on the Charles City Road. The unexpected assault hit the Yankees like a tornado, and the bluecoats reeled backward from the blow.[29] The entire Rebel line was restored.

The very next day, Grant advanced at Petersburg, hoping to turn Lee's western flank and sever his link via the Weldon Railroad to the south. The Confederate army received most of their supplies over this line, and Lee took frantic steps to keep the tracks out of Northern hands. He recalled not only all of the men just sent to Ewell's front but also pulled two of Field's brigades (and Field) from their breastworks above the James. The supreme effort was of no avail. The Federals captured four critical miles of the railroad and all efforts to dislodge them failed.[30]

In the midst of this bad news, the Confederacy received encouragement from the North. Grant's hammering had resulted in huge casualties, and support for the war had dimmed above the Mason-Dixon Line. On August 29th, McClellan was nominated by the Democrats to oppose Lincoln in the fall elections. Their platform stated "after four years of failure to restore the Union by the experiment of war . . . [we] demand that immediate efforts be made for a cessation of hostilities."[31] Even if the Rebels could not win on the battlefield, they were in position to gain their independence through the ballot. Most thought Lincoln was doomed to defeat, but just two days later, Sherman drove the Army of Tennessee under Hood (who had taken charge from Joe Johnston) from Atlanta. His success changed the mood up north and when Sheridan overwhelmed Early in the third battle of Winchester on September 19th, citizens in the Union realized they were winning the war, and all thought of Federal capitulation disappeared. Three days later, Sheridan attacked Early at Fisher's Hill. The Yankees again shattered the Rebels ranks, and as the Confederates fled south, they left both Sandie Pendleton and Robert Rodes dying on the field.

Ewell was devastated by the death of his two former subordinates, especially that of Sandie Pendleton. "The men in my old corps said it is not [me] but Sandie who commands," he wrote the young man's father, "but I never felt a pang of jealousy."[32]

What Ewell did not say but certainly felt was the absolute certainty that the Confederates were losing the war. Where once the South controlled their own actions, choosing if they would attack or assume the defense, now the Rebels could only react whenever the Federals decided to assault. And with the loss of the Weldon Railroad, even standing up to the enemy had become questionable. How could Lee keep his army supplied with food and ammunition? "We [were] already meager and emaciated . . . ," John Jones wrote, "but there is a mournful gloom upon the brow of many since Gen. Grant holds the Weldon Road."[33]

Despite his discouragement, Ewell remained dedicated to regaining field command. He proved this when the enemy again attacked his front on September 29th. They crept forward at 3:00 a.m., their numbers concealed by both the darkness and a dense fog. The Yankees moved slowly toward a new line Ewell was erecting. He was entrenching in between Signal Hill and the Varina Road to keep the Federals' from using the canal they were still digging across Dutch Gap. When Ewell learned of the bluecoats' approach, he assumed that they were only checking out his almost finished breastworks. He had stationed a force there, and he was sure they could handle a raiding party. But after sending a note to Lee to tell him about the Yankee foray, Ewell decided that he had better reinforce his guard, and he roused several companies of artillerymen and started them to Signal Hill.[34]

A few hours later, as Ewell was eating his breakfast, a

messenger arrived with sinister news. Brigadier General John Gregg, defending his upper flank with the two brigades Field had left behind and Gary's cavalry, reported that the Yankees were gathering in force between the New Market and Kingsland Roads. The dispatch was an alarming one. Ewell knew at once that he had miscalculated the intent of the Federals' early morning movement. They were about to launch a massive assault against him, and their blow would fall at any moment. With only 4,400 troops at hand plus 1,500 men three miles to the rear in reserve along the intermediate arc, Ewell lacked the force to defend the entire length of his line. He had to concentrate his meager numbers where he thought the Federals might charge. Recalling Grant's prior strategy of assaulting his flank, Ewell ordered Gregg to cover the north; he would rush south with his artillerymen to make a stand by the river at Chaffin's Bluff.[35]

Ewell guessed wrong. The Union attack was divided into two wings: Major General David Birney's 12,400 infantry plus a cavalry division under Brigadier General August Kautz came up the New Market Road toward Gregg's line. A force of 8,000 men under Major General Edward Ord were on the Varina Road en route to Fort Harrison, the center of the Confederate front, the area just vacated by Ewell in his attempt to strengthen his flank.[36] Ewell's transfer of about one thousand artillerymen south had created a weak link in his defense.

The Federals attacked both Gregg and Ewell at 5:30 a.m. Protected behind breastworks, Gregg managed to repel Birney's assault, but the handful of artillerymen left behind at Fort Harrison never had a chance against Ord's inexorable numbers. The enemy came en masse up to the dry moat fronting the parapets, dropped down into the ditch, climbed the eighteen-foot high dirt rampart (improvising ladders by jabbing their bayoneted rifles into the earthen wall), and then poured into the works. As the bluecoats entered the bastion, the few Rebels at hand fled for their lives.[37]

Ewell had gone with the artillerymen to Fort Maury, a small bulwark below Chaffin's Bluff to await the Federal blow. He watched with horror as the enemy easily overran the area he had just left. When Fort Harrison fell, he knew that the road to

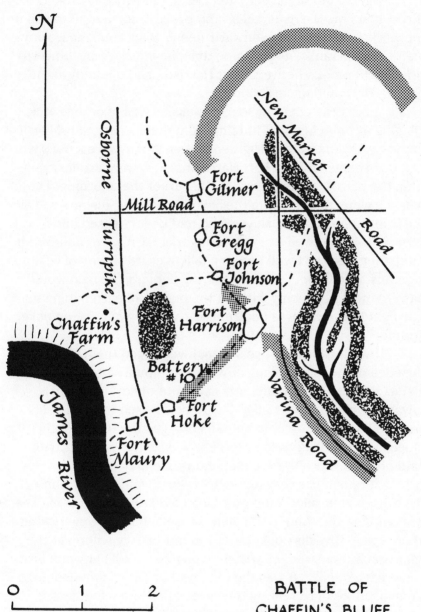

N

Osborne Turnpike

New Market

Mill Road

Fort
Gilmer

Road

Fort
Gregg

Fort
Johnson

Chaffin's
Farm

Fort
Harrison

Battery
#10

James River

Fort
Hoke

Fort
Maury

Varina Road

0   1   2

Miles

BATTLE OF
CHAFFIN'S BLUFF

Sept. 29 – Oct. 2, 1864

333

Richmond lay essentially open to the Yankees.

He barked out orders: tell Lee the enemy has broken through at Fort Harrison, telegraph Bragg in Richmond to call up the clerks and rush them onward, see if Gregg could spare any men from his ranks. At the same time, he mounted his horse to ride for the woods between Fort Harrison and the path to the capital. He would make a stand.

Under the cover of soaring oaks, leaves of orange still clinging to branches that hid him from the enemy's view, Ewell found a conglomerate of frightened men. Some were troops who had been expelled from Fort Harrison; a few were artillerymen from the patrol driven off Signal Hill earlier that morning. The balance were infantry from the Seventh Georgia, just arrived at the front to reclaim the slaves who had been pressed into service to build Ewell's new breastworks.[38] Only two hundred in total, they were all Ewell had to challenge Ord's army of 8,000 veterans. And if this was not sobering enough, the men would have to meet the enemy without the benefit of entrenchments. The fight that Ewell was determined to wage would be on naked ground.

Herding his men like sheep, Ewell urged them forward to the edge of the forest. They moved tremulously into the open just as a line of Federal soldiers came out of Fort Harrison toward Ewell's motley ranks. The Rebels raised their muskets and fired a volley, a feeble but effective gesture that sent the bluecoats scurrying back into the works. Ewell's bluster had paid off. Ord's troops were momentarily at bay.

"I remember very distinctly how [Ewell] looked," one of the skirmishers said. "Mounted on an old gray horse, as mad as he could be, shouting to the men and seeming to be everywhere at once . . . . [By] his cool courage and presence wherever the fight was hottest, [he] contributed as much . . . as any one man could have done."[39] It was the old Ewell of '61, summoned forth from his place of retreat by the necessities of the moment.

Ewell's impertinent bluff did not end the fighting, but it did change the enemy's strategy. Instead of continuing on the open path to Richmond, they turned to attack the Rebel flanks, which Ewell had wisely kept manned. Federal soldiers started advancing on Fort Maury. Halfway to their objective, they were met by grape and canister fired from Ewell's guns. The barrage was so fierce, the Yankees were forced to abandon their assault.[40]

To the north Gregg had extended his line downward into Fort Johnson. When the enemy tried to turn Ewell's center by charging this bastion, the attack, delivered piecemeal, one brigade at a time, was easily repelled. And as Ewell's front stabilized, reinforcements began to arrive. Hughs' infantry, Gary's cavalry, and the Rebels' gunboats sailing on the James River joined the fray. Ewell skillfully directed everything, knitting an impenetrable defense, turning what had started as a calamity into a brilliant success.

"Yet great as were his [prior] accomplishments, they do not equal his achievement this day," Richard Sommers has commented. This leading authority on the 1864 battles at Richmond observed, "Acting in the face of imminent disaster to forge and sustain a continuous line to contain the Federal breakthrough and save Richmond was the greatest contribution Ewell ever rendered to the Confederate cause."[41]

About 11:00 a.m., Anderson, First Corps commander, rode up from Petersburg below the James. He came with orders from Lee to take charge of the front, to marshall the forces under Ewell and Gregg and make an attempt to retake Fort Harrison. Lee's instructions read like a denunciation of Ewell for losing the key bastion.

Knowing full well that he had been a hero, that he had proved his capability for field command by his performance that morning, Ewell was incensed that Lee had sent Anderson to replace him. He refused to either step aside or to cooperate in an attack on the fort, a foolhardy scheme given the overwhelming number of Union soldiers gathered behind the best entrenchments the South could build. His angry stand convinced Anderson to not only defer the assault on Fort Harrison but also to accept a division of command responsibilities. He would direct Confederate operations from Fort Gilmer north; Ewell would remain in charge below that line.[42]

Lee's concern for recapturing the key bastion along the exterior line lay with his recognition that if the enemy continued to occupy the fort, he would have to commit troops to contain the Federals above the James River. He had no men to spare.

335

When he first learned of the disaster, Lee sent a wire to Ewell to "endeavor to retake Fort Harrison."[43] Ewell replied that this was not possible with the force at hand. Lee, no doubt disappointed with Ewell's answer, then started reinforcements, 16,000 men, one-third of his whole army, forward. "It will take time for troops from here to reach [the] north side," Lee advised Ewell. "Can you not draw . . . from your left to retake Fort Harrison?"[44]

The men to Ewell's left (now under Anderson) were busy defending against attacks by the Federals determined to break through the Rebels' line at Fort Gilmer. The enemy assaults began with a noisy artillery bombardment about noon, followed by three infantry charges an hour apart. After all had been repelled, the Union decided to end their ventures that day.

All this time Southern reinforcements continued to pour into the area. Ewell guided the troops into position, and by 3:00 p.m., saw that a sufficient force was finally at hand to attempt to recapture Fort Harrison. "We will take the offensive . . . soon," he wired Lee.[45]

When he rode to Fort Maury to set up the assault, Ewell met Lee, who had come north to direct the advance. Snowden's Twenty-Fifth Tennessee, Montague's brigade, plus a hardy contingent of Ewell's artillerymen, moved out at 5:00 p.m. They quickly recaptured Fort Hoke, conceded by the Yankees without a fight, then hurried on for Fort Harrison. As they closed on the well-built bastion, the Union gunners fired a cruel barrage that was so devastating, the Rebels saw that they had no chance of dislodging the enemy, and that they would absorb needless casualties by continuing to press forward. Montague, leading the charge, ordered a retreat.[46]

While Lee accepted Montague's decision, he had not given up his hopes of retaking the fort. He decided to make a full scale attack the next morning when all of his reinforcements were available. Field, who reached the front with three brigades about 7:00 p.m., disagreed with the delay, and went to Lee to urge an immediate assault. He argued that the Yankees would use the night to strengthen their position. His pleas were so similar to Gordon's suggestions at Gettysburg, Ewell, who had been denounced for turning down that recommendation, must have listened with singular interest for Lee's reaction. Lee now did exactly as Ewell had done at Gettysburg. He noted that the troops were exhausted after marching all day, that more men were due soon, and that he preferred to wait until dawn.[47] While the Rebels retired for the night, the enemy stayed up to dig in.

Ewell arose before sunrise to ride the field and survey his dispositions. About 9:00 a.m., Lee and some of his aides joined Ewell. The commander questioned Ewell intently on his opinions. Eager to flaunt his expertise, to demonstrate that he was recovered and able to resume command, Ewell became so absorbed in their discussion, he failed to spot the gaping hole in his path. And when his horse swerved to avert the crater, Ewell flew off his mount to land headfirst on a rock on the ground. He was not seriously hurt. "No bones broken," Moxley Sorrel recalled, "but . . . his head [was] scratched, bruised, torn, and bloody."[48]

As Ewell tried to collect himself, Lee looked down from above. "[Go] back to Richmond," Lee ordered, "and stay there until [you are] completely well."

Completely well! Lee still considered him frail, unfit for command. The valiant performance of yesterday which should have proven him fully capable of resuming duty in the field had been transcended by the fall from his horse. Ewell saw that unless he demonstrated immediate recuperative powers from his injuries, his career was finished.

Ewell was taken by ambulance to a hospital in Richmond. Upon his arrival, he insisted on immediate treatment, and his impatience probably hurried the doctor into a stopgap effort, winding bandages around his head from bald pate to shoulders, poking holes in the cloth so he could see and breathe. With little concern that he looked like a mummy, Ewell rushed back to the front. He had been gone for only several hours.

"Painfully comic [he] was," Sorrel remembered. "But indifferent . . . to such mishaps, [Ewell] was sharp about his work . . . lisping out directions."

Ewell no doubt heard the low titters. But fully driven now by his own personal demons, he felt he must show himself as stalwart as anybody. Lee could not presume him to be feeble.

While Ewell was absent, Lee settled on his strategy for retaking Fort Harrison. He would start at 11:00 a.m. with an artillery barrage, using both his field cannons and the navy gun ships. The infantry, 9,000 troops charging from the west and northwest, would then assault. While the plan was sound, the execution was faulty. The cannonade opened on schedule, but when most of the shells fell short, the fort was unharmed and the Yankee defenders remained at their posts, ready to receive the attack. And when Lee's forces charged at 2:00 p.m., their leaders failed to coordinate the movement. Those from the northwest hurried forward while the regiments to the west remained in place. Lee rode frantically from point to point to personally mold a united effort, but these efforts were fruitless, and by 3:00 p.m., with his losses mounting, he saw that the battle was lost. He called a halt.[49]

As the dejected Rebels trudged back toward their camps, the sky grew dark and a cold rain began to fall. That night, as the storm continued overhead, Lee called a meeting of his generals (including Ewell) to discuss plans. Lee had decided to give up his attempt to retake Fort Harrison. He proposed digging a new trench between Forts Hoke and Johnson. Most agreed with Lee, but Pemberton (Ewell's artillery chief) urged that they make one last try at repelling the enemy. "I made my effort . . . and failed," Lee answered. "There shall be no more blood shed . . . unless you can show me a practical plan of capture."[50] Pemberton had no proposal in mind. Work on the new line started the following morning, and by dusk the next day, October 1st, the entrenchment was finished. Stalemate returned to Ewell's front.

A week later, October 7th, Lee did mount another attack on Fort Harrison. Ewell was in reserve behind the newly completed line when Hoke and Field charged the enemy's position. Their advance, however, was just as disjointed as before, and the Rebels suffered not only a rebuff but also casualties of over 1,000 men, including the fatal wounding of Brigadier General John Gregg. About two weeks later, even worse news came from the Valley. Early had charged Sheridan at Cedar Creek, but after routing the enemy in the morning, he paused while his men plundered the Federal camps. The Yankees regrouped to counterattack. In a fierce battle, they almost destroyed the Second Corps as they drove Early back up the Valley. Ramseur, one of

Ewell's favorites, lost his life in that fray.[51]

On October l9th, the same day that Early was so roundly crushed in the Valley, Longstreet returned to duty. Although he had not completely recovered from wounds received during the Wilderness Battle (he would never regain the use of his right arm), Longstreet was mentally fit, and Lee put him in command of all troops north of the James River, which included Ewell and his tiny force. Longstreet was soon tested by the Federals, who tried to take advantage of his "rusty" military skills by mounting a two-pronged attack: one element feinted a charge up the New Market Road while the second moved north to make a real assault on the Williamsburg Pike. Longstreet was not fooled by the enemy's strategy. When he saw that the initial Yankee thrust lacked spirit, he quickly pulled Field's men out from behind their breastworks and rushed them north. They were in line on the Williamsburg Pike when the bluecoats began their charge. Shocked by finding the Rebels in force, the Federals withdrew with embarrassing speed, and when a cold rain began to fall, they totally abandoned the front.[52]

This attack was the last by the Yankees against Ewell's front that year. Grant's reasons for relaxing his efforts to capture the Confederate capital were related to happenings in the deep south. Sherman and Hood were duelling in Georgia. Seeing that he was too weak to crush Sherman in battle, Hood attempted to lure his adversary out of Georgia by taking his troops north, hoping the enemy would follow him. "Damn him!" Sherman said when he learned of the move, "[But] if he will go to the Ohio River, I'll give him rations."[53] His cockiness stemmed from having already dispatched two of the three armies in his command north to deal with Hood. While Thomas at Nashville and Schofield at Pulaski awaited the Army of Tennessee, Sherman would be unopposed in Georgia. He planned to head southeast, marching to the sea to reestablish his supply line, then come north to unite with Grant against Lee. Anticipating massive and veteran reinforcements, Grant could afford a delay in his campaign against Richmond.

Ewell's November quiet was broken by a summons from Lee to army headquarters. Probably expecting that he was finally being restored to field command, Ewell rushed to report.

He was bitterly disappointed. Lee suggested that Ewell accept a new post as Chief of the Bureau of Cavalry, a desk job in the capital. Longstreet had recommended the appointment, noting that Ewell could not "get about well on foot . . . . "[54]

"I prefer active duty," Ewell snorted as he refused the post. "I have been exclusively on similar duty for a quarter of a century, and have no experience . . . as a bureau officer."[55]

Based on their prior discussions, Lee had expected that Ewell would reject the duty, and to show that he bore no hard feelings, he asked his former subordinate to share his lunch, two sweet potatoes. Ewell could not resist such a delectable treat (a pitiful commentary on the depths to which the South had fallen), and for the first time in months, he said "yes" to a proposal by Lee.

As Christmas approached, Ewell continued to stay in the field at Chaffin's Farm. He attended to his ordinary duties, one of which was supervising the testing of a new gun, a big rifled cannon. A large group was present for the firing, and during the exercise, a courier approached Ewell with news of a Rebel victory in a battle fought between Mackey's Point and Pocotaligo. Ewell had never heard of either place, and asked if anyone present knew where they were located.

"South Carolina," a young officer called out.[56]

Turning toward the speaker, Ewell thought he recognized the lad. "Aren't you the man who came so near shooting me at Ashland?" he questioned.

"I am."

Ewell remembered that incident very well. While he was training recruits early in the war, he had issued orders that no one was to enter camp through a particular gate. When he returned that night from visiting the village, however, Ewell decided he would use that post. He was stopped by the guard, George Eggelston, the youth at his side. Ewell tried to push past, but the sentry refused to yield, pointing his rifle at Ewell's stomach, holding him at bay while he called for help. The officer of the day soon arrived. Ewell ordered the lieutenant to throw the private in irons, but he refused.

"The sentinel has only done his duty," the officer protested, "obeying the orders you have given him."

Ewell saw that he was in the wrong, offered an apology, and galloped away to come into camp through another gate. He had not seen Eggleston since that night. Now, recalling the episode, Ewell offered a droll postscript. "I'm glad you did not [shoot me]."

In mid-December, Lee made an organizational change that again revived Ewell's hopes for a field command. Lee relieved Early as head of the Second Corps. Because of his series of defeats by Sheridan in the Valley, influential people in the Confederacy had lost confidence in Early, and Lee felt compelled to respond to their demands for a new general. He recalled the Second Corps to Richmond, but postponed naming Jubal's replacement until their arrival. Early stayed in the Valley in charge of a small army composed of just Wharton's brigade, an artillery section, and Rosser's cavalry.[57] While Ewell probably did not really think that he would be put in charge of his old corps, he still wanted the post, and the days of waiting for Lee's pronouncement were no doubt agonizing for him. His dreams were soon dashed. Lee placed John Gordon in the coveted command.[58]

Even though Ewell was not surprised by the appointment, he was crushed by the snub, and he sought solitude by sending his aides back to Richmond for the holidays. He remained alone on duty on the exterior line. When a nearby farmer saw Ewell in isolation, he sent him a Christmas present, a big turkey leg. Ewell had expected to eat the drumstick by himself, but later that day as he rode along the stream to check out his cannon emplacements, he met his young friend, Robert Stiles and invited him to share in his meal. Stiles eagerly accepted, thus providing Ewell companionship when he needed it most.[59]

As Ewell sat alone in his headquarters on Christmas Eve, a picket burst into the house to report that a Northern force was approaching the exterior line. Ewell sent an urgent message to Richmond to assemble the clerks and rush them forward to his side. Knowing that Ewell was not a man to "cry wolf," the local officials immediately rang the tocsins to summon the citizen-soldiers to arms. Led by the officers that Ewell had put on leave, they raced to the front, but as they filed into the trenches, the supposed peril vanished. The Yankee patrol had returned to its camp. The cold winter night became still once more, and Christmas was as peaceful as it ought to be.

Lizinka was at a party in Richmond when the bells began ringing to alert the clerks to assemble. Knowing that Ewell was alone at the front, Lizinka decided to go to him, and she brought some of the other guests with her. One was a distant relative of Ewell's, a doctor named Smith. After the Federal threat had vanished, the two held a prolonged conversation in which Ewell revealed his feelings that the South's attempt to win its freedom had been in vain. "The Confederacy is lost," he concluded. "[I think] Lee should ask for peace."[60]

Most Southerners agreed with Ewell that they had little chance of winning the war. They saw that while their capital remained out of Grant's reach, Lee could not drive the enemy away from the city's gates. Richmond's defense would fail in time.

Out west, Hood had staggered to a halt below Nashville. His ranks were decimated by losses from a November 30th fight at Franklin, where he had rashly assaulted impregnable works, and he was too weak to risk an attack on George Thomas' force to his front. His men lay shivering in the cold, waiting for the enemy to come to them. Thomas advanced on December 15th, and in the most decisive battle of the war, he shattered the only meaningful Confederate army other than Lee's east of the Mississippi.[61]

Sherman was still in Georgia, just outside of Savannah, about to enter the city and reestablish his supply lines from the sea. His next move would be to proceed north, join with Grant, and confront Lee.

And, so with the reality of certain defeat confronting the South, sagging morale finally began to break. All over the Confederacy, as if by mutual consent, people simply gave up the struggle in their minds. Richmond itself became an odd bedlam city where fear of imminent battle mixed with the desperate search for food. In the field, many of the Southern generals preferred death to living under Northern rule and seemed to be recklessly exposing their persons. "Lee to the rear!" was a cry heard more than once since the battle at the Wilderness, where the army's leader had first sought the grandeur of dying in battle. "If we are to be conquered," Jeb Stuart had stated, "[I do] not want to live."[62] A.P. Hill was destined to die, too. When the enemy finally broke through the lines below Petersburg, he rode to the front, where he was shot while offering no resistance.

Ewell was so depressed and disillusioned at this time that like the others, he may have been considering a glorious death, too. Lizinka, however, induced him to make a different decision—one that viewed in the strictest sense was probably traitorous. Late that Christmas Eve, after all the guests had gone, she and Ewell talked about their future. Lizinka noted that because she was the wife of a Confederate officer, all of her properties would be confiscated after the war was over. But if she rejected the South now, before the Cause was lost, she could recover her multiple estates. They could live out their years in great comfort. Lizinka stated that she intended to take the Oath of Allegiance to the Union to regain her Federal citizenship![63]

Ewell must have known that Lizinka's act would probably result in his being branded a traitor and that he faced being shunned by old friends for the rest of his life. While this was an unthinkable fate, he could not help but admit that her proposal made realistic sense. Why should they live in poverty to demonstrate fidelity to a lost cause, to honor those people who had demoted him from his command? Whatever arguments Lizinka offered, she was bound to win. Ewell could not refuse her a thing in normal times; in his present debilitated and disillusioned condition he acceded to Lizinka's plan to go back North.

* * * *

Was Ewell a traitor? What is treasonous behavior in a political entity never officially recognized as a nation by outsiders and facing certain disintegration? How long must a cause's adherents sacrifice especially as the cause dies? Lizinka saw the futility of the situation, and she did not hesitate to desert the South. Ewell, however, could not bring himself to take that step. While he would help his wife in every way, he would remain at his post and fight the war to its bitter end. Ewell paid a price for his decision. Already harassed by mounting pressure as the enemy tightened their death grip on the Confederacy, his distress was now magnified because of the fearful secret he bore. Ewell was working with Union officials to secure Lizinka's citizenship and to regain her properties. Ewell's effectiveness as an officer was certainly compromised. Perhaps he thought that he could sustain his duty as he preserved some sort of a future, and that he would not be called upon to deal with issues of importance. If so, Ewell would soon find that he was wrong.

Appomattox

Lizinka had decided to take the Oath of Allegiance to the Union in order to gain the restoration of her many properties. She probably felt that since the North was anxious to end the war, they would encourage highly placed Confederates (such as herself) to leave the South, serving as examples for the masses to follow. There had been indications that in this crucial pre-peace phase of the war, the winning of prominent civilians to the Federals' side was just as vital to the North as military victories in the field. She had to act quickly, however, because once the shooting stopped, the enemy would have no further use for her. They would most likely treat the Confederate elite, especially the wife of a Rebel general, most harshly.

The first step in her plan was to contact Thomas Gantt, her lawyer cousin in St. Louis, Missouri, to represent her to the Lincoln administration.[1] Gantt had managed her financial affairs for years, and like Lizinka, was a personal friend of influential people (such as the Blairs) in the Union capital.

As Gantt opened a dialogue with Montgomery Blair, Lizinka took steps to restore Tarpley, her plantation located below Nashville, with fields that stretched into Mississippi. She needed workers to replace the former slaves. Hiring any free blacks was out of the question, as she shared her son Campbell's deep prejudices. "If the negro is put under the same laws against theft and perjury [that apply to whites]," he had written, "we will have to build extra penitentiaries everywhere . . . ."[2] The only means for hiring new hands was up North, where agencies specialized in placing Irish, Swede, and German emigrantes.

Campbell volunteered to travel to New York City to meet with the agencies and hire white employees. Crossing Federal lines would be easy, as passports were being issued every day to wealthy Southerners, who made the trip to buy provisions.[3] Several days after Christmas, Campbell left Richmond for New York, Philadelphia, and then Baltimore. To keep Ewell's name out of any record of his treachery, he sent his first report to Lizinka. He informed her that on January 10, 1865, he had met with Harris and Ashby in New York. "They [can] furnish farm hands for $12 to $15 per month for men and $7 to $10 for women or boys," he wrote. "[They] advise getting two or three families to form a center and the rest, men. [They can provide] Germans or Irish on a day's notice but might be a week in filling an order for Swedes, Norwegians, Hollanders, etc. . . . [We] will have to furnish .. . passage money to Nashville . . . five dollars per head . . . . They [suggest employing a guide] as these peoples are so ignorant of our styles of travelling . . . they might get lost."[4]

Prior to calling on Harris and Ashby, Campbell had gone to another agent, whom he found disgusting. "His sign was too large for the office," the lad wrote. "[He] told me the emigrants would not be contented to live on what the negro [ate] . . . they would want meat to eat now and then . . . . I left him in his ignorance . . . that we never gave our negroes meat."

Other tasks Campbell completed during his trip included purchasing bags of seed for spring planting, which he shipped to W.T. Berry and Company in Richmond, and visiting brokers to determine the price trends for cotton and gold. Both were going down, and Campbell suggested investing in gold futures, "at least $5,000," for the moment. He ended his note by saying that he would return to Richmond the next day, coming by boat through Williamsburg or by car if he could catch a night train.

The Ewells were not the only ones who were watching out for themselves in January, 1865. But while their treason was driven by greed, to save a fortune so large they could afford to speculate in gold futures, most of those who abandoned the Rebel Cause were motivated by the need for food and clothing. Every night, hundreds of Lee's starving troops took advantage of the dark to climb out of their trenches and cross over to the Federal lines and surrender just to get a warm meal. The Confederate officials, tacitly admitting that their soldiers were justified in deserting, let them go, choosing to neither pursue the men nor punish them when caught.[5] The times were ripe for overtures of peace.

Frank Blair, one of Lizinka's influential friends, made the first move by visiting Richmond on January 12th to try to convince Jefferson Davis to open a dialogue with Lincoln. The Confederate President agreed to an early February conference, and appointed three emissaries, Robert Hunter, John Campbell, and Alexander Stephens, to represent the South. They passed through the Northern lines on January 31st, but when the trio reached City Point, the Federal supply depot at the mouth of the James River, they were stopped. The meeting with Lincoln had been cancelled. He would not accept the South's description of the negotiations as being between "our two countries."[6] This impasse was broken by Grant. Touched by the spontaneous and joyful cheers of his men as the Southern statesmen entered his lines, he appealed to Lincoln to ignore semantics and proceed with the conference.

Grant's entreaty caused Lincoln to change his mind and within an hour, he and William H. Seward, Secretary of State, were on board the River Queen, sailing for Virginia. They met with the Rebel spokesmen on that ship, the morning of February 3rd. The Southern contingent opened the conference by proposing that they set aside the war to combine forces and drive the French out of Mexico. Napoleon III had seized advantage of the American conflict to take over the capital of that country and install Maximilian, the Archduke of Austria, as emperor. Lincoln, however, refused to even consider this offer. He would do nothing until the Rebels had capitulated and come back into the Union.

Hunter tested the Federal leader's resolve. "You think that we of the Confederacy have committed treason," he asked, "that we are traitors . . . and are proper subjects for the hangman?"[7]

"That is about the size of it," Lincoln replied grimly, showing no sign of his usual humor.

The Confederate emissaries were so stunned by Lincoln's chilling remark, they decided to end the conference and return to the safety of Richmond. Federal shells accompanied their arrival as the enemy bombarded the capital to show their displeasure with the failed meeting. When Jefferson Davis spoke at Metropolitan Hall on February 6th, he used the impasse as proof that Union retribution was sure to come should the Confederates lose the war, that the Southern people had to keep fighting to the bitter end. He also offered hope, announcing that same day that Lee had been placed in command of all the Confederate armies. While the people were heartened by Lee's new role, he was less impressed by the promotion. "I do not know what he [Davis] wants me to undertake," Lee mournfully wondered when told of the assignment.[8]

Lee had reason to be apprehensive. How could he worry about troops far away when those directly under his command were so bitterly harassed? Grant had resumed his attacks, trying to cut off Lee's only remaining line of supply, a wagon trail west of Petersburg. In a three day fight near Hatcher's Run, the Rebels at first held the Yankees at bay, then drove them back from the front. The victory, however, forced Lee to extend his lines further west, and since his ranks were already thin everywhere else, he had few men to fill the new trenches.

Ewell took note of the problem. Showing his loyalty to the Cause (while paradoxically awaiting Lizinka's desertion), he offered to raise a force of clerks from the capital to man the exterior lines above the James, freeing veterans now in place to guard the more threatened trenches to the south. Lee refused this proposal. Ewell's idea was not impractical, but Lee saw that continuing a patchwork defense of Richmond was futile. Sherman had come out of Savannah on February 1, 1865, and was on his way north to unite with Grant against Lee. If Joe Johnston, back in charge of what remained of the Confederate Army of Tennessee, did not stop Sherman, which was improbable, the capital was doomed. The city was a trap. Lee had to go now, before Sherman arrived. When he issued his last ditch plans, Lee gave Ewell a key role.

Ewell had left his Chaffin's Farm headquarters and moved to Richmond where he could be with his wife during their few remaining hours together in the city, as she awaited approval of her petition to come north. He was in his office at the corner of Seventh and Franklin Streets when Lee's orders arrived on February 25th. "The emergency [alluded to yesterday] . . . has arisen . . . " Lee announced. "The cotton and tobacco which owners cannot remove must be destroyed."[9]

Lee's instructions, to burn the contraband so the enemy could not have it, meant that the Yankees were about to enter Richmond. The distressing orders must have terrorized Ewell. Lizinka had not yet received her pardon, and if she was still in the city when the bluecoats marched into the capital, all of their detailed plans would collapse. Lizinka would never regain her properties; they would face a penniless future.

There must have been a certain bitter relief in the dismal orders to fire the stores and leave the city. Ewell probably felt guilty because of his involvement in Lizinka's treason, and Lee's drastic orders meant that he would at least be spared from being branded a traitor. Sending Campbell to the mayor of Richmond, he requested an assembly of the common council to discuss destroying the tobacco and cotton stored in the capital. He knew that the local officials would undoubtedly panic upon learning of both the imminent arrival of the Yankees and the torching of valuable property. Ewell told Campbell to pretend that his visit was only an exercise, and that all he needed was a list of those people owning contraband.

Campbell handed his message to Mayor Mayo, then hovered outside the government's chambers to await an answer from the council. A committee of six, led by James D. Scott, emerged after an hour-long session, and demanded an audience with Ewell.[10] Campbell took them to Ewell's office where, after giving him the requested list, Scott added a warning. He said that when Ewell set fire to the cotton and tobacco, flames would soon spread to the rest of the city.

Ewell ignored the protest by introducing the council members to Major Isaac Carrington, his Provost Marshall. He explained that Carrington was ready to burn the contraband now, and they must accompany him to provide assistance should anyone try to stop the destruction. Shocked by Ewell's blunt pronouncement, the committee challenged his authority to torch private property. He had anticipated resistance. Each member was given a copy of Lee's orders plus the text of the bill that gave Ewell the right to carry out these instructions. The officials had no choice but to accept Ewell's decision, and the unhappy body left his office to go with Carrington on his mission.

Shortly after their departure, Ewell received another letter from Lee. The "emergency" he had cited in his earlier note was not at hand; Lee had only meant for Ewell to start planning to burn the tobacco and cotton, not to set any fires today.[11] Aides were hurriedly dispatched to find Carrington and stop him from applying the torch. He was found in time.

Despite the unexpected reprieve, Ewell saw that Scott's warning about flames spreading to other buildings in the city had merit. He decided to take a look at all the warehouses, to see if any should be spared because they were too close to other structures. His inspection took all the next day, and he personally checked every site. Ewell picked only four for burning: the Public Warehouse close to the Petersburg Depot, Shockoe Warehouse in the heart of the business district, and Mayo's and Dibrell's Warehouses, located on Clay Street.[12]

After returning to his offices, Ewell called Carrington to his side. He gave the Provost Marshal the list of buildings to be torched, asked him to make plans to destroy these warehouses, but told him to be sure to obtain advice from the common council. If there were any claims of miscarriage, he intended to see that no blame fell on him. With that issue in mind, Ewell went to see Mayor Mayo. The tiny, wasted, eighty-year-old-man, known for his elaborate dress which usually included "a white cravat and irrepressible ruffles,"[13] sat quietly as Ewell outlined his concerns. While the warehouses marked for firing were sufficiently isolated from other buildings, once the Confederate army abandoned Richmond, mob violence was likely. Unrestrained vandals would probably burn homes and businesses. To prevent this from happening, Ewell suggested a volunteer force to protect the city. He promised to supply arms for every man Mayo recruited.

The mayor attempted to follow Ewell's advice. But when he issued his appeal for citizens to come forward to serve on the volunteer force, only one person answered Mayo's call.[14] There would be no local police force in the interval between Lee's departure and Grant's arrival in the Confederate capital. Richmond would be at the mercy of her worst elements.

The same Sunday that Ewell spent inspecting the tobacco and cotton warehouses, President Davis, Lee, Longstreet, and John Breckinridge (Confederate Secretary of War) secretly met to discuss a new peace proposal suggested by Federal General Edward Ord. The General had made his offer to Longstreet at the front with a flag of truce. "[Since] the politicians of the North are afraid to touch the question of peace,"

Ord began, "there is no way to open the subject except through officers of the armies."[15] He recommended a face-to-face meeting between Lee and Grant that he felt sure would result in the two reaching an honorable agreement for ending the war. Lee was attracted by Ord's idea, and he sent Grant a letter on March 2nd asking for a conference. The Union general, however, refused to cooperate. His reply gruffly noted that only Lincoln held the authority to make terms, and there would be no meeting except on the battlefield.

Lee must have despaired at Grant's rejection of this chance to make peace, especially upon receiving the latest news from the Valley. Sheridan had attacked Early again. In a battle of unequal forces, he had captured most of Early's troops, removing any further need for the Yankees to remain in the Shenandoah. Sheridan was on the way to Richmond to add to Grant's already dominant numbers.

Early rode into the capital on March 16th. Accompanied by only a few aides, his arrival presented a pitiful contrast to his departure nine months ago, when Jubal took Ewell's thousands north to pursue glory. "Your reverses in the Valley . . . which the public and the army [must] judge chiefly by the results have, I fear, impaired your influence," Lee wrote, "and I deem a change in commanders in your Department necessary."[16] Lee was sending Early home and out of the army. Ewell, while not one to gloat over others' troubles, must have received at least some pleasure from Early's disgrace.

In addition to Sheridan, even more Union reinforcements were approaching Richmond. Sherman had hurried through South Carolina, stopping only to torch Columbia, the state capital, and was now in North Carolina, waiting for Schofield's troops to arrive from Wilmington where they had landed by sea. Once these two armies were joined together, they would come north, blasting Johnston aside, to unite with Grant.

As the Yankee noose tightened, a courier passed through the lines. He came from St. Louis carrying a copy of a telegram to Lizinka Ewell, living in Dr. Hancock's house on Main Street, Richmond, Virginia. The March 22nd message was brief:

Thomas Gantt:

*The president gave the order to General Dodge yesterday
by telegram which we supposed you desired in relation
to Mrs. Ewell.*

Montgomery Blair[17]

There was no turning back. Lizinka would leave at once
for St. Louis to take the Oath of Allegiance. She would then seek
a court decision to restore her properties, and if that was favorable, go on to Nashville to begin the restoration of her plantation at Spring Hill.

The same night that Ewell and Lizinka received the
telegram from Montgomery Blair, John Gordon had approached
Lee to suggest a means of easing the siege of Richmond. He
proposed an attack on Fort Stedman, the Union line east of
Petersburg. If Gordon could open a hole through the Federal
defenses, he could force Grant to abandon his positions to the
south and west, giving Lee a shorter front to protect. This
would also open communications to Johnson, contesting
Sherman's position in North Carolina. The scheme had almost
no chance of success, but Lee was so impressed by Gordon's
fervor, he decided to take the risk.

The assault was launched before dawn on March 25th. As
Gordon had predicted, the Yankee line was quickly penetrated.
Grant, however, rushed thousands of soldiers into the breach,
and Gordon found himself assailed from all sides. His troops
wavered, then turned to run for the safety of their trenches.
They left 3,500 comrades killed, wounded or captured in enemy
hands.[18]

Gordon's drubbing at Fort Stedman convinced Lee that
he could no longer cope with Grant's numbers. He had to abandon Richmond while there was still the opportunity to escape
and unite with Johnson in confronting the enemy. Since he could
not move through Grant's lines, Lee planned to load his army on
the cars of the Southside Railroad and hurry west to Danville.
He would then switch to the Piedmont Railroad and ride south
to Greensboro where he would meet Johnson. Lee had to go by

train because he had little chance of evading the Yankees on foot.

Grant, however, saw the same picture, and he planned to thwart Lee's move. He quickly sent Sheridan's cavalry riding in a wide arc southwest, then northwest, to block Lee's path to Danville. When Lee learned that the Union was enroute to cut off his line of escape, he countered by dispatching both Pickett's infantry and Fitz Lee's troopers right, toward Five Forks, to intercept the enemy and push them south, away from the Rebels' avenue of retreat.

Pickett made contact with Sheridan's troops the night of March 30th. Marching southwest for Dinwiddie Court House the next morning, hoping to turn the enemy's left, Pickett found that he could not get around the Union, which remained in touch throughout the day. That night, as he planned a daybreak attack, Pickett learned that troops from Warren's Fifth Corps had been captured late that afternoon. His foe included infantry, not just Sheridan's cavalry. The disturbing information caused Pickett to grow leery, and he decided that instead of taking the offense on April 1st, he had better fall back to Five Forks where he could set up a stronger defense. The Union followed, keeping close contact.[19]

The following morning, as Pickett guided his force into position, he received an invitation to lunch from Tom Rosser, Ewell's artilleryman at First Manassas. Rosser, now head of a cavalry division under Fitz Lee, had gone fishing late the night before and caught a "mess of shad." Not expecting Sheridan's men to attack him, Pickett rode to the rear to join with Fitz Lee and Rosser in eating fish. They were all still enjoying their meal when Sheridan charged about 4:00 p.m. The Yankees broke through the Rebel's left, isolating Pickett's men from the rest of Lee's army and capturing the Southside Railroad—the Confederate path out of Richmond.[20]

Lee's response was a massive shuffling of his army west to try and retake the vital tracks, and over the next twenty-four hours, the Confederates traded positions with desperate speed: Anderson, located in front of Petersburg, rushed west to extricate Pickett; Longstreet hurried south with Field's Division to secure the gap left in the Rebel line; and Ewell was asked to summon the clerks out of Richmond and cover the ground

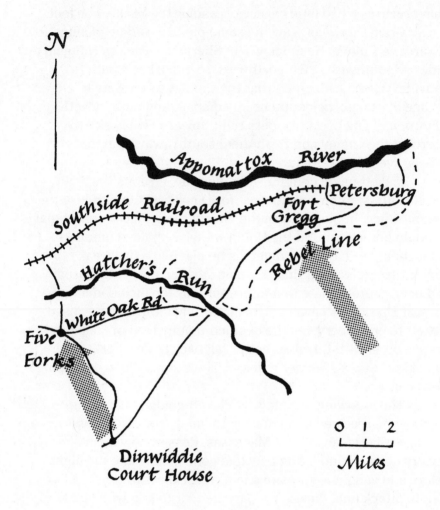

FEDERAL BREAKTHROUGHS: FIVE FORKS
                           April 1, 1865

                           FORT GREGG
                           April 2, 1865

vacated by Longstreet north of the James River. Lee's efforts, however, proved futile. At 4:00 a.m. on April 2nd, Grant attacked the line in front of Petersburg. Longstreet's force had not yet arrived, and the Union troops broke through the unmanned works to head unopposed for the capital.[21]

Ewell received his orders about 7:30 p.m. on April 1st. Unsure of their significance and hesitant to provoke panic by ringing the tocsin calling the reserves from their homes, he decided to quietly rally troops from the Chimborazo Hospital. Many of the wounded soldiers confined there were well enough for light duty. Expecting assembly in case of a crisis, they had been organized into a unit under Captain Woods.[22] Ewell met the contingent in Capitol Square about 1:00 a.m., ordered them to rush to the trenches on the exterior line, then rode ahead to find Longstreet, who could tell him what was happening. When Ewell arrived at the field headquarters, he found that Longstreet had gone without relating why he had left the front.

At sunrise, just as the convalescents came up, fighting exploded to the southwest. Ewell decided to check on the men he had at hand, to be ready in case the Yankees attacked his line. He hurried south, below Fort Harrison, to where Custis Lee's makeshift division was posted. The young Lee's 1,300 militia were divided into two brigades: one of former artillerymen headed by Colonel Stapleton Crutchfield, the second composed of reserves mixed with veteran troops under Brigadier General Seth Barton.[23]

Ewell next went to the center of his line where Kershaw and his South Carolina division of 4,000 experienced men were on watch. He then rode north to his headquarters to be sure that the soldiers from the hospital were all in trenches, replacing Field's Division which had gone to Petersburg. His final stop was on the upper flank where Gary's cavalry was on patrol.

About 10:00 a.m., after he had finished his tour of the front, Ewell received a message that he must rush back to the capital. No reason was given for the hasty recall. When he arrived at his city headquarters, Ewell learned that the Federals had broken through the Petersburg line and were coming unchecked toward Richmond. Lee had decided against trying to halt the onslaught. He would yield the capital. Ewell must burn the cotton and tobacco.

While Ewell was no doubt shocked by this terrible news, he showed great presence of mind. He knew that most citizens would be in church that Sunday morning, so he sent a courier to each of the many services to tell the preachers to read an announcement he had prepared: all reserves must assemble in Capitol Square by 3:00 p.m.[24] Ewell anticipated a panic when he lit his fires, and he wanted troops in place to quell the probable riots.

After alerting his provost marshall to Lee's decision, Ewell remained at his headquarters. He was by himself planning, when an impassioned officer burst into his offices. Josiah Gorgas, Chief of the Ordnance Bureau, had come to plead with Ewell not to burn the contraband, that the flames were likely to spread and ignite all of Richmond. Ewell refused to recall his arsonists. His orders gave him no option. He could have asked his visitor why he was so concerned now, when only five weeks ago, Gorgas had suggested dousing the cotton and tobacco with turpentine so the flames would burn more briskly.[25]

By now, rumors were rampant that the army would abandon Richmond that evening, and crowds had gathered in the streets around Ewell's offices. They blocked the path of the French Consul to Richmond, Elfred Paul, causing him to push through their midst, using his elbows to make a passage into Ewell's headquarters. The bureaucrat was infuriated. He had learned that the Confederates planned to torch all the tobacco in town, and he wanted assurances that the large inventory owned by the French government would be spared. He said that Ewell had to make provisions to protect their property.

"Speak to the provost marshal before he disappears . . . ." Ewell answered with obvious sarcasm. "He will put a guard at your disposition."[26] He was not about to yield to the greed of special interests, particularly the French, who had done so little to aid the Confederate Cause.

Paul was livid over Ewell's refusal to do more, but the words, "before he disappears" had their effect. Paul hurried out the door to find the provost marshal.

About 3:30 p.m., Ewell received a message from Lee. "I wish you to make all preparations quietly and rapidly to abandon your position tonight . . . . Have your . . . troops prepared for battle or marching orders . . . . "27

Your troops! With Longstreet located on the Petersburg line, Ewell was now officially in charge of every Confederate soldier above the James River. Ironically, and at this extreme moment, he had at last resumed field command. Ewell was also assigned responsibility for the hundreds of Union captives locked up in Libby and Castle Thunder prisons. Most of them were no doubt angry and desperate men, and Ewell knew he could not leave any behind when he left the city. They would be released immediately when the bluecoats occupied Richmond, and would either seek revenge on the local citizens or swell the ranks of those pursuing the Confederate retreat. Ewell would have to add them to his entourage. He also recognized that these prisoners would tend to be uncooperative, and would try to slow his march. He had to put them on the road just as soon as possible. But who would guard the Yankee captives? The troops located out along the exterior line could never return to Richmond in time to start the prisoners forward; the reserves, just now assembling in Capitol Square, were unsuited for watching dangerous, veteran Union soldiers. And the provost marshal's, although able to carry out such an assignment, could not be spared. They were required to preserve order during the final hours of Ewell's stay in the city. Ewell made his decision. The provost marshal's would convey the enemy prisoners; his reserves would have to take on the police duty. His orders were issued, and the task begun.28

Ewell had intended to go to Capitol Square to meet with the reserves, but before he could leave his headquarters, Lee sent him new orders. "Move your command to [the] south side of [the] James River tonight," Lee's message read. "Take . . . your troops . . . to Branch Church, via Gergory's, to Genito road, via Genito Bridge to Amelia Court House . . . . Wagons . . . will take the Manchester Pike and Buckingham Road . . . to Amelia Court House. The movement will commence at 8 o'clock, the artillery moving out first . . . infantry following . . . . General Stevens will . . . furnish guides."29

Ewell selected Manchester, a village south of Richmond, west of the James, as a rendezvous point for his command, and sent instruction to Kershaw, Custis Lee, and Gary as to how to get there. Kershaw and Gary would come into the capital, then leave over Mayo's Bridge; Lee would avoid the city, crossing the river via a pontoon bridge near Chaffin's Bluff. After dispatching an aide to locate General Stevens and arrange for the guides mentioned in Lee's order, Ewell finally left his headquarters late in the afternoon for Capitol Square.

As he limped outside through his office door, Ewell was confronted with chaos. "The streets [were] filled with men," remembered one observer, " . . . and behind them excited negroes with trunks, bundles, and luggage of every [kind]."[30] Everyone seemed to know that the army was about to leave Richmond, and they intended to do the same. Mounting his horse, Ewell pushed his way through the throngs to Capitol Square. He had expected to find twelve hundred reserves waiting for him, but only about two hundred men had answered his call.[31] As they stood in ragged formation, buffeted by the noisy, constantly surging crowd, Ewell saw that they were too few to handle the riots he was sure would start at any minute.

Ewell sent the reserves to the armory to pick up rifles before taking to the streets. He would remain at the square, astride his horse, to help control the crowds. As he looked down at the mass of milling people, Ewell suddenly thought of a way to keep order. The Commissary! The army no longer had a need for the facility, and if it were opened to the hungry citizens, they would run there for free food and have no time for other mischief. Mayor Mayo was contacted, and he agreed to Ewell's ploy. About 7:00 p.m., the doors to three depots, the Commissary, the Government Bakery, and the Quartermaster Store were unlocked. Crowds formed at once, and a desperate scramble for free goods began. Ewell's means to contain the locals was at least momentarily successful.[32]

No sooner was one problem solved, however, when another appeared. The aide sent to bring back the guides promised by General Stevens returned to Capitol Square to look for Ewell. He found him, conspicuous among the packed crowd in the growing darkness because he was still on horseback, and reported that Stevens had no one available who knew the road to Amelia Court House. Stevens could not even provide a map.

Because Ewell had never been southwest of Richmond, he needed help in leading his troops to Lee's rendezvous point, and he tried to think of someone else who could furnish assistance. The provost marshal came to mind, and shouting above the din, Ewell told the aide to go find Isaac Carrington and ask if he could supply a man who was familiar with the route to Amelia Court House.[33]

The sun had set by now, and Ewell had to go back to his office to issue the orders to burn the tobacco and cotton. As he slowly pushed his way through the noisy throngs blocking the streets, Ewell saw "fierce crowds of skulking men and coarse, half-drunken women [breaking into] . . . the stores . . . [fighting] among themselves over the spoils."[34] The riots that Ewell had tried to avert were beginning. He must have known that burning buildings would only spur the mobs, yet he issued these orders when he arrived at his headquarters. In this time of anarchy and error, Ewell fell back on his military training. He did not question instructions; he obeyed them blindly.

About 8:30 p.m., smoke started to billow down along the water front. Shockoe Warehouse was on fire. The other three warehouses that Ewell had condemned were soon in flames, and as the sparks from these infernos drifted like hosts of fireflies onto the roofs of adjacent buildings, they, too, began to burn. The residents easily doused the fires.[35]

Three hours passed by, anxious hours for Ewell, who had expected to see Kershaw and his men marching into the city by now. The veteran troops leaving the exterior line were late, which put Ewell's retreat from Richmond behind schedule.

All at once, about midnight, a red glow burst into view at a site far away from those marked for destruction. Flames soon flashed in other locations supposedly safe from Ewell's torches. The looters, having emptied the shops of their contents, had started to burn the ransacked outlets. With only a small force available to repress the arsonists, Ewell could not have been blamed if he chose to let the flames run their course, but he sprang into action. Aides and any soldiers he could find were rushed into the streets to restore order. The convalescents, led by Major Sullivane, were dispatched to Mayo's Bridge to keep the mobs from setting it afire, and an officer was sent to

Kershaw to ask him to speed his regiments into the city.[36]

Waiting anxiously for signs that his efforts would bear fruit, Ewell found his hopes were shattered about 2:00 a.m., when the ground shuddered from a series of explosions along the river front. Huge, black billows of smoke arose as the detonations boomed. The arsenal had been blown.[37]

Horrified by the demolition of the city, Ewell left his headquarters and rode to the War Department to seek more men. He found John Breckinridge, the Secretary of War, surrounded by hundreds of scared citizens outside his offices. Breckinridge was calm, oblivious to the mounting holocaust. Ewell, "like the wreck he was, his thin narrow face wizened and worn . . . ,"[38] must have wondered if Breckinridge blamed him for the conflagration, the result of his setting fire to the tobacco and cotton. Still, Breckinridge had said earlier, "I don't care a damn if every house is . . . consumed. The Warehouses must be burned."[39]

Ewell then left Breckinridge, but instead of continuing his search for troops, he gave up on saving the city and went to Mayo's Bridge. He would hold that span, his only way out of Richmond, until Kershaw reached town. While Ewell watched and waited by Mayo's Bridge, he received a message from Carrington that he could not provide a guide to show the path to Amelia Court House. Major Archer of the Quartermaster Corps, however, might have man who knew the way. Carrington would make that inquiry.[40]

Dawn was breaking when Kershaw's troops finally marched into view. They saw the city in flames, their path to Mayo's bridge blocked by an ugly mob. Ewell was at the foot of the crossing, challenging the crowd by shouting, "I'll shoot down the first man that puts a torch to this bridge."[41] His dire threats rang hollow as the wooden span was already aglow, set aflame by a burning barge mired against girders that reached up from the waters. Kershaw rushed up to Ewell, who gave him these orders: dispatch some of the men to suppress this mob, try to put out the fire, start the troops over the river.

After dispersing two battalions to open the way through the milling hordes, Kershaw turned to the burning bridge. He asked for help from the boatmen in the river, and they responded by dislodging the flaming barge. As the blackened boat began to drift slowly downstream, the infantry moved onto the span. The last of Kershaw's troops were stepping off the smoldering bridge just as Gary's troopers galloped up. Without a pause, they rode onto the wooden viaduct and thundered across to the far bank. Only Ewell, Kershaw, and Breckinridge remained on the Richmond shore. As Ewell, along with the others, guided his mount onto the span, he might as well have been heading for oblivion. He had just heard from Carrington that Major Archer could not supply him with guides. Ewell would have to grope his way to Amelia Court House.[42]

April 2nd was a sunny, warm day. By mid-morning, Ewell had led Kershaw and Gary to Manchester, where they joined with Custis Lee's Division, the supply trains, the artillery, and the Yankee prisoners. Ewell formed his command into columns for the march west, but before starting, he turned to take a final look at the capital. Richmond was ablaze. In addition to the four warehouses that he had torched, many other buildings were also on fire, the most spectacular being Crenshaw's flour mill. Nine stories high, it rose above the capital on a site as far from the structures Ewell had ordered destroyed as possible. As he watched the city blacken, forming a dark silhouette against the cloudless, blue sky, Ewell wondered if he would be blamed for the ravaged city. He had tried to warn Mayor Mayo and the common council, and would later argue that if only they had listened to him and formed a civilian guard, most, if not all, of the devastation could have been avoided.

Ewell was not bereft of funds. He wore a money belt stuffed with six hundred dollars in gold coins, all he had left to his name.[43]

Suddenly, the air was rent by a tremendous explosion, a blast quickly followed by a series of detonations. Ewell saw flames soaring above the James River, east of the city. The Navy had just blown their ironclads. This was the final disgrace, a stabbing realization that Richmond was lost.[44]

Ewell could stand it no more. Wheeling his horse about, he galloped to the head of the van where he ordered the march to commence. Ewell's whole force started down the Manchester Pike, but he soon split his columns in two. Lee's orders called

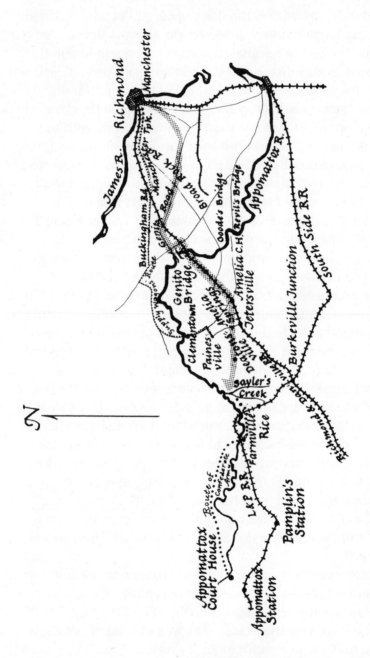

EWELL'S RETREAT FROM RICHMOND
TO LITTLE SAYLER'S CREEK

April 3-6, 1865

for separate routes for the infantry and wagon trains, so while the teamsters and prisoners continued down the road, the cavalry, the artillery, and the infantry dropped below to move cross country, interposed between the likely approach of the enemy, coming from Petersburg, and the wagon trains.[45]

Using his meager knowledge of the country, knowing that he had to cross the Appomattox River up ahead, Ewell told his non-combatants to ford the water at Meadville, then go south toward Amelia Court House. The soldiers, acting as a shield between the wagons and the enemy, would use the Genito Bridge over the water, then swing in left parallel to the trains as they moved to Lee's rendezvous point. Ewell's plan was good, showing that he was mentally alert, that he was enjoying this odd, last-ditch return to field command, that he had at least a vestige of the quick thinking military virtuosity that had won renown throughout the war. He seemed so confident that his men caught his spirit, and they went forward with equal courage toward the unknown.

Ewell rode with his infantry, cavalry, and artillery as they plodded through the fields. They were interrupted often by woods, which gave them cover, but the obstacles in their path slowed their progress. After three hours, with no sign of the Federals advancing on him, Ewell decided to risk using the roads. He veered south to the Brock Road, followed it west to the Genito Road, then took that artery toward the river. He camped that evening at Tomahawk Church. The weary troops with Ewell had nothing to eat that night. Custis Lee had brought 20,000 rations with him, but all these provisions were in the wagons to the north. While the men suffered hunger pangs that night, their lack of food proved an advantage in the morning. With no breakfast to fix, they were ready to start marching again at dawn.[46]

There was no sunrise. A cold rain was falling, and the already rutted road was soon a mire of mud. The men trudged for nine hours before covering the ten miles to what remained of the Genito Bridge over the Appomattox River. Confederate troops traveling in front of Ewell had torched the span after crossing to the far shore. As he looked down at the still smoldering timbers and deep, fast-flowing stream, Ewell realized he could not go forward. He had to detour north or south, and he chose the latter path. While this way was more dangerous because it took him closer to his Yankee pursuers, it was also the fastest way to Lee.

Following the winding Appomattox River, Ewell soon came to the Richmond and Danville Railroad, where a bridge over the stream was still in place. There was one problem. The span had no planking between the ties. One could look down to see the brown, swirling waters below. Men might be able to jump from tie to tie to get across the river, but without a floor, the cannons and their teams could never be driven over to the opposite bank. Unwilling to abandon his artillery, Ewell began looking for materials to fill in the gaps, and he quickly spotted an old barn nearby whose gray, weathered boards were exactly what he needed. The building was torn down, the wood was laid in place, and horses pulled the guns across the bridge. Walking in single file, trodding gingerly on the wet and wobbling boards, the men followed the artillery onto the span. Their progress was so slow that the last man did not step on the opposite shore until 9:00 p.m.[47]

Ewell decided to camp that night by the river. Knowing that Lee would be wondering whether he was coming, Ewell sent an aide ahead to report his position. Supper, a scanty menu gleaned from a few wagons that had come south from the trains to join Ewell's columns, was cooked. The troops then sought refuge from the still pouring rain by making their beds and trying to get some sleep.

Dawn was gray and sodden. In the cold drizzle, the troops formed and began plodding southwest. About 10:00 a.m., the sound of a spirited skirmish exploded to the west. Ewell halted his columns. His wagon trains were going through that area, and he was worried that they might be under attack. He waited in place while Kershaw went with one of his regiments to investigate. Within an hour, Kershaw came back to report that enemy cavalry had charged Ewell's trains. All of the teamsters had been captured, their wagons had been set afire, and the Union prisoners had been set free.[48] The loss was great, but Ewell could do nothing now. Expecting an attack from either east or west, Ewell put his men in battle array, then resumed marching. His troops were in this formation when Ewell finally reached Amelia Court House. While the men set up camp, Ewell rode ahead to see Lee.

When Ewell reported to Lee, he was told that the Rebels were in desperate straits. They had no food. Although ample provisions had been sent to Amelia Court House, the supplies were mistakenly shipped back to Richmond just before Lee's army reached the town. Foraging proved futile, as the area was barren. Lee's men had eaten nothing for two days. Worse yet, the enemy was coming up much faster than anticipated. Sheridan's cavalry and an imposing host of infantry lay south at Jetersville. They were blocking the way to Danville, where Lee had hoped to load his force on railroad cars and ride to North Carolina. Too weak to open a passage through the Federal line, Lee's only option was to hurry west to Lynchburg and use the trains there. He had to move fast, to get around the Yankees before they were positioned to dispute the path. Lee's army would have to begin on an all-night trek, starting just after dark, to create a gap between the Rebels and "those people."[49]

As Ewell turned to go back to his troops and prepare for the imminent march, Lee asked a favor. Four hundred sailors, led by Commodore Tucker, had scuttled their ironclads moored in the James River, and then come west to link with the army. Would Ewell take them under his wing? He agreed to the additional responsibility, assigning the tars to Custis Lee.[50]

Lee's march started about 8:00 p.m. Longstreet led the parade, followed by Anderson, Ewell, the army's wagon trains, and finally Gordon with the Second Corps. The cavalry under Fitz Lee rode along both flanks.[51] Beset by a steady rain, the difficulties of a narrow road, and the weakened condition of starving soldiers, the pace of the columns was excruciatingly slow. Ewell's men progressed only to Amelia Springs by 8:00 a.m.

As he rode into the small village that morning of April 6th, Ewell whirled in the saddle to look back at his trudging columns. He was shocked to see that his numbers had greatly diminished during the night. Almost half of his force had deserted.[52] Ewell had no means of retrieving those who were gone. He could only continue to plod ahead.

The rain kept falling. But where mud had been the only

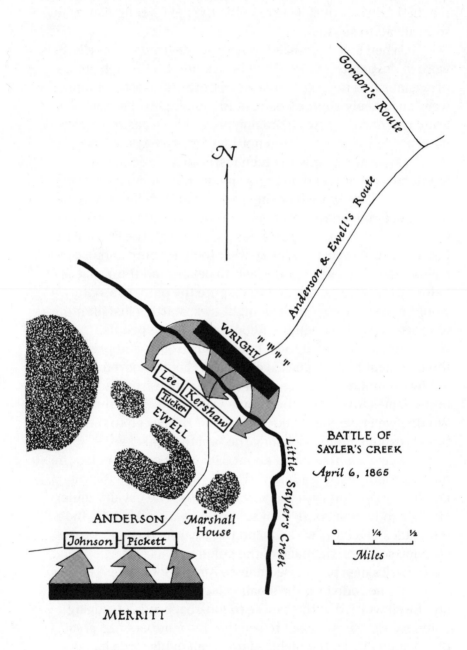

N

Gordon's Route

Anderson & Ewell's Route

WRIGHT

Lee Kershaw

Tucker

EWELL

Little Sayler's Creek

BATTLE OF
SAYLER'S CREEK

April 6, 1865

ANDERSON

Marshall
House

Johnson Pickett

o   ¼   ½

Miles

MERRITT

enemy most of the way from Richmond, the presence of Northern troopers was now painfully apparent. Yankee horsemen
sniped at Lee's columns, and Ewell was repeatedly forced to halt
and beat off their darting assaults. Ewell became so frustrated
by the enemy's audacity that about 11:00 a.m. he stopped, put
his men into battle formation, and faced his tormentors. As
Ewell was sparring with the Federals, the wagons rumbled past
to fall in behind Anderson. When John Gordon came up, Ewell
pulled his men back into column and hurried down the road to
pass the trains and get back in line.[53]

A fork in the road loomed ahead. The left lane, marked
by two gate posts, was a farm path while the main road veered
to the right. Anderson had taken the country lane, but when
Ewell turned to follow him, he found that he soon was forced to
stop. A small creek lay ahead, and Anderson was halted on the
opposite shore. Just as Ewell was about to ride ahead to find out
what the delay in the march was, Fitz Lee galloped up.

"A large force of [Yankee] cavalry [hold] the road just in
front of General Anderson," Fitz announced. "They are . . .
strongly posted."[54]

At almost the same moment, a messenger from Gordon
rode up from the rear. He reported that inordinate pressures
were being applied by the trailing Yankees. Could Ewell move
forward a bit faster?

Ewell realized that the enemy had sprung a trap. Since he
could not advance, both Gordon and the trains were doomed.
When the wagons closed on his rear, the trains would have to
halt. Bluecoats by the thousands would swoop down from every
direction to capture them all. Making a quick and courageous
decision, Ewell sent the wagons northwest onto the main road.
Gordon would go with them to provide protection. Ewell would
await the Yankees, inviting their "attention upon his little command to save . . . the trains."[55]

After posting his men in battle lines, ready to meet the
oncoming bluecoats, Ewell rode forward to meet with Anderson.
He found him on a small knoll south of the path, studying the
front through binoculars. "At least two divisions of cavalry are
in my front," the tall, lightly-bearded officer observed. "[We
have] two modes of escape—either to unite our forces to break

through or to move right through the woods . . . . "[56]

Ewell quickly recommended they take to the trees. When Anderson hesitated to accept this suggestion, Ewell offered a disclaimer. Anderson was more familiar with the ground; he must choose their path to safety. As the two were discussing their options, however, Federal troops were spotted swarming on Ewell's rear. There was no time for an informed decision. Anderson rode ahead to mount an attack to force an opening up front; Ewell galloped to the rear to hold off the bluecoats until the way was cleared.

After reaching his lines, Ewell rode along the front to check his dispositions. Custis Lee had placed his artillerymen facing east, posted behind a small hill on the north. The navy squadron was located to his right rear in reserve. Kershaw's veterans lay south, astride the narrow lane. A modest brook, Little Sayler's Creek, bubbled a hundred yards ahead of their position. Except for the scrub trees growing along the small stream, a clear field of fire extended to the rise across the water.[57] Satisfied that everyone was ready, Ewell called his key officers together to discuss their situation. They assembled down by the stream, out of sight of the enemy. As they were talking, the Federals opened with their artillery, the shells exploding nearby. "I must confess I felt somewhat excited," one observer recalled. "But General Ewell [made a remark] in his ordinary tones . . . [that] at once calmed my excitement, and with great difficulty, I restrained [a] laugh."[58]

"Tomatoes are very good," Ewell observed casually. "I wish I had some." The comment had no relation to the peril faced and several observers took it as a typical display of eccentricity by Ewell. Perhaps, though, he could see that his officers were frightened and he made his remark as a diversion, to allay their fears. Or maybe it was only the deeply felt yearning for the normalcies of life in a horrendously abnormal situation.

After sending the regimental leaders back to their men, Ewell, Lee, and Kershaw remained down by the stream, awaiting Crutchfield, who was looking for cannons to add to their defense. He soon rode up to report that he could not provide any pieces. "The guns that got past the [Union] cavalry got stuck in the roads," he groaned, "or had to be left behind as the horses gave out."[59]

As Jackson's former Chief of Artillery was speaking, an enemy shell swooped down from overhead and struck the mounted Crutchfield. The ball hit his right thigh, went through his horse, cleanly severed the Colonel's left leg, and then burst into fragments beyond the group of horrified observers. Both rider and beast crumpled to the ground. Ewell and the others hurriedly dismounted and ran to Crutchfield's side. "Take my watch and letters for my wife," the old colonel gasped with his last breath, "[and] tell her how I died, at the front."[60] The sorrowful moment passed. Ewell rose, and in a quiet voice, ordered the men to their posts. While they fought the enemy, he would return to Anderson to see if a path was open ahead.

The Union assault came about 4:00 p.m. Charging in two lines (front and rear), their numbers so many they overlapped both Rebel flanks, they advanced, confident of success. Some even waved their handkerchiefs at the Confederates to suggest that they surrender. Ewell's men, however, stood like rocks. Never acknowledging the bluecoats' impertinent gestures, they held their fire until the Yankees were almost on top of them. Then they opened as one. The leading Northern line vanished, literally blown away by the blast of Confederate rifles. The trailing enemy ranks fled back to their starting point. Kershaw's veterans calmly reloaded their pieces, but Lee's innocent artillerymen could not restrain their just-acquired zeal for fighting. They bolted forward, harassing the retiring enemy until they were out of sight, and then walked back to the Southern line.[61]

The Rebels had repulsed the center of the Union attack, but no one had contested the Federal troops who were enveloping both Southern flanks. The enemy soldiers moved past the front line, then whirled inward to infiltrate the Confederates' rear. When Kershaw's troops saw the bluecoats coming toward them from the south, they abandoned their post and ran northwest, where they soon met the Yankees coming down from above. The South Carolinians knew they were caught in a pincer, and they fought frantically to escape the vise.[62]

At the same time, the enemy renewed their attack on the Rebel front. Lee's artillerymen and the former sailors bravely held their ground, but as the North fed more and more troops into the fray, the pressure became too much. The Confederate reserves were pushed back into the center of the melee, where Kershaw's force was fighting front and rear. Every semblance of a distinguishable military line was lost. The adversaries were hopelessly intermingled, no longer under the command of their leaders, each man fighting his own individual battle to the death.[63]

In the interim after the Federals' initial attack, when they were retiring after being repulsed by the Rebels, Ewell's called Campbell Brown and several other aides to his side to ride back to the hill where he had first met Anderson. Ewell wanted to see if Anderson had succeeded in breaking through the roadblock that was ahead. They met Anderson just as he learned that his assault had failed and that the enemy was mounting a counterattack. The bluecoats were closing in on the knoll where he stood. After a hurried shout to let Ewell know he was in danger, Anderson spurred his horse down the hill to go rally his troops. Ewell and his aides started to gallop back to their lines.[64]

After riding only about 200 yards, Ewell found that his party could go no farther as shot and shell were raining down on the path. Ahead he could see that his lines had vanished, that his men, while still battling, were engulfed by waves of enemy soldiers. Blocked from the front and rear, Ewell knew that his only chance for escape was north or south. He first looked to the woods on the north, where he saw bluecoats pouring out from under the trees. He then peered south, and found that avenue closed, too. A formidable wave of Federal troops was advancing toward him. He was surrounded.

Spotting a momentary haven, a farmhouse that lay almost hidden in a grove of elms below the lane, Ewell led his aides to the shelter of the budding trees. He knew that he had no chance of escape, that he had to surrender before his troops absorbed more needless casualties. Ewell asked Major Pegram to perform the perilous mission. Tying a white handkerchief to the tip of his sword, Pegram cantered into the open and began waving his banner toward the Yankee soldiers approaching from the north.[65] Ewell watched as Pegram moved ahead.

All at once, Ewell had an eerie feeling of eyes staring at

his back. Whirling in the saddle, he found himself facing six bluecoated soldiers with rifles pointed at Ewell and his staff.

"Are any of you officers?" Ewell asked. Sergeant Angus Cameron, in command of a squad composed of himself, corporals John J. Cosat, August Brocker, and Charles Roughan, and privates H.W. True and John W. Davis, said, "No."[66] Ewell was involved in an ultimate ignominy. He was being captured by common soldiers. Stoically he made his formal statement, "I surrender myself and 5,000 men unconditionally."

* * * *

Among all the Confederate leaders serving in Lee's Army during those last, agonizing days of the war, Ewell's burdens were certainly the greatest. He commanded raw troops. Only Ewell was beset by panicked citizens, as well as the riffraff of Richmond. He was responsible for significant numbers of hostile Union prisoners. He was charged with burning the tobacco and cotton in the city, a move that was sure to arouse citizen rage and inspire arsonists to action, adding to his problems. Ewell was the last one to leave the capital, which made his force the most likely to be attacked by the pursuing Federals. He had no guides to lead the way to Amelia Court House. He had no food for his hungry men. And in addition to all these pressures, Ewell bore the terrible onus of Lizinka's treason and his own certain implication.

There was a certain loyal, stoic greatness in Ewell's last stand. Not only did he perform all of his assignments in the capital, but he also led his men to Amelia Court House on time. Even the Union prisoners and the wagons almost made it to Lee's camp. But instead of finally finding relief after all his problems, Ewell was saddled with more trouble: a forced march, sniping attacks by enemy cavalry en route, and finally an overwhelming, uneven battle. Ewell had no choice but to surrender, not to save his own life but to end the needless slaughter of his troops.

Success is not often recognized when failure is the end result. But since Lee's retreat from Richmond had no chance,

Ewell's accomplishments rise above defeat. He was truly a hero during these final days.

Fort Warren

Ewell and his aides were herded northward by the squad of Union soldiers, who showed pride at having captured a famous Rebel general. After traveling only a short distance, however, the procession was intercepted by a Federal detachment following Major Pegram south to look for Ewell. The officer in charge offered hurried congratulations to Sergeant Cameron and his men for the capture of Ewell and his staff, but quickly relieved them of their prisoners. The battle was still raging and he wanted to take these important captives out of the line of fire. Ewell, however, refused to budge. He insisted on sending a suggestion to Custis Lee to surrender his troops before there was further needless bloodshed. Even as a prisoner, Ewell followed military procedure. He noted that as a captive, he could not order Custis to lay down his arms. The Yankees holding Ewell were happy to honor his request as the lives at risk included those of their comrades.

"You are surrounded," Ewell wrote, "General Anderson's attack has failed. I have surrendered and you had better do so, too, to prevent useless loss of life."[1] After finishing his note, Ewell handed it to a Union courier, who rode under a white flag toward the melee. Only then would Ewell submit to being led south to safety.

When the entourage arrived at a farmhouse several miles below the battlefield where Major General Horatio G. Wright's Sixth Corps was headquartered, the prisoners were ordered to dismount and their horses were confiscated. The rules of war declared the mounts belonged to the United State Army. Ewell lost Rifle, his favorite, the bony gray whom he considered a more friend than beast. While Ewell was saddened by losing his horse to the Yankees, he found some cheer in the bitter moment. Rifle would finally be fed a full meal. "I expect when he got his fill of good oats and hay," Ewell would write later, "[Rifle] thought the millennium had come."[2]

The Rebel captives were taken to a campfire in the yard where Ewell found five Southern generals (Kershaw, Simms, and Du Bose from his command plus Hunton and Corse of Anderson's Corps) sitting and talking with Yankee officers. The Rebel aides hovered just outside this circle. Custis Lee, Barton, and Commodore Tucker soon arrived, bringing the total of Confederate general officers captured at Sayler's Creek to nine. In the growing darkness, the Rebel leaders quietly discussed their experiences of the day. Custis Lee was particularly vocal, noting with pride that his artillerymen and the sailors had counterattacked after the initial assault by the Yankees. Federal officers who had joined the circle agreed that the Southern charge had been daring. "I was never more astonished," General Wright confirmed in his official report. "Those troops were surrounded . . . . Looking upon them as already our prisoners, I had ordered the artillery to cease firing . . . [yet] this force charged our front."[3]

Ewell was intrigued. Who had led the impetuous attack? Someone replied that it had been Stiles! Ewell asked that his young friend, taken prisoner in the battle, be brought to the campfire. He was led to a group of generals seated by the fire. The youthful artilleryman stood at attention in front of Ewell.

"I have summoned you," Ewell explained, "to say, in the hearing of these officers, that [your] conduct . . . has been reported to me and I . . . congratulate you . . . . "[4]

The other Confederate officers no doubt enjoyed Ewell's commendation of Stiles, a kindly act normal to his character. He surprised them, however, when he next spoke. Ewell understood his role as a prisoner of war, as he had shown earlier when he had refused to order Custis Lee to surrender. Yet, when he was asked the size of his force, he eagerly revealed, "Six thousand . . . left Richmond with [me]."[5] When his captors noted that only 2,800 men had been taken prisoner during the battle, Ewell explained, "thousands straggled away during the march."

Why did Ewell give the enemy information that would be useful against the South? The question has intrigued many.

Ewell's imprudent admissions could be attributed to any number of rationales: he was in great shock because of being

374

captured; he was suffering from both the mental pressure of the past weeks and the physical rigors of a forced march, the lack of food, and the recent battle; and he was emotionally drained, no longer caring who won or lost the war. While all of these were certainly true, the fact was Ewell retained full control of his faculties. He had decided to curry the favor of his enemy. Why?

Lizinka was certainly the key. Worried that his status as a prisoner posed a threat to her interests, that the Union would have no reason now to return the properties of a captured general, and that she would blame him for her loss, Ewell sought to prevent the worst from happening. His only chance was to become a suddenly converted Union man—or at the very least, friendly and obliging to his former enemies.[6]

After dark, General Philip Sheridan joined the group by the fire. He was weary from fighting throughout the day, and without a comment to the Rebel prisoners, he wrapped himself in a blanket and lay down to sleep. Ewell saw the chance to make a good impression. Trying to engage the Yankee cavalry chief in conversation, he suggested, "To avoid further sacrifice, send a flag of truce to Lee." Sheridan ignored Ewell's comment, causing him to make a stronger appeal. "Demand his surrender."[7]

Sheridan raised his head. "[I] hope . . . Grant will drive on faster," he snapped, then lay back down to sleep.

While the others also stretched out on the ground, Ewell sat with "his hands clasped about his knees, his head lowered, in an attitude of utter despondency."[8] Sheridan's remarks were devastating, as they revealed that many of Ewell's friends who were running from the Yankees were doomed to die. Ewell was also no doubt agonizing over his decision to turn his back on these same friends by seeking favor from the enemy to insure Lizinka's fortune and his own personal future. The war, to all events and purposes, was over. The years stretched on, and he had to have some future in them. He could not change his mind. Ewell was on a course of no return, and he did not waver.

The next morning, the nine Confederate general officers and their aides formed to leave the front and head for a Federal prison. As they started marching up the road, Major General George Custer and his cavalry approached from the rear. They saluted as they galloped past the Rebel column. Ewell waved in return, shouting a cheer to the Northern horsemen, and his comrades, unaware of his plan to endear himself to the enemy, followed his example. When a Northern band accompanying the troopers began performing "The Bonnie Blue Flag," a Confederate tune, Ewell yelled even louder.[9]

While most of the prisoners walked, Ewell and the other generals rode in wagons as they moved toward Union Army Headquarters, located just outside Nottaway Junction. Snow fell throughout the day, and the Rebels were both frozen and tired when they finally arrived at their destination. Apologizing because Grant was not there to greet them (he was away stalking Lee), Colonel Badeau, Grant's military secretary, set up stools for the officers to sit on in the grass around a blazing bonfire. A whiskey punch was served. Later that night, the prisoners were taken into town and housed in the home of Wither Waler. Their supper consisted of warm soup.[10]

On April 8th, Ewell and his companions started for City Point, a port at the mouth of the James River. About an hour after they set out, they encountered a group of Northern officers who halted the procession to speak to Ewell. Looking to make a good impression, he made an outrageous comment. "Our troops devastated Yankee territory more than the Yankees devastated ours," he asserted.[11] His statement, intended to ingratiate him with his captors, infuriated the other Rebels.

"You know that is not true!" Eppa Hunton howled. "Will you tell me what [Northern] territory we devastated more than the valley of Virginia was devastated . . . ?"

Ewell's remarks brought his changed allegiance out into the open, but he was not about to debate his reasons for the switch in loyalty. He ignored the enraged Hunton. The march to City Point was restarted. As the Rebel captives continued along the road, a second band of Union officers brought them to a halt. They wanted to talk to Ewell, too, and he eagerly obliged with another shocking remark. "Our government [has] been cruel to . . . prisoners."[12]

Hunton exploded with fury. "While Yankee prisoners may have fared badly at our hands," he bellowed, "they have fared just as well as our soldiers . . . . We have called upon the Union over and over . . . to exchange them."

Again, Ewell refused to retract his comments. And while none of the other officers seemed as dismayed as Hunton about Ewell's comments, when the entourage stopped by the roadside that night to set up camp, Ewell found that he was ostracized by all except Campbell.

The trek continued. On April 10th, as the Confederates neared Petersburg, a courier rode up to the Yankee officer in charge to hand him a note. He read it quickly, then smiled, and announced that Lee and his force had surrendered to Grant yesterday at Appomattox Court House.

"I was a prisoner once before," McHenry Howard, an aide to Custis Lee, cautioned. "False rumors [were reported] to us then, too."[13]

Most concurred with Howard that the tale was a lie, but when their guard added that Lee's army had been paroled, they were less sure. The Yankee would not have said that if it were not so. Ewell more than anyone stood to lose in the surrender. He was not free. He was the highest ranking captive held by the North, and if the government decided to punish the South for starting the war, Ewell would bear the brunt of their wrath. Lizinka's wealth would never be returned to her under these circumstances.

The parade of prisoners walked into Petersburg on April 11th. Determined to put on a good show, the captives marched in cadence, their heads held high. One even dressed for the occasion. Major Costin, an aide of Kershaw's, wore a pair of once white, now torn and dirty, kid gloves.[14]

The group of Rebel officers was broken up in Petersburg. The generals and their immediate aides composed one band that would go on to Fort Warren in Boston Harbor; the others were headed for imprisonment at Johnson's Island at Lake Erie. As Ewell and his party were waiting for further orders, a Yankee officer, trailed by an orderly leading a spare horse, came up and asked, "Is General Custis Lee here?"

Lee stepped forward, and the officer reported, "Your mother is dying in Richmond. I have brought you your parole and you are ordered to mount this horse and go to her . . . ."[15]

"I cannot leave my fellow prisoners," Lee protested, "I must share the hardships of prison life with them."

"Don't hesitate to leave us," his comrades cried in unison. "Go to your ill mother."

Custis reluctantly agreed to go see his mother, and he mounted up, waved farewell, and rode off to the north. While Ewell certainly felt sorry that Mrs. Lee was so ill, he must have despaired at seeing Custis go free. The only target for Yankee vengeance other than himself had departed, leaving him alone to bear whatever was to come. Had Ewell known that the tale of Mrs. Lee's dying was a hoax, hatched by Custis' friends to keep him out of prison, Ewell would have been outspokenly angry over this show of favoritism.

Ewell, the other generals, and their aides moved on to City Point where they boarded a boat for Washington, D.C. As the ranking officer, (and possibly due to his currying favor from the Federals), Ewell received special amenities on ship. He sat at a table when eating, while his fellow officers were forced to squat on the floor; and Ewell was the only one who slept in a bed each night. While he could have shared these advantages with his comrades, Ewell kept them all to himself, which served to increase their growing animosity toward him. Ewell also gave his companions a new reason for feeling resentful about his attitude. Throughout the ocean voyage, he kept bemoaning, "The property of . . . Mrs. Brown will be confiscated."[16] Disgusted by Ewell's unseemly concern for wealth, his fellow generals were even more incensed when they belatedly realized that Ewell was alluding to his wife.

The ship carrying the captives reached Washington, D.C. on April 14th. Taken into the Union capital to the office of the Provost Marshal to fill out forms, Ewell took advantage of this opportunity to write a note to Lizinka. He described the surrender, said that he felt fine, and told Lizinka that she must not worry about him.[17] After spending the whole day in Washington, Ewell then returned to the Potomac wharves to board a boat for New York.

As the ship slipped into New York harbor about dawn the next morning, the prisoners sensed a tension in the air. Whispers of those around, a general air of pall, seemed to show that during the night, something terrible had happened. Already unnerved by the ominous atmosphere, Ewell and his fellow companions were then further intimidated by being quickly taken off the boat and onto a ferry for shore. Union Major General Benjamin Butler, one-time head of the Army of the James was aboard. His eyes red from crying, Butler showed the Rebels a newspaper whose headlines screamed, "Lincoln Assassinated!" The Southerners were shocked by the dire news, and they begged Butler for details. He tearfully told them that the President had been shot while attending a play the night before at Ford's Theater in the capital. He added that a different assailant had entered Seward's home about the same time, slashed the Secretary of State's throat, then disappeared into the night. Assuming that these attacks were a Confederate conspiracy, a last, inhuman attempt to win the war, many Northern people were demanding revenge. Butler warned the generals that their lives were in peril, that they were handy candidates for the gallows.[18]

At first, Butler's predictions seemed hasty. Ewell and his companions were fed a good breakfast, then started toward the depot to catch a train north to Boston. No one tried to impede the Rebels' path as they drove through the city. When they arrived at the station, however, an unruly crowd was on hand.

"Hang them!" rose the cry.[19]

The throng was large enough to overwhelm Ewell's guards and carry out their demands, but when challenged, the mob meekly parted as ordered to allow the Confederates to climb into the cars. The train left the terminal in peace.

The locomotive pulling its load of Confederate soldiers and miscellaneous citizens thundered northward toward Boston. When it came to the towns along the way, however, it slowed and stopped at the stations to let non-military passengers on or off the train. Hordes of angry people swarmed at each of the depots, and when they spotted the Confederate officers on board, they cried out for revenge for Lincoln's murder. At one of the earlier stops, a burly individual whose courage was no doubt bolstered by liquor, climbed onto the train to ride for the next sixty miles. At every subsequent depot, he tried to rally the gathered populace by shouting, "Hang them!" at the top of his lungs. Fortunately, this fellow was so wild-eyed that he served more to quiet than rouse the crowds. Ewell and the other captives breathed easier when this self-appointed prosecutor finally left the train.[20]

Their relief was premature. When the train pulled into Providence, Rhode Island, the next morning, April 16th, a host of angry people were waiting to greet them. The throngs were disorderly, but no more than at any of the prior stops. Then a voice rose above the rest. "Three groans for Ewell!" The cry ignited the mob. Men grabbed rocks from the roadbed and hurled them as they advanced toward the cars. Ewell and the other Rebels fell to the floor. Death seemed inevitable. At that instant, Campbell saw that the conductor was huddled on his knees among the Southerners. He cried out to the trainman to do something.

Fearing for his own life, the conductor rose and yelled through a broken window at the throng to fall back. "There's only some blockade runners aboard," he lied. As he bellowed to the crowd, the trainman yanked the cord that ran along the ceiling of the car, his signal to the engineer to move ahead. The train lurched, then began to inch forward. The would-be-lynchers pressed against the coach, trying to look inside, to identify Ewell. But before they could spot his telltale bald head, the locomotive came up to speed and flew out of sight.[21]

When the Confederates finally reached Boston, they were rushed off the cars, loaded into closed hacks, and hurried to the waterfront. A ferryboat took them seven miles out in the bay to George's Island and Fort Warren.

The sun was shining brightly when Ewell stepped off the boat and onto a wharf extending into the sea. Looking up, he saw the tall, gray, stone walls of his prison. The fort had five sides, each six-hundred feet long, eight feet thick, and twenty feet high, and occupied most of the island. Bulwarks made of mounds of dirt, covered with loose stone, sloped in front of each wall. Atop the ramparts, cannons were in line shoulder-to-shoulder facing the water.[22]

The captives entered a gate to the left of the landing, marched along a narrow aisle between the wall and its earthen cordon, and halted at the guardhouse, built in the coverface, where they checked their meager possessions. They were then herded north to the first bastion. They turned east, staying left of a deep, dry moat, until they came to the footbridge over the ditch. The Confederate prisoners crossed over to the sallyport, stepped through, and came out of the shadows onto the edge of an expansive parade ground that filled the center of the fort. Turning right, Ewell and his comrades followed the path next to the stone edifice to a stairway leading down into a walled passageway. They descended the thirteen steps and continued along the corridor to where wooden doors on the right opened to cells.[23]

When Ewell entered his assigned compartment, he found a dark, dank room split into two sections, front and back. The forward chamber had cots hung from the walls; the inner alcove contained a table, a stove, and some chairs. Slots in the far wall allowed a dim light to enter the room, but when Ewell looked outside through open, narrow, barred vents, only the grassy slopes of the dry moat were visible.[24]

Kershaw, Corse, DuBose, Barton, and Hunton shared these quarters with Ewell; Simms and Commodore Tucker resided next door. Six other Confederate leaders (John Marmaduke, George Gordon, William Cabell, John Jones, Henry Jackson, and Edward Johnson) were lodged in a third cell along the outside corridor. While the generals were allowed to enter the passageway to visit the other rooms, they were kept isolated from their aides. Campbell and the others were imprisoned in a separate dungeon in the fort.

Immediately after his arrival, Ewell sat down and wrote a letter to General Grant, in which he condemned the murder of Lincoln. Ewell was certainly sincere in stating that "of all the misfortunes which could befall the Southern people . . . the greatest, in my judgment, would be the prevalence of the idea that they could entertain any other than feelings of unqualified abhorrence and indignation for the assassination of the President of the United States."[25] Afraid that the Southern generals (including himself) would be charged with the wrong, he went on to claim that "we are no assassins . . . we would be ashamed of our own people, were we not assured that they will reprobate this crime." He then closed by hinting at this stance as a covert expression of acquiescent loyalty to the conquering Union. "I could not refrain from some expression of my feelings," he

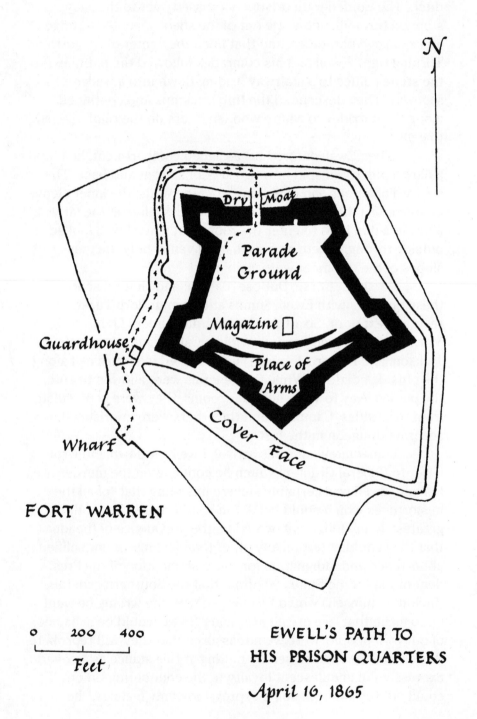

N

Dry Moat

Parade
Ground

Magazine □

Guardhouse

Place of
Arms

Cover Face

Wharf

FORT WARREN

0   200   400

Feet

EWELL'S PATH TO
HIS PRISON QUARTERS

April 16, 1865

wrote. "I thus utter them to a soldier who will comprehend them."

Ewell paused at this point, wondering if his companions in captivity felt the same as he did. He concluded that they held similar sentiments, and he added their names and states as "concurring with me . . . . "

Before posting the letter, however, Ewell began to have second thoughts. He did not regret writing to Grant; he was concerned over speaking for the other generals without their permission. He decided to discuss his note with them, and he called a meeting of the prisoners.

"We should declare by resolution that we had no complicity in the assassination of Abraham Lincoln," Ewell started the meeting, "and that we deplore the act."[26]

Ewell should have known that this proposal would not be acceptable to the others, that it seemed to convey a position of groveling to the Federals. "Do you think it becoming for thirteen gentlemen, thought worthy to wear the stars of general officers of the Confederate Army, to declare to the world that they are not assassins?" Hunton's sneer started an argument which lasted for hours. In the end, the others refused to join Ewell's resolution.

Hunton added a final jeer. "Where is the leg you lost at Manassas buried?" he demanded. Before Ewell could answer the bizarre query, Hunton snarled, "I wish to pay honor to that leg for I have none to pay to the rest of your body!"[27]

Despite the rebuttal, perhaps because of Hunton's acrid insults, Ewell sent his message to Grant without deleting the names of those imprisoned with him. His timing was perfect. Grant was about to seek revenge upon the South, assuming that "assassination remains the order of the day with the Rebels."[28] Ewell's note, however, not only calmed his vindictive spirit but also served to put Ewell in Grant's good graces.

Ewell did not know of his good fortune. He expected to be executed because of the South's rebellion against the Federal Union, an opinion shared by his fellow prisoners. "I'm convinced they'll hang us," one general confided. "The only thing left is [for us all] to die gracefully."[29]

Ewell wondered what it would be like to die by a noose.

Would it hurt? He asked that question in a letter he sent to his younger brother, "Parson" Stoddart, who wrote that Ewell need not worry. He remembered bushwackers once tied a rope around his neck, and it had not been painful.[30]

Just as Ewell probably thought that things could get no worse, Lizinka sent him dreadful news. She had been arrested by the Federal authorities! She had reached St. Louis about a week after leaving Richmond, took the oath of allegiance to the United States (attested to by Lieutenant George Richardson, an assistant provost marshal), remained in Missouri for five days to take care of personal affairs, then went to Nashville to begin legal proceedings of the restoration of her properties. The courts ruled in her favor on April 20th, but just two days later, Lizinka was arrested under direct order from Edwin Stanton, the Secretary of War.[31] Because she had done nothing wrong, Lizinka told Ewell not to worry. She was sure she would soon be freed. Lizinka's only concern was that her troubles might add to the rigors of Ewell's confinement.[32]

Ewell was convinced that he was the cause of her arrest, that if he had not been taken prisoner, the Union authorities would never have bothered Lizinka. Worse yet, she no longer was of value to the Federals. The war was almost over. Johnson had surrendered to Sherman on April 26th; Taylor had agreed to a truce with Canby in Alabama on April 30th.

This was the nadir of Ewell's life. From this point on, his lot would improve. The first sign of better times was an unexpected relaxing of Ewell's confinement. His captors allowed him to not only leave his cell and wander the grounds within Fort Warren, but also to visit the other prisoners. Ewell asked that he and Campbell be reunited, and his request was granted. On May 7th, Ewell moved into new quarters which he shared with Campbell, Gordon, Cabell, Marmaduke, and Smith.[33] Ewell was finally rid of the annoying Hunton.

About the same time, Lizinka wrote she had been charged with exacting rent from the Negroes who had built shanties on vacant land she owned near Nashville. "Of course it is untrue," she pouted. "From the Negroes living in small brick houses and keeping shops on my lots, I have neither demanded nor received one dollar of rent."[34]

Ewell was somewhat relieved. If Lizinka had not broken any laws, then her detention must be because he was being held prisoner. She would be freed upon his release from Fort Warren. To hasten that happening, Ewell applied for a pardon by signing the Oath of Allegiance.[35] His request was denied.

Ewell took the rejection of his appeal in stride. He even began to joke in his notes to Lizinka. When she sent him some candles to light his dark cell, Ewell chided her for shipping a box of twelve after he had asked for only two. "I'd hate to have to be a prisoner," he wrote, "until I burnt them all."[36]

Ewell even found the potential of his death by hanging, an event still hovering over him, a subject for humor. When Lieutenant William H. Woodman, the Yankee liaison officer between the prisoners and their captors, volunteered to make arrangements for Ewell to purchase a new, artificial leg (his makeshift peg had finally given out and he was hobbling about on crutches), Ewell made a droll quip. "I'll wait to see if the authorities are going to hang me," he jested. "If I am going to be hung, I do not care to go to the expense."[37]

Early in June, Ewell received a letter from Lizinka, in which she revealed that she was not as innocent of charges as she had first claimed. "Seeing you were sent to Fort Warren, I wrote President Johnson, asking that you and Campbell might be allowed to leave this country," she confessed. "Five days afterwards, to my astonishment, I was arrested . . . . Judge Blair [said] that my proposal had given offense, and [advises that I] cultivate a national feeling . . . . Having done mischief instead of good . . . I shall keep quiet and make no further useless efforts."[38]

Ewell knew his wife. Lizinka was not about to stop her efforts to gain their freedom. Contemplating what Lizinka's next audacious impulse might be must have alternately cheered and alarmed Ewell.

A few days later Ewell received a note from one of the old dragoons who had served with him in New Mexico before the war. The soldier offered to help Ewell. Touched by a voice from his prior days, Ewell answered the letter by recalling some of his actions. "My health suffered terribly," he remembered, "not much to the improvement of my temper, and I regret much harsh language and conduct toward men . . . [who were] better able to control themselves than I could."[39] He went on to claim that he had joined the Confederacy because of allegiance to his State, "a painful sense of duty . . . . Few were more devoted to the old country than myself." Having affirmed his position as a now firm supporter of the Union, Ewell then revealed that he was very bitter about his current status as a captive. "Now I see persons, who did all they could to bring about the war, in high favor in the North, holding high office . . . while I am [held in Fort Warren] with no good prospects of getting out . . . My wife is under arrest in St. Louis . . . ."

Ewell's letter was published in newspapers all over the country. His words brought him sympathy, established his reputation as a repentant citizen, and helped offset Lizinka's request that he and Campbell be allowed to leave the country.

On June 21st Lizinka received a telegram from Stanton, the Secretary of War. His wire read, "The President is willing for Mrs. General Ewell to visit Washington or . . . wherever she pleases except Tennessee . . . ."[40] She was no longer under arrest and could leave St. Louis to work for Ewell's release.

Lizinka left town immediately. Traveling by train, she and her daughter, Hattie, arrived in Baltimore the evening of June 23rd and checked into the Barnum Hotel. Lizinka was so weak from excitement and fatigue, however, when family friends (the Reynolds) offered her the more comfortable surroundings of their home, she readily accepted. Lizinka rested one day. Up at dawn on June 25th, she took the early morning train for Washington to call on Andrew Johnson. She headed straight to the White House, but when she arrived, Lizinka was told that the President was "indisposed."[41] She would not be denied an audience with Johnson. When would he be "disposed"? He was consulted, and agreed to see Lizinka three days later on June 28th at 11:00 a.m.

When she returned to Washington that Wednesday, Lizinka was again rebuffed. The President was still too sick to talk to visitors. Lizinka was undaunted. She badgered Johnson's staff, insisting on another appointment. The new date set was July 1st.

The President finally admitted Lizinka into his offices that Saturday morning. Expecting to charm Johnson, a man she had known for years, into granting the releases of both Ewell and Campbell from Fort Warren plus the return of her northern properties, Lizinka was shocked when he opened their meeting with a heartless query. "Tell me," Johnson asked with a smug grin, "why did you ever marry a one-legged man?"[42]

The President would neither intercede in Ewell's behalf nor assist Lizinka in regaining her properties. But when she left the White House, Lizinka did not head back to Baltimore. She went next door to the War Department to see Grant and ask for his help. In relating her story, Lizinka put particular emphasis on Ewell's frail health. Grant was aware of Ewell's weakened condition. Back in April, when Lee had sent a note requesting the parole of the Confederate officers captured at Sayler's Creek, giving them the same terms afforded the army that surrendered three days later at Appomattox, he had noted that Ewell was not well.[43] Grant may have also recalled the time twenty years ago when Ewell had given him a furlough to visit his bride-to-be.

"It will be my pleasure," Grant assured Lizinka, "to do what I can for my old friend, General Ewell."[44]

Encouraged by Grant's promise, plus the announcement on July 1st that all captives confined at Fort Warren excepting the Rebel generals and their aides would be released, Lizinka decided to head north to be closer to Ewell. She and Hattie boarded a train in Baltimore on July 4th. When they reached Providence, Rhode Island, five days later, they went south by carriage to Wakefield on the Atlantic coast.[45]

President Johnson tried to contact Lizinka to tell her that Ewell would be set free during this time. "If you will visit Washington tomorrow or Monday," he wrote in a July 7th wire, "I will see if some arrangement cannot be made for [releasing] General Ewell and your son."[46] Because Lizinka had already left Baltimore, she never received the telegram. The President repeated his offer by letter on July 12th, but this message, too, went astray.

On the night of July 18th, the generals and their aides were sitting in their cells when a chorus of cheers broke out overhead. The sounds of celebration came from the quarters of the Yankee enlisted men. Frail and apprehensive from four years of war plus three months as a prisoner, Ewell probably cringed as the shouts reverberated off the stone walls of his dungeon. But as he listened more carefully, his fears turned to relief and exhilaration.

"Bully, boys," a voice boomed. "The Rebel generals are to be released!"[47]

* * * *

The days at Fort Warren were very difficult for Ewell, especially because of the anguishing suspense over Lizinka's arrest. The general's frail health was further stressed by the likelihood that he would be executed, and he left prison with the fire of his life burning low. But that small flame would blaze anew as never before. While others might look back to what could have been, Ewell's sight was fixed on the future, to long-awaited marital bliss, to a different and more modest road to glory.

Epilogue

Although Ewell was no longer a prisoner at Fort Warren, he was not a free man. Ewell was on parole, confined to Virginia, forbidden to go beyond the state's boundaries without special permission from the War Department. He was too feeble to work, and since Lizinka's wealth had not been returned to her, the two were impoverished. They were forced to live off the generosity of their friends. Late in August, however, a court in Nashville ordered that because Lizinka's estates had been taken after she pledged allegiance to the Federal Union, the seizure had been illegal. Title to her 4,500-acre Spring Hill plantation, three substantial plots of land in Virginia, two prime lots in Washington, D.C. and another 200-acre farm in Tennessee were returned to her. She became, as Ewell wryly noted, "tolerably flush."[1]

The Ewells remained in Virginia through October. While his parole had been transferred to Tennessee so the two could live in Lizinka's house, Tarpley, at Spring Hill, they delayed leaving until after the wedding of Lizinka's daughter, Hattie, to Tom Turner, a former aide of Ewell's. When they finally started for Spring Hill that October, they made an important stop on the way home. Ewell was fitted with a fine artificial leg in Philadelphia.[2]

Beginning in the fall of 1865, Ewell became a gentleman farmer who specialized in breeding cattle and horses. He was the first to introduce Jersey cows to Tennessee, and he nurtured the "Hal" strain of thoroughbreds, the most famous being the pacer, "Little Brown Jug."[3] In recognition of his efforts, Ewell's peers elected him President of the Maury County Agriculture Society. Ewell also served on the Board of Trustees for the Columbia Female Institute. All the while, Ewell ignored the war. He made no effort to claim credit or to defend his record. He traveled only three times in the next seven years, going to visit good friends in Virginia, New Orleans, and Mississippi.

January 8, 1872, was an unseasonably warm day for winter in Tennessee. Taking advantage of the spring-like condition, Ewell set out on a long gallop over the fields. He wore his thin army desert uniform. While he was miles away from home, the skies clouded and the temperature fell. Ewell shivered from the cold as he hurried back to the house. The next morning, he awoke to both pneumonia and pleurisy.[4]

Over the next six days, Lizinka stayed at Ewell's side, working untiringly to try to restore his health. Ewell grew stronger, but when Lizinka became ill with the same flu-like symptoms, the family's concern shifted to her and away from Ewell. He took advantage of the situation by opening up the window in his bedroom to get fresh air. This exposure to the cold brought on a relapse, and Ewell started to sink rapidly. At the same time, Lizinka took a turn for the worse, and despite desperate treatment by the family, she died the night of January 22nd.[5]

This tragedy was kept from Ewell, but he quickly sensed that something was awfully wrong. He called William "Parson" Stoddert (his brother) to his room. Lying on his back, his pale eyes on the ceiling, Ewell whispered, "A pall has fallen on this house."[6] William told him the sad news. When Ewell tried to get up to go and see his dead wife, William, seeing that Ewell was too weak to leave his bed, restrained him. He had Lizinka's casket brought to Ewell's side.

After looking at his beloved wife, Ewell turned to face the grieving family that had gathered in his room. "It's all right," he assured them. "Delay her funeral so mine can take place at the same time."[7]

Cries of protest that he would soon recover were raised, but Ewell silenced them with just a feeble wave of his hand. He made a last jest. Recalling all the perils he had faced during the war, Ewell averred, "It's strange that an old pair of infantry pantaloons should kill me."[8]

Forty-eight hours later, Richard Stoddert Ewell passed away. As Lizinka once said, "In death as in life, we are not meant to be apart."

Footnotes

PROLOGUE

[1] Marietta Minnigerode Andrews, *Scraps of Paper*, (New York: E.P. Dutton and Company, Inc., 1929), p.112.

[2] Ibid., p. 111.

[3] Richard Taylor, *Destruction and Reconstruction*, (New York: D. Appleton & Company, 1879), p. 78.

[4] Andrews, p. 112.

[5] *War of the Rebellion: A Compilation of the Official Records of the Union and Confederate Armies*, (Washington, D.C.: Government Printing Office, 1880-1901), vol. XII, pt. 3, p. 890.

ANTEBELLUM

[1] Letter/Unidentifed, No Date, Benjamin Ewell Papers, Earl Gregg Swem Library, College of William and Mary, Williamsburg, Virginia.

[2] Ibid.

[3] J.T. Stoddert to Elizabeth Ewell, December 15, 1868, Benjamin Ewell Papers, Earl Gregg Swem Library.

[4] *Webster's Biographical Dictionary*, (Springfield, Massachusetts: G. & C. Merriam Company, 1957), p. 1415.

[5] Jesse Ewell to Thomas Ewell, April 8, 1808, Benjamin Ewell Papers, Earl Gregg Swem Library.

[6] Percy G. Hamlin, *Old Bald Head*, (Strasburg, Virginia: Shenandoah Publishing House, 1940), p. 7.

[7] Rebecca Ewell to Benjamin Ewell, May 15, 1835, Benjamin Ewell Papers, Earl Gregg Swem Library.

[8] *Biographical Register of the Officers and Graduates of the United States Military Academy, 1802-1867*, (New York: James Miller Publishers, 1879), vol. I, p. 602.

[9] Percy G. Hamlin, *The Making of a Soldier*, (Richmond, Virginia: Whittet & Shepperson, 1935), p. 27.

[10] Ibid., p. 27.

[11] *Biographical Register . . . United States Military Academy, 1802-1867,* vol. I, p. 602.

[12] Lloyd Lewis, *Captain Sam Grant,* (Boston: Little, Brown and Company, 1950), p. 110.

[13] Hamlin, *The Making of a Soldier,* p. 53.

[14] Hamlin, *Old Bald Head,* p. 38.

[15] Ibid., p. 39.

[16] Thomas Gantt to Lizinka Brown, November 2, 1855, Ewell-Brown Papers, Tennessee State Library and Archives, Nashville, Tennessee.

[17] Hamlin, *The Making of a Soldier,* p. 85.

PROFILE OF A SOLDIER

[1] R. Taylor, p. 37.

[2] John S. Wise, *The End of an Era,* (Cambridge, Massachusetts: Houghton, Mifflin & Company, 1899), p. 332.

[3] John B. Gordon, *Reminiscences of the Civil War,* (New York: Charles Scribners' Sons, 1904), p. 38.

[4] Thomas Gantt to Lizinka Brown, November 2, 1855, Ewell-Brown Papers, Tennessee State Library and Archives, Nashville, Tennessee.

[5] Campbell Brown, "Military Reminiscences From 1861 to 1865," Unpublished/Tennessee State Library and Archives, Nashville, Tennessee, p. 8.

[6] Robert G. Tanner, *Stonewall in the Valley,* (Garden City, New York: Doubleday & Company, 1976), p. 182.

[7] Gordon, p. 39.

[8] George Gary Eggleston, *A Rebel's Recollections,* (Cambridge, Massachusetts: Hurd and Houghton, 1875), p. 158.

[9] Ibid., p. 159.

[10] Lewis, p. 102.

[11] R. Taylor, p. 39.

[12] Wise, p. 332.

[13] Frank M. Myers, *The Commanches,* (Marietta, Georgia: Continental Book Company, 1956), p. 37.

[14] Hamlin, *Old Bald Head,* p. 60.

15 *The Missouri Republican*, January 28, 1872, Polk-Brown-Ewell Papers, Southern Historical Collection, University of North Carolina, Chapel Hill, North Carolina.

FIRST MANASSAS

1 Military Service Records, National Archives and Records Service, Washington, D.C.

2 Brown, "Military Reminiscences," p. 3.

3 Hamlin, *Old Bald Head,* p. 78.

4 Brown, "Military Reminiscences," p. 5.

5 Robert Johnson and Clarence Buel, Eds. *Battles and Leaders of the Civil War*, (New York: Thomas Yoseloff, 1956), vol. I, p. 175.

6 Ibid., p. 176.

7 Brown, "Military Reminiscences," p. 4

8 Gordon, p. 39.

9 Ibid., p. 39.

10 *Official Records*, vol. LI, pt. 2, p. 186.

11 Brown, "Military Reminiscences," p. 7.

12 Jeffery E. Wert, "Robert E. Rodes," *Civil War Times Illustrated*, vol. XVI, no. 8. December, 1977, p. 4.

13 Taylor, p. 85.

14 Millard K. Bushong, *Fightin' Tom Rosser*, (Shippensburg, Pennsylvania: Beidel Printing House, 1983), p. 13.

15 Brown, "Military Reminiscences," p. 7.

16 Gordon, p. 39.

17 Ibid.

18 Ibid., p. 40.

19 Newton Martin Curtis, *From Bull Run to Chancellorsville*, (New York: G.P. Putnam and Sons, 1906), p. 48.

20 Gordon, p. 42.

21 Ibid.

22 *Official Records*, vol. II, p. 565.

23 George F. Harrison, "Ewell at First Manassas," (Richmond, Virginia: *Southern Historical Society Papers*), vol. 14, p. 357.

24 *Official Records*, vol. II, p. 537.

25 Brown, "Military Reminiscences," p. 11.

26 Campbell Brown, *The First Manassas: Correspondence Between Generals R.S. Ewell & P.G.T. Beauregard*, (Nashville, Tennessee: Wheeler,Osborn & Duckworth, 1885), p. 5.

27 Brown, "Military Reminiscences," p. 11.

28 Richard S. Ewell to Joseph E. Johnston, August 15, 1866, Polk-Brown-Ewell Papers, Southern Historical Collection.

29 Ibid.

30 Brown, "Military Reminiscences," p. 5.

31 Richard S. Ewell to Joseph E. Johnston, August 15, 1866, Polk-Brown-Ewell Papers, Southern Historical Collection.

32 Harrison, '"Ewell at First Manassas," *SHSP,* p. 358.

33 Ibid.

LIZINKA BROWN

1 John S. Mosby, *Memoirs*, (Bloomington, Indiana: Indiana University Press, 1959), p. 90.

2 Brown, "Military Reminiscences," p. 17.

3 Ibid., p. 16.

4 Ibid., p. 17.

5 C. Vann Woodward, *Mary Chesnut's Civil War*, (New Haven, Connecticut: Yale University Press, 1981), p. 528.

6 Brown, "Military Reminiscences," p. 18.

7 *Official Records*, vol. V, p. 913.

8 Brown, "Military Reminiscences," p. 25.

9 Ibid.

10 Ibid.

11 Ibid.

12 Ibid.

[13] Ibid.

[14] Photograph, Ewell-Brown Papers, Tennessee State Library and Archives.

[15] Hamilin, *Old Bald Head*, p. 78.

[16] Ibid., p. 73.

[17] Ibid., p. 74.

[18] Ibid., p. 73.

[19] Military Service Records, National Archives and Records Service, Washington, D.C.

[20] R. Taylor, p. 37.

[21] Ezra J. Warner, *Generals in Gray*, (Baton Rouge, Louisiana: Louisiana State University Press, 1983), p. 310.

[22] John O. Cassler, *Four Years in the Stonewall Brigade*, (Dayton, Ohio: Morningside Press, 1971), p. 19.

[23] Douglas Southall Freeman, *Lee's Lieutenants*, (New York: Charles Scribner's Sons, 1942), vol. I, p. 349.

[24] Charles L. Dufour, *Gentle Tiger*, (Baton Rouge, Louisiana: Louisiana State University Press, 1957), p. viii.

[25] R. Taylor, p. 25.

[26] Douglas Southall Freeman, *R.E. Lee*, (New York: Charles Scribner's Sons, 1934), vol. II, p. 26.

[27] Brown, "Military Reminiscences," p. 26.

[28] Ibid., p. 39.

[29] Ibid., p. 38.

[30] R. Taylor, p. 38.

[31] Oliver O. Howard, *Autobiography*, (New York: The Baker and Taylor Company, 1907), vol. I, p. 198.

[32] McHenry Howard, *Recollections of a Maryland Confederate Soldier*, (Baltimore, Maryland: Williams & Wilkens Company, 1914), p. 218.

[33] Brown, "Military Reminiscences," p. 28.

[34] Ibid., p. 29.

[35] R. Taylor, p. 39.

[36] Brown, "Military Reminiscences," p. 31.

STONEWALL JACKSON

[1] Wiley Sword, *Shiloh: Bloody April*, (New York: William Morrow and Company, 1974), pp. 460-461.

[2] Jefferson Davis, *The Rise and Fall of the Confederate Government*, (New York: D. Appleton & Company, 1874), vol. II, p. 67.

[3] Freeman, *R.E. Lee*, vol. II, p. 34.

[4] Brown, "Military Reminiscences," p. 30.

[5] *Official Records*, vol. XII, pt. 3, p 847.

[6] Ibid., p. 852.

[7] Ibid.

[8] Ibid., p. 853.

[9] Brown, "Military Reminiscences," p. 32.

[10] *Official Records*, vol. XII, pt. 3, p. 854.

[11] Brown, "Military Reminiscences," p. 32.

[12] Kyd Douglas, *I Rode With Stonewall*, (Chapel Hill, North Carolina: University of North Carolina Press, 1940), pp. 42-45.

[13] *Official Records*, vol. XII, pt. 3, p 858.

[14] Brown, "Military Reminiscences," p. 32.

[15] Ibid., p. 33.

[16] R. Taylor, p. 49.

[17] Ibid., p. 38.

[18] Freeman, *Lee's Lieutenants*, vol. I, p. 350.

[19] Archie P. McDonald, *Make Me A Map Of The Valley*, (Dallas, Texas: Southern Methodist University Press, 1973), p. 35.

[20] Freeman, *Lee's Lieutenants*, vol. I., p. 350.

[21] Myers, p. 37.

[22] *Official Records*, vol. XII, pt. 3, p. 878.

[23] J. William Jones, "Reminiscences," (Richmond, Virginia: *Southern Historical Society Papers*), vol. 9, pp. 364-365.

[24] *Official Records*, vol. XII, pt. 3, p. 879.

[25] Ibid., p. 881.

[26] Ibid., p. 882.

[27] Ibid., p. 884.

[28] Ibid., p. 885.

[29] Ibid., p. 135.

[30] Freeman, *Lee's Lieutenants*, vol. I, p. 353.

[31] Myers, p. 38.

[32] Ibid., p. 38.

[33] Hamlin, *The Making of a Soldier*, p. 108.

[34] *Official Records*, vol. XII, pt. 3, p. 180.

[35] Thomas T. Munford, "Jackson's Valley Campaign," (Richmond, Virginia: *Southern Historical Society Papers*), vol. 7, p. 526.

[36] Ibid., p. 526.

[37] Ibid.

[38] Ibid. p. 527.

[39] Hamlin, *The Making of a Soldier*, p. 108.

[40] *Official Records*, vol. XII, pt. 3, p. 888.

[41] Ibid., p. 889.

[42] Ibid., p. 890.

[43] Ibid.

[44] Ibid., p. 889.

[45] Ibid., p. 893.

[46] Robert L. Dabney, *Life and Campaigns of Lieutenant General Thomas J. Jackson*, (New York: Blelock and Company, 1866), p. 359.

[47] *Official Records*, vol. XII, pt. 3, p. 897.

[48] Brown, "Military Reminiscences," p. 37.

[49] Frank Vandiver, *Mighty Stonewall*, (New York: McGraw-Hill Company, 1957), p. 235.

[50] *Official Records*, vol. XII, pt. 3, p. 896.

[51] Myers, p. 48.

[52] Ibid.

[53] *Official Records*, vol., XII, pt. 3, p. 897.

THE VALLEY BATTLES

[1] Varina Davis, *Jefferson Davis*, (New York: Belford Company, Publishers, 1890), vol. II, p. 269.

[2] Tanner, p. 204.

[3] Ibid. p. 211.

[4] Douglas, p. 204.

[5] Brown, "Military Reminiscences," p. 38.

[6] Tanner, p. 213.

[7] Myers, p. 50.

[8] *Official Records*, vol. XII, pt. 1, p. 779.

[9] Ibid., p. 779.

[10] Ibid., p. 780.

[11] Brown, "Military Reminiscences," p. 42.

[12] Ibid., p. 42.

[13] *Official Records*, vol. XII., pt. 1, p. 779.

[14] Ibid., p. 705.

[15] Ibid., p. 617.

[16] Ibid., p. 706.

[17] Ibid., p. 707.

[18] Ibid., p. 793.

[19] Tanner, p. 271.

[20] Ibid., p. 272.

[21] R. Taylor, p. 64.

[22] Ibid., p. 37.

[23] Ibid., p. 65.

[24] Ibid.

[25] Ibid., p. 67.

[26] Tanner, p. 277.

[27] Myers, p. 61.

[28] Ibid., p. 61.

[29] The Comte De Paris, *History of the Civil War in America,* (Philadelphia: Porter and Coates, 1876), vol. II, p. 48.

[30] Brown, "Military Reminiscences," p. 47.

[31] R. Taylor, p. 37.

[32] *Official Records*, vol. XII, pt. 1, p. 781.

[33] Ibid., p. 796.

[34] Brown, "Military Reminiscences," p. 52.

[35] Dabney, p. 421.

[36] *Official Records*, vol. XII, pt. 1, p. 786.

[37] R. Taylor, p. 75.

[38] Robert Stiles, *Four Years Under Marse Robert,* (New York: Neale Publishing Company, 1903), p. 246.

[39] Douglas, p. 91.

[40] Munford, "Jackson's Valley Campaign," *SHSP*, p. 530.

[41] Brown, "Military Reminiscences," p. 55.

[42] Stiles, p. 246.

[43] Brown, "Military Reminiscences," p. 47.

[44] *Official Records*, vol. XII, pt. 1, p. 778.

[45] Ibid., p. 779.

[46] Ibid., p. 781.

[47] Myers, p. 51.

THE SEVEN DAYS BATTLES

[1] Brown, "Military Reminiscences," p. 56.

[2] George Gary Eggleston, *The History of the Confederate War*, (New York: Sturgis & Walton, 1910), p. 398.

[3] Brown, "Military Reminiscences," p. 57.

[4] Douglas, p. 97.

[5] *Battles and Leaders*, vol. II, p. 348.

[6] Vandiver, p. 292.

[7] Joseph P. Cullen, *The Peninsula Campaign 1862*, (New York: Bonanza Books, 1968), p. 79.

[8] Clifford Dowdey, *The Seven Days*, (Boston: Little, Brown & Company, 1964), p. 201.

[9] Freeman, *Lee's Lieutenants*, vol. I, p. 505.

[10] G.F.R. Henderson, *Stonewall Jackson*, (London: Longman, Green & Company, 1913), vol. II, p. 18.

[11] Brown, "Military Reminiscences," p. 61.

[12] Hamlin, *Old Bald Head*, p. 109.

[13] *Official Records*, vol. XI, pt. 2, p 621.

[14] Ibid., p. 614.

[15] Brown, "Military Reminiscences," p. 62.

[16] Ibid., p. 64.

[17] Ibid.

[18] Freeman, *Lee's Lieutenants*, vol. I, p. 520.

[19] Brown, "Military Reminiscences," p. 65.

[20] *Official Records*, vol. XI, pt. 2, p. 605.

[21] Ibid. p. 614.

[22] Dowdey, *The Seven Days*, p. 230.

[23] *Official Records*, vol. XI, pt. 2, p. 605.

[24] Dufour, p. 195.

[25] *Official Records*, vol. XI, pt. 2, pp. 605-606.

[26] Ibid., p. 614.

[27] Ibid., p. 606.

[28] Ibid.

[29] Ibid., p. 595.

[30] Brown, "Military Reminiscences," p. 67.

[31] Ibid., p. 68.

[32] Alexander S. Webb, *The Peninsula*, (New York: Charles Scribner's Sons, 1881), p. 136.

[33] *Official Records*, vol. XI, pt. 2, p. 617.

[34] Ibid., p. 516.

[35] Brown, "Military Reminiscences," p. 68.

[36] Ibid., p. 69.

[37] Ibid.

[38] *Official Records*, vol. XI, pt. 2, p. 617.

[39] Ibid., p. 561.

[40] Brown, "Military Reminiscences," p. 71.

[41] *Official Records*, vol. XI, pt. 2, p. 611.

[42] Brown, "Military Reminiscences," p. 71.

[43] Ibid., p. 75.

[44] Ibid., p. 74.

[45] Ibid., p. 73.

[46] Ewell-Brown Papers, Tennessee State Library and Archives.

[47] *Official Records*, vol. XI, pt. 2, p. 612.

[48] Vandiver, p. 322.

[49] Brown, "Military Reminiscences," p. 77.

[50] Moxley Sorrel, *Recollections of a Confederate Staff Officer*, (New York: The Neale Publishing Company, 1903), p. 53.

[51] Brown, "Military Reminiscences," p. 79.

[52] Ibid.

[53] Hamlin, *The Making of a Soldier*, p. 111.

SECOND MANASSAS

[1] Edward Pollard, *The Lost Cause*, (New York: E.B. Treat and Company, 1866), p. 300.

[2] Henderson, vol. II, p. 82.

[3] Hamlin, *Old Bald Head*, p. 117.

[4] Edward J. Stackpole, *From Cedar Mountain to Antietam*, (Harrisburg, Pennsylvania: The Stackpole Company, 1959), p. 24.

[5] J. Davis, *Rise and Fall of the Confederate Government*, vol. II, p. 316.

[6] Joseph Durkin, *Confederate Chaplain*, (Milwaukee, Wisconsin: Bruce Publishing Company, 1960), p. 2.

[7] Ibid., p. 2.

[8] Brown, "Military Reminiscences," p. 35.

[9] Burke Davis, *They Called Him Stonewall*, (New York: Rinehart and Company), p. 274.

[10] Brown, "Military Reminiscences," p. 82.

[11] Hamlin, *Old Bald Head*, p. 117.

[12] Freeman, *Lee's Lieutenants*, vol. II, p. 24.

[13] Myers, p. 88.

[14] *Official Records*, vol. XII, pt. 2, p. 229.

[15] Ibid., p. 182.

[16] Ibid., p. 229.

[17] Myers, p. 89.

[18] Hamlin, *Old Bald Head*, p. 119.

[19] Tunstall Smith, *Richard Snowden Andrews*, (Baltimore Maryland: The Sun Job Printing Office, 1910), p. 54.

[20] Brown, "Military Reminiscences," p. 85.

[21] *Official Records*, vol. XII, pt. 2, p. 227.

[22] Ibid., p. 184.

[23] Myers, p. 95.

[24] Hamlin, *Old Bald Head*, p. 121.

[25] Freeman, *Lee's Lieutenants*, vol. II, p. 56.

[26] Douglas, p. 130.

[27] Brown, "Military Reminiscences," p. 89.

[28] Susan Leigh Blackford, *Letters from Lee's Army*, (New York: Charles Scribner's Sons, 1947), p. 122.

[29] Brown, "Military Reminiscences," p. 89.

[30] Jubal A. Early, *Autobiographical Sketch and Narrative of the War Between the States*, (Philadelphia: J.B. Lippincott Company, 1912), p. 108.

[31] Ibid., p. 111.

[32] Ibid., p. 112.

[33] Ibid.

[34] Ibid.

[35] Brown, "Military Reminiscences," p. 90.

[36] Douglas, p. 133.

[37] Brown, "Military Reminiscences," p. 91.

[38] Burke Davis, *The Last Cavalier*, (New York: Rinehart and Company, 1957,) p. 175.

[39] Hamlin, *Old Bald Head*, p. 124.

[40] Durkin, p. 10.

[41] Brown, "Military Reminiscences," p. 92.

[42] Ibid., p. 92.

[43] Ibid., p. 93.

[44] Ibid.

[45] Freeman, *Lee's Lieutenants*, vol. II, p. 102.

[46] Brown, "Military Reminiscences," p. 95.

47 Ibid., p. 95.

48 *Battles and Leaders*, vol. II, p. 508.

49 William W. Blackford, *War Years With Jeb Stuart*, (New York: Charles Scribner's Sons, 1945), p. 119.

50 Ibid., p. 120.

51 Alan T. Nolan, *The Iron Brigade,* (New York: The McMillan Company, 1961), p. 54.

52 Vandiver, p. 364.

53 Brown, "Military Reminiscences," p. 101.

54 Shelby Foote, *The Civil War*, Vol. I, (New York: Random House, 1958), p. 627.

55 Brown, "Military Reminiscences," p. 103.

56 Early, *Autobiographical Sketch*, p. 212.

57 William W. Hassler, *A.P. Hill: Lee's Forgotten General*, (Richmond, Virginia: Garrett & Bassie, 1962), p. 88.

58 Brown, "Military Reminiscences," p. 102.

59 J. Early, *Autobiographical Sketch*, p. 121.

60 Brown, "Military Reminiscences," p. 102

61 Ibid., p. 102.

62 Ibid.

63 Ibid.

64 Ibid., p. 103.

65 Ibid.

66 Ibid.

67 Ibid., p. 104.

68 *Official Records*, vol. XII, pt. 2, p. 183.

69 Hamlin, *Old Bald Head*, p. 121.

70 *Official Records*, vol. XII, pt 2, p. 664.

RECUPERATION

[1] "How Ewell Lost His Leg," *Civil War Times Illustrated*, vol. IV, no. 5, June, 1965, p. 18.

[2] Lawrence W. Friedmann, M.D., *The Psychological Rehabilitation of the Amputee*, (Springfield, Illinois: Charles C. Thomas Publishers,1978), p.21.

[3] "How Ewell Lost His Leg," *CWTI*, p. 20.

[4] Ibid., p. 19.

[5] Brown, "Military Reminiscences," p. 106.

[6] Vandiver, p. 399.

[7] Lizinka Brown to Richard Ewell, September 21, 1862, Ewell-Brown Papers, Tennessee State Library and Archives.

[8] "How Ewell Lost His Leg," *CWTI, p. 20.*

[9] Brown, "Military Reminiscences," p. 104.

[10] Ibid., p. 105.

[11] Hamlin, *Old Bald Head*, p. 130.

[12] R. Taylor, p. 78.

[13] Hamlin, *The Making of a Soldier*, p. 120.

[14] Ibid., p. 116.

[15] Ibid., p. 118.

[16] Hamlin, *Old Bald Head*, p. 131.

[17] Ibid., p. 137.

[18] Constance Cary (Mrs. Burton Harrison), *Recollections Grave and Gay*, (New York: Charles Scribner's Sons, 1911), p. 111.

[19] Mary Conner Moffett, *Letters of General James Conner*, (Columbia, South Carolina: The R.L. Bryan Company, 1950), p. 111.

[20] John B. Jones, *A Rebel War Clerk's Diary*, (New York: Old Hickory Bookshop, 1935), vol. I, p. 285.

[21] Richard Ewell to P.G.T. Beauregard, May 8, 1863, Washington, D.C.: National Archives and Records Services.

[22] Hamlin, *The Making of a Soldier*, p. 120.

[23] Freeman, *Lee's Lieutenants*, vol. II, p. 695.

[24] Hamlin, *Old Bald Head*, p. 136.

[25] Richard Ewell to P.G.T. Beauregard, May 8, 1863, National Archives and Records Service.

[26] Military Service Records, National Archives and Records Service, Washington, D.C.

[27] Hamlin, *Old Bald Head*, p. 136.

[28] McDonald, p. 146.

PENNSYLVANIA

[1] W.G. Bean, *Stonewall's Man Sandie Pendleton*, (Chapel Hill, North Carolina: University of North Carolina Press, 1959), p. 128.

[2] *Official Records*, vol. XXVII, pt. 2, p. 439.

[3] Ibid.

[4] Ibid.

[5] John W. Schildt, *Roads to Gettysburg*, (Parsons, West Virginia: McClain Printing Company, 1978), p. 31.

[6] McDonald, p. 148.

[7] Ibid., p. 149.

[8] Bean, p. 133.

[9] Campbell Brown, "My Confederate Experiences," Unpublished/Tennessee State Library and Archives, Nashville, Tennessee), p. 21.

[10] McDonald, p. 150.

[11] *Official Records*, vol. XXVII, pt. 2, p. 295.

[12] Ibid., p. 546.

[13] Brown," My Confederate Experiencess," p. 21.

[14] Wilber S. Nye, *Here Come the Rebels!*, (Baton Rouge, Louisiana: Louisiana State University Press, 1965), p. 142.

[15] McDonald, p. 151.

[16] Nye, p. 79.

[17] Bean, p. 129.

[18] W. Blackford, p. 179.

[19] Brown, "My Confederate Experiences," p. 25.

[20] Harry Gilmor, *Four Years in the Saddle*, (New York: Harper & Brothers, 1866), p. 90.

[21] Ibid., p. 90.

[22] *Official Records*, vol. XXVII, pt. 2, p. 442.

[23] Brown, "My Confederate Experiences," p. 29.

[24] *Official Records*, vol. XXVII, pt. 3, p. 894.

[25] Ibid., p. 914.

[26] Ibid., p. 912.

[27] Hamlin, *Old Bald Head*, p. 141.

[28] Freeman, *Lee's Lieutenants*, vol. III, p. 30.

[29] Hamlin, *The Making of a Soldier*, p. 121.

[30] Brown, "My Confederate Experiences," p. 41.

[31] Stiles, pp. 205-206.

[32] Glenn Tucker, *High Tide at Gettysburg*, (Indianapolis, Indiana: The Bobbs-Merrill Company, 1958), p. 63.

[33] McDonald, p. 155.

[34] Brown, "My Confederate Experiences," p. 47.

[35] Ibid.

[36] Ibid.

[37] Ibid.

[38] *Official Records*, vol. XXVII, pt. 3, p. 943.

[39] Charles W. Thompson, *The Fiery Epoch*, (Indianapolis, Indiana: The Bobbs-Merrill Company, 1931), p. 133.

[40] Freeman, *Lee's Lieutenants*, vol. II, p. 690.

[41] Ibid.

[42] Bean, p. 133.

[43] *Official Records*, vol XXVII, pt. 3, p. 914.

[44] Nye, p. 79.

⁴⁵ Bean, p. 133.

GETTYSBURG: DAY ONE

¹ Tucker, *High Tide at Gettysburg*, p. 81.

² John Cabell Early, "A Southern Boy at Gettysburg," *Civil War Times Illustrated*, vol. IX, no. 3, June, 1970, p. 35.

³ Nye, p. 359.

⁴ *Official Records*, vol. XXVII, pt. 2, p. 444.

⁵ Isaac R. Trimble, "The Battle and Campaign of Gettysburg," (Richmond Virginia: *Southern Historical Society Papers*), vol. 26, p. 122.

⁶ Nye, p. 361.

⁷ *Official Records*, Vol. XXVII, pt. 2, p. 552.

⁸ Ibid.

⁹ Ibid., p. 444.

¹⁰ Brown, "My Confederate Experiences," p. 51.

¹¹ *Official Records*, vol. XXVII, pt. 2, p. 444.

¹² Warren W. Hassler, Jr., *Crisis at the Crossroads*, (Tuscaloosa, Alabama: University of Alabama Press, 1970), p. 90.

¹³ Ibid., p. 92.

¹⁴ Ibid., p. 102.

¹⁵ Brown, "My Confederate Experiences," p. 55.

¹⁶ McDonald, p. 156.

¹⁷ Hassler, *Crisis at the Crossroads*, p. 106.

¹⁸ Ibid., p. 96.

¹⁹ *Official Records*, vol. XXVII, pt. 2, p. 582.

²⁰ Stiles, p. 211.

²¹ *Official Records*, vol. XXVII, pt. 2, p. 469.

²² Ibid., p. 555.

²³ Ibid., p. 445.

²⁴ Trimble, "The Battle and Campaign of Gettysburg," *SHSP*, p. 123.

25 Douglas, p. 247.

26 Gordon, p. 157.

27 Tucker, *High Tide at Gettysburg*, p. 176.

28 Trimble, "The Battle and Campaign of Gettysburg," *SHSP*, p. 123.

29 James S. Montgomery, *The Shaping of a Battle*, (Pennsylvania: The Chilton Company, 1959), p. 72.

30 Trimble, "The Battle and Campaign of Gettysburg," *SHSP*, p. 123.

31 Ibid., p. 124.

32 Ibid.

33 James Power Smith, *With Stonewall Jackson in the Army of Northern Virginia*, (Gaithersburg, Maryland: Zullo and Van Sickle Books, 1982), p. 56.

34 *Official Records*, vol. XXVII, pt. 2, p 445.

35 Smith, *With Stonewall Jackson in the Army of Northern Virginia*, p. 57.

36 Brown, "My Confederate Experiences," p. 61.

37 Walter H. Taylor, *Four Years With General Lee*, (New York: Bonanza Books), p. 95.

38 *Official Records*, vol. XXVII, pt. 2, p. 318.

39 Jubal Early, "The Battle of Gettysburg," (Richmond, Virginia: *Southern Historical Society Papers*, vol. IV, no. 6, December, 1877), p. 256.

40 Ibid.

41 Hamlin, *Old Bald Head*, p. 149.

42 J. Early, "The Battle of Gettysburg," *SHSP*, p. 272.

43 J.C. Early, "A Southern Boy at Gettysburg," *CWTI*, p. 39.

44 J. Early, "The Battle of Gettysburg," *SHSP*, p. 273.

45 Brown, "My Confederate Experiences," p. 71.

46 Hamlin, *Old Bald Head*, p. 149.

47 Montgomery, p. 75.

48 *Official Records*, vol. XXVII, pt. 2, p. 445.

49 Tucker, *High Tide at Gettysburg*, p. 215.

[50]   *Official Records*, vol. XXVII, pt. 2, p. 446.

[51]   Gordon, p. 156.

[52]   *Official Records*, vol. XXVII, pt. 2, p. 446.

[53]   Brown, "My Confederate Experiences," p. 65.

[54]   Glenn Tucker, *Lee and Longstreet at Gettysburg*, (Indianapolis, Indiana: Bobbs-Merrill Company, 1968), p. 209.

[55]   Edwin B. Coddington, *The Gettysburg Campaign*, (New York: Charles Scribner's Sons, 1968), p. 209.

[56]   Terry L. Jones, "Going Back Into The Union At Last," *Civil War Times Illustrated*, vol. XXIX, no. 6, January/February, 1991, pp. 56-57.

DAY TWO AND AFTER

[1]   Montgomery, p. 92.

[2]   Brown, "My Confederate Experiences," p. 65.

[3]   Tucker, *High Tide at Gettysburg*, p. 219.

[4]   Brown, "My Confederate Experiences," p. 69.

[5]   Trimble, "The Battle and Campaign of Gettysburg," *SHSP*, p. 125.

[6]   J. Early, *Autobiographical Sketch,* p. 272.

[7]   Fairfax Downey, *The Guns at Gettysburg,* (New York: David McKay Company, 1958), p. 97.

[8]   Walter Lord, *The Fremantle Diary*, (Boston: Little, Brown and Company, 1954), p. 206.

[9]   *Official Records*, vol. XXVII, pt. 2, p. 555.

[10]   Ibid., p. 556.

[11]   Stiles, p. 215.

[12]   *Official Records*, vol. XXVII, pt. 2, p. 447.

[13]   Ibid.

[14]   J. Early, *Autobiographical Sketch*, p. 273.

[15]   *Official Records*, vol. XXVII, pt. 2, p. 470.

[16]   Ibid., p. 447.

[17] Coddington, p. 454.

[18] Jennings Cropper Wise, *The Long Arm of Lee*, (Lynchburg, Virginia: J.P. Bell Company, 1915), vol. II, pp. 652-653.

[19] Tucker, *High Tide at Gettsburg*, p. 306.

[20] *Official Records*, vol. XXVII, pt. 2, p. 447.

[21] Brown, "My Confederate Experiences," p. 79.

[22] *Official Records*, vol. XXVII, pt. 2, p. 447.

[23] Coddington, p. 470.

[24] *Official Records*, vol. XXVII, pt. 2, p. 448.

[25] Ibid., p. 447.

[26] Ibid., p. 448

[27] Brown, "My Confederate Experiences," p. 81.

[28] Freeman, *R.E. Lee*, vol. III, p. 133.

[29] McDonald, p. 158.

[30] Brown, "My Confederate Experiences," p. 83.

[31] Bean, p. 140.

[32] Brown, "My Confederate Experiences," p. 83.

[33] Ibid, p. 85.

[34] Freeman, *R.E. Lee*, vol. III, p. 137.

[35] McDonald, p. 159.

[36] *Official Records*, vol. XXVII, pt. 2, p. 558.

[37] Ibid.

[38] Eppa Hunton, *Autobiography*, (Richmond, Virginia: Privately Printed, 1933), p. 98.

VIRGINIA

[1] Samuel Carter III, *The Final Fortress*, (New York: St. Martin's Press, 1980), p. 302.

[2] McDonald, p. 161.

[3]   Jennings Wise, vol. II, p. 653.

[4]   E.B. Long, "The Battle That Almost Was—Manassas Gap," *Civil War Times Illustrated*, vol. XI, no. 8, December, 1972, p. 22.

[5]   *Official Records*, vol. XXVII, pt. 2, p. 449.

[6]   Ibid., p. 626.

[7]   Ibid., p. 449.

[8]   Frederick Maurice, *An Aide-de-camp of Lee*, (Boston: Little Brown & Company, 1911), p. 247.

[9]   McDonald, p. 164.

[10]   John W. Schildt, *Roads From Gettysburg*, (Privately printed, 1979), p. 160.

[11]   McDonald, p. 160.

[12]   Brown, "My Confederate Experiences," p. 87.

[13]   Foote, *The Civil War*, vol. II, p. 637.

[14]   Durkin, p. 54.

[15]   Casler, p. 193.

[16]   John W. Worsham, *One of Jackson's Foot Cavalry*, (Jackson, Mississippi: McCowat-Mercer, 1964), p. 112.

[17]   Clifford Dowdey and Louis H. Manarin, *The Wartime Papers of R.E. Lee*, (Boston: Little, Brown and Company, 1961), p. 602.

[18]   Fairfax Downey, *Storming of the Gateway*, (New York: David McKay Company, 1960), p. 96.

[19]   Durkin, p. 58.

[20]   Ibid., p. 63.

[21]   H.B. McClellan, *I Rode With Jeb Stuart*, (Bloomington, Indiana: Indiana University Press, 1958) p. 393.

[22]   A.L. Long, *Memoirs of Robert E. Lee*, (New York: J.M. Stoddart & Company, 1886), p. 311.

[23]   M. Howard, p. 234.

[24]   McDonald, p. 179.

[25]   M. Howard, p. 235.

[26]   *Official Records*, vol. XXIX, pt. 1, p. 632.

[27]   Ibid., p. 624.

[28]   Hamlin, *Old Bald Head*, p. 162.

[29]   *Official Records*, vol. XXIX, pt. 1, p. 834.

[30]   Bean, p. 154.

[31]   Hamlin, *The Making of a Soldier*, p. 124.

[32]   *Official Records*, vol. XXXIII, p. 1095.

[33]   Ibid., p. 1096.

[34]   Moffett, p. 115.

[35]   Ibid.

[36]   Stiles, p. 236.

[37]   Durkin, p. 75.

[38]   Bean, p. 189.

[39]   Freeman, *Lee's Lieutenants*, vol. III, p. 333.

[40]   E.B. Long, *The Civil War Day by Day*, (Garden City, New York: Doubleday & Company, 1971), p. 478.

[41]   Freeman, *Lee's Lieutenants*, vol. III, p. 333.

[42]   *Battles and Leaders*, vol, IV, p. 118.

[43]   Freeman, *Lee's Lieutenants*, vol. III, p. 345.

THE WILDERNESS

[1]   *Official Records*, vol. XXXVI, pt. 2, p. 372.

[2]   *Official Records*, vol. LI, pt. 2, p. 888.

[3]   *Official Records*, vol. XXXVI, pt. 1, p. 1070.

[4]   Ibid., p. 1080.

[5]   Freeman, *Lee's Lieutenants*, vol. III, pp. 237-238.

[6]   Douglas, p. 274.

[7]   *Official Records*, vol. XXXVI, pt. 2, p. 948.

[8]   Stiles, p. 245.

[9]   *Official Records*, vol. XXXVI, pt. 1, p. 1070.

[10] Ibid.

[11] Ibid.

[12] Edward Steere, *The Wilderness Campaign*, (Harrisburg, Pennsylvania: The Stackpole Company, 1960), p. 144.

[13] Ibid., p. 145.

[14] Ibid., p. 162.

[15] Gordon, p. 239.

[16] *Official Records*, vol. XXXVI, pt. 1, p. 1077.

[17] Steere, p. 170.

[18] Hamlin, *Old Bald Head*, p. 171.

[19] Ibid.

[20] Steere, p. 159.

[21] Ibid., p. 174.

[22] Ibid., p. 246.

[23] Ibid.

[24] Ibid., p. 248.

[25] *Official Records*, vol. XXXVI, pt. 1, p. 952.

[26] Ibid, p. 953.

[27] Edward P. Alexander, *Fighting For the Confederacy*, (Chapel Hill, North Carolina: University of North Carolina Press, 1989), p. 353.

[28] Ibid., p. 354.

[29] *Official Records*, vol. XXXVI, pt. 1, p. 1028.

[30] McDonald, p. 201.

[31] Steere, p. 319.

[32] Ibid., p. 323.

[33] *Official Records*, vol. XXXVI, pt. 1, p. 1081.

[34] J. Early, *Autobiographical Sketch*, p. 348.

[35] Gordon, p. 243.

[36] *Official Records*, vol. XXXVI, pt. 2, p. 962.

[37] Gordon, p. 247.

[38] Campbell Brown memo, Ewell-Brown Papers, Tennessee State Library and Archives, Nashville, Tennessee.

[39] J. Early, *Autobiographical Sketch,* p. 348.

[40] Campbell Brown memo.

[41] Ibid.

[42] Ibid.

[43] Morris Schaff, *The Battle of the Wilderness,* (New York: Houghton Mifflin Company, 1910), p. 253.

[44] Campbell Brown memo.

[45] *Official Records*, vol. XXXVI, pt. 1, p. 1055.

[46] J. Early, *Autobiographical Sketch,* p. 348.

[47] Steere, p. 440.

[48] *Official Records*, vol. XXXVI, pt. 1, p. 1071.

[49] Schaff, p. 338.

[50] McDonald, p. 202.

[51] Foote, *The Civil War*, vol. III, p. 190.

[52] Gordon, p. 258.

[53] Steere, p. 435.

[54] Gordon, p. 364.

SPOTSYLVANIA

[1] William D. Matter, *If It Takes All Summer,* (Chapel Hill, North Carolina: The University of North Carolina Press, 1988), p. 75.

[2] *Official Records*, vol. XXXVI, pt. 1, p. 1071.

[3] *Official Records*, vol. LI, pt. 2, p. 902.

[4] Clifford Dowdey, *Lee's Last Campaign,* (Boston: Little, Brown and Company, 1960), p. 189.

[5] Matter, p. 87.

6   Jeffery Wert, "Emory Upton's Fight for a Brigadier's Star," *Civil War Times Illustrated*, vol. XXII, no. 2, April, 1983, p. 13.

7   Matter, p. 103.

8   *Official Records*, vol. XXXVI, pt. 1, p. 1072.

9   *Official Records*, vol. XXXVI, pt. 1, p. 1072.

10   Matter, p. 165.

11   Wert, "Emory Upton's Fight for a Brigadier's Star," *CWTI*, p. 21.

12   Ibid.

13   *Official Records*, vol. XXXVI, pt. 1, p. 1072.

14   Ibid.

15   Matter, p. 190.

16   Hamlin, *Old Bald Head*, p. 178.

17   Freeman, *R.E. Lee*, vol. III, p. 316.

18   *Official Records*, vol. XXXVI, pt. 1, p. 1080.

19   Ibid., p. 1086.

20   Ibid., p. 335.

21   Ibid., p. 1072.

22   Gordon, p. 276.

23   Gary W. Gallagher, *Lee's Gallant General*, (Chapel Hill, North Carolina: The University of North Carolina Press, 1985), p. 108.

24   *Official Records*, vol. XXXVI, pt. 1, p. 336.

25   Gordon, p. 40.

26   Casler, p. 214.

27   Emory M. Thomas, *Bold Dragoon*, (New York: Harper and Row, 1986), p. 293.

28   Matter, p. 267.

29   Gallagher, p. 112.

30   Hamlin, *Old Bald Head*, p. 181.

31   Thomas L. Connelly, *The Marble Man*, (New York: Alfred A. Knopf, 1977), p. 215.

32 *Official Records*, vol. XXXVI, pt. 1, p. 338.

33 Campbell Brown to Lizinka Ewell, May 20, 1864, Polk- Brown-Ewell Papers, Southern Historical Collection.

34 Ibid.

35 *Official Records*, vol. XXXVI, pt. 1, p. 1073.

36 McDonald, p. 206.

37 J. Early, *Autobiographical Sketch,* p. 359.

38 Freeman, *R.E. Lee*, vol. III, p. 356.

39 U.S. Grant, *Personal Memoirs*, (New York: Charles L. Webster & Company, 1886), vol. II, p. 252.

40 *Official Records*, vol. XXXVI, pt. 1., p. 1074.

41 Robert E. Lee to Richard S. Ewell, May 29, 1864, Polk- Brown-Ewell Papers, Southern Historical Collection.

42 Robert E. Lee to Richard S. Ewell, May 31, 1864, Polk- Brown-Ewell Papers, Southern Historical Collection.

43 *Official Records*, vol. XXXVI, pt. 3, p. 863.

44 Robert E. Lee to Richard S. Ewell, June 1, 1864, Polk- Brown-Ewell Papers, Southern Historical Collection.

45 Hamlin, *The Making of a Soldier*, p. 130.

RICHMOND

1 J. Early, *Autobiographical Sketch,* p. 362.

2 *Battles and Leaders*, vol. IV, p. 217.

3 Hamlin, *The Making of a Soldier*, p. 127.

4 Ibid., p. 128.

5 Campbell Brown to Richard Ewell, June 13, 1864, Polk-Brown-Ewell Papers, Southern Historical Collection.

6 Ibid.

7 Jubal Early to Richard Ewell, June 5, 1864, Polk-Brown-Ewell Papers, Southern Historical Collection.

8 Campbell Brown to Richard Ewell, June 13, 1864, Polk-Brown-Ewell Papers, Southern Historical Collection.

[9] *Official Records*, vol. XL, pt. 2, p. 646.

[10] Richard J. Sommers, *Richmond Redeemed*, (Garden City, New York: Doubleday & Company, 1981), p. 14.

[11] John C. Pemberton III, *Defender of Vicksburg*, (Chapel Hill, North Carolina: University of North Carolina Press, 1945), p. 262.

[12] *Official Records*, vol. XL, pt. 2, p. 671.

[13] Ibid.

[14] *Official Records*, vol. XL, pt. 3, p. 745.

[15] Ibid., p. 750.

[16] Ibid., p. 764.

[17] *Official Records*, vol. XXII, p. 1017.

[18] *Official Records*, vol. XL, pt. 1, p. 795.

[19] Hamlin, *The Making of a Soldier*, p. 131.

[20] Lew Wallace, *An Autobiography*, (New York: Harper & Brothers, 1906), vol. II, p. 710.

[21] *Official Records*, vol. XL, pt. 3, p. 794.

[22] Ibid., p. 796.

[23] Ibid., p. 807.

[24] Ibid., p. 813.

[25] Ibid.

[26] Ben Perley Poore, *Life of Burnside*, (Providence, Rhode Island: J.A. & R.A. Reed, Publishers, 1882,) p. 247.

[27] Official Records, vol. XLII, pt. 1, p. 873.

[28] Official Records, vol. XXII, pt. 2, p. 1180.

[29] Manly Wade Wellman, *Giant in Gray*, (New York: Charles Scribner's Sons, 1949), p. 154.

[30] Official Records, vol. XLII, pt. 2, p. 1194.

[31] Lloyd Paul Stryker, *Andrew Johnson*, (New York: The Macmillan Company, 1930), p. 145.

[32] Bean, p. 219.

33 Jones, vol. II, p. 280.

34 Sommers, p. 28.

35 Ibid., p. 28.

36 *Official Records*, vol. XLII, pt. 1, p. 793.

37 Ibid., p. 794.

38 Sommers, p. 61.

39 Ibid., p. 62.

40 Ibid.

41 Ibid., p. 63.

42 Ibid., p. 72.

43 *Official Records*, vol. XLII, pt. 2, p. 1303.

44 Ibid., p. 1304.

45 Ibid.

46 Sommer, p. 98.

47 Freeman, *R.E. Lee*, vol. III, p. 501.

48 Sorrel, p. 268.

49 Sommers, p. 146.

50 Freeman, *R.E. Lee*, vol. III, p. 504.

51 Gallagher, p. 165.

52 Longstreet, p. 577.

53 *New York Times*, November 16, 1864.

54 *Official Records*, vol. XLII, pt. 3, p. 1268.

55 *Official Records*, vol. XLII, pt. 2, p. 1174.

56 Eggleston, A *Rebel's Recollections*, p. 137.

57 Bushong, p. 168.

58 Allen B. Tankersley, *A Study in Gallantry*, (Atlanta,Georgia: The Whitehall Press, 1955), p. 172.

[59] Stiles, p. 245.

[60] Burke Davis, *To Appomattox*, (New York: Rinehart and Company, 1959), p. 295.

[61] Stanley F. Horn, *The Decisive Battle of Nashville*, (Knoxville, Tennessee: University of Tennessee Press, 1978), p. 153.

[62] B. Davis, *The Last Cavalier*, p. 390.

[63] Lizinka Ewell to Andrew Johnson, July 1, 1865, Polk- Brown-Ewell Papers, Southern Historical Collection.

APPOMATTOX

[1] Hattie Brown to Lizinka Ewell, April 8, 1865, Polk-Brown-Ewell Papers, Southern Historical Collection.

[2] Campbell Brown to Lizinka Ewell, June 23, 1865, Polk-Brown-Ewell Papers, Southern Historical Collection.

[3] Jones, vol. II, p. 345.

[4] Campbell Brown to Lizinka Ewell, January 10, 1865, Polk- Brown-Ewell Papers, Southern Historical Collection.

[5] *Official Records*, vol. XLVI, pt. 2, p. 1254.

[6] Foote, *The Civil War*, vol III, p. 772.

[7] Ibid., p. 777.

[8] Dowdey/Manarin, *The Wartime Papers of R.E. Lee*, p. 889.

[9] *Official Records*, vol XLVI, pt. 2, p. 1260.

[10] Louis Manarin, *Richmond At War*, (Chapel Hill, North Carolina: The University of North Carolina Press, 1966), p. 571.

[11] *Official Records*, vol. XLVI, pt. 2, p. 1293.

[12] Rembert W. Patrick, *The Fall of Richmond*, (Baton Rouge, Louisiana: Louisiana State University Press, 1960), p. 44.

[13] Philip Van Dorn Stern, *An End to Valor*, (Boston: Houghton Mifflin Company, 1958), p. 177.

[14] *Official Records*, vol. XLVI, pt. 1, p. 1293.

[15] Longstreet, p. 584.

[16] J. Early, *Autobiographical Sketch*, p. 468.

17 Montgomery Blair to Thomas Gantt, March 22, 1865, Polk-Brown-Ewell
    Papers, Southern Historical Collection.

18 *Official Records*, vol. XLVI, pt. 1, p. 51.

19 Ibid., p. 1299.

20 Joshua L. Chamberlain, *The Passing of the Armies*, (Dayton, Ohio: The
    Morningside Press, 1982), p. 156.

21 Burke Davis, *The Long Surrender*, (New York: Random House, 1985),
    p. 16.

22 Ibid., p. 93.

23 M. Howard, p. 354.

24 A.A. and Mary Hoehling, *The Day Richmond Died*, (New York: A.S.
    Barnes and Company, 1981), p. 113.

25 *Official Records*, vol. XLVI, pt. 1, p. 1293.

26 Hoehling, p. 121.

27 *Official Records*, vol. XLVI, pt. 3, p. 1380.

28 *Official Records*, vol. XLVI, pt. 1, p. 1293.

29 *Official Records*, vol. XLVI, pt. 3, p. 1380.

30 B. Davis, *To Appomattox*, p. 101.

31 Ibid., p. 110.

32 Alfred Hoyt Bill, *The Beleaguered City*, (New York: Alfred A. Knopf,
    1946), p. 271.

33 *Official Records*, vol. XLVI, pt. 3, p. 1380.

34 Hoehling, p. 143.

35 *Official Records*, vol. XLVI, pt. 1, p. 1294.

36 *Official Records*, vol. XLVI, pt. 1, p. 1293.

37 Bill, p. 273.

38 B. Davis, *To Appomattox*, p. 128.

39 Patrick, p. 43.

40 *Official Records*, vol. XLVI, pt. 3, p. 1381.

41 B. Davis, *To Appomattox*, p. 109.

[42] *Official Records*, vol. XLVI, pt. 3, p. 1381.

[43] Hunton, p. 128.

[44] Bill, p. 223.

[45] M. Howard, p. 369.

[46] *Official Records*, vol. XLVI, pt. 1, p. 1296.

[47] Ibid., p. 1296.

[48] M. Howard, p. 372.

[49] *Official Records*, vol. XLVI, pt. 1, p. 1294.

[50] M. Howard, p. 373.

[51] Colonel Joseph B. Mitchell, "Sayler's Creek," *Civil War Times Illustrated*, vol., IV, no. 5, October, 1965, p. 11.

[52] M. Howard, p. 377.

[53] *Official Records*, vol. XLVI, pt. 1, p. 1294.

[54] Ibid., p. 1294.

[55] Mitchell, "Sayler's Creek," *CWTI*, p. 13.

[56] *Official Records*, vol XLVI, pt. 1, p. 1294.

[57] Ibid., p. 1295.

[58] Colonel R.T.W. Duke, *Burning of Richmond*, (Richmond, Virginia: *Southern Historical Society Papers*, vol. 25), p. 137.

[59] B. Davis, *To Appomattox*, p. 251.

[60] Ibid.

[61] *Official Records*, vol. XLVI, pt., 1, p. 1297.

[62] Ibid., p. 1284.

[63] Ibid., p. 1297.

[64] Ibid., p. 1295.

[65] Ibid., p. 984.

[66] Ibid., p. 953.

FORT WARREN

[1] *Official Records*, vol. XLVI, pt. 1, p. 1295.

[2] Hamlin, *The Making of a Soldier*, p. 136.

[3] *Official Records*, vol. XLVI, pt. 1, p. 906.

[4] Stiles, p. 335.

[5] B. Davis, *To Appomattox*, p. 258.

[6] Hunton, p. 129.

[7] Joseph Hergesheimer, *Sheridan*, (New York: Houghton Mifflin Company, 1931), p. 354.

[8] Ibid., p. 354.

[9] Stern, p. 229.

[10] M. Howard, p. 390.

[11] Hunton, p. 125.

[12] Ibid., p. 125.

[13] M. Howard, p. 392.

[14] Ibid., p. 393.

[15] Hunton, p. 128.

[16] Ibid., p. 129.

[17] Richard Ewell to Lizinka Ewell, April 15, 1865, Polk-Brown-Ewell Papers, Southern Historical Collection.

[18] Ibid., p. 130.

[19] Ibid.

[20] Ibid.

[21] Hamlin, *Old Bald Head*, p. 194.

[22] *History and Master Plan, George's Island and Fort Warren, Boston Harbor*, (Boston: Shurcliff & Merrill, Landscape Architects, May, 1960), p. 14.

[23] Ibid.

[24] Edward Rowe Snow, *The Islands of Boston Harbor*, (New York: Dodd & Mead & Company, no date), p. 12.

25 *Official Records*, vol. XLVI, pt. 3, p. 787.

26 Hunton, p. 137.

27 Ibid.

28 Bruce Catton, *Grant Takes Command*, (Boston: Little, Brown & Company, 1968), p. 477.

29 Richard Ewell to Lizinka Ewell, May 27, 1865, Polk-Brown-Ewell Papers, Southern Historical Collection.

30 Hamlin, *The Making of a Soldier*, p. 138.

31 *Official Records*, Series II, vol. VIII, p. 507.

32 Lizinka Ewell to Richard Ewell, May 4, 1865, Polk-Brown-Ewell Papers, Southern Historical Collection.

33 Campbell Brown to Hattie Brown, May 8, 1865, Polk-Brown-Ewell Papers, Southern Historical Collection.

34 Lizinka Ewell to Richard Ewell, May 4, 1865, Polk-Brown-Ewell Papers, Southern Historical Collection.

35 Richard Ewell to Lizinka Ewell, May 17, 1865, Polk-Brown-Ewell Papers, Southern Historical Collection.

36 Richard Ewell to Lizinka Ewell, May 21, 1865, Polk-Brown-Ewell Papers, Southern Historical Collection.

37 Myrta Lockett Avery, *Recollections of Alexander Stephens*, (New York: Doubleday, Page and Company, 1910), p. 220.

38 Lizinka Ewell to Richard Ewell, May 25, 1865, Polk-Brown-Ewell Papers, Southern Historical Collection.

39 *The New Orleans Times*, July 11, 1866, in the Louisiana State Library.

40 John Pope to Lizinka Ewell, June 21, 1865, Polk-Brown-Ewell Papers, Southern Historical Collection.

41 Lizinka Ewell to Richard Ewell, June 25, 1865, Polk-Brown-Ewell Papers, Southern Historical Collection.

42 Mosby, p. 391.

43 *Official Records*, vol. XLVI, pt. 3, p. 1013.

44 Mosby, p. 392.

45 Lizinka Ewell to Richard Ewell, July 9, 1865, Polk-Brown-Ewell Papers, Southern Historical Collection.

46 Andrew Jonhson to Lizinka Ewell, July 7, 1865, Polk-Brown-Ewell Papers, Southern Historical Collection.

47 Hunton, p. 139.

EPILOGUE

1   Hamlin, *The Making of a Soldier*, p. 144.

2   Military Division of the Atlantic, Orders, October 17, 1865.

3   The sign stands by the road in Spring Hill, Tennessee.

4   *The Missouri Republican*, January 28, 1872, in the Tennessee State Library and Archives.

5   Hamlin, *Old Bald Head*, p. 198.

6   *The Missouri Republican*, January 28, 1872, in the Tennessee State Library and Archives.

7   Ibid.

8   Ibid.

Bibliography

MANUSCRIPT MATERIALS

Ewell-Brown Papers, State Library and Archives, Nashville, Tennessee.

The Polk, Brown, and Ewell Family Papers, #605, The Southern Historical Collection, Library of The University of North Carolina at Chapel Hill.

Swem Library's Ewell and Rouzie Papers, The College of William and Mary, Williamsburg, Virginia.

Records of the War Department, Adjutant General's Office, National Archives, Washington, D.C.

GOVERNMENT PUBLICATIONS

War of the Rebellion: A Compilation of the Official Records of the Union and Confederate Armies, Washington, D.C.: Government Printing Office, 1880-1901.

Atlas to Accompany The Official Records of the Union and Confederate Armies, Washington, D.C.: Government Printing Office, 1891-1895.

PERIODICALS AND MAGAZINES

The Missouri Republican, 1872, St. Louis, Missouri.

The New Orleans Times, 1865, New Orleans, Louisiana.

Civil War Times Illustrated, Harrisburg, Pennsylvania.

Southern Historical Society Papers, Richmond, Virginia.

The New York Times, 1864, New York.

PAMPHLETS

Brown, Campbell, *The First Manassas*, Nashville, Tennessee: Wheeler, Osborn & Duckworth, 1885.

History and Master Plan, George's Island and Fort Warren, Boston Harbor, Boston: Shurcliff & Merrill, Landscape Architects, May 1960.

BOOKS

Alexander, Edward P., *Fighting For The Confederacy*, Chapel Hill, North Carolina: The University of North Carolina Press, 1989.

Andrews, Marietta Minnigerode, *Scraps of Paper*, New York: E.P. Dutton and Company, 1929.

Avery, Myrta Lockett, *Recollections of Alexander Stephens*, New York: Doubleday, Page and Company, 1910.

Bean, W.G., *Stonewall's Man Sandie Pendleton*, Chapel Hill, North Carolina: The University of North Carolina Press, 1959.

Bill, Alfred Hoyt, *The Beleaguered City*, New York: Alfred A. Knopf, 1946.

Biographical Register of the Officers and Graduates of the United States Military Academy, 1802-1867, New York: James Miller Publishers, 1879.

Blackford, Susan Leigh, *Letters From Lee's Army*, New York: Charles Scribners' Sons, 1947.

Blackford, William W., *War Years With Jeb Stuart*, New York: Charles Scribners' Sons, 1945.

Bushong, Millard K., *Fightin' Tom Rosser*, Shippensburg, Pennsylvania: Beidel Printing House, 1983.

Carter, Samuel (III), *The Final Fortress*, New York: St. Martin's Press, 1980.

Cassler, John O., *Four Years in the Stonewall Brigade*, Dayton, Ohio: Morningside Press, 1971.

Catton, Bruce, *Grant Takes Command*, Boston: Little, Brown and Company, 1968.

Chamberlain, Joshua L., *The Passing of the Armies*, Dayton, Ohio: Morningside Press, 1982.

Coddington, Edwin B., *The Gettysburg Campaign*, New York: Charles Scribners' Sons, 1968.

Comte De Paris, *History of the Civil War in America*, Philadelphia: Porter and Coates, 1876.

Connelly, Thomas L., *The Marble Man*, New York: Alfred A. Knopf, 1977.

Cullen, Joseph P., *The Peninsula Campaign*, New York: Bonanza Books, 1968.

Curtis, Newton Martin, *From Bull Run to Chancellorsville*, New York: G.P. Putnam and Sons, 1906.

Dabney, Robert L., *Life and Campaigns of Lieutenant General Thomas J. Jackson*, New York: Blelock and Company, 1866.

Davis, Burke, *The Last Cavalier*, New York: Rinehart and Company, 1957.

Davis, Burke, *The Long Surrender*, New York: Random House, 1985.

Davis, Burke, *They Called Him Stonewall*, New York: Rinehart and Company, 1954.

Davis, Burke, *To Appomattox*, New York: Rinehart and Company, 1959.

Davis, Jefferson, *The Rise and Fall of the Confederate Government*, New York: D. Appleton & Company, 1874.

Davis, Varina, *Jefferson Davis*, New York: Belford Company Publishers, 1890.

Douglas, Kyd, *I Rode With Stonewall*, Chapel Hill, North Carolina: The University of North Carolina Press, 1940.

Dowdey, Clifford, *Lee's Last Campaign*, Boston: Little, Brown and Company, 1960.

Dowdey, Clifford and Manarin, Louis H., *The Wartime Papers of R.E. Lee*, Boston: Little, Brown and Company, 1961.

Dowdey, Clifford, *The Seven Days*, Boston: Little, Brown and Company, 1964.

Downey, Fairfax, *Storming the Gateway*, New York: David McKay Company, 1961.

Downey, Fairfax, *The Guns of Gettysburg*, New York: David McKay Company, 1958.

Dufour, Charles L., *Gentle Tiger*, Baton Rouge, Louisiana: Louisiana State University Press, 1957.

Durkin, Joseph, *Confederate Chaplain*, Milwaukee, Wisconsin: Bruce Publishing Company, 1960.

Early, Jubal A., *Autobiographical Sketch and Narrative of the War Between the States*, Philadelphia: J.B. Lippincott Company, 1912.

Eggleston, George Gary, *A Rebel's Recollections*, Cambridge, Massachusetts: Hurd and Houghton, 1875.

Eggleston, George Gary, *The History of the Confederate War*, New York: Sturgis & Walton, 1910.

Foote, Shelby, *The Civil War*, New York: Random House, 1958.

428

Freeman, Douglas Southall, *Lee's Lieutenants*, New York: Charles Scribners' Sons, 1942.

Freeman, Douglas Southall, *R.E. Lee*, New York: Charles Scribners' Sons, 1934.

Friedmann, Lawrence W., M.D., *The Psychological Rehabilitation of the Amputee*, Springfield, Illinois: Charles C. Thomas Publishers, 1978.

Gallagher, Gary W., *Lee's Gallant General*, Chapel Hill, North Carolina: The University of North Carolina Press, 1985.

Gilmor, Harry, *Four Years in the Saddle*, New York: Harper & Brothers, 1866.

Gordon, John B., *Reminiscences of the Civil War*, New York: Charles Scribners' Sons, 1904.

Grant, Ulysses S., *Personal Memoirs*, New York: Charles L. Webster & Company, 1886.

Hamlin, Percy, *Old Bald Head*, Strasburg, Virginia: Shenandoah Publishing House, 1940.

Hamlin, Percy, *The Making of a Soldier*, Richmond, Virginia: Whittet & Shepperson, 1935.

Harrison, Mrs. Burton (Constance Cary), *Recollections Grave and Gay*, New York: Charles Scribners' Sons, 1911.

Hassler, Warren W., *Crisis at the Crossroads*, Tuscaloosa, Alabama: The University of Alabama Press, 1970.

Hassler, William W., *A.P. Hill: Lee's Forgotten General*, Richmond, Virginia: Garrett & Massie, 1962.

Henderson, G.F.R., *Stonewall Jackson*, London: Longman, Green & Company, 1913.

Hergesheimer, Joseph, *Sheridan*, New York: Houghton Mifflin Company, 1931.

Hoehling, A.A. and Mary, *The Day Richmond Died*, New York: A.S. Barnes and Company, 1981.

Horn, Stanley F., *The Decisive Battle of Nashville*, Knoxville, Tennessee: University of Tennessee Press, 1978.

Howard, McHenry, *Recollections of a Maryland Confederate Soldier*, Baltimore, Maryland: Williams and Wilkens Company, 1914.

Howard, Oliver O., *Autobiography*, New York: The Baker and Taylor Company, 1907.

Hunton, Eppa, *Autobiography*, Richmond, Virginia: Privately Printed, 1933.

Johnson, Robert and Buel, Clarence, Editors, *Battles and Leaders of the Civil War*, New York: Thomas Yoseloff, 1956.

Jones, John B., *A Rebel War Clerk's Diary*, New York: Old Hickory Bookshop, 1935.

Lewis, Lloyd, *Captain Sam Grant*, Boston: Little, Brown and Company, 1950.

Long, A.L., *Memoirs of Robert E. Lee*, New York: J.M. Stoddart & Company, 1886.

Long, E.B., *The Civil War Day By Day*, Garden City, New York: Doubleday & Company, 1971.

Lord, Walter, *The Fremantle Diary*, Boston: Little, Brown and Company, 1954.

Manarin, Louis, *Richmond At War*, Chapel Hill, North Carolina: The University of North Carolina Press, 1966

Matter, William D., *If It Takes All Summer*, Chapel Hill, North Carolina: The University of North Carolina Press, 1988.

Maurice, Frederick, *An Aide-de-camp of Lee*, Boston: Little, Brown and Company, 1911.

McClellan, H.B., *I Rode With Jeb Stuart*, Bloomington, Indiana: Indiana University Press, 1958.

McDonald, Archie P., *Make Me a Map of the Valley*, Dallas, Texas: Southern Methodist University Press, 1973.

Meyers, Frank M., *The Commanches*, Marietta, Georgia: Continental Book Company, 1956.

Moffett, Mary Conner, *Letters of General James Conner*, Columbia, South Carolina: The R.L. Bryan Company, 1950.

Montgomery, James S., *The Shaping of a Battle*, Philadelphia: The Chilton Company, 1959.

Mosby, John S., *The Memoirs of Colonel John S. Mosby*, Bloomington, Indiana: Indiana University Press, 1959.

Nolan, Alan T., *The Iron Brigade*, New York: The Macmillan Company, 1961.

Nye, Wilber S., *Here Come The Rebels!* Baton Rouge, Louisiana: Louisiana State University Press, 1965.

Patrick, Rembert W., *The Fall of Richmond*, Baton Rouge, Louisiana: Louisiana State University Press, 1960.

Pemberton, John C. (III), *Defender of Vicksburg*, Chapel Hill, North Carolina: The University of North Carolina Press, 1945.

Pollard, Edward, *The Lost Cause*, New York: E.B. Treat and Company, 1866.

Poore, Ben Perley, *Life of Burnside*, Providence, Rhode Island: J.A. & R.A. Reed, 1882.

Schaff, Morris, *The Battle of the Wilderness*, New York: Houghton Mifflin Company, 1910.

Schildt, John W., *Roads From Gettysburg*, Privately Printed, 1979.

Schildt, John W., *Roads To Gettysburg*, Parsons, West Virginia: McClain Printing Company, 1978.

Smith, James Power, *With Stonewall Jackson in the Army of Northern Virginia*, Gaithersburg, Maryland: Zullo and VanSickle Books, 1982.

Smith, Tunstall, *Richard Snowden Andrews*, Baltimore, Maryland: The Sun Job Printing Office, 1910.

Snow, Edward Rowe, *The Islands of Boston Harbor*, New York: Dodd, Mead & Company.

Sommers, Richard J., *Richmond Redeemed*, Garden City, New York: Doubleday & Company, 1981.

Sorrel, Moxley, *Recollections of a Confederate Staff Officer*, New York: The Neale Publishing Company, 1903.

Stackpole, Edward J., *From Cedar Mountain to Antietam*, Harrisburg, Pennsylvania: The Stackpole Company, 1959.

Steere, Edward, *The Wilderness Campaign*, Harrisburg, Pennsylvania: The Stackpole Company, 1960.

Stern, Philip Van Dorn, *An End To Valor*, Boston: Little, Brown and Company, 1958.

Stiles, Robert, *Four Years Under Marse Robert*, New York: Neale Publishing Company, 1903.

Stryker, Lloyd Paul, *Andrew Johnson*, New York: The Macmillan Company, 1930.

Sword, Wiley, *Shiloh: Bloody April*, New York: William Morrow and Company, 1974.

Tankersley, Allen B., *A Study in Gallantry*, Atlanta, Georgia: The Whitehall Press, 1955.

Tanner, Robert G., *Stonewall in the Valley*, Garden City, New York: Doubleday & Company, 1976.

Taylor, Richard, *Destruction and Reconstruction*, New York: D. Appleton & Company, 1879.

Taylor, Walter H., *Four Years With General Lee*, New York: Bonanza Books.

Thomas, Emory M., *Bold Dragoon*, New York: Harper and Row, 1986.

Thompson, Charles W., *The Fiery Epoch*, Indianapolis, Indiana: The Bobbs-Merrill Company, 1931.

Tucker, Glenn, *High Tide at Gettysburg*, Indianapolis, Indiana: The Bobbs-Merrill Company, 1958.

Tucker, Glenn, *Lee and Longstreet at Gettysburg*, Indianapolis, Indiana: The Bobbs-Merrill Company, 1968.

Vandiver, Frank, *Mighty Stonewall*, New York: McGraw-Hill Company, 1957.

Wallace, Lew, *An Autobiography*, New York: Harper & Brothers, 1906.

Warner, Ezra J., *Generals in Gray*, Baton Rouge, Louisiana: Louisiana State University Press, 1983.

Webb, Alexander S., *The Peninsula*, New York: Charles Scribners' Sons, 1881.

Webster's Biographical Dictionary, Springfield, Massachusetts: G. & C. Merriam Company, 1957.

Wellman, Manly Wade, *Giant in Gray*, New York: Charles Scribners' Sons, 1949.

Wise, Jennings Cropper, *The Long Arm of Lee*, Lynchburg, Virginia: J.P. Bell Company, 1915.

Wise, John S., *The End of an Era*, Cambridge, Massachusetts: Houghton, Mifflin & Company, 1899.

Woodward, C. Vann, *Mary Chesnut's Civil War*, New Haven, Connecticut: Yale University Press, 1981.

Worsham John W., *One of Jackson's Foot Cavalry*, Jackson, Mississippi: McCowat-Mercer, 1964.